MW00447939

Supreme Justice

Supreme Justice

Speeches and Writings

THURGOOD MARSHALL

Edited by J. Clay Smith, Jr.

PENN

University of Pennsylvania Press

Philadelphia

Publication of this volume was assisted by a grant from The Olender Foundation

10 9 8 7 6 5 4 3 2 1

Published by
University of Pennsylvania Press
Philadelphia, Pennsylvania 19104-4011

Library of Congress Cataloging-in-Publication Data

Marshall, Thurgood, 1908–1993.
  Supreme Justice : speeches and writings : Thurgood Marshall /
edited by J. Clay Smith, Jr.
    p. cm.
  Includes bibliographical references and index.
  ISBN 0-8122-3690-4 (cloth : alk. paper)
    1. Civil rights—United States. 2. African Americans—Legal status, laws, etc. 3.
United States—Race relations. I. Smith, J. Clay (John Clay), 1942– II. Title.

KF213.M37 S63 2003
347.73'2634—dc21
[B]
                                                                    2002027103

Frontispiece: Thurgood Marshall, Arthur B. Spingarn Papers, Howard
University. Photograph by Moss Photo, New York.

To the Marshall Family

Contents

Preface

Thurgood Marshall is best known as the first African American to sit on the Supreme Court of the United States.[1] He was an indefatigable proponent of equality, and his ideals were meticulously expressed in his writings, speeches, interviews,[2] and opinions, particularly those written prior to his elevation to the federal judiciary. Through these texts Marshall provides a panoramic view of American history, especially as it concerned race, law, and social justice in the twentieth century, and offers acute insights about the society into which he was born and in which he practiced law and served his country.

Supreme Justice presents Thurgood Marshall's aspirations, dreams, demands, concerns, and warnings to the nation in his own words. This is Marshall's book. It presents him as he was: a brilliant law student, untiring civil rights lawyer, federal judge, U.S. Solicitor General, and Justice of the Supreme Court of the United States. In each of these roles, Marshall taught the nation and the world how to advance social justice. Indeed, Marshall was challenging lay and political leadership to secure equality for all. This book shows the broad reach of Marshall's efforts to achieve these goals and to spread his ideals to a wide audience throughout his life.

Marshall was a strategist and an architect in the modern civil rights movement in the tradition of Charles Hamilton Houston.[3] The "social

---

1. Marshall has been ranked among lawyers "who have had the most impact on the elevation of Western, particularly Anglo-American law." DARIEN A. WHITER, THE LEGAL 100: A RANKING OF THE INDIVIDUALS WHO HAVE MOST INFLUENCED THE LAW ix, 230–234 (1997), at 230.

2. One of the most comprehensive interviews of Justice Marshall was done in the 1970s. *See* Transcript, Thurgood Marshall, on file at Columbia University Library, February 1977 (Ed Edwin, interviewer). He touches on some of the incidents that appear in Marshall's early speeches and writings in this book.

3. J. Clay Smith, Jr., *Forgotten Hero*, 98 HARV. L.J. 482, 487–490 (1984) (reviewing Genna Rae McNeil, GROUNDWORK: CHARLES HAMILTON HOUSTON AND THE

engineers" that Houston trained at Howard Law School or otherwise influenced included many of the key figures in the civil rights struggle, the "noble efforts of a particular group of men and women lawyers who have dedicated and are now dedicating their lives to erase the 'badges of slavery.'"[4] Civil rights lawyers, who persuaded citizens and the government that equality is a right due to all persons in the nation, contributed much more to society than has been reflected in modern legal and political history. Schools of legal thought have also neglected the historic contributions of Marshall as scholar.[5] Yet Marshall is a towering figure in the development of our country's core values; his contributions clearly put him in the category of nation-builder.

Marshall believed that law could—and should—change society for the better, and he recognized that if law was to be the instrument of social and political improvement, his clients had to believe in its transformative power as strongly as he did. The documents reproduced here constitute a valuable source for the study of Marshall's efforts, aided by an army of NAACP lawyers and volunteers committed to the rule of law, toward increasing general awareness of social and legal injustice. Marshall and his supporters interpreted the law without fixing on one approach but, rather, by drawing on a combination of methods, legal

STRUGGLE FOR CIVIL RIGHTS [1983]). Note, *Legal Realism and the Race Question: Some Realism About Realism on Race Relations*, 108 HARV. L. REV. 1607, 1624 n.118 (1995), citing J. Clay Smith, Jr., *In Memoriam: Professor Frank D. Reeves—Towards a Houstonian School of Jurisprudence and the Study of Pure Legal Existence*, 18 HOW. L.J. 1, 6 (1973). Houston, Marshall, and a legion of other black lawyers trained at Howard's law school drew other lawyers within the Houston's net and created a "broader jurisprudential movement." *Id.*

4. *Id.* at 7 (*In Memoriam: Professor Frank D. Reeves*). The *Memoriam* reads: "While the complete blueprint was made by several hands . . . [including] Leon Ransom, William H. Hastie, James Madison Nabrit, Jr. . . . all . . . were on the faculty of Howard University School of Law." In addition, Justice Marshall stated, "'It was Charlie who taught us,' referring to Houston's ability to turn the classroom into a courtroom." *Id.* at 18 n. 9, citing E. PEEKS, THE LONG STRUGGLE FOR BLACK POWER 277, 278 (1971). One can see the underlying philosophy of Marshall's work in this explanation of pure legal existence: "Pure legal existence looks to the future but studies the present and the past of the law that touches black people and those similarly situated, in order to trace, to ascertain and to analytically assess the growth of how near they are to an existence which is free from racial discrimination." *Id.* at 5 (*In Memoriam*). Charles H. Houston is also listed among the most influential lawyers in Western history. THE LEGAL 100 *supra* note 1, at 227.

5. This is not surprising: legal and social scholars have tended to interpret the contributions of black lawyers in story form, assigning the study and application of theory to others. *See* JAMES T. PATTERSON, BROWN V. BOARD OF EDUCATION: A CIVIL RIGHTS MILESTONE AND ITS TROUBLED LEGACY xxiv–xxv (2001) (citing examples).

actions, group consensus, and public opinion they strove to rectify inequities suffered by minorities and persons similarly situated. Realizing that often their circumstances kept many of these individuals from even realizing that they were entitled to civil rights, Marshall and supporters of his agenda provided crucial leadership in the struggle to eliminate Jim Crow.

Marshall applied a variety of jurisprudential approaches to advance the cause of equality. Certain speeches tend to cast him as a realist,[6] who "placed a premium on public policy, ethical and institutional concerns."[7] In these remarks, the abstractions of law served real, practical ends that made a difference in people's lives. Yet other speeches tilt him toward textualism, urging the courts to interpret the Reconstruction Amendments strictly to secure equality for the slave progeny. For Marshall, the goal of justice and equality for all was an unassailable good, and throughout his life he used whatever legal methods were at his disposal to make the courts realize this goal.

Marshall's fidelity to the Constitution was not shared by some members of the black community, who believed that white people controlled the application of the law and the meaning of the Constitution. Black people who had witnessed public lynchings, endured unfair treatment in local courts, and lived in communities where pleas for simple justice led to various forms of harassment and sometimes death must be forgiven if they were not all persuaded by Marshall that the Constitution was a living document. In the minds of some, the courts acted as though the Constitution operated "solely for whites"[8] as it applied to civil and human rights. For Marshall, "[t]he judicial system does not exist as an end in itself. It does not exist to serve lawyers and judges, but to serve the public, our own constituency."[9] Ultimately, as we know, Marshall's philosophy of the role of the courts in the adjudication of racial discrimination claims gained the support of other members of the Supreme Court.

To win the support of skeptics and to keep existing supporters from losing faith, Marshall traveled extensively during the 1950s to keep

6. *See* EDWIN N. GARLAN, LEGAL REALISM AND JUSTICE 5 (1941). Garlan writes: "Essentially, the realists have taken seriously the practical techniques of the lawyer and have transformed them into generalized and critical methods of research, thereby opening avenues of insight hitherto virtually untouched by an analytical and formal jurisprudence and affecting profoundly our settled convictions about law." *Id.*

7. Note, *Legal Realism, supra* note 3, at 1607.

8. This perception is: "True law, in [the opinion of Negroes], operated . . . never for Negroes. When applied to Negroes, its dispensation depended upon the whims of white court officials, never the weight of the evidence." ALFRED E. CAIN AND WALTER CHRISTMAS, THE NEGRO HERITAGE LIBRARY 128 (1966).

9. Thurgood Marshall, Speech: The Fifty-Year Fight for Civil Rights (1950), at 1

NAACP members informed about the strategies being developed and actions waged to defeat Jim Crow. In the face of local retaliatory conduct, protected by the principle of state's rights, Marshall inspired black people to shed their fears and become agents of change. His speeches were sometimes taped, transcribed by the press, or handed out to local leaders and members of the NAACP, broadening the reach of his message.

Marshall's speeches reveal a man of strength, confidence, character, and loyalty to and undivided love for his country and its citizens.[10] Themes frequently sounded are the call for peaceful rebellion against those who threaten the legitimacy of the equal rights of humankind and an intolerance of racial exclusion in a democratic community. Even in the face of contradiction, Marshall never appears to lose faith in America's fundamental principles, though from time to time he conveys disappointment in its leadership and judicial decisions.

Even his early writings reveal his basic belief that segregation mandated by law and the conduct of government were barriers that lawyers relying on the Constitution had to tear down. Marshall made clear to those committed to the tactics of interposition and nullification[11] that they were victims of false indoctrination and misunderstood the Reconstruction Amendments. He believed that those arguing for segregation as a positive national good relied on the logic used in earlier centuries to justify slavery.[12] Driven by a sense of legal and political history, Marshall hoped that society would demand an inclusive reading of the Constitution that would eventually unfold in actuality, with or without legal pressure. In addition, he hoped that the majority of Americans would adopt

---

in the P. L. Prattis Papers, Box 144–22, Folder 32, Amistad Research Center, Tulane University.

10. For a detailed discussion on style and rhetoric of Thurgood Marshall's speeches, *see* Erma Waddy Hines, Thurgood Marshall's Speeches on Equality and Justice Under Law 1965–1967, diss., Louisiana State University and Agricultural and Mechanical College, May 1979. *See also* Jamye Coleman Williams, A Rhetorical Analysis of Thurgood Marshall's Arguments Before the Supreme Court in the Public School Desegregation Controversy, diss., Ohio State University 80–89 (1959) (discussing Marshall's forensic ability).

11. After the Brown decision was decided, "[o]ne hundred and ten members of Congress . . . issued a 'Southern Manifesto' encouraging massive resistance to Brown." Herbert Brownell, *Civil Rights in the 1950s*, 69 TUL. L. REV. 781, 787 (1995). This nullifying statement reads as follows: "We pledge ourselves to use all lawful means to bring about a reversal of this decision which is contrary to the Constitution and to prevent the use of force in its interpretation." *Id.* at 787. *See also* Peyton McCary, *Freedom: Constitutional Law: Yes, But What Have They Done to Black People Lately? The Role of Historical Evidence in the Virginia Board Case*, 1995 CHI.-KENT L. REV. 1275, 1293 n. 97 (referring to Virginia's opposition to the U.S. Supreme Court's decision in Brown v. Board of Education, 347 U.S. 483 (1954)).

12. CARLYLE MCKINLEY, AN APPEAL TO PHARAOH xiv (1906).

the same Judeo-Christian ethic that guided the abolitionist movement to advocate an end to slavery.[13]

Nor does Marshall in his speeches lay blame solely on Southern racial policies.[14] He saw that "Albany, the capital of New York, is about as prejudiced a place as you want to find" because it welcomed only the "right type of Negro." He was critical of New York and the industrial states in the North that had adopted civil rights laws but never vigorously enforced them, observing that "the civil rights statutes in these states meant nothing."[15]

Marshall's actions and those of the NAACP lawyers mark the early 1930s as the point in American history when African Americans began collectively to assert their claims as citizens, attacking restrictions nationwide on black access to the vote and breaking down economic discrimination and segregation.[16] This assault on prejudices about the inability of blacks to participate in the political process and the need for economic protectionism began to have effect by 1948, when at least 1.3 million black people in the South voted in the presidential election. African Americans' reliance on political power resulted in national legislative reforms, such as the Fair Employment Practice Commission, the initial drive to secure freedom from discrimination in the work place on the basis of race or color.[17]

Marshall expected conflict in the South following the Brown decision. He realized that desegregation and the implementation of the Brown orders would take time but was hopeful that hostilities against Negroes would not last. To Marshall, the momentum of history favored continued progress toward equality even as "[t]he struggle to obtain justice in the courts for Negro Americans cover[ed] practically the entire span of the fifty-year history of the NAACP."[18] Nonetheless, he did not hide his impatience at its slow pace.

---

13. *See* Allen C. Guezo, *A Reluctant Recruit to the Abolitionist Cause*, WASH. POST, Feb. 11, 2001, at B3 (addressing the conflicting personalities of the abolitionist and President Lincoln).
14. *See, e.g.*, WILLIAM M. TUTTLE, JR., RACE RIOT: CHICAGO IN THE RED SUMMER OF 1919, at 43–66 (1970).
15. *Infra*, at 30.
16. Segregation and Desegregation, *infra* note 13, at 78.
17. *See, e.g.*, MERL E. REED, SEED TIME FOR THE MODERN CIVIL RIGHTS MOVEMENT: THE PRESIDENT'S COMMITTEE ON FAIR EMPLOYMENT PRACTICE 1941–1946, at 21–46 (1991). *See also* Harold A. McDougall, *Social Movements, Law, and Implementation: A Clinical Dimension for the New Legal Process*, 75 CORNELL L. REV. 83, 108 (1989).
18. Thurgood Marshall, Speech: The Fifty-Year Fight for Civil Rights (1950), at 1 in the P. L. Prattis Papers, Box 144–22, Folder 32, Amistad Research Center, Tulane University.

Beginning in the 1950s, Marshall's speeches articulate a determination to eliminate all racial distinctions in America. He knew that *de jure* and *de facto* segregation, which isolated the races in public schools and elsewhere, was a dangerous public policy. Peering into the future, he predicted that a segregated society would forever be unable to live up to its fundamental principles, a point later reinforced by Dr. Martin Luther King, Jr.[19] While this stance was not Marshall's alone, it confirmed the beliefs of descendants of slaves and of liberals that they should continue to rely on the Declaration of Independence, Emancipation Proclamation, and the Reconstruction Amendments to transform America into a nation that embodied the creed it was preaching around the world to lead communist and emerging nations to democratic values.[20]

The speeches and commentaries by Marshall address not only adults but also youth at historically black colleges and universities, whose role "is significantly important."[21] He wanted black youth taught "the facts of life" to prepare them to assume leadership in their communities and to support and participate in the desegregation movement.[22] Marshall, the realist, encouraged youth to believe in a bright future, but he warned them that "the world is waiting for you with outstretched arms, with a club in each hand."[23] Although he argued for open admission policies to universities, he told black young people that they had to study longer, read more, and work harder than other students to succeed. While Marshall opposed violence, he was not opposed to students bringing

19. MARTIN LUTHER KING, JR., WHERE DO WE GO FROM HERE: CHAOS OR COMMUNITY 135–166 (1968). *See also* Anthony E. Cook, *Beyond Critical Legal Studies: The Reconstructive Theology of Dr. Martin Luther King, Jr.*, 103 HARV. L. REV. 985, 1036 (1990); J. Clay Smith, Jr., Why Is Equality So Assiduously Avoided, Speech before NAACP, Maricopa County Branch, Phoenix, Ariz., May 18, 1979, at 4.
20. In 1979, during the twenty-fifth anniversary celebration of the Brown v. Board of Education, 347 U.S. 483 (1954) decision, James Madison Nabrit, Jr., one of the leading lawyers in Bolling v. Sharpe, 347 U.S. 497 (1954) (the companion case of Brown v. Board of Education), commented on the impact of these decisions: "I think they have meant a great deal to our struggle for civil rights, and for the opportunities which all citizens should face, without the racial discrimination and hatred with which we fought for so long. I think, to put it bluntly, today we have made enough progress where we are now in a position to really fight for our civil rights. And, that is what we have to do, from this point on." Transcript of Proceedings, Program in Commemoration of Twenty-Fifth Anniversary of Brown vs. Board of Education, sponsored by the NAACP Legal Defense and Education Fund, Howard University School of Law, May 15, 1979, at 52. *See also* ARGUMENT: THE ORAL ARGUMENT BEFORE THE SUPREME COURT IN BROWN V. BOARD OF EDUCATION OF TOPEKA, 1952–55, at 122 (Leon Friedman ed., 1969) (regarding Nabrit).
21. *See* The Future Lies with Our Youth, *infra* at 67.
22. *Id.* at 67–68.
23. *Id.* at 68.

attention to injustices by the use of public demonstrations in public forums. He encouraged young people to exercise their freedom of speech "in a most effective way," reminding them that the right of protest was "basic to a democratic form of government."[24]

During the civil rights movement of the 1950s Marshall's speeches began to emphasize the economic and political stake that African American youth had in the nation. Drawing on this realization, he reminded the nation that it was unjust to treat people of the darker races in America as second-class citizens and then require them to fight for democracy in times of international conflict.[25]

Marshall often recalled "the dark past" of history, comparing it to modern times,[26] even though others were quick to extol the hard-won progress for civil and human rights in America. Toward the end of his life, in 1992, he returned to themes he had been sounding for decades:

America must get to work. In the chilled climate in which we live, we must go against the prevailing winds. We must dissent from the indifference. We must dissent from the apathy. We must dissent from the fear, the hatred, and the mistrust. We must dissent from a nation that buried its head in the sand waiting in vain for the needs of its poor, its elderly, and its sick to disappear and just blow away. We must dissent from a government that has left its young without jobs, education, or hope. We must dissent from the poverty of vision and timeless absence of moral leadership. We must dissent.[27]

In 1992 Justice Marshall graciously agreed to write the foreword to my book *Emancipation: The Making of the Black Lawyer, 1844–1944.* At the time I told the Justice that I would attempt to find as many speeches of his as I could and compile them into a book. (With characteristic modesty, he did not seem to think the speeches would be as valuable as I suggested.) So in a sense this volume is the fulfillment of a promise made to Justice Marshall.

Supreme Justice covers seven decades of Thurgood Marshall's career. The forty speeches and writings (and two interviews) include several historic panel discussions in which Marshall participated with other noted figures. Part I is composed of writings by Marshall during his days in law

---

24. Thurgood Marshall, The Cry for Freedom: Shame if You Don't, speech before the NAACP Meeting in Charlotte, N.C., March 20, 1960, at 2.
25. *See* excerpt of Marshall *et al.*'s argument before the U.S. Supreme Court in Morgan v. Virginia *in* RICHARD KLUGER: SIMPLE JUSTICE: THE HISTORY OF BROWN V. BOARD OF EDUCATION 238 (1975).
26. The words "the dark past" appear in "Lift Every Voice and Sing" (the Black National Anthem), written by James Weldon Johnson in 1921, connoting strength in time of tribulation.
27. *See* We Must Dissent, *infra*, at 313, 316.

school through the period on the road to *Brown v. Board of Education,*
roughly the 1930s to 1950s. Part II covers Marshall's tenure as federal
judge, solicitor general, and U.S. Supreme Court Justice (including two
transition speeches made just prior to his elevation to the federal court).
The order of the selections is thematic within the decade groupings,
each of which is preceded by a brief introduction to situate the speeches
in their historical and legal context. Unless otherwise indicated, footnotes have been supplied by the volume editor. Also, Thurgood Marshall
refers to the National Association for the Advancement of Colored
People and the NAACP throughout this book, although in 1940 the
organization changed its name to its present form, the NAACP Legal
Defense and Education Fund, Inc.

Certain selections were included because they document a specific
time in Marshall's career or the progress in the civil rights struggle.
Some speeches, including the panel discussions, are important dialogue
in the emerging consensus that equality for all Americans could not be
postponed indefinitely. Others, such as his later statement on the death
penalty, address issues relevant to the legal profession and general
domestic or international concerns.

Thurgood Marshall, 1908–1993

Thurgood Marshall was born in Baltimore, Maryland, on July 2, 1908, the son of William C. and Norma A. Marshall. On September 4, 1929, he married Vivian Burney, who died in February 1955. On December 17, 1955, he married Cecelia A. Suyat, with whom he had two children: Thurgood, Jr., and John William. They made their home in Northern Virginia.

After attending public schools in Baltimore, Marshall graduated with honors from Lincoln University in 1930, where he had gone with the intention of becoming a dentist. His aims changed to law, and in 1933 he graduated at the head of his class from Howard University School of Law in Washington, D.C. He subsequently received numerous honorary degrees.

Upon graduation he entered the private practice of law in Baltimore and, in 1934, became counsel for the Baltimore branch of the National Association for the Advancement of Colored People (NAACP). In 1936 he joined the organization's national legal staff and, in 1938, was appointed chief legal officer. He served as Director-Counsel of the NAACP Legal Defense and Educational Fund from 1940 until his appointment to the federal bench.

President John F. Kennedy nominated Thurgood Marshall to the Second Circuit Court of Appeals on September 23, 1961. He was given a recess appointment in October 1961 and his nomination was confirmed by the Senate on September 11, 1962.

President Lyndon B. Johnson nominated Judge Marshall for appointment as Solicitor General of the United States on June 13, 1965. He took the oath of office on August 24, 1965. He was the first African-American to hold this post.

Marshall was nominated by President Johnson as Associate Justice of the Supreme Court of the United States on June 13, 1967, was confirmed by the Senate on August 30, 1967, and took the Constitutional oath and was seated on October 2, 1967, as successor to Justice Tom C. Clark. Marshall was the first African American to become a Justice of the Supreme Court.

Justice Marshall's government service aside from the courts took many forms over the years. In 1951 he visited Japan and Korea to investigate court-martial cases involving black soldiers. He served as consultant at the Constitutional Conference of Kenya in London in 1961 and as President Kennedy's personal representative to the independence ceremonies of Sierra Leone in 1961. Just prior to becoming Solicitor General he was Chief of the United States delegation to the Third United Nations Congress on the Prevention of Crime and the Treatment of Offenders, which convened in Stockholm in August 1965. He was President Truman's personal representative to the laying of the cornerstone ceremony at the Center for the Advancement of Peace (Harry S. Truman Center) in Jerusalem on July 11, 1966. He attended the funeral of the late Prime Minister Sangster of Jamaica on April 17, 1976, as Special Ambassador and head of the United States delegation.

Justice Marshall was a member of the Board of Directors of the John F. Kennedy Library. He was a member of the American Bar Association, National Bar Association, Association of the Bar of the City of New York, New York County Lawyers Association, the Research Institute, Alpha Phi Alpha Fraternity, and the College of Electors, Hall of Fame, New York University. He was the recipient of scores of national and local medals, awards, and citations for his work in the field of civil rights.

Justice Marshall submitted his resignation from the Supreme Court on June 27, 1991, effective upon the qualification of his successor. Justice Marshall's career continued, however. For a short period after retirement, the Court by special order assigned Justice Marshall to perform duties in the United States Court of Appeals for the Second Circuit during the period of December 2–4, 1992, and to hear cases in the Fourth Circuit Court of Appeals in Baltimore, Maryland.

Thurgood Marshall died on January 24, 1993, and is buried at Arlington National Cemetery.

Part I
The Lawyer, 1930s–1950s

1. Thurgood Marshall, 1946 NAACP convention, Atlantic City, N.J. Collection of Moorland-Spingarn Research Center, Howard University. Photograph by Fred Hess & Son.

THE 1930s–1940s

Thurgood Marshall graduated from Howard University School of Law in 1933. Marshall was a man of humor, a brilliant student, and the only one of his classmates to graduate with honors.[1] While in law school, Marshall wrote a complex paper entitled "The Fairness of the Reorganization Plan in Industrial Corporations,"[2] which demonstrates his acumen in legal writing and corporate law at the threshold of his distinguished career. In 1935 he asked the acting law school dean to be considered for a position on the faculty, a request that was apparently denied. The letter (the only one included in this book) is important because it causes one to wonder about the significant contribution Marshall might have made to further the science of law as a teacher instead of or in addition to a civil rights lawyer.

During his second year in law school, Marshall—led by his mentor, Charles Hamilton Houston—learned that street protests could communicate injustice to the public. In the first selection in the book, Marshall describes his baptism as an activist protesting the lynching of blacks.

The early 1940s found the world at war against Adolf Hitler and American soldiers were being drafted to defend freedom, including black Americans. The Jim Crow policies of the military, which treated blacks like second-class citizens, infuriated the NAACP, the Urban League, and other groups. Their leaders complained to President Franklin Roosevelt about the discriminatory conditions in the armed services, arguing that if blacks were drafted to fight for democracy, then it was time to give them full rights as citizens of that democracy on American soil.[3] The protest of these leaders may have resulted in the appointment of Judge William Henry Hastie as civilian aide to the Secretary of War (although

---

1. *Howard University Bulletin, The School of Law*, 1932–1933, at 30 (Thurgood Marshall graduating *cum laude*).
2. This paper appears in the appendix of this book.
3. *See* JOHN HOPE FRANKLIN, FROM SLAVERY TO FREEDOM: A HISTORY OF NEGRO AMERICANS 575–576 (1967).

2. Black lawyers at the 1947 National Bar Association convention. Front row:
Richard Atkinson, Margaret Haywood, Thurman L. Dodson, William Powell,
Maurice Weeks, Hubert Pair. Middle row: Ollie May Cooper, Roy Gavin,
Thurgood Marshall. Back row: David W. Williams, George W. Peterson, LeRoy
McKinney, Lewis Ferrell. Collection of J. Clay Smith, Jr.

he eventually resigned from that post because of continued segregation
in the military).[4]

As blacks migrated to the North to work in the cities, such as Detroit,
they encountered the same racist conditions they had hoped to leave
behind in the South. Marshall, writing for the NAACP, sheds light on
the bloody violence against blacks when a mob of white persons armed
with rocks, sticks and other weapons attacked Negro tenants attempting

4. Hastie was later Dean of the Howard University School of Law and one of the
shining lights in major civil rights cases. GILBERT WARE, WILLIAM HASTIE:
GRACE UNDER PRESSURE 93–95, 98, 104–105, 109 (1984). Constance Baker Motley, who also made a significant contribution in the movement to desegregate the
schools in the South and other achievements for racial equality, credits Robert
W. Ming, a member of the law faculty of Howard University School of Law and
later the University of Chicago Law School. See Constance Baker Motley, Standing on His Shoulders: Thurgood Marshall's Early Career, in THURGOOD MARSHALL:
MEMORIAL TRIBUTES IN THE CONGRESS OF THE UNITED STATES 254, 259 (1994).

to move into the projects in Detroit. "Negro Status in the Boilermakers Union" demonstrates the efforts of the civil rights community to end the Jim Crow exclusionary labor union membership rules. Marshall's words help us to understand the reality of the era, "the same old story of discrimination tied up with the evil of segregation."[5]

The memorandum reproduced here under the title "Saving the Race" reveals a great deal about the challenges faced by civil rights lawyers moving around the South while attempting to keep lawyers and the people informed on the need to "save the race."[6]

---

5. *See* Thurgood Marshall, Negro Status in Boilermaker Union, *infra*, at 17, 19.
6. *Infra* at 22.

Marshall and Houston Jailed

When I was in law school, 1932 I think it was, the Anti-Crime Conference or something by the then Attorney General, Homer Cummings;[1] and they would not put lynching on their calendar or their agenda. And we protested, and my law school, Howard University Law School, set up a picket line, headed by our dean, Charlie Houston, and about twenty of us went out on the picket line in front of the meeting which was held here in Washington, D.C., in the Pan-American Building. The captain of police said it was an illegal picket line, and we told him, so what? He was very nice. He asked us to stop and we wouldn't. And the second day he got instructions, and he said, "Well, look—you either stop or you're under arrest."

And we said, "Well, what are you waiting for? What do you think we picketed for? That's what we picketed for. Go ahead." And he called up the patrol, and put the guys in, and there were three of us for whom there wasn't room in the two wagons. So we said, "What about us?"

We got a taxi and followed the patrol to the precinct and got back into line. He said, quote, "This is the damnedest bunch of criminals I've ever run across."

Transcription of interview of Justice Thurgood Marshall, April 13, 1977, at 131–132 (interviewed by Ed. Edwin, on file at Columbia University).
1. For information regarding Cummings's views, *see generally* HOMER CUMMINGS AND CARL McFARLAND, FEDERAL JUSTICE: CHAPTERS IN THE HISTORY OF JUSTICE AND THE FEDERAL EXECUTIVE (1937).

Letter to Dean Taylor
Applying for Law School Position

I do not know whether or not there is, at present, a vacancy on the faculty of the Law School, nor whether there will be one in the near future. I am, however, taking this means to making an application for consideration for a position on the faculty whenever a vacancy occurs.

It is my belief that there should be at least one graduate of the Law School as a full-time professor on the faculty. I do not believe that there are, at present, any graduates serving in this capacity.

I was graduated from the Law School in 1933 with the degree of Bachelor of Law *cum laude*. While in the Law School I served as student assistant librarian for two years,[1] was a member of the Court of Peers for one year and Chief Justice of the Court of Peers during the last year. My record in the Law School, I am certain, is available.

My primary education consisted of high school work in the Douglass High School of Baltimore City and a Bachelor of Arts degree from Lincoln University in Pennsylvania. Under these circumstances, it seems that my education has not been obtained solely at Howard, but rather, consists of education in the two universities, Howard and Lincoln. Therefore, my application for a position would not be guilty of "in breeding." On the other hand, it would give an opportunity for a Howard Law School graduate to serve on the faculty of the School.

In 1933, after graduating in the early part of June, I took the Maryland Bar examination within the next two weeks and passed.[2] I was admitted to the Bar of the Court of Appeals of Maryland in October, 1933, and to the Supreme Bench of Baltimore City in November of the

Thurgood Marshall wrote this letter, dated December 27, 1935, to William E. Taylor, acting dean of Howard University School of Law, located at 420 Fifth Street, N.W., Washington, D.C. Marshall's letterhead indicates that his law office was located at 604 Phoenix Building, 4 E. Redwood Street, Baltimore, Maryland.
1. Thurgood Marshall worked for Professor A. Mercer Daniel, who was both a law teacher and the law librarian at Howard University School of Law.
2. According to the 1930 census, there were thirty-three black lawyers in the State of Maryland and 2,697 white lawyers. J. CLAY SMITH, JR., EMANCIPATION: THE MAKING OF THE BLACK LAWYER, 1844–1944, at 631, app. 2 (1993).

same year, after which time I immediately started active practice of the law. Since that time, my experience has been more or less diversified. I have tried several criminal cases, most important of which were two murder cases and one rape case. The last case was by appointment of Judge Owens of the Supreme Bench who certified to me the highest fee possible to be paid for a case involving capital punishment.

My civil work has included personal injury cases, property damage cases, contract actions, relevant actions and insurance actions. I am, at present, counsel for the colored laundry in Baltimore City reputed to be the second largest Negro enterprise in the City, counsel for the only colored building association in the City and counsel for several prominent individuals including the treasurer of the Afro-American company. I have also taken part in the trial of several cases of more or less national importance. Associated with Dr. Charles Hamilton Houston,[3] we tried a case involving the disbarment of one Bernard Ades, a white attorney.[4] This, I have been informed, is the first time Negro attorneys have represented a white attorney in such a procedure.

In September of this year I took part in the civil action against a white policeman charged with shooting and killing a Negro while under arrest, which case resulted in a verdict and judgment of $1,200 in favor of the widow. I was also associated in the case of Murray vs. the University of Maryland, which case is, at present, pending in the Court of Appeals of Maryland.[5] I am, at present, counsel for the local branch of the NAACP, and chairman of the legal committee thereof.

Last August at the Convention of the National Bar Association I was elected secretary of this Association,[6] and I am acting in that capacity at the present time. I am also secretary of the Monumental City Bar Association and a member of the Bar Association, a branch of the National Bar Association.

As to my personal history, I am 27 years of age, married and at present, living in Baltimore City.

3. See J. Clay Smith, Jr., *Thurgood Marshall: An Heir of Charles Hamilton Houston*, 20 HASTINGS CONST. L.Q. 503 (1993).
4. EMANCIPATION, *supra* note 1, at 251 n. 71 (regarding attempt to disbar Ades).
5. Pearson v. Murray, 169 Md. 478, 182 A. 590 (1936). (The court ordered that Donald G. Murray be admitted into the University of Maryland Law School.)
6. Marshall was National Secretary of the National Bar Association from 1935 to 1937. *Roster of National Bar Association Officers*, 3 N.B.A.J. 303 (Sept. 1945).

The Gestapo in Detroit

Riots are initially the result of many underlying causes, yet no single factor is more important than the attitude and efficiency of the police. When disorder starts, it is either stopped quickly or permitted to spread into serious proportions, depending upon the actions of the local police.

Much of the blood spilled in the Detroit riot is on the hands of the Detroit police department. In the past the Detroit police have been guilty of both inefficiency and an attitude of prejudice against Negroes. Of course, there are several individual exceptions.

The citizens of Detroit, white and Negro, are familiar with the attitude of the police as demonstrated during the trouble in 1942 surrounding the Sojourner Truth housing project. At that time a mob of white persons armed with rocks, sticks and other weapons attacked Negro tenants who were attempting to move into the project. Police were called to the scene. Instead of dispersing the mob which was unlawfully on property belonging to the federal government and leased to Negroes, they directed their efforts toward dispersing the Negroes who were attempting to get into their own homes. All Negroes approaching the project were searched and their automobiles likewise searched. White people were neither searched nor disarmed by the police. This incident is typical of the one-sided law enforcement practiced by Detroit police. White hoodlums were justified in their belief that the police would act the same way in any further disturbances.

In the June riot of this year, the police ran true to form. The trouble reached riot proportions because the police once again enforced the law with an unequal hand. They used "persuasion" rather than firm action with white rioters, while against Negroes they used the ultimate in force: overturning and burning automobiles on Woodward Avenue. This is arson. Others were beating Negroes with iron pipes, clubs, and rocks.

50 Crisis 246, August 1943. The editor wishes to thank The Crisis Publishing Co., Inc., the publisher of the magazine of the National Association for the Advancement of Colored People, for authorizing the use of this work.

This is felonious assault. Several Negroes were stabbed. This is assault with intent to murder.

All these crimes are matters of record; many were committed in the presence of police officers, several on the pavement around the City Hall. Yet the record remains: Negroes killed by police—seventeen; white persons killed by police—none. The entire record, both of the riot killings and of previous disturbances, reads like the story of the Nazi Gestapo.

Evidence of tension in Detroit has been apparent for months. The *Detroit Free Press* sent a reporter to the police department. When Commissioner [Julian] Witherspoon was asked how he was handling the situation he told the reporter: "We have given orders to handle it with kid gloves. The policemen have taken insults to keep trouble from breaking out. I doubt if you or I could have put up with it." This weak-kneed policy of the police commissioner coupled with the anti-Negro attitude of many members of the force helped to make a riot inevitable.

Sunday Night on Belle Isle

Belle Isle is a municipal recreation park where thousands of white and Negro war workers and their families go on Sundays for their outings. There had been isolated instances of racial friction in the past. On Sunday night, June 20, there was trouble between a group of white and Negro people. The disturbance was under control by midnight. During the time of the disturbance and after it was under control, the police searched the automobiles of all Negroes and searched the Negroes as well. They did not search the white people. One Negro who was to be inducted into the army the following week was arrested because another person in the car had a small pen knife. This youth was later sentenced to ninety days in jail before his family could locate him. Many Negroes were arrested during this period and rushed to local police stations. At the very beginning the police demonstrated that they would continue to handle racial disorders by searching, beating and arresting Negroes while using mere persuasion on white people.[1]

---

1. Reporting on the riots in the *Detroit Free Press* and the *Detroit News* reflected negatively on the Negro. See *Six More Get Riot Terms*, DETROIT NEWS, July 16, 1943, at 4; Mayor Jefferies appointed the Inter-Racial Peace Board on July 20, 1943, "to find the guilty in 13 unresolved race riot deaths . . . 6 of the 13 were white," *Race Riot Jury Quiz Advocated*, DETROIT NEWS, July 20, 1943, at 1; the press even inferred that the riot was a plot by blacks and Germans (with whom the United States was at war) and blamed the riots on "the work of hoodlum minorities." *Civic Leaders Blame 5th Column and Ku Klux Klan for Riots*, DETROIT NEWS, June 22, 1943, at 6; *Must Have Order*, DETROIT NEWS, June 22, 1943, at 18. Michigan appealed to President Franklin D. Roosevelt to send federal troops to quell

The Riot Spreads

A short time after midnight disorder broke out in a white neighborhood near the Roxy Theatre on Woodward Avenue. The Roxy is an all-night theatre attended by white and Negro patrons. Several Negroes were beaten and others were forced to remain in the theatre for lack of police protection. The rumor spread among the white people that a Negro had raped a white woman on Belle Island and that the Negroes were rioting.

At about the same time a rumor spread around Hastings and Adams streets in the Negro area that white sailors had thrown a Negro woman and her baby into the lake at Belle Isle and that the police were beating Negroes. This rumor was also repeated by an unidentified Negro at one of the nightspots. Some Negroes began to attack white persons in the area. The police immediately began to use their sticks and revolvers against them. The Negroes begin to break out the windows of stores of white merchants on Hastings Street.

The interesting things is that when the windows in the stores on Hastings Street were first broken, there was no looting. An officer of the Merchants' Association walked the length of Hastings Street, and noticed that none of the stores with broken windows had been looted. It is thus clear that the original breaking of windows was not for the purpose of looting.

Throughout Monday the police instead of placing men in front of the stores to protect them from looting contented themselves with driving up and down Hastings Street from time to time, stopping in front of the stores. The usual procedure was to jump out of the squad cars with drawn revolvers and riot guns to shoot whoever might be in the store. The policemen would then tell the Negro bystanders to "run and not look back." On several occasions, persons running were shot in the back. In other instances, bystanders were clubbed by police. To the police, all Negroes on Hastings Street were "looters." This included war workers returning from work. There is no question that many Negroes were guilty of looting, just as there is always looting during earthquakes or as there was when English towns were bombed by the Germans.

---

the riot, pointing to blacks as the cause. Roosevelt's response was neutral; he sent federal troops and issued a proclamation which stated in part: "I do hereby command all persons engaged in said unlawful and insurrectionary proceedings to disperse and retire peaceably to their respective abodes immediately." *President Order Dispersing Rioters*, Detroit News, June 22, 1943, at 26; *Order Returns to Detroit as the U.S. Troops Move In*, Detroit News, June 22, 1943, at 36 (photos).

Cars Detoured into Mobs

Woodward Avenue is one of the main thoroughfares of the city of Detroit. Small groups of white people began to rove up and down Woodward beating Negroes, stoning cars, and yanking Negroes from them, and stabbing and shooting Negroes. In no case did the police do more than try to "reason" with these mobs, many of which were, at this stage, quite small. The police did not draw their revolvers or riot guns and never used any force to disperse these mobs. As a result of this, the mobs got larger and bolder and even attacked Negroes on the pavement of the City Hall in demonstration not only of their contempt for Negroes, but of their contempt for law and order as represented by the municipal government.

During this time, Mayor [Edward J.] Jeffries was in his office in the City Hall with the door locked and the window shade drawn. The use of nightsticks or the drawing of revolvers would have dispersed these white groups and saved the lives of many Negroes. It would not have been necessary to shoot, but it would have been sufficient to threaten to shoot into the white mobs. The use of a firehose would have dispersed many of the groups. None of these things was done and the disorder took on the proportions of a major riot. The responsibility rests with the Detroit police.

At the height of the disorder on Woodward Avenue, Negroes driving north on Brush Street (a Negro street) were stopped at Vernor Highway by a policeman who forced them to detour to Woodward Avenue. Many of these cars are automobiles which appeared in the pictures released by several newspapers showing them overturned and burned on Woodward Avenue.

While investigating the riot, we obtained many affidavits from Negroes concerning police brutality during the riot. It is impossible to include the facts of all of these affidavits. However, typical instances may be cited. A Negro soldier in uniform who had recently been released from the army with a medical discharge was on his way down Brush Street Monday morning toward a theatre on Woodward Avenue. The soldier was not aware of the fact that the riot was still going on. While in the Negro neighborhood on Brush Street, he reached a corner where a squad car drove up and discharged several policemen with drawn revolvers who announced to a small group on the corner to run and not look back. Several of the Negroes who did not move quite fast enough for the police were struck with nightsticks and revolvers. The soldier was yanked from behind by one policeman and struck in the head with a blunt instrument and knocked to the ground where he remained in a stupor. The police then returned to their squad car and drove off. A

Negro woman in the block noticed the entire incident from her window, and she rushed out with a cold, damp towel to bind the soldier's head. She then hailed two Negro postal employees who carried the soldier to a hospital where his life was saved.

There are many additional affidavits of similar occurrences involving obviously innocent civilians throughout many Negro sections in Detroit where there had been no rioting at all. It was characteristic of these cases that the policemen would drive up to a corner, jump out with drawn revolvers, striking at Negroes indiscriminately, oft times shooting at them, and in all cases forcing them to run. At the same time on Woodward Avenue, white civilians were seizing Negroes and telling them to "run, nigger, run." At least two Negroes, "shot while looting," were innocent persons who happened to be in the area at the time.

One Negro who had been an employee of a bank in Detroit for the past eighteen years was on his way to work on a Woodward Avenue streetcar when he was seized by one of the white mobs. In the presence of at least four policemen, he was beaten and stabbed in the side. He also heard several shots fired from the back of the mob. He managed to run to two of the policemen who proceeded to "protect" him from the mob. The two policemen, followed by two mounted policemen, proceeded down Woodward Avenue. While he was being escorted by these policemen, the man was struck in the face by at least eight of the mob, and at no time was any effort made to prevent him from being struck. After a short distance this man noticed a squad car parked on the other side of the street. In sheer desperation, he broke away from the two policemen who claimed to be protecting him and ran to the squad car begging for protection. The officer in the squad car put him in the back seat and drove off, thereby saving his life.

During all this time, the fact that the man was either shot or stabbed was evident because of the fact that the blood was spurting from his side. Despite this obvious felony, committed in the presence of at least four policemen, no effort was made at that time either to protect the victim or arrest the persons guilty of the felony.

In addition to the many cases of one-sided enforcement of the law by the police, there are two glaring examples of criminal aggression against innocent Negro citizens and workers by members of the Michigan State police and Detroit police.

Shooting in YMCA

On the night of June 22 at about 10 o'clock, some of the residents of the St. Antoine Branch of the YMCA were returning to the dormitory. Several were on their way home from the YWCA across the street. State police were searching some other Negroes on the pavement of the YMCA when two of the YMCA residents were stopped and searched for weapons. After none was found they were allowed to proceed to the building. Just as the last of the YMCA men was about to enter the building, he heard someone behind him yell what sounded to him like, "Hi, Ridley." (Ridley is also a resident of the Y.) Another resident said he heard someone yell what sounded to him like "Heil, Hilter."

A state policeman, Ted Anders, jumped from his car with his revolver drawn, ran to the steps of the YWCA, put one foot on the bottom step, and fired through the outside door. Immediately after firing the shot he entered the building. Other officers followed. Julian Witherspoon, who had just entered the building, was lying on the floor, shot in the side by the bullet that was fired through the outside door. There had been no show of violence or weapons of any kind by anyone in or around the YMCA.

The officers with drawn revolvers ordered all those residents of the YMCA who were in the lobby of their building to raise their hands in the air and line up against the wall like criminals. During all this time these men were called "black b—— and monkeys," and other vile names by the officers. At least one man was struck, another was forced to throw his lunch on the floor. All the men in the lobby were searched.

The desk clerk was also forced to line up. The officers then went behind the desk and into the private offices and searched everything. The officers also made the clerk open all locked drawers, threatening to shoot him if he did not do so.

Witherspoon was later removed to the hospital and has subsequently been released.

Vernor Apartment Siege

On the night of June 21 at about eight o'clock, a Detroit policeman was shot in the two hundred block of Vernor Highway, and his assailant, who was in a vacant lot, was, in turn, killed by another policeman. State and city policemen then began to attack the apartment building at 290 E. Vernor Highway, which was fully occupied by tenants. Searchlights were thrown on the building and machine guns, revolvers, rifles, and deer guns were fired indiscriminately into all of the occupied apartments facing the outside. Tenants of the building were forced to fall to the floor and remain there in order to save their lives. Later slugs from the machine guns, revolvers, rifles, and deer guns were dug from the inside walls of many of the apartments. Tear gas was shot into the building and all the tenants were forced out into the streets with their hands up in the air at the point of drawn guns.

State and city policemen went into the building and forced out all the tenants who were not driven out by the tear gas. The tenants were all lined up against the walls, men and women alike, and forced to remain in this position for some time. The men were searched for weapons. During this time these people were called every type of vile name and men and women were cursed and threatened. Many men were struck by policemen.

While the tenants were lined up in the street, the apartments were forcibly entered. Locks and doors were broken. All the apartments were ransacked. Clothing and other articles were thrown around on the floor. All these acts were committed by policemen. Most of the tenants reported that money, jewelry, whiskey, and other items of personal property were missing when they were permitted to return to their apartments after midnight. State and city police had been in possession of the building in the meantime.

Many of these apartments were visited shortly after these events. They resembled part of a battlefield. Affidavits from most of the tenants and lists of property destroyed and missing are available.

Although a white man was seen on the roof of an apartment house up the street from the Vernor apartments with a rifle in his hand, no effort was made to either search that building or its occupants. After the raid on the Vernor apartments, the police used as their excuse the statement that policeman Lawrence A. Adams had been shot by a sniper from the Vernor apartments and that for that reason, they attacked the building and its occupants. However, in a story released by the police department on July 2 after the death of Patrolman Lawrence A. Adams, it was reported that "The shot that felled Adams was fired by Homer Edison, 28 years old, of 502 Montcalm, from the shadows of a parking lot. Edison, armed with a shot gun, was shot to death by Adams' partner." This is merely another example of the clumsy and obvious subterfuges used by the police department in an effort to cover up their total disregard for the rights of Negroes.

Justification for our belief that the Detroit police could have prevented the trouble from reaching riot proportions is evidenced in at least two recent instances. During the last month in the town of Atlanta, Georgia, several white youths organized a gang to beat up Negroes. They first encountered a young Negro boy on a bicycle and threw him to the ground. However, before they could beat this lone Negro, a squad car drove up. The police promptly arrested several of the white boys, and dispersed the group immediately, thus effectively forestalling and preventing what might have resulted in a riot. On the Sunday preceding the Detroit riots, Sheriff [Andrew C.] Baird, of Wayne County, Michigan, with jurisdiction over the area just outside of Detroit, suppressed a potential riot in a nearby town. A large group of Negroes and a large group of white people were opposing each other and mob violence was threatened. The sheriff and his deputies got between the two groups and told them that in case of any violence, the guilty parties would be handled and that the law-enforcement officers would do everything possible to prevent the riot. Because of this firm stand, the members of both groups dispersed.

If similar affirmative action had been taken by the Detroit police when the small groups were running up and down Woodward Avenue beating, cutting, and shooting Negroes, the trouble never would have reached the bloody and destructive magnitude which has shocked the nation.

This record by the Detroit police demonstrates once more what all Negroes know only too well: that nearly all police departments limit their conception of checking racial disorders to surrounding, arresting, maltreating, and shooting Negroes. Little attempt is made to check the activities of whites.

The certainty of Negroes that they will not be protected by police, but instead attacked by them, is a contributing factor to racial tensions leading to overt acts. The first item on the agenda of any group seeking to prevent rioting would seem to be a critical study of the police department of the community, its record in handling Negroes, something of the background of its personnel, and the plans of its chief officers for meeting possible racial disorders.

Negro Status in Boilermakers Union

The status of the Negro in the Boilermakers union recently reached the front page as a result of Judge [Alexander] Churchill's decision that "the purpose and effect of the so-called 'auxiliary' was to segregate Negroes and persons of no other race and color" and that therefore "auxiliaries" "are illegal and void." This decision is epoch making, for it is the first one of its type involving the legal status of "auxiliary unions."

At least fifteen unions exclude Negroes from membership by provisions in either their constitution or ritual. Nine international unions bar Negroes from admission to their regular unions and locals, admitting them only to "Jim Crow" auxiliary bodies. Herbert R. Northrop, in the *Journal of Political Economy,* June 1943, has summarized the discriminatory tactics used by labor unions against Negroes as follows: (1) exclusion of Negroes by provision in the ritual; (2) exclusion by provision in the constitution; (3) exclusion by forcing the Negro to join a segregated auxiliary.[1]

The International Brotherhood of Boilermakers, Iron Shipbuilders and Helpers of America, AFL, refuses to admit qualified Negroes to membership in its regular locals. Although union officials claim they exclude Negroes pursuant to provision in the ritual, a careful examination of their ritual reveals no mention whatever of race or color. This makes it clear, therefore, that Negroes are relegated to "Jim Crow" auxiliary unions as a result of the whims of officers of the International.

51 Crisis 77 (March 1944). The editor thanks The Crisis Publishing Co., Inc., the publisher of the magazine of the National Association for the Advancement of Colored People, for authorizing use of this work.
1. Herbert R. Northrop, *Organized Labor and Negro Workers,* 51 J. Pol. Econ. 206, June 1943, at n.7, 207. *See also* F. Ray Marshall and Vernon M. Briggs, Jr., The Negro and Apprenticeship (1967), where the authors state: "A number of developments during the 1950s and 1960s focused attention on the problem of equal apprenticeship opportunities. The clashes between increasingly militant civil rights organizations and discriminatory unions during the 1950s drew attention to the absence of Negroes from many unions." *Id.* at 3.

Further investigation of the practices of the Boilermakers reveals the adoption of a new constitution at their 1937 convention. According to this constitution, membership in the Boilermakers is open to male citizens "of some civilized country between the ages of 16 and 70 years, working at some branch of the trade at the time of making application." No reference is made to race or color anywhere in the constitution, nor even in the by-laws adopted by the International. They have, however, issued another book labeled "By-Laws Governing Auxiliary Lodges," which purports to have been adopted by the Executive Council of the Boilermakers. These rules profess to restrict membership to "colored male citizens."[2]

A comparison of these two sets of rules shows clearly that the only equality between the auxiliary lodges and the regular lodges is in the amount of dues paid. Though members of an auxiliary, Negroes have to pay the same dues as the white members of the regular lodges. After this, all semblance of equality vanishes.

Other Inequities

In addition to segregation, there are other glaring inequalities. Insurance policies provide for Negro members about half the benefits they do for white members, and Negro auxiliary lodges are all under the direct control of the white local lodges, designated as "supervising lodges." "Auxiliaries" are also denied the right to have a business agent of their own; the right to have a grievance committee; and the right to promotion on the job without the permission of the supervising local. Membership in auxiliaries is limited to persons under sixty years of age, while white persons are eligible for membership in a local up to seventy years of age. Clinching proof of the ephemeral status of an auxiliary is found in the fact that the International president has the uncontrolled discretion to suspend any auxiliary or any officer or member. He may do this upon a mere whim, since he is answerable to no one. But a local, which consists exclusively of members of the white race, may be suspended by the International president only when he acts in conjunction with the Executive Council, and then only after such a local shall have been proved guilty of violation of the constitution and by-laws. Handicaps are even placed on the right of employment of "auxiliary members" in other cities.

In view of the fact that more and more Negroes are being employed

2. *Id.* The exact language quoted above does not appear in the text of the Northrop article, but it does confirm that the text of the 1937 *By-Laws Governing Auxiliary Lodges* excluded black males.

in the shipbuilding industry, these discriminatory practices of the Boilermakers union, since they hold a closed shop contract in most of the shipyards, have become the target of attack by the NAACP and other liberal organizations.

Discrimination against Negroes in the Boilermakers union is the same old story of discrimination tied up with the evil of segregation. And past experience teaches us that with a reduction in the number of contracts for ships, and the consequent reduction in employment, the members of the Negroes' auxiliary are not going to have the protection of the union, and the old story of the Negro's being "the first to go" will again face us.

During the earlier months of the war emergency, Negroes were excluded from most skilled jobs in shipyards. However, need for workers became so acute that it became necessary to employ Negroes, and the Boilermakers, being unable to secure a sufficient number of white workers, had to admit Negroes to these jobs. While the Boilermakers permitted the Negroes to work, they did not intend for them to have full membership in the union. So in order to protect their closed-shop agreements, they began to inaugurate the policy of setting up "Jim Crow" auxiliary unions. On the West Coast many Negroes, while paying their dues, including initiation fees to the regular locals of the Boilermakers, at the same time refused to be relegated to the status of members in auxiliary locals. This situation prevailed for some time.

Complaint Filed

Finally the Portland, Oregon, branch of the NAACP, in conjunction with the National Office, filed formal complaints with the FEPC [Fair Employment Practices Commission] concerning this type of discrimination, and full hearings by the FEPC were held in Portland and Los Angeles in November of 1943. The Boilermakers, however, on November 28, 1943, ordered the Marinship Corporation in San Francisco, Calif., to discharge all non-members, which included all of the Negroes who had refused to join the auxiliary. The Negro workers, then, led by Joseph James, a shipyard worker, secured a temporary injunction in the local federal court preventing the discharge of these men. But the case was dismissed on the ground that no diversity of citizenship was involved nor sufficient federal question to warrant such action in the federal courts.[3] Through their lawyers the Negroes workers applied for and secured a

3. James v. International Brotherhood of Boilermakers, 54 F. Supp. 94 (N.D. Calif. 1944). This case turned on a lack of diversity of citizenship, the basis of dismissal by the court. Also reported in James v. International Brotherhood of Boilermakers, Iron Shipbuilders, and Helpers of America, 13 LRRM 738 (Sept. 1943 to Feb. 29, 1944).

second temporary injunction, this time from the local courts. This case is now pending.

While the federal case was pending, FEPC, on December 9, 1943, issued its findings and directives in regard to the Boilermakers union, ordering the union to "take such necessary steps and put in course of execution such required procedures as will effect elimination of the discriminatory policies and practices found to be in conflict with and in violation of Executive Order 9346."[4]

Despite this ruling by FEPC, the Boilermakers have refused to discontinue their discriminatory policies.

Providence Case

In the shipyards in Providence, R.I., the Boilermakers union was anxious to win the election among the workers in order to be designated as the bargaining agent. Preceding the election the Boilermakers had admitted all persons, regardless of race or color, and was more than anxious to sign up Negroes. These Negroes were admitted into the regular union, attended meetings, made motions, voted, and were treated as any other members. After the election had been won by the Boilermakers and the closed-shop agreement signed, officers of the International of the Boilermakers attempted to set up an auxiliary, though a majority of the local officers of the union, as well as the Negro members of the local and a majority of white members, were opposed to this move. As a matter of fact a large majority of both Negro and white members had adopted in September 1943, a resolution to the effect that there should be no distinction as to race in the membership of the local. Yet the International officers continued their efforts to remove Negro members from the local, and it was soon discovered members, after paying their dues as members of the local, were receiving "auxiliary cards." These "auxiliary cards" were ignored by the Negroes and other members of the local, and Negroes continued to attend meetings along with others and were ostensibly considered regular members.

When the December election of officers was held, the International made efforts to have men elected who would discriminate against Negroes. In order to insure the election of such men, International representatives challenged all ballots cast by Negro members and refused to permit them to be counted. A case challenging this type of discrimination is now pending in the local Providence court.

On January 13 Judge Churchill handed down this epoch-making decision. He said, among other things, "That the purpose and effect of the

4. 8 FR 7183 (May 27, 1943) (Issued by President Franklin D. Roosevelt).

so called 'auxiliary' was to segregate Negroes and persons of no other race and color, in a position less favorable in substantial matters than the position enjoyed by other members [white] of Local 308. . . . It is clear beyond doubt that such acts at this election of December 14, 1943, in respect to ballots offered Negro voters, under instructions of the officials of the International, constitutes a discrimination based on race and color, and the question is, is this discrimination illegal? . . . I rule that the conduct at the election of December 14, 1943, and that the by-laws and constitution of the so-called 'auxiliary,' in so far as they discriminate between members of the colored race, Negroes, and persons of all other races, as compared with the by-laws and constitution of the Brotherhood, are illegal and void." In concluding his decision, Judge Churchill said: "I rule that colored members of the so-called auxiliary are members of the so-called auxiliary are members of Local 308, and that their dues ought to be kept in Rhode Island."[5]

Negro shipyard workers on the West Coast[6] and in Providence, R. I., have refused to be discriminated against by the Boilermakers and have shown their willingness to fight this un-American practice through legal means. Negro members of the Boilermakers union are anxious to contribute their part toward the war effort by building ships, but at the same time they insist on being accorded their full rights as American citizens while building ships to enable the United Nations to win the war for freedom abroad.

5. The citation for this case could not be found. No reference to Judge Churchill was discovered. However, Robert Weaver has written: "In January, 1944, a court in Providence, Rhode Island, declared that the purpose of auxiliary lodges of the boilermakers was to segregate Negroes in a position less favorable than that of white members. It then rules illegal and void a union election which the international had challenged and refused to count the votes of colored members. . . . In California a similar decision was in the offing." ROBERT C. WEAVER, NEGRO LABOR: A NATIONAL PROBLEM 229 (1946).

6. The West Coast case referred to appears to be James v. Marinship Corp., 24 Cal. 2d 721, 155 P. 2d 329 (1944). This case upheld the temporary restraining order challenging the racially discriminatory treatment of black workers. The Supreme Court of California stated: "The fundamental question in this case is whether a closed union coupled with a closed shop is a legitimate objective of organized labor." *Id.* at 334. The court ruled as it did because the union admitted on the record that it excluded Negroes from its membership and from membership in Local 6 and required them to organize in segregated locals. *Id.* at 338. The Court ruled that "If a union may not directly exclude certain workers [*see* Steele v. Louisville & Nashville R.R. Co., 323 U.S. 192 (1944) and Tunstall v. Brotherhood of Locomotive Firemen, 323 U.S. 210 (1944)], it may not do so indirectly by prescribing intolerable or unfair conditions of membership for such persons." *Id.* (James). For a more detailed discussion on the Steele and Tunstall cases, *see* J. Clay Smith, Jr., and E. Desmond Hogan, *Remembered, Forgotten Contribution: Charles Hamilton Houston, Legal Realism and Labor Law*, 14 HARV. BLACKLETTER L.J. 1, 5 (1998).

Saving the Race

New Orleans: Only two questions involved in the motion to dismiss: (a) that there was no diversity of citizenship, and (b) that there was no cause of action. We prepared a short memorandum brief in opposition to motion to dismiss, which was filed with the court.

On Tuesday the Assistant City Attorney called and told [A. P.] Tureaud[1] that one of the Assistant Attorney Generals was sick and requested another continuance. We refused to agree. On Wednesday when the case was called there were no lawyers to represent the defendants. However, one assistant attorney general and one Assistant City Attorney showed up with both arms loaded with law books. They presented a doctor's certificate showing that one of the lawyers was sick and made a long argument to the court that the case should be continued. I pointed out that the defendants already had the attorney general's office and the city attorney's office representing them and that the case had been pending for more than five months. Also pointed out that this was an action for a declaratory judgment and should be advanced for hearing rather than postponed. So ruled the court.

The entire burden of their argument on motion to dismiss was that since the school board was violating the laws of the State of Louisiana there was no violation of the Fourteenth Amendment—a point decided

NAACP Legal Files, Library of Congress Group II: B99, Folder: Thurgood Marshall General 1940–41. Memorandum to Office from Thurgood Marshall, Nov. 22, 1941. Marshall traveled throughout the South, consulting with black lawyers on various cases and using their offices as his own. This memorandum was on the letterhead of Arthur Davis Shores, whose office was located at 1630 Fourth Avenue, No. Birmingham, Alabama. Concerned about the desegregation of the schools in Alabama, Marshall was in Alabama to argue against the motion of the state to dismiss his case.

1. A. P. Tureaud was one of the leading civil rights lawyers in Louisiana. *See* "Journey for Justice: The A. P. Tureaud Story" (1997), a documentary produced by Rachel Emanuel on the life of Tureaud. *Neighbors Note: Emanuel Documentary to Premiere in New York*, THE ADVOCATE (Baton Rouge, La.), Oct. 19, 1997 (Metro Edition).

several times by the Supreme Court against them.[2] They argued that we should bring our action in the Louisiana State Courts "where we would get justice"—and how.

The Assistant Attorney General who is sick is to file a brief within a week and we have a week thereafter to file a reply brief which gives us the last say. I never saw so many teachers at a hearing before[.] [T]hey filled the entire court-room, filled the space within the bar reserve for lawyers, and were at least five deep standing around the walls of the court-room. All day Wednesday and Thursday we were busy explaining to them what was going on. They are with us and mean business.

The Assistant City Attorney says the School Board does not want to settle but he thinks something can be arranged. He asked for an offer and I told him we could not make an offer because our teachers wanted back money for about ten years. He says he will make us an offer in writing in the near future. Looks like this one is over too if the judge rules with us on the motion. If he rules against us we will of course appeal.

The Assistant Attorney General is also interested in settling the case if possible. All of this is "off the record."

When the brief for the defendant is filed it will be mailed to the [NAACP] office [in New York City]. Please hold until I get there. If Frank[3] has any time he had better start on the question of answering their brief and I will take it up when I get back.

Birmingham: Our committee here has requested a conference with the State Superintendent, which has not been granted. Dr. [E. W.] Taggert,[4] as usual, is in the front of this fight. From every indication the daily press will be with us in this fight.

We are now preparing the petition to the school board here in Birmingham. We have the client for here and another one for Andalusia, Alabama. We are on our way.

Will be in Atlanta late tomorrow and Monday. Regards to the office.

---

2. Such arguments were in defiance of any federal directives to the state, even if the state action violated the Constitution.

3. Probably referring to Frank Daniel Reeves, a 1939 law graduate of Howard University who was on the NAACP law staff. *See* HOWARD UNIVERSITY DIRECTORY OF GRADUATES 1870–1976, at 396 (1977).

4. "Dr. E. W. Taggert was a dentist, who is one of heroes of the civil rights movement in Birmingham." Telephone interview with Judge U. W. Clemon, U.S. District Judge of the Northern District of Alabama, Oct. 11, 2000. For more on Judge Clemon, *see* SYLVIA STEIN AND ANGELA DORN, EDS., FROM SLAVERY TO THE SUPREME COURT: THE AFRICAN-AMERICAN JOURNEY THROUGH THE FEDERAL COURTS 36 (1992).

3. Civil rights conference at Howard University, Rankin Chapel, late 1940s–early 1950s. Phineas Indritz, (next three unidentified), Thurgood Marshall, Marjorie McKenzie Lawson, (unidentified), George Johnson, Spottswood W. Robinson III. Collection of Moorland-Spingarn Research Center, Howard University.

THE 1950s

In the 1950s, Thurgood Marshall emerged to leave his own extraordinary contributions in the larger world. The legal principles that he learned at Howard, as well as the approaches and the law practiced by his mentor and friend Charles Hamilton Houston, the acknowledged leader of the modern civil rights movement, greatly influenced him in the legal trials and challenges throughout his life.

For nearly twenty years, Houston had led a tireless fight to eliminate *de jure* discrimination in education, transportation, and other areas. Houston died on April 22, 1950,[1] of an "acute coronary thrombosis"[2] after being warned by his doctor to withdraw from the heavy civil rights litigation in which he was involved. Although Houston died before the historic *Brown* decision in 1954, he had trained and inspired a legion of predominantly African American lawyers who ushered in a new era of civil rights and protracted civil rights litigation.

Three months after Houston's death, at a major conference at Fisk University's Institute on Race Relations, Thurgood Marshall summarized the desegregation cases that Houston had brought in the areas of higher education, public transportation in interstate commerce, and restrictive covenants. For Marshall, the time had come to out-litigate the Dixiecrats. Taking renewed courage from these Supreme Court decisions, the NAACP and its allies could apply the law to destroy the basis of their opponents' political strength—the segregated system and dual citizenship.[3]

Marshall had realized that equality could be achieved in the South not by political means but through the force of judicial review before the Supreme Court of the United States. This statement may have been Marshall's declaration to continue his mentor's work, for he applied

1. J. Clay Smith, Jr., *Forgotten Hero*, 98 Harv. L. Rev. 482, 487 (1984) (*reviewing* Genna Rae McNeil, Groundwork: Charles Hamilton Houston and the Struggle for Civil Rights (1983)).
2. Groundwork at 211.
3. Thurgood Marshall, Racial Integration in Education Through Resort to the Courts, *infra*, at 45, 56.

Houston's strategies and drew inspiration from Houston, whom William Henry Hastie referred to as Moses leading his people to freedom across the Red Sea.[4]

Also in 1950, in what may be the first law review article written by a black lawyer in the *Michigan Law Review*, Marshall drew on jurisprudence of Justice Frank Murphy. Marshall stated that "To [Justice Murphy], the primacy of civil rights and human equality in our law and their entitlement to every possible protection in each case, regardless of competing considerations, was a fighting faith."[5] Marshall, quoting Thurmond W. Arnold, drew attention to three qualities of Justice Murphy: "The first was simplicity; the second was courage; and the third was insight into the substance of the problems of the changing times in which he lived."[6]

While Marshall believed in the rule of law and judicial review, he also realized that Black people could influence politics only when they got involved and challenged the status quo. He believed that where law was openly violated, protest by the people was an appropriate measure to bring about change. Marshall, recognizing that a *sine qua non* to education was to have good teachers, followed the model of his mentor, Houston. Marshall used speeches to teach the people about the law and the strategies of the NAACP. He informed adults and youth of the substance and progress of the cases, before and after the Brown decisions.

The 1954 Brown decision was a historic victory for Marshall. It should be noted several lawyers contributed their considerable talents preparing the cases at both the trial and appellate levels and writing the brief, especially Robert L. Carter, the lead counsel in the Supreme Court case *Brown v. Board of Education*.[7] However, it was Marshall, the chief lawyer of the NAACP, who crossed the country teaching people about the significance of the decision and raising funds for the NAACP to continue to fight for equality for all people in the courts and other forums.

The 1950s was a busy and exciting decade for Marshall. Toward the end of the decade he began to believe that the NAACP and its lawyers had the South on the run.

In "Judicial Methods in Due Process," Marshall expresses his agreement that courts should restrict themselves from overreaching in the exercise of judicial review. However, Marshall asserts that judicial restraint has its limits and should be balanced against the general principle of

4. William H. Hastie, *Charles Hamilton Houston*, 35 J. NEGRO HIST. 355, 356 (July 1950).

5. Thurgood Marshall, *Justice Murphy and Civil Rights*, 48 MICH. L. REV. 745 (1950).

6. *Id.* at 745–746, *quoting* Thurmond W. Arnold, *"Mr. Justice Murphy,"* 63 HARV. L. REV. 289, 293 (1949).

7. *See also* OLIVER W. HILL, SR., THE BIG BANG: BROWN V. BOARD OF EDUCATION AND BEYOND 148–188 (2000) (edited by Jonathan K. Stubbs).

due process. In "The Rise and Collapse of the White Democratic Primary," Marshall declares that a democratic process that excludes Blacks from voting in primary elections to select candidates for the general election results in political parties being white men's parties. Yet, even after the Supreme Court declared this device unconstitutional, Marshall reminds us that the struggle to overcome new devices continued to exist. Finally, in "Summary Justice: The Negro GI in Korea," perhaps one of Marshall's most passionate writings, he chronicles the disparate treatment in the sentencing process in military courts-martial during the Korean War, including the application of the death penalty. Marshall's aim here was to preserve the honor of Black servicemen who bravely fought for their country while being demeaned as cowards by racist commanders.

From Law to Social Reality
and Panel Discussion

What I want to do this morning is to give some of the time to Loren Miller.[1] He has been in most of these cases, and he has been around the fringes at least, of all of them. We have talked about it over the past two days, and there are some things that I think he can give much better than I can. The real problem surrounding cases of the type we have been discussing is that in the past we have been unable to translate these victories . . . into actual patterns, or into the social life of the communities. . . . I want to, first of all, give you just a brief outline of what we want.

So far as I am concerned, I cannot do too much of telling you what can be done, from the non-legal side. . . . I can, however, give you the problems. In the first place, the lawyers who try these cases are considerably hamstrung by what is known as a "Code of Ethics." Clarence Darrow once told us, when I was in Law School, that the code, or the "Canon of Ethics" as they are called, are merely a group of rules promulgated by a group of lawyers who couldn't make it to keep lawyers who were making it from continuing to make it.[2] I think this is pretty close to being accurate. For example, we are prohibited from stirring up litigation. As a matter of fact, there are three different rules on it. They have very nice sounding names, Champerty, Barratry, and Maintenance.[3]

Opening remarks by Thurgood Marshall at the Seventh Annual Institute of Race Relations, Fisk University, Nashville, Tenn., June 26–July 8, 1950. Reproduced courtesy of the Race Relations Department, United Church Board for Homeland Ministries (UCBHM) Archives, Amistad Research Center, Tulane University.
1. Loren Miller, a 1928 graduate of Washburn University School of Law and one of the most respected civil right lawyers in California, was one of the lawyers on the brief in Shelley v. Kraemer, 334 U.S. 1 (1948) that struck down racial covenants. He is also the author of THE PETITIONERS: THE STORY OF THE UNITED STATES AND THE NEGRO (1966).
2. In January 1930, during Marshall's first year as a law student, Clarence Darrow lectured at Howard Law School. It may be these lectures to which Marshall refers. See J. Clay Smith, Jr., *The Early Days of the Law Alumni Association*, 1 THE JURIST 7, 9, Dec. 1986 (listing subject of lectures). See also OLIVER W. HILL, SR., THE BIG BANG: BROWN V. BOARD OF EDUCATION AND BEYOND 78–79 (2000) (edited by Jonathan K. Stubbs) (visit of Clarence Darrow).
3. *See, e.g.*, Note, *Ambulance Chasing*, 30 N.Y.U. L. REV. 561 (1955).

Translated into plain understandable English, a lawyer is not supposed to go up and chase ambulances or do anything to get business; he is supposed to sit there and wait until the business comes in. If you starve in the meantime, it is just your hard luck. These rules, of course, were made for commercial practice, not for cases of our type, but we still are bound by them. While the case is pending in court, we are usually prohibited from discussion of those cases. . . . That rule is not as strict, and it varies, and you can take certain leeway with it.

For example, the three cases I discussed the other night, which we have been discussing off and on . . . are still pending in the Supreme Court. The reason they are still pending is because motions for rehearing have been filed, the usual procedure when lawyers lose a case. It's one of the few things you can do . . . to file a motion for rehearing, and tell the courts that you think they are wrong. That's about as far as you can go. Well, when the mandates go down on the cases and they are finally completed, lawyers are then free to discuss the case and do whatever can be done. All of which adds up to the fact that the lawyers, as such, are prevented from doing the type of effectual social action within the community surrounding a case that other people can do. None of the rules that I have mentioned apply to anyone but lawyers and, to a part, judges.

Let me give you background of one other item, and then we'll get to these cases. In many states, as you know, we have civil rights statutes, which prohibit discrimination on the basis of race, creed, or color in places of public accommodation. In most of these states these statutes have been on the books for many years. But let's see what has happened as a result of inaction on the community level. For example in California, in Los Angeles and in San Francisco, you can enforce the civil rights statutes; and they have been enforced. But in all other sections of California Negroes are prohibited from eating in establishments and staying in decent hotels. In other words, the law is just openly violated, and nobody does anything about it. You can come across the country and touch any other states with civil rights statutes, and you will find the same thing is true. In Illinois there is only one place that the Illinois civil rights statutes is enforced, and that is in Chicago . . . For example in the capital of Illinois, in Springfield, there is one legislative member there, Corneal A. Davis,[4] who every year introduces a resolution in the

4. Corneal A. Davis, also known as "Deacon" because he was a minister, was a Democratic state representative in 1950. He served in the Illinois State Assembly from 1943 to 1979. In 1969, he influenced passage of the first Fair Employment Practice Act. During the 1940s Davis led the fight to end discrimination against black students at the University of Illinois Medical School in Chicago by threatening to have the college's funds cut off. In addition, " in 1944, he fought

legislature of Illinois asking that Lincoln's tomb be removed from Springfield because of the considerable discrimination against the Negroes in
that city. In Michigan the same is true. In the rural areas, the civil rights
statutes [might] just as well . . . not be on the books. I am of course more
familiar with New York. The civil rights statute in New York was enforced
in the Metropolitan City of New York, and that is all. You leave Metropolitan New York and you have no civil rights to be protected. Albany,
the capital of New York, is just about as prejudiced a place as you want
to find. In recent years we have broken through in some of the hotels.
One or two of them will tolerate the "right type of Negro." In other
words, if you have sufficient backing, and you are a great person, then
you can stay there. The average person cannot.

So, for all intents and purposes, the civil rights statutes in these states
mean nothing, and it is understandable, the legislature—pressure that
was put on the legislature—brought about these statutes. The people
sat down and let the statutes sit on the books and rot. As to whether anything can be done at this late date, of course something can be done.
How can it be done is a matter for well-trained community personnel to
work out; the lawyers can't work it out. We can't even win a lawsuit in
these rural areas because the people there have just not been educated.
Whereas they have been educated that if a man steals a watch, that is not
only against the statutes, but it is against their principles. A jury will convict, if of course the man is guilty. However, if a restaurant owner refuses
to permit a Negro to eat a dinner, that is not against the policy of the
general community level, and the jury will just not convict.

I know the case for example in Brooklyn. Where Ted Poston—I think
some of you know him—he has won several awards in the recent months
as a result of his writings in the *New York Post*.[5] For some years back he
went to "Minnie's Kitchen," in Brooklyn, a restaurant, and he was told by
the proprietor that the only place (she was from Virginia) Negroes ate
in Virginia was in the kitchen, and that was the only place they could
eat in her restaurant, was in the kitchen. She was told by Poston about

---

in behalf of black school teachers in Downstate Cairo who were being paid less
than white faculty members. He contacted . . . a[n] [NAACP] lawyer to file a suit
that was sent to future Supreme Court Justice Thurgood Marshall. Together, they
won the case." *Corneal A. Davis, Civil Rights Leader, State Rep,* CHI. SUN-TIMES,
April 19, 1995, at 78. *See also Former State Rep. Corneal A. Davis, 94,* CHI. TRIB.,
April 19, 1995, at 11.
5. Ted Poston was one of the "first black reporters for a big city daily." Letter
from William H. A. Carr to AM. JOURNALISM REV. 5 (July–Aug. 1999). Poston,
who died in 1974, also wrote short stories, which were published posthumously.
TED POSTON, THE DARK SIDE OF HOPKINSVILLE: STORIES (1991) (edited by
Kathleen Hauke).

the civil rights laws: they meant nothing to her. He had her arrested, and he had her tried, and she admitted exactly that on the witness stand. And the jury promptly acquitted her—in Brooklyn. . . . The same is true in every state. The lawyers can give you examples where we have civil rights statutes.

Now let's get back to these school cases. If we run along the same channel we have been running on these, we'll have much of the same effect. When the University of Maryland case was tried to get Donald Murray in the University of Maryland, while the case was pending, after argument on an appeal, we got a letter from a very good friend of the NAACP, in Washington. He said that he realized that the lawyers were interested in the legal side of the case, but had any of us stopped to realize that the decision in the case meant nothing. It was completely unimportant. The important thing was, what would happen when Murray was admitted to the Law School? Many of us had been worrying about that problem. For example, when Donald Murray was admitted to the Law School, back in '36,[6] the Dean of the University of Maryland Law School[7] was quite worried. He said he was worried. He wanted Murray to sit either in the front or the back of the classroom; to sit to the side, or something—after all, they had problems. Donald Murray told him, one thing, he might submit to segregation, but he would never ask for it. After much argument, it was agreed that Murray would be put in the middle of the classroom. As a matter of fact, he was put in the exact middle. And the Dean said, he did not want any trouble, so would it be all right if he asked around—at least among the students whom he knew—to see if he could find some—imagine this, now, if he could find any American citizen who had no objection to sitting beside an American. Murray said, "I don't care what you do," he was going to sit there. And that very afternoon the Dean called up and said, "Guess what happened. The first young man I asked merely asked me, in return, was this the man he had been reading about in the [press]; was this the same one who had brought the lawsuit, and I said, yes. And he said, 'There is just one more question that I want to ask you. Does he have any contagious disease?' And he said, 'No.' Then he said, 'Well why can't I sit beside him?'" That young man represented the student body, that same young man became the president of his class, and was president for three years and I for one, believe that he spoke for the whole class.

6. *See* Pearson v. Murray, 169 Md. 478, 182 A. 590 (1935) (Maryland Court of Appeals orders the University of Maryland to admit Donald G. Murray to the School of Law).
7. Dean Roger Howell. *See Tributes to Professor John M. Brumbaugh*, 55 Md. L. Rev. 519, 524 (1999) (includes information about Dean Howell).

Murray was accepted freely; he was taken into the law clubs along with everyone else, and he was taken into the social clubs along with everyone else, and nothing happened. He got along fine. There have been Negroes there ever since. So maybe something was accomplished. But, again, the community did little. The University of Maryland's Law School is not on the [main] campus of the University of Maryland, it's thirty some miles from it; it is in Baltimore. The campus of the University of Maryland is at College Park, practically in Washington. So that a Negro in the University had no effect on the campus because they were too far apart. With that principle established in that case, the State of Maryland offered out-of-state scholarships to students, and we never could get, for years, a Negro willing to apply to the Medical School, the Dental School, or any other school. And the lawyers couldn't go out and ask them to apply, we couldn't go out and solicit business. And so, as of this year, there are no Negroes on the campus of the University of Maryland. We have another case against the School of Nursing this year,[8] but the School of Nursing is again in Baltimore, and not on the [main] campus.

To go from Maryland let's jump a little distance down and go to Oklahoma—go to Missouri, let's stop at Missouri on the Gaines case.[9] Another victory won. Nothing was done in the general community; nothing has been done in Missouri to educate either side until just a year ago, when there was agitation in the legislature to amend the law to permit Negroes to attend the University. Then this year, as a result of that agitation, and the result of constant pressure over a year's period of time, the Board of Regents of the University of Missouri filed a lawsuit, not the Negroes. They filed the lawsuit asking for declaratory judgment, for the court to tell them whether they should admit Negroes. They knew full well what the court would say, and the court promptly ruled that they had to admit qualified Negroes.[10] But that same type of action had it been going on from '38 when the Gaines case was decided, would have at least cleaned up Missouri long before now.

8. This case was ultimately won. See McCready v. Byrd, 195 Md. 131, 73 A.2d 8 (1950).

9. Missouri law required separate education for blacks and whites in higher education. Thus, Lloyd Gaines's application to the University of Missouri Law School was denied. However, state policy provided modest subsidies for black students to attend professional schools outside the state if no black institution existed therein. The U.S. Supreme Court struck down the state law as unconstitutional, stating that "a denial of the equality of legal right to the enjoyment of privilege which the state has set up, and the provision for the payment of tuition fees in another state does not remove the discrimination." Missouri ex rel. Gaines v. Canada, 305 U.S. 337, 349–350 (1938).

10. The case referred to by Marshall is no doubt associated with State ex rel. Gaines v. Canada, 305 U.S. 337 (1938).

In Oklahoma, in that case, when the case was filed, the Negro community was completely behind it. They put their money in the case, they stuck to it, when Miss Sipuel's case[11] went up to the Supreme Court and when they set up a little piece of a law school in the state capital and their community action defeated the state just as well as the Law School. Because it became—I use this word carefully, and I guess we'll understand it—became "unhealthy" for Negroes to go to that law school—the Jim Crow. Negroes made it known to everybody that they would have no respect, and do [nothing] else for a Negro who had applied to the law school. And no one applied, with the exception of one. And it was developed that the one Negro who had applied was working as a bellboy in the club where all of the big officials stayed. And then it just so happened that he belonged to a Negro college fraternity, and it just so happened, that they had a special meeting of that fraternity. And since I am not a member of that fraternity and wasn't there, I don't know what happened at the fraternity meeting, but I do know that on the next day, he withdrew from the school. I don't know what the segment of the community in that fraternity said that night, but the gentleman withdrew the next day.

On the other hand, the white students at the University of Oklahoma, without any prodding by any group except a Methodist social action group,[12] conducted a poll, . . . held meetings and, if you will remember, they burned the Fourteenth Amendment when Miss Sipuel was refused admission. The community level around the Oklahoma University is located around a town called Norman. Norman, Oklahoma, is a city [like other cities] in this country that Negroes are not allowed to live in. During the war, they had a few of them who were allowed to stay there because of a war plant that was nearby. But when the Sipuel case was tried, there was a serious question as to where the Negro witness, the Negro lawyers, and the Negroes interested in the case would eat lunch. And the largest church in that city—one of the social clubs of that church—opened the doors of the church and served lunch to all of the Negroes who were present at that trial on the first day of that trial. As a result of that, on the second day of the trial, we had lunch in the largest

11. After Ada Lois Sipuel's application to the state law school in Oklahoma was denied because she was black, she sued. The matter reached the U.S. Supreme Court, which applied the principle that it had held in Gaines. Sipuel v. Board of Regents, 332 U.S. 631 (1948). The Court dismissed as irrelevant the fact that the state had established a law school for blacks. Fisher v. Hurst, 333 U.S. 147 (1948).
12. For more on the attitude of the law students, *see* ADA LOIS SIPUEL FISHER, A MATTER OF BLACK AND WHITE: THE AUTOBIOGRAPHY OF ADA LOIS SIPUEL FISHER 107–108, 114–117, 146–148 (1996).

restaurant in Norman, Oklahoma. That is the type of community level action that, to my mind, is important—where not only the University itself had a terrific drive, but that the drive from the University reached over into the church, and the leadership of the church made it possible for us to at least break open—and I say advisably, temporarily at least— the ban against Negroes.

At the University of Texas, the *Daily Texan,* the local newspaper run by the University student body, carried at least two dozen editorials urging that [Heman] Sweatt[13] be admitted to the University of Texas. The student body had mass meetings, they organized a college chapter of the NAACP, and I had the honor of giving them their charter in the chapel at the University of Texas.[14] The student body almost wholeheartedly supported the right of this young Negro not to be excluded. At the hearing on this case, you couldn't get into the courtroom for the students from the University of Texas—mostly law school students. On the second day of the trial, the bailiff of the court—I don't know what happened— the record shows that he went up and talked to the judge on the side, Judge Archer,[15] and went back and told two of the white students, who were sitting beside a group of Negroes whom they knew, that that was the Negro side of the courtroom, and they had to move. And these two young men told the bailiff that the only grounds upon which they would move would be if the Negroes told them that they weren't welcome. And after a few words backward and forward, every day, on both sides of the courtroom, Negro and white spectators would spread themselves

13. This case was ultimately decided by the U.S. Supreme Court in Sweatt v. Painter, 339 U.S. 629 (1950).
14. Thurgood Marshall's account of the student support at the university is supported by Michael L. Gillette, who writes: "The prospect of a Negro attending law school did not concern the students. . . . In the fall of 1946, a variety organizations became involved in the *Sweatt* case. . . . [T]hey held a rally in support of Sweatt's admission. . . . To NAACP officials the quintessence of support from the University community was the formation of a University of Texas chapter of the NAACP. Suggested by the national youth secretary, the organization apparently evolved from the Sweatt Fund Drive. . . . The University of Texas branch was the only one on a segregated campus." Michael L. Gillette, *Blacks Challenge the White University,* 86 Sw. HIST. Q. 111 (Oct. 1982). Letter from Stephanie Towery to J. Clay Smith, Jr., Oct. 26, 1999. In 1946, the *Dallas Morning News* reported that a group of white students at the University of Texas adopted the following resolution in support of Heman Sweatt: "We hereby endorse and intend to support the National Association for the Advancement of Colored People's efforts for equal educational opportunities, as evidenced in the case of Heman Sweatt, seeking admission to the University of Texas law school." Dawson Duncan, *UT Students Group Would Admit Negro,* DALLAS MORNING NEWS, Nov. 20, 1946, at 1.
15. This judge is likely Judge Roy C. Archer, Chief Justice, 3rd District, Texas Court of Civil Appeals.

out over two seats apiece, so that we had a complete cross-section like this across the courtroom. Those students from the University of Texas listened to the Dean of the Law School, at that time, Dean Charles T. McCormick, justify segregation, justify the practices, and booed him openly in the court room—their own Dean. They booed the President of the University, his name was Shickel Painter, I don't know about "Shickel Goober," but his name was Shickel Painter anyhow. And when, for example, Dean Errol Harrison of the University of Pennsylvania Law School testified for Sweatt, they cheered him. And the students, I should add, were so jammed in there that they were sitting all around the floor in the courtroom, which of course was against the law but they found difficulty in getting them up and getting them out. (You know young people just don't move unless they want to move.)

Now these decisions in the McLaurin case[16]—when Miss Sipuel was admitted, they told her that she would be segregated, and she said, "Well, let me see about this, because I'm not going to take segregation." And they said, "Well around that seat where you sit is an imaginary wall, and you sit inside of that imaginary wall, and you're thereby segregated, and we comply with the law." And the white students wouldn't even accept that, as many of them as could, walked through the wall and sat down with her. In the cafeteria, there was one table with a sign marked "reserved for colored." Of course the sign got misplaced, lost, and pushed around. Finally, the last and most interesting thing before the decision in Oklahoma, was that as a result of having these "reserved for Negro" signs in the library, the cafeteria, and every place else the largest social group on the campus, a club by the name of which I don't remember, sent out invitations for people to come on "O.U. party," meaning Oklahoma University, and nobody could understand what an "O.U. party" was, until everybody came to the recreation room, and when they came in they found out the significance of the O.U. party was because on every table in the room was a sign "reserved for colored."

So, the court decision as to the University itself was a little bit behind the University. The faculty and student body settled the problem when those Negroes were admitted. So that as to the particular Universities involved in these cases, we needed no community action other than supporting action. What are you going to do on the other levels? How are we going to break down segregation on the collegiate level? How on the high school and elementary level? And that is our problem. I don't

16. The McLaurin case laid the foundation for the Sipuel case. The Court held that to separate McLaurin from the white students while in the Department of Education of the University of Oklahoma limited "his ability to study, to engage in discussions and exchange views with other students, and, in general, to learn his profession." McLaurin v. Oklahoma State Regents, 339 U.S. 637, 641 (1950).

know the answer, and before I yield the time to Loren Miller, I'll say in advance that he has admitted that he cannot answer this question, but I'm leaving it out for those of you to be thinking over before we have a discussion, because I seriously want an answer. And the question is: . . . assume that in the near future, as a result of these decisions, I get a letter from little Mary Jones, in "Podunk" County, Mississippi, who would say, "I read about the decisions, I heard about what my rights are to attend a non-segregated school. You've been around talking about we should apply to these schools, I want to go to the white high school in 'Podunk,' Mississippi, what are you going to do about it?" Now, I have the first two answers, but I want the third answer, and I seriously want this third answer from somebody. I take the extreme case because I think from the extreme case we will get the type of machinery to use in other cases. I said I have the first two answers, one is "I'm in conference and can't be disturbed." But now, when I get by that, what do I tell that young lady and what can all of us do on it, not legally, we know what we can do legally, but what we can do from a community level, and when Loren gets through, I hope somebody will have an answer. He won't, but I hope somebody will.

Panel Discussion Following Marshall's Comments Re: Supreme Court Decisions—Sweatt, McLaurin, and Henderson Cases

Panel: Saville Davis, George Schermer, Alexander Looby, Loren Miller, R. Alexander Miller, P. L. Prattis, Thurgood Marshall[17]

Mr. L. Miller: What are your impressions of the recent Supreme Court decisions and how was it received in the city of Chicago?

17. Saville Davis was on the editorial staff of the CHRISTIAN SCIENCE MONITOR. *See Saville Davis, Was Managing Editor of Christian Monitor,* BOSTON GLOBE, Dec. 4, 1991, at 17. George Schermer was a race relations specialist. *George Schermer, Race Relations Expert,* CHI. TRIB., June 9, 1989, at 12C. Dr. Zephaniah Alexander Looby was a leading black lawyer, politician and civil rights leader in Nashville. His civil rights advocacy almost cost him his life when his house was blown up in the 1960s. *Looby-Westbrook, Civil Rights Leader Dies,* THE TENNESSEAN, Jan. 14, 1997, at 6B. (This obituary for Dr. Looby's former wife reports on the bombing.) Dr. Looby died in 1972. For more on Looby, *see* Tim Chavez, *Movements Are of People, Not Leaders,* THE TENNESSEAN, Aug. 14, 1997, at arc. and J. CLAY SMITH, JR., EMANCIPATION: THE MAKING OF THE BLACK LAWYER, 1844–1944, at 62, 343–344, 364 n. 209 (1993). Loren Miller was a leading publicist and civil rights lawyer from Los Angeles and the author of a leading account of *Brown v. Board of Education. See* LOREN MILLER, THE PETITIONERS, *supra* note 1. P. L. Prattis was the editor of the powerful PITTSBURGH COURIER. He is mentioned in Michael Marsh, *Writer Helped Robinson Along,* CHI. SUN-TIMES, March 30, 1997, at 17; and George H. Hill, BLACK MEDIA IN AMERICA: A RESOURCE GUIDE 14 (1984).

Mr. Carey [a member of the audience]: There were three reactions that I might note. One is that as far as the dining car case [Henderson] was concerned, it failed to say anything about travel within the state. The second is that none of the decisions took the step of saying that segregation is unconstitutional and un-American. The third is the failure of the Supreme Court to agree to review the case of the three Negro American veterans who were denied admission to Stuyvesant Town in New York by the Metropolitan Life Insurance Company.[18] The decisions were hailed by everybody, who believes in fair play and equal opportunity, and they were saluted as great milestones in the American people's march towards complete equality; but these are three definite shortcomings.

Mr. Looby: It seems to me that in spite of the fact that the Supreme Court [*Sweatt*] did not definitely say that segregation was unconstitutional, recognizing that the Court does not pass upon these constitutional cases unless it is forced to, nevertheless it did rule it unconstitutional, if not in words at least in effect. While the Supreme Court sets certain standards by which the course of law schools can be measured, those standards cannot be met by setting up a separate school. To meet the Supreme Court decision, it would be absolutely necessary that Negro applicants be admitted to the law school. With respect to the other cases, it seems to me, especially in the McLaurin case, that the education being offered certainly was equal but the psychological effect it had on the segregated person was the determinant. Consequently, if that is to be removed, it simple means that segregation must be removed. I think the same reasoning would follow through in the dining car case.[19] While we do not have a definite decision saying that segregation is unconstitutional in itself, we have in effect certain decisions, which make it impossible to comply with the standards set [by] the Supreme Court without establishing equality.

Mr. R. A. Miller: And do you think the South will accept this decision?

Mr. Looby: I think the South definitely will accept it. In fact, I believe that the South has been ready for these decisions for some time; only a

---

18. *See* Dorsey v. Stuyvesant Town Corp., 299 N.Y. 512, 87 N.E. 2d 541 (1949), *cert. den.*, 339 U.S. 981 (1950).

19. Referring to Henderson v. United States, 339 U.S. 816 (1950), holding that interstate carriers such as railroads that discriminate on the basis of race in dining-room cars deny equal protection and violate the equal protection clause of the Constitution. This case is discussed in Seth P. Waxman, *Twins at Birth: Civil Rights and the Role of the Solicitor General*, 75 IND. L.J. 1297, 1306, n. 54 (2000). See also *Segregation in Interstate Commerce*, 8 NAT'L BAR J. 1 (March 1950) (contains argument of Philip B. Perlman, Solicitor General of the United States, who argued before the Supreme Court that passengers of different races should not be served meals at different times).

few politicians and a few other reactionaries have been retarding the South in its progress. I believe the masses are generally ready.

Mr. L. Miller: I'm not nearly as optimistic about the fact that the masses of the South are ready to break down segregation in the public school systems of the South tomorrow, in a month, or in a year, without considerable struggle. However, despite any reactions, we have to press forward. It is not these segregation cases that will provide the fuel for the demagogues. They will find fuel, no matter what the situation is. Look at the Florida elections: before the segregation cases were decided, the race issue was played up in Pepper's campaign to a higher point than it has been played up for some six or eight years.[20] We're going to meet a good many set-backs and some difficult tension situations, Mr. Marshall has said, we have to continue pressing forward as vigorously and as courageously as we know how.

Mr. Davis: It seems to me that it is necessary to look at these decisions not only in the remedial and social context but in the political context surrounding it. Before the war the Supreme Court would not have, under any circumstances, given the decisions which are now being discussed. This means that the Supreme Court follows what we as citizens do. All of the advancing with its limitations is part of a process by which society is slowly but absolutely moving on the problems of inequality.

Mr. Schermer: These cases haven't touched us directly, but those affecting housing have; and we are just beginning to feel the impact of them in the past few years. The loosening up of the housing market has been very decided, as a result in part of the restrictive covenants decision[21] and the changing financial situation insofar as FHA [Federal Housing Administration] is concerned. As far as reactions on the recent decisions are concerned, I noticed that the people in the Negro community and the people whom we consider as "good folks" perhaps expressed a little disappointment in the cases. I think they expected a forthright outlawing of the whole concept of "separate but equal." The decisions will have a terrific impact on the thinking and attitudes of the people who disliked them, those who might be called the reactionary forces in the community. There the full meaning of these decisions seems to have registered. If you can get the power forces of the community to take a position on the side which is right, then you get a lot of people going along. The Supreme Court is significant as a force of power; people accept its decisions.

Through the years, we have had a segregated public housing program in Detroit. There have been definite indications in the last few years that

20. Apparently referring to Claude Pepper's run for the U.S. Senate in 1950.
21. See, e.g., Shelley v. Kraemer, 334 U.S. 1 (1948).

the City Council and the Mayor would like to get away from that practice; but for political reasons they don't dare to. Under present law in cities or towns, any time the Mayor or a city councilman takes a position against segregation in Detroit he's through politically. But the Supreme Court decisions help pave the way for towns; and it's just a little matter of processing one case or more and we hope to be able to get out from under segregation in Detroit.

Mr. Prattis: I believe we have the rascals on the run and can keep them running. Justice Black in the '30s in a case involving exclusion of Negroes from jury service in the South went far beyond presentations which had been made as to whether or not Negroes were systematically excluded from juries in the South.[22] The fact was they did not serve on them. It seems to me that the Supreme Court in most recent decisions has followed this thinking of Justice Black and is getting beyond legalistic formalism to reach the equation of justice. There is also something else in the air; the white people of the South can no longer ignore the very powerful forces which are at work in the world today and which are running counter to the established traditions of the South. The Supreme Court justices cannot consider what is happening among the nations of the world, in the United Nations, in respect to human rights, without being, unconsciously or consciously, moved to apply those developments to our domestic problems.[23] I don't believe that what has happened in Florida and in North Carolina is representative of the mass thinking of the South. We have existing in our country at this time a certain political condition, which has put a minority party into the position of seeking to regain power by any means possible. Political interests outside the South exploited the race issue in North Carolina and in Florida. The southern masses of people jumped through the hoop for the advantage of a certain political party. But where the masses of southern people are appealed to on the basis of fairness, of rightness, and of human relations, I believe we would get very different results. We must back up the Supreme Court by continuing to file cases and, more importantly, by continuing to supply the NAACP with the sinews of war, which is money.

22. Smith v. Texas, 311 U.S. 128, 130 (1940) (describing a jury as a body "truly representative of the community").
23. Black lawyers of this generation were probably quite aware of the Universal Declaration of Human Rights, G.A. Res. 217A, U.N. Doc. A/810, at 71 (1948). The text of the Declaration can be found in LOUIS HENKIN, ET AL., HUMAN RIGHTS 287 (1999). It proclaimed, in part, "Everyone is entitled to all the rights and freedoms set forth in this Declaration, without distinction of any kind, such as race, colour, sex, language, religion, political or other opinion, national or social origin, property, birth or other status" (Art. 2).

Question from the audience: Can the Supreme Court decisions form the basis for attacking segregation on the undergraduate, elementary, and high school levels?

Mr. Marshall: Among the quarrels of lawyers that studied these decisions the opinion is that they would be the basis for such legal action, but that we would be obliged to produce the same type of expert testimony on those levels. We'll have to get experts in the field of collegiate, elementary, and high school education, for example, to show that each cannot get education without an interchange of thoughts and ideas. I am informed that we can get more experts to show even more clearly the necessity for all ethnic groups being educated together on the lower levels. We will have to go to court and fight it out, but these decisions will be the precedents. *Plessy* is through.[24]

Question from the audience to Mr. R. Alexander Miller: . . . Mr. Miller, you seem to disagree with me when I say that the masses of the South are ready for integration that is, terminate segregation. I should like to ask if—in your opinion—the legislature of any of the southern states—let's say Tennessee, for example—in 1951 should abolish all its segregation laws, do you think the people would accept it?

Mr. R. A. Miller: . . . I would say that there might be a little more opposition that some people might think but. . . . If the legislature of Tennessee, in 1951, representing all the people of this state, were to abolish segregation, I think the people—and Mr. Crump—would obey their dictates.[25]

Mr. Carey: I think that what Mr. Miller says is there is no depletion in the accumulation of power in the decisions of the Supreme Court by an acknowledgment of the fact that it would take time for the people to catch up with the idea. It's a two-way street—the Supreme Court follows the election results and the election results follow the Supreme Court. When a law is passed some people learn for the first time that a given type of action is disapproved in our society. From that point on they have a different attitude toward the particular thing that is in question. In that sense the Supreme Court not only follows the mores of the people but helps to fix these mores in many instances. . . .

Question from the audience: [Inaudible.]

Mr. Marshall: So as far as I'm concerned, right now—as they now stand—we have a case where, for example, a Negro was refused admission

24. Plessy v. Ferguson, 163 U.S. 547 (1896).
25. Referring to E. H. "Boss" Crump, who served as Mayor of Memphis for several years. "The black-white battles are recounted during the reign of E. H. 'Boss Crump' from 1909 until his death in 1954." Nate Hobbs, *Story of '91 Election Reveals the City*, THE COMM. APPEAL, Oct. 31, 1996, at 1C. Mayor Crump was "an avowed segregationist who tolerated no power position for an African American in his political machine." *Id.*

to a law school in—well, let's say Tennessee; we're in Tennessee. I think then you'd go like we did in the McLaurin case—allege that the statute is unconstitutional. Carry that case straight to the Supreme Court, and the Supreme Court will then do what it does all the time—say that as applied to that particular person, the statute is unconstitutional. I can't change that procedure and, honest to goodness, the Supreme Court itself can't change it. They can only decide the case as to the individual involved. We expect the people to follow. The best example I love to give is the Texas primary decision, by which not only Negroes in Texas have been voting but they have been voting in most other southern states, as a result of that decision.[26] Yet here is what actually happened. That suit was against two registrars . . . and the case ended in a five dollar judgment against both of them—which, incidentally was not collected; and yet Negroes are voting all over the South.

Question from the audience: What can students do to help in the integration of schools?

Mr. Marshall: I can give you two examples: one in the South and one in the North. In one of the best academies in the North, young students got a few of their teachers, the president, and, eventually, the trustees straightened out. It took them four years, but they did it by pressuring their parents, who in turn pressured the trustees by threatening to cut off money; but the students started it. In the University of Oklahoma case one of the officials indicated himself that he was going to do all right because he was sick and tired of his son giving him a fit three times a day about being out of step with the times. Your biggest job as students, to my mind, is an affirmative campaign within your own group and student body on the necessity of having Negroes in your classes to help you and them. Students themselves can bring the faculty and the board of trustees in line with their thinking. You can do a lot about it, but you have to convince your own students first.

Mr. L. Miller: There is pretty general agreement among the members of this panel that the support is not only for the particular rights established in these decisions but also indicates a trend on the part of the Supreme Court toward enlarging the freedoms that are contained in the Fourteenth and Fifteenth Amendments. There is agreement also that a decision of the Supreme Court, because of the tremendous prestige that such a pronouncement has, will have a great effect in shaping the thinking and the attitudes of Americans. There is some disagreement as to how ready the South is to accept this decision and all it implies. But there is agreement everywhere that every effort must be made to push

26. *See* Smith v. Allwright, 321 U.S. 649 (1944); Alan Robert Burch, *Charles Hamilton Houston, the Texas White Primary, and Centralization of the NAACP's Litigation Strategy*, 21 T. MARSHALL L. REV. 95 (1995).

this decision to its ultimate limits to finally erode the whole fabric of the "separate but equal" doctrine. There is the opinion also expressed here that the Supreme Court does, in the popular phrase, follow the election returns but also that it helps make attitudes and shape the mores of the people. There is also the opinion expressed that any Supreme Court opinion rendered these days, or any other opinion by the government, must be weighed in the light of the grave international events that confront us on all sides.

Second Day Panel Discussion

Panel: Loren Miller, Thurgood Marshall

Question from the audience: Why is community support so lacking or so difficult to mobilize?

Mr. Marshall: The reason we do not get the type of implementation from our local organizations and the individual people as well is because as much as we shout and as much as we do, we do not actually in our minds have that necessary *crusading, driving* spirit. That is what we must have. We must have a period of believing in our own lines of discussion, of working every day on it, and I think there is a page we can take out of any study that has been made of well-disciplined groups—they work at their job twenty-four hours a day wherever they go. We have people who deep in their own minds believe in equality but are not willing to actually go out and work at it. That is the real problem.

Question from the audience: Can you give any estimates on the costs of these civil rights cases?

Mr. Marshall: The University of Maryland case cost around $10,000; the University of Missouri case was over $30,000. That indicates everything except counsel fees, which the lawyers do not get. When the final count comes through the University of Texas case comes to about $25,000 or $26,000.[27] The McLaurin case was a "quickie" case, costing a low $10,000.[28] Cases testing segregation on the lower level, to get through the lower courts would be $5,000; through the Circuit Court of Appeals, $10,000–15,000; and through the Supreme Court about $5,000–10,000. Every man is entitled to his day in court, if he has the money.

Mr. L. Miller: We also have to face the school problem that exists up North. Every Northern city districts its schools, drawing boundary lines roughly in accordance to the manner in which the Negro population is spread. If in the average Northern city I knew nothing at all except the original location of the school and its original boundary lines, I could trace the direction of Negro population, assuming that there was a small

27. Sweatt v. Painter, 339 U.S. 629 (1950).
28. McLaurin v. Oklahoma State Regents for Higher Educ., 339 U.S. 637 (1950).

nucleus of Negroes in that city in the beginning. That is true in my home state [California] and I know is true in most states. Of course if you are going to have a high concentration of residential segregation, you obviously are going to get school boundary lines drawn accordingly. Where you have peripheral areas, something might be done by community organizations if they bothered to scrutinize and call the Board of Education to account on the mapping of school districts.

It is almost impossible in most cities for a Negro student to get transferred out of an all-Negro school. This is school segregation, about which something could be done by social action and groups in any community. Then you have another problem in most communities about the integration of teacher staff—the tendency to send Negro teachers to what are known as "Negro schools" and to send white teachers elsewhere. Here's a problem in which there is no legal question involved at all, unless your state has a nonsegregation law. Still segregation is built up and maintained by these very obvious devices. There is nothing involved here except the arbitrary drawing of school boundary lines which arrives at that segregation in lower schools. We like to complain about this state of affairs so much in the South and yet do so little about it in the North.

Question from the audience: Don't you think, though, that the civil rights laws in northern states can help remedy this situation?

Mr. R. A. Miller: You are perfectly right, provided community groups act to increase the enforcement of these laws. The longer you delay action, the less the law becomes effective. There must be a point somewhere at which some action is undertaken, or the law will fall into such complete disuse that its value becomes almost negative.

Mr. Marshall: Some years ago, in Washington, D.C., . . . a law was found that had been passed in 1873 which prohibited a restaurant from refusing service to any person because of color on penalty of $100 fine and losing his license for one year. That law was passed when the City of Washington was operated and governed by a city council. Since that time Congress has changed the District's form of government, and the city is now operated by Commissioners appointed by the President of the United States, with Congress passing laws for the District. The question arose, after discovery of this law passed in 1873, when is a law not a law? Is that law still in operation? It had never been repealed. It had never been enforced. In fact it had never been discovered, as far as the present generation is concerned, except accidentally. When Joseph Lohman[29] was in Washington making the survey of segregation in the nation's capital, folks began talking about this law and decided to test it. The testing committee went downtown to a large restaurant, one of the most prominent in the city, and were refused service. They then presented the case

29. Joseph Lohman was a professor of sociology at the University of Chicago.

to the District of Columbia Corporation Attorney for prosecution, under the old statute of 1873. He hemmed and hawed and tried to walk out of the snow without making any tracks. But the committee was persistent, and the Commissioners ordered the Corporation Counsel to make a study of the old law and decide whether or not it was feasible to prosecute under it. While the case was being studied, the committee withdrew its request for prosecution. Several months later, the Corporation Counsel came up with the opinion that the law is valid: he could find no record of repeal and, therefore, the law was still in force.[30] Consequently, the committee went back to the same restaurant, and once again presented themselves for service and once again were denied. They immediately filed complaint again and the prosecutor brought [a criminal] suit against this restaurant owner. The owner had the backing of the Washington Restaurant Association, an affiliate of the National Restaurant Association, and had one of the most prominent lawyers they could get. Up until now the judge has not rendered a decision, but that case is pending and sooner or later I suppose—there is no such thing as a judge not giving a decision.[31]

That is a case of the community's attempting to implement a law one might say was almost obsolete.

30. This statute can be found in THE GENERAL INDEX OF THE LAW OF THE DISTRICT OF COLUMBIA 97, 98, 151 (1912). Section 150 of THE COMPILED STATUTES IN FORCE IN THE DISTRICT OF COLUMBIA INCLUDING THE ACTS OF THE SECOND SESSION OF THE FIFTIETH CONGRESS, 1887–89, at 183 (1894) reads: "Any restaurant keeper or proprietor, any hotel keeper or, proprietors or keepers of ice-cream saloons or places where soda-water is kept for sale, or keepers of barber shops and bathing houses, refusing to sell or wait upon any respectable well-behaved person, without regard to race, color, or previous condition of servitude, or any restaurant, hotel, ice-cream saloon, or soda fountain, barber shop or bathing-house keepers, or proprietors, who refuse under any pretext to serve any well-behaved respectable person, in the same room, and at the same prices as other well-behaved and respectable persons served, shall be deemed guilty of a misdemeanor, and upon conviction in a court having jurisdiction, shall be fined one hundred dollars, and shall forfeit his or her license as keeper or owner of a restaurant, hotel, ice-cream saloon, or soda fountain, as the case may be, and it shall not be lawful for the Assessor [Register] or any officer of the District of Columbia to issue a license to any person or persons, or to their agent or forfeited their license under the provisions of this act until a period of one year shall have elapsed after such forfeiture."
31. The matter was decided by the U.S. Supreme Court in 1953. Reversing the U.S. Circuit Court of the District of Columbia, the Court held that under the Constitution, Congress was within its powers to delegate its authority reflected in the antidiscrimination statutes of June 20, 1872, and June 1873. The formation of a reformed D.C. government was of no moment since the laws saved the civil rights provisions of the relevant acts. District of Columbia v. John R. Thompson Co., Inc., 346 U.S. 100, 103 (1953).

Racial Integration in Education Through Resort to the Courts and Summit Discussion

In order to evaluate recent efforts to achieve racial integration in education through legal action, it is necessary first to consider the legal background of these cases. There are three distinct periods to be considered: the period between 1896 and 1930; the period between 1930 and 1945; and the period from 1945 to date.

1896–1930 Period

The Supreme Court in 1896 in the case of *Plessy v. Ferguson*[1] involving the validity of a statute of Louisiana requiring segregation in intrastate transportation used certain state cases upholding segregation in public education as the basis for its decision upholding the statute. This decision started the "separate-but-equal" doctrine. During the period between 1896 and 1930, this separate-but-equal doctrine became ingrained in our case law through a lack of carefully planned legal action. Many cases were decided in state and Federal courts during that period; and almost without exception these courts cited with approval the separate-but-equal doctrine. The important point to be considered during this period is that no effort was made in any of these cases to present to the court testimony and other evidence aimed at challenging the validity of these segregation statutes in these states. A good example of this is the case of *Gong Lum v. Rice*[2] in which the Supreme Court followed the separate-but-equal doctrine. An examination of the record and briefs in this case

Thurgood Marshall, *An Evaluation of Recent Efforts to Achieve Racial Integration in Education Through Resort to the Courts*, 21 J. NEGRO EDUC. 316 (1952). Copyright © 1952 by Howard University. Jack Greenberg writes: "In April 1952, under the sponsorship of the *Journal of Negro Education*, Charles Thompson assembled at Howard University a group of scholars, lawyers, journalists, organizational leaders . . . black and white . . . advocates of extreme gradualism and those who demanded an immediate end to segregation." JACK GREENBERG, CRUSADERS IN THE COURTS 112 (1994). This speech by Marshall was given at the summit. The discussion that followed is also included here.
1. 163 U.S. 537 (1896).
2. 275 U.S. 337 (1938).

demonstrates that the Chinese complainant did not object to the segregation statutes of the State of Mississippi but objected to being assigned to the Negro school.

This period can be summed up for our purposes by recognizing that the separate-but-equal doctrine of *Plessy v. Ferguson* was set forth without critical analysis on the part of the Supreme Court and with a record which did not give them an opportunity to consider the question adequately. This doctrine established in a case involving intrastate transportation was seized upon and used by state and federal courts in school cases again and again without any effort being made to analyze the legality of the segregation statutes involved. This separate-but-equal doctrine thus became a rule of law sacred and apparently beyond legal attack.

1930–1945 Period

The NAACP in 1930 started the attack on the inequalities in public education. A special fund was set up to begin the campaign. A careful study was made by the late Nathan Margold.[3] This study formed the groundwork for the first attack which was aimed at the professional school level. The late Charles H. Houston, armed with the Margold report, amplified this report and began the blueprint for the extended legal attack against the inequalities in public education. Many of Houston's associates and students at Howard University Law School worked closely with him on this new project.[4]

The first case in this campaign was the [Thomas] Hocutt case against the law school of the University of North Carolina in 1933.[5] This case was handled by William H. Hastie and Conrad O. Pearson.[6] The case was lost on a technicality when the President of the Negro college in North Carolina refused to certify the scholastic record of the plaintiff in the case. Thus, the plaintiff was ineligible for admission to the law school.

This case was followed by the Donald Murray case which opened the law school of the University of Maryland in 1935[7] and the Gaines case against the law school of the University of Missouri in 1938.[8] At that time

3. *See* RICHARD KLUGER, SIMPLE JUSTICE: THE HISTORY OF BROWN V. BOARD OF EDUCATION AND BLACK AMERICANS' STRUGGLE FOR EQUALITY 133–138 (1976).
4. *See* J. Clay Smith, Jr., *In Tribute: Charles Hamilton Houston*, 111 HARV. L. REV. 2178 (1998).
5. Kluger, *supra* note 3, at 157–158 (discussing the Hocutt case).
6. *See* GILBERT WARE, WILLIAM HENRY HASTIE: GRACE UNDER PRESSURE 47–53 (1984).
7. Pearson v. Murray, 169 Md. 478, 182 A. 590 (1936).
8. State *ex rel.* Gaines v. Canada, 305 U.S. 337 (1938).

the best overall strategy seemed to be an attack against the segregation system by lawsuits seeking absolute and complete equalization of curricula, faculty, and physical equipment of the white and Negro schools on the theory that the extreme cost of maintaining two "equal" school systems would eventually destroy segregation.

It did not take long to discover that this approach would not produce the necessary results. Because of the unaccounted disappearance of Lloyd Gaines,[9] the plaintiff in the Gaines case, that case could not be followed through and ended with the establishment of a Jim Crow law school at the University of Missouri. The Bluford case[10] in Missouri which followed the Gaines case did not open the University of Missouri but ended with the establishment of a school of journalism at the Negro college. The cases against the University of Tennessee were lost on the highly technical point of failing to exhaust administrative remedies. The case against the University of Kentucky resulted in the establishment of a makeshift engineering course at the Negro college. So that, insofar as the university level was concerned, the only graduate or professional school opened to Negroes was the law school of the University of Maryland.

This campaign moved along slowly for three reasons: (1) There was a lack of full support from the Negro community in general; (2) few Negroes were interested enough to ask to be plaintiffs; and (3) there was a lack of sufficient money to finance the cases.

An evaluation of this period would be that it marked the beginning of the period of planned legal strategy against racial segregation. It was the beginning of the period of the closing of doors used by the courts in disregarding the fundamental principles of equality of law. The greatest gain from this period was the public education of school officials, the courts, and the general public in the lawlessness of school officials in depriving Negroes of their constitutional rights. It is the period whereby all of us found by experience that the tangential approach to this legal problem did not produce results in keeping with time, effort, and money expended.

This period is also noted for the cases to equalize the salaries of white and Negro public school teachers. The theory behind these cases was twofold—one, it was hoped that these cases would add to the cost of the segregated school system and be an additional burden making segregation too costly to survive. At the same time, these cases were establishing

9. *See* Robert W. Tabscott, *Unfinished Business*, St. Louis Post-Dispatch, Feb. 23, 1992, at 1C (stating: "In 1938 Lloyd Gaines was poised to become a major figure in the desegregation of America. But then he vanished").
10. Bluford v. Canada, 32 F. Supp. 707 (D.C. Mo. 1940), *app. dism'd*, 119 F.2d 779 (8th Cir. 1941).

the basic principle of equal pay for equal work without regard to race and color in the hope that these principles established in public school education would filter down into other phases of life and employment.

1945–1952 Period

During the period between 1930 and 1945, this legal program was being checked and rechecked and was constantly being evaluated. It shortly became obvious that the only solution to the problem was an all-out attack against segregation in public education so that by 1945 plans were ready for a direct attack on the validity of segregation statutes insofar as they applied to public education on the graduate and professional school level.

It appeared that the university level was the best place to begin a campaign that had as its ultimate objective the total elimination of segregation in public educational institutions in the United States. In the first place, at the university level no provision for Negro education was a rule rather than the exception. Then, too, the difficulties incident to providing equal educational opportunities even within the concept of the "separate-but-equal" doctrine were insurmountable. To provide separate medical schools, law schools, engineering schools, and graduate schools with all the variety of offerings available at most state universities would be an almost financial impossibility. Even if feasible, it would be impractical to undertake such expenditures for the few Negroes who desired such training. It was felt, therefore, that if effort at this level were pressed with sufficient vigor many states would capitulate without extended litigation. Here also it was easy to demonstrate to the courts that separate facilities for Negroes could not provide equal training to that available in the state universities, which for many years had been expanding and improving their facilities in an effort to compete with the great educational centers of the North and West.

The first case filed in this program was the Sweatt case against the law school of the University of Texas in 1946.[11] When the case was first filed, the state of Texas assumed that it was a case seeking a separate-but-equal law school. Consequently, the Legislature met and merely changed the name of the Negro state college from Prairie View to "Prairie View University" without doing anything in the line of increased appropriations or building funds. After preliminary hearings on the case and after an amendment to the pleadings, it became evident that this case was actually making a direct attack on the segregation laws as they applied to the

11. Ultimately decided by the U.S. Supreme Court: Sweatt v. Painter, 339 U.S. 629 (1950).

University of Texas. Upon discovering this, the same Texas Legislature reconvened and appropriated $2,600,000 plus $500,000 per annum to establish a brand new university for Negroes.

These two moves in and of themselves demonstrated that a direct attack on segregation would produce more in dollars and cents than the other method of seeking equal facilities. It was, therefore, clear, at least in Texas, that the new approach not only produced more education for Negroes than the other approach but also presented the opportunity to break down segregation itself at the same time.

As all of you know, the University of Texas set up a Jim Crow law school and made every effort to show that if it was not equal to the University of Texas law school insofar as physical facilities were concerned, it would be made equal in short order.[12] During the trial of the Sweatt case, the first efforts were made to give to the court the necessary expert testimony to make a competent judgment of the validity of segregation statutes as applied to law schools. To do this, it was necessary to demonstrate that segregation of students on the basis of race was an unreasonable classification within the accepted rules for measuring classification statutes by the states. Experts in anthropology were produced and testified that given a similar learning situation a Negro student tended to react the same as any other student, and that there were no racial characteristics which had any bearing whatsoever to the subject of public education. Experts in the field of legal education testified that it was impossible for a Negro student to get an equal education in a Jim Crow law school because of the lack of opportunity to meet with and discuss their problems with other students of varying strata of society. These witnesses also testified that even if two law schools could be made absolutely equal insofar as physical facilities, equipment, curricula, and faculties, the Jim Crow law school would nevertheless not offer an education equal to that offered at the other school for the reasons set forth above. Although the Texas courts refused to follow this testimony, the United States Supreme Court reversed these decisions and ordered Sweatt admitted to the law school of the University of Texas.[13]

You also remember the McLaurin decision, which was in many respects an even more clear-cut decision on the question of segregation.[14] For in the McLaurin case, the plaintiff had the same teacher, the same curricula, was in the same building, and, and as a matter of fact, was in the same classroom, although set apart from the other students.

---

12. The school referred to is Texas Southern School of Law. In 1976 the school was renamed Thurgood Marshall School of Law. Lydia Lum, *TSU Law School to Get Visit from High Jurist*, HOUSTON CHRON., Jan. 29, 1998, at A22.
13. Sweatt, *supra* note 11.
14. McLaurin v. Oklahoma State Regents of Higher Ed., 339 U.S. 637 (1950).

It is significant that the decisions in both the McLaurin and Sweatt cases were unanimous. In the Sweatt case the court held: ". . . petitioner may claim his full constitutional right: legal education equivalent to that offered by the State to students of other races. Such education is not available to him in a separate law school as offered by the State. . . . We hold that the Equal Protection Clause of the Fourteenth Amendment required that petitioner be admitted to the University of Texas Law School."[15] The McLaurin decision asserted:

> But they signify that the State, in administering the facilities it affords for pro-fessional and graduate study, sets McLaurin apart from the other students. The result is that appellant is handicapped in his pursuit of effective graduate instruction. Such restrictions impair and inhibit his ability to study, to engage in discussions and exchange views with other students, and, in general, to learn his profession.
>
> We conclude that the conditions under which this appellant is required to receive his education deprive him of his personal and present right to the equal protection of the laws. See *Sweatt v. Painter.* We hold that under these circum-stances the Fourteenth Amendment precludes differences in treatment by the state based upon race. Appellant, having been admitted to a state-supported graduate school, must receive the same treatment at the hands of the state as students of other races. The judgment is reversed.[16]

What effect have these university cases had upon the general public? In the first place, it is significant that in each university case the local white student bodies have openly shown their willingness to accept Negro students. Despite dire predictions of horrible catastrophes by die-hard state officials, the admission of qualified Negroes had been smooth and without incident. For example, when the appeal of the University of Maryland case was pending the Attorney General of Maryland told the Maryland Court of Appeals that if Murray was admitted many white stu-dents would withdraw and there would be much trouble. Donald Murray was admitted and later testified in another case as follows:

> My experience, briefly, was that I attended the University of Maryland Law School for three years, during which time I took all of the classes with the rest of the students, and participated and at no time whatever did I meet any attempted segregation or unfavorable treatment on the part of any student in the school, or any professor or assistant professor.

When the Sweat and McLaurin cases were pending in the Supreme Court the attorneys-general for the Southern states filed a joint brief alleging that: "The Southern States trust that this Court will not strike

15. *Id.* at 641.
16. *Id.* at 642.

down their power to keep peace, order and support of their public schools by maintaining equal separate facilities. If, the states are shorn of this police power and physical conflict takes place . . . the states are left with no alternative but to close their schools to prevent violence." What happened to this dire prediction? No schools have been closed. More than a thousand Negroes are now attending graduate and professional schools in the South. Benjamin Fine recently reported in the *New York Times* that a survey made by him showed:

> This situation would have been considered impossible ten years ago. Responsible educators had warned that any breaching of the segregation line would prove dangerous and might even lead to campus or community riots. Today, these same officials report that the Negroes have not disturbed normal collegiate life in any manner.[17]

In the recent case against the University of Tennessee, application was made for a special three-judge court to hear the attack against the validity of an order of the Trustees of the University of Tennessee excluding Negroes from admission. The three-judge court decided that the attack could not be made on the validity of the order of the University of Tennessee, or the statutes of the State of Tennessee requiring segregation. The court therefore referred the case to a single judge for decision. The single judge held that the statutes and order were not in question and wrote an opinion upholding the right of Negroes to attend the University of Tennessee on the grounds that no other school had been furnished them. The original order of the three-judge court was appealed to the Supreme Court where during argument, the lawyers for the University of Tennessee stated in open court that the University had at last agreed to admit Negro students. The Supreme Court stopped argument at this point and refused to hear any further argument from petitioners. The Supreme Court subsequently issued an order vacating the judgment of the lower court and ordering the case dismissed as moot. Although the action of the Supreme Court is far from clear, by vacating the order of the lower court the Supreme Court nullified a bad precedent of a decision denying the right to challenge the constitutionality of such orders and statutes.

While the right of Negroes to attend state graduate and professional schools has now been established, most Negroes who have received their early education in segregated schools are handicapped because their

---

17. This is not an exact quote from the Fine article, but it does reflect that improvements in the physical plant of black schools and salary increases of black teachers were being made in several Southern states. *See* Benjamin Fine, *Negro Education in South on Rise*, N.Y. TIMES, March 16, 1952, at 82.

early training was inadequate and inferior. It became increasingly apparent that the supreme test would have to be made—an attack on segregation at the elementary and high school levels. Acceptance of segregation under the "separate but equal" doctrine had become so ingrained that overwhelming proof was sorely needed to demonstrate that equal educational opportunities for Negroes could not be provided in a segregated system.

It is relatively easy to show that a Negro graduate student offered training in a separate school, thrown up overnight, could not get an education equal to that available at the state universities. Public elementary and high schools, however, present a more difficult basis for comparison. They are normally not specialized institutions with national or even statewide reputations. Public school teachers at these levels are not likely to gain eminence in the profession comparable to that of teachers in colleges and universities. For years, however, exposure of the evils of segregation and discrimination has come from social scientists, and their help was elicited for this phase of the campaign. Social scientists are almost in universal agreement that segregated education produces inequality. Studies have been made of the personality problems caused by discrimination and segregation and most social scientists have reached the conclusion that artificial and arbitrary barriers, such as race and color bars, are likely to have an adverse effect on the personality development of the individual. The energy and strength which the individual might otherwise use in the development of his mental resources is dissipated in adjustment to the problems of segregation.

Unfortunately, the effects of segregation in education have not been isolated for study by social scientists. They have dealt with the whole problem of segregation, discrimination and prejudice, and although no social scientist can say that segregated schools alone give the Negro feelings of insecurity, self-hate, undermines his ego, make him feel inferior and warp his outlook on life, yet for the child the school provides the most important contact with organized society. What he learns, feels, and how he is affected there is apt to determine the type of adult he will become. Social scientists have found that children at a very early age are affected by and react to discrimination and prejudices. Thus they have agreed that it is sound to conclude that segregated schools, perhaps more than any other single factor, are of major concern to the individual of public school age and contribute greatly to the unwholesomeness and unhappy development of the personality of Negroes which the color caste system in the United States has produced.

The elimination of segregation in public schools may not remove all of the causes of insecurity, self-hate, etc., among Negroes, but since this is a state-sponsored program, certainly the state, consistent with the requirements of the Fourteenth Amendment, should not be a party to a system which does help produce these results. This is the thesis which is now being used to demonstrate the unconstitutionality of segregation at the public elementary and high school levels.[18]

Preliminary test cases in Virginia and Texas demonstrated the ineffectiveness of the failure to push for a clear-cut determination of the validity of the segregation statutes. I believe that an appraisal of these cases will show that their success was limited by the same difficulties as were encountered in the earlier university cases. After considerable and costly litigation and appeals, these cases ended in court orders limited to the equalization of physical facilities. These facilities in each instance were not equalized so that it was necessary to file motions for further relief to reopen the cases for a new determination of whether or not the Fourteenth Amendment was being complied with. It is significant that in these latter proceedings it was found necessary to make a frontal attack on the validity of segregated statutes.

The Clarendon County school case was the first test case to make a direct attack against segregation on the elementary and high school level.[19] That case, which was tried in Charleston, South Carolina, in May of last year, was based upon the theory that the Sweatt and McLaurin decisions have pointed the way toward consideration of the validity of segregation on all levels of education. In order to extend this principle it was necessary to produce equally competent testimony to show the unreasonableness of segregation and impossibility of equality of Jim Crow education on lower levels.

Therefore, in the Clarendon County case competent expert testimony was produced to show that segregation on the elementary and high school levels was just as unequal as segregated education on the graduate and professional school level when measured by the criteria set forth in the Sweatt and McLaurin decisions. In other words, competent expert testimony was produced to show in detail the injury to the Negro pupil attending the segregated schools in Clarendon County and to show that this injury was a permanent and continuing one which prevented the Negro child from obtaining an education equal to that obtained by other students. Of course, testimony was also produced to show that there was no reasonable basis for racial segregation in public education. Two of the three judges deciding this case held that despite this testimony the separate-but-equal doctrine was still a valid doctrine supported by decisions of the Supreme Court and that although the schools were

18. *See generally Desegregation: An Appraisal of the Evidence*, 9 J. Soc. Issues (1953) (Kenneth B. Clark, issue author).
19. Briggs v. Elliott, 98 F. Supp. 529, 538 (E.D.S.C. 1951).

not equal in physical facilities, the Negroes were entitled to equal facilities and they should be given equal physical facilities. The majority of the court therefore refused to enjoin the enforcement of the segregation statutes of South Carolina but ordered that the physical facilities be equalized and ordered the school board to report within six months on this equalization of physical facilities.[20] Judge J. Waites Waring, however, in a most vigorous dissenting opinion held that the segregation laws were unconstitutional and stated that segregation was *per se* unconstitutional.[21] A direct appeal from the majority judgment was made to the United States Supreme Court where, on January 26, 1952, the United States Supreme Court issued an order vacating the judgment of the lower court and remanding the case to that court for a consideration of the report made by the school officials and any other additional facts in order that the district court "be afforded the opportunity to take whatever action it may deem appropriate in light of that report."[22]

A hearing was promptly held in the district court with Judge [Armistead M.] Dobie of Virginia replacing Judge Waring, who had previously retired from the bench.[23] After argument, the new three-judge court issued a unanimous decree again refusing to declare the statutes unconstitutional but again ordering the school board to furnish equal facilities. An appeal is now being prepared to the Supreme Court form this latest decision.[24]

The second case in this line of cases is the Topeka, Kansas, case, which was tried in June of last year. Again similar testimony from other expert witnesses in larger number was produced and in this case the three judges unanimously found as a fact that:

20. *Id.*

21. *Id.*

22. Briggs v. Elliott, 98 F. Supp. 529 (1951), *vacated*, 342 U.S. 350, 351 (1952).

23. Judge J. Waites Waring retired from the bench on February 15, 1952, 101 F. Supp. x, n. 2 (1952).

24. Briggs v. Elliott, 103 F. Supp. 921 (S.D. S.C. 1952). For commentary on the Clarendon school case, *see* Jesse L. Jackson, *Thurgood Marshall Commemorative Issue: Justice Thurgood Marshall: The Struggle Personified*, 35 How. L.J. 73 (1991). Jackson states: "For me . . . it begins in my home state of South Carolina, in Clarendon County, where in 1947, a minister-teacher Joseph Albert DeLaine rallied the black community to file suit agasint racial discrimination in the Clarendon County public school." *Id.* Others have commented on the Clarendon County case and the courage of people like Rev. DeLaine. See generally Kluger, *supra* note 3, at 4, 8; Janet Reno, *Civil Rights: A Challenge of Conscience*, 27 Cumb. L. Rev. 381, 393 (1996–1997). The Briggs case was decided with other cases under the U.S. Supreme Court's decision in Brown v. Board of Education, 347 U.S. 483 (1954). "Briggs v. Elliott (Case No. 8) was argued by Thurgood Marshall." J. Clay Smith, Jr., *Thurgood Marshall: An Heir of Charles Hamilton Houston*, 20 Hastings Const. L.Q. 503, 515 (1993).

Segregation of white and colored children in public schools has a detrimental effect upon the colored children. The impact is greater when it has the sanction of the law; for the policy of separating the races is usually interpreted as denoting the inferiority of the Negro group. A sense of inferiority affects the motivation of a child to learn. Segregation with the sanction of law, therefore, has a tendency to retard the education and mental development of Negro children and to deprive them of some of the benefits they would receive in a racial[ly] integrated school system.[25]

The same court, however, felt obliged not to follow this finding but to follow the antiquated decisions of the Supreme Court, which seem to uphold the validity of segregation in elementary education. That case is now pending before the United States Supreme Court.

The third case was the Wilmington, Delaware, case, which was tried on October 22, 1951, and which was decided week before last in an exhaustive twenty-six page opinion by Chancellor Collins J. Seitz ordering the admission of the Negroes in the previously all white schools.

The fourth case was the Prince Edward, Virginia, case tried before a three-judge court in Richmond, Virginia, last month. In this case, which was tried for a full week, more expert testimony was produced than in any other of the cases. For the first time the other side produced expert testimony which while opposing the immediate removal of segregation, nevertheless admitted the inequality inherent in a segregated school system in addition to the regular inequalities in physical equipment. This court in unanimous opinion refused to enjoin the segregation statutes but ordered the equalization of facilities. This case is also being prepared for appeal to the United States Supreme Court.

It should be pointed out that in the second hearing in the Clarendon County case the court was urged to abolish segregation in public school on either of two grounds: (1) that the testimony showed that segregation laws were invalid or (2) that the absence of equality in the segregated facilities required the application of the Sipuel doctrine. The court rejected both arguments and accepted the school board's assurances that the physical facilities would be equalized by September.

On the other hand, Chancellor Seitz in the Wilmington, Delaware, case while refusing to hold segregation invalid as such did extend the Sipuel doctrine to give effective relief. He held:

It seems to me that when a plaintiff shows to the satisfaction of a court that there is an existing and continuing violation of the "separate but equal" doctrine, he is entitled to have made available to him the State facilities which have been shown to be superior. To do otherwise is to say to such a plaintiff: "Yes, your Constitutional rights are being invaded, but be patient, we will see whether in

25. *See, e.g.,* Brown v. Board of Education, 347 U.S. 483, 494–495 (1954).

time they are still being violated." If, as the Supreme Court has said, this right is personal, such a plaintiff is entitled to relief immediately, in the only way it is available, namely, by admission to the school with the superior facilities. To postpone such relief is to deny relief, in whole or in part, and to say that the protective provisions of the Constitution offer no immediate protection.[26]

The school officials have decided to appeal this decision. The Supreme Court will, therefore, have an opportunity to pass upon this question presented in varying forms in these four cases.

I will, of course, not speculate as to either the outcome of the individual cases or the general decision of the Supreme Court on this point. Getting back to an appraisal of the recent cases in line of the objective sought, we can appraise these cases in the light of their immediate effect. In South Carolina, Governor [James] Byrnes, in an effort to circumvent these cases, last year succeeded in getting through the legislature approval for seventy-five million dollars which will be used in both Negro and white schools. It is admitted that this fund is for the purpose of equalizing physical facilities, a large proportion of the fund will no doubt go to white schools. At any rate, if nothing more is done in the legal field; the schools of South Carolina, both Negro and white, will be seventy-five million dollars better off. On the other hand, Governor Byrnes, followed by Governor Talmadge of Georgia, had put through a plan whereby they hope to turn over the public schools to private institutions such as churches in the event that the Supreme Court declares the segregation statutes invalid. Many of us are convinced that this move to turn over the public schools to private institutions will be declared invalid by the Supreme Court. There are even more people who are convinced that the white citizens in these states are not insane enough on the segregation issue to be willing to turn over millions of dollars of their tax money invested in schools to private institutions where they will have little, if any, control over the education of their children.

Many of the people who believe that segregation is invalid and should be declared unconstitutional are moved by this threat of a few Southern governors. It seems to me that the best answer to this threat is that the same threat was made by the attorneys-general of the Southern states while the Sweatt and McLaurin cases were pending in the Supreme Court. The specific threat was that if segregation was destroyed on the graduate and professional level "the states are left with no alternative but to close their schools to prevent violence." The record shows that no state universities were closed and nothing happened except that Negroes were admitted just as if they had been attending the schools for years back. In the face of these facts, the argument is now made that elementary and

26. Belton v. Gebhart, 32 De. Ch. 343, 359, 87 A.2d. 662, 869 (1952).

high school education is different and that the South will not stand for it. There is an answer to this argument also. Many junior colleges in Texas have recently opened their doors to Negroes and nothing happened. This brings us to another phase of the objective of this litigation and that is the education of the general public to the evils of segregation, its harmful effects, and the reasons why this segregation should be abolished.

The pendency of the Sipuel, Sweatt, and McLaurin cases over a period of some five years brought about wide newspaper coverage and discussion in daily press, the weekly magazines, the professional magazines and college newspapers. This education of the general public played a large part in making it possible for the Negro students to be admitted without incident, to have no trouble while in school, and to encourage other public and private colleges and universities to open their doors to qualified Negroes.

The pending cases have likewise received wide and broad coverage in the same channels. In addition, articles are now appearing in scientific journals on the validity of the scientific testimony in this field. It is doubtful that this issue will be resolved overnight, but the pendency of these cases will continue to educate the general public along the lines suggested above.

It has been most encouraging to find that whereas the earlier cases on the university level failed to attract the attention and support of most of the Negro communities, the present litigation has had 100 percent cooperation in each area where these cases have been pending. For example, the courage of the Negroes in Clarendon County, South Carolina, and the support of the Negroes in other areas in South Carolina; the courage of the Negroes in Farmville, Virginia, and the support from the other areas in Virginia will stand as a landmark in the struggle for full citizenship. Any appraisal of the actual cases in these fields must include an appraisal of the community support commanded by the cases.

Neither the Sipuel nor the McLaurin decisions struck down the separate-but-equal doctrine. There are many who hoped this would happen. However, all legal minds will agree that the Supreme Court is not obliged to make far sweeping decisions but rather tends to limit its decisions to the matter before it in the pending cases. So it is apparent that the whole segregation problem cannot be solved in one lawsuit. It would, of course, be easier and cheaper to do it that way. If we view the problem from a realistic standpoint, it means that the best possible course is a step-by-step approach on each level of education to be followed by a step-by-step approach at each other area of segregation.

In addition, it is necessary to implement the precedents on each level, and this will require additional lawsuits on each level. The present cases on the elementary and high school levels show the varied approach to this problem, varied as to area, and varied as to testimony.

The university cases not only opened the state universities in twelve Southern states but many private institutions in states like Kentucky and Maryland have opened their doors to qualified Negroes. There are other private colleges willing to open their doors to Negroes but are prevented from doing so by state statutes. It is expected that in the near future there will be cases filed to enjoin the enforcement of these statutes as applied to the private colleges anxious to admit qualified Negroes. There has also been some discussion as to the eventual possibility in the future of requiring a private college to admit Negro students despite its ban upon the admission of Negro students. I imagine that this suggestion when and if made will split the legal profession in half.

In states like Alabama, Florida, South Carolina, and Mississippi, the time when the universities in these states will be opened to Negroes depends solely upon when qualified Negroes apply to those universities and are refused admission and bring suit against these universities. As soon as that is done they will be opened up. Such a case is now ready for filing in Georgia and it is expected that additional cases will be filed in Florida in order to open the University of Florida.

The primary objective of this recent litigation has been to obtain full and complete integration of all students on all levels of public education without regard to race or color. The stumbling block in the path toward this objective is the separate-but-equal doctrine. In the beginning the courts prevented litigants from either attacking the doctrine head on or circumventing the doctrine. In the next phase of this program the courts eventually permitted the tangential approach by ordering equality of physical facilities while upholding segregation.

Finally in the Sweatt and McLaurin decisions the tangential approach was discarded and segregation on the graduate and professional school levels was removed. Even there the Supreme Court refused to strike down the separate-but-equal doctrine as such. The elementary and high school cases are the next steps in this campaign toward the objective and complete integration of all students.

The earlier legal approach to this problem failed to bring about either integration or equality of physical facilities. The direct attack on segregation, even if not successful in its all-out attack on segregation, nevertheless produced immediate serious efforts toward physical equality.

In evaluating these recent cases we must always bear in mind that we are dealing with a brand new field of law both as to substantive law and procedural law. Although the separate-but-equal doctrine still stands in the road blocking full equality or opportunity, recent cases have been closing the doors of escape from a clear-cut determination of the validity or invalidity of this doctrine. While evaluating the recent decisions we must constantly look to the future.

Summit Discussion of Papers[27]

Chairman [Homer S.] Brown:[28] Our discussion leaders will follow in the position you find them on the program. I have the honor now of introducing Mr. Will Maslow, Director, Commission on Law and Social Action, American Jewish Congress.

Mr. Will Maslow: The two brilliant papers by Professor John Frank[29] and Thurgood Marshall open up so many pathways . . .

I agree with Professor [John] Frank that the fear of violence is not the real deterrent in judicial action. I would suggest to him that in addition to the three deterrents he mentioned, there is, perhaps, a fourth and a more important one and that is the fear of the Supreme Court that its mandates may be publicly and contemptuously disregarded. I think the Supreme Court is extremely unlikely to issue a decision, which it may not be able to enforce. As you know, the Supreme Court has no means of enforcing its mandates when a state throws down the gauntlet. All it can do is ask its marshals to help and then, in turn, call upon the President.

The last time there was a defiance of the Supreme Court mandate was in 1832 and then, too, on an issue of race relations when the Supreme Court handed down a decision involving the Cherokee Indians[30] the state refused to comply and the President of the United States refused to lend his assistance.

I am not intimating that the State of South Carolina, for example, would refuse to obey a Supreme Court decision, but I think it is one of the things that we might think about. And when you think about the presidential candidates you wonder which one would call out the Army to enforce a decision of the Supreme Court.

---

27. Follows Marshall's article at 21 J. Negro Educ., at 327.
28. Homer S. Brown was a judge on the Allegheny County Court, Pittsburgh, Pa., in 1948. Christopher W. Riley, *Markers for Those Who Left Their Mark*, Post-Gazette, July 13, 1997, at A10 (on Judge Brown).
29. John Frank was an Associate Professor of Law at Yale University. *See* Peter S. Canellos, *A. L. Higginbotham, Jr., Civil Rights Voice; at 70*, Boston Globe, Dec. 15, 1998, at D8. Canellos reports that Professor Frank "gave Judge [Leon] Higginbotham the money for the train ride from New Haven to Washington, [D.C.,] and introduced the young student to both Thurgood Marshall and Supreme Court Judge Hugo Black." *Id.*
30. Worcester v. State, 31 U.S. (6 Peters) 515 (1832) (held that treaties and laws of the United States consider Indian territories to be completely separated from that of the states).

I would also disagree with the advice given by John Frank, that we should be careful about cases in the next six months. The reason I do not think it is important to be careful is that the Supreme Court will exercise all the care that is necessary. No matter what decisions we bring there, they have infinite capacity not only for passing the buck, but for searching the records, for sending things back, for hearing, for reargument, for postponing jurisdiction, so that we really should not concern ourselves with an unfortunate political repercussion. They are past masters on that bench of judging political reactions.

I do believe, however, that there is one point which we might consider and that is the question of selecting cases particularly the most difficult cases involving segregation on the primary school level, and whether the wisest strategy is to take states like South Carolina where there is a risk. Perhaps Governor [James] Byrnes is bluffing, but perhaps he is not bluffing. He does not have to give the school system away to private groups. He can refuse to obey the mandates.

In view of that risk, and the good poker players do not call every bluff, are we wise in pressing in South Carolina instead of attempting to win the victors on the border, as they have been won by Marshall and his associates in Kansas and particularly this magnificent decision in Delaware? That type of strategy where you win your victories on the circumference, on the periphery, aid in preparing public opinion and the courts for the victory in the hard land.

The strategy of the NAACP has been, in these particular cases in Virginia, in Delaware, in Kansas, in South Carolina, and so on, to make a frontal assault on segregation as such. I think we all here would agree that the days of fighting for equalization have gone; that more can be achieved even if our objective is equalization by asking for elimination of segregation. But I would refine that strategy in one respect. If, in addition, you present the courts with an alternative and you present it as forcefully as you present the attack on segregation, the alternative being that you want equality now. If you say to the courts, "These two schools are unequal; we are not asking that they be equalized because it may take years for them to be equalized; we are asking that this particular student, this Negro child, sent to an inferior school in the first and second grade be given equal facilities right here and now."

The Court can then be persuaded without passing upon the doctrine of segregation, to admit the Negro child into the white school. That is what was ordered by the Chancellor in Delaware. The net result of the decision is the same as if the Court outlawed segregation because what the Court is saying is that the Negro child must go to the white school. That was the effect of the whole thing in the McLaurin case. The Court refused to pass upon the doctrine of Plessy against Ferguson. The net result, however, is in the guise of eliminating inequality in the school. If you are more interested in decisions—in results than in words—that alternative should be presented formally to the courts.

I want to make one final observation. We have talked about the education cases as though they were the only way of attacking segregation in the courts. I submit to you that John Frank's suggestion about pursuing alternative remedies has a great deal of weight. Thirty years ago the Supreme Court refused segregation in housing in the famous case of Buchanan against Warley.[31] Thirty years ago, before there was any great interest in civil rights and without any record of the harmful effects of segregation!

Yet those cases have not been adequately followed up. A decision in Detroit involving housing would not present the Court with the severe political and psychological problem that the primary school cases do. A decision by the Supreme Court declaring that segregation in housing is unconstitutional would have great weight in the whole field of segregation in education.

Thank you. (Applause)

Chairman Brown: The next leader of our panel discussion, well known to practically all of us, Miss Marjorie McKenzie, attorney-at-law, feature writer for the *Pittsburgh Courier*.[32] Miss McKenzie:

Miss McKenzie: I suppose a few of you know why I am here. I represent what might be termed in this area of thought the loyal opposition.

There is a distinct advantage in being both a lawyer and columnist in this area of discussion, because I can have the last word.

Last summer, after the decision in the Clarendon case, one hot July day when I was feeling very much discouraged about it, I sat down and wrote a column that expressed what I thought about the decision and about the legal theory that was involved. I left town immediately so that when the story broke over my head I was safely away on an island.

By the time the storm had cleared it was safe for me to come back to Washington. I have been misunderstood in that column. It was said of me that I was in favor of segregation or of gradual efforts to eliminate segregation. That is not true. What did I say in that column? Basically, four things: First, that I thought the Supreme Court was not yet ready for

---

31. U.S. 60 (1917).

32. *See* J. Clay Smith, *Black Women Lawyers: 125 Years at the Bar; 100 Years in the Legal Academy*, 40 How. L.J. 365 (1997), states: "In 1962, a landmark appointment to the Juvenile Court of the District of Columbia was marked with the confirmation of Marjorie McKenzie Lawson, at age 50, to the newly organized Juvenile Court of the District of Columbia Court." *Id.* at 393. Lawson graduated from the Robert H. Terrell School of Law in 1939. Telephone interview, November 1995.

an all-out decision with regard to segregation, an across-the-board decision. We remembered that the Supreme Court had a chance in June, 1950, in the Henderson case[33] to say segregation was unconstitutional, and it had not taken advantage of that opportunity. That does not mean that I did not want the Court to say that it thought so, but I thought the Court was not ready to say it.

The second thing I said was that I thought efforts to force the Court—briefs designed to force the Court were unwise and caused risk where none was necessary.

As Professor Frank has pointed out, I underestimated the Court's ingenuity, and in that respect, I may have been wrong. It seemed to me that the possibility of having a number of district courts' decisions which revived the doctrine of *Plessy v. Ferguson* and gave it a modern-day interpretation was a dangerous thing to have happen.

In the third place, I thought that we had in the Sweatt and McLaurin decisions a formula for success and so there was no reason to change horses in midstream. Nothing succeeds like success. What I could see was that there were hundreds of Negro students and now a thousand Negro students in graduate schools in the South and that McLaurin and Sweatt had achieved what we had set out to do for them. I saw no reason why this legal theory could not have been attempted in the high schools and in grammar school-level cases. I thought we should have given it a whirl.

In the fourth place, I said that our leadership—our civil rights leadership—maybe I had better be clear on it and say our lawyers had allowed too much distance to come between them and their plans, and the people to be affected by this planning. You know, we lawyers get very interested in legal theories. They are very beautiful things sometimes. We can look at a lot of decisions like the whole line in this field of education, beginning with the Murray case, and on through Gaines, McLaurin, and Sweatt, and say that here at the end of this line there is a little hole to be filled in and we say let us fill in the hole; let us wash this up; let's make this a perfect legal theory.

We got into a rarefied atmosphere of thinking and we got more interested in our mental gymnastics than in the social and political realities. So I said that we needed to consult with more groups and with more thinking on this subject. Take this conference, for instance; it is a wonderful thing. It is not too little and too late. It is just too late. When should we have had this conference? In June 1950 or no later than July. We should have sat right down to assess our gains in Sweatt and McLaurin and to have applied them to a plan of action, because in this kind of group we have the kind of social thinking which will remove

33. Henderson v. United States, 339 U.S. 816 (1950).

the fight from one point of view, from one organization, so that it becomes our joint fight with our joint view and techniques available for its solution.

What has happened since last July? We have learned that the Clarendon case has gone back on very flimsy grounds. The Kansas case will not be decided until Clarendon comes up again, and we are pretty sure that will not happen until next November. The District of Columbia case is now pending trial on whether or not we are going to have a three-judge court, so we are not going to have any kind of definitive action so far as most of us can see until after next November and that may be a good thing.

That brings me to another of my points. Even if we should put pressure on the Court to solve the problem of segregation in this case, we must also remember that this is a government of divided powers and that it is our duty to press on the executive and on the legislative branches as well while we push the Court. The Court is responsible for *Plessy v. Ferguson*, and it should erase it. Perhaps this Court is not the one that will give us the definitive across-the-board decision, outlawing *Plessy v. Ferguson*.

There is one further thing I think that we should do in terms of technique and that is to understand the nature of the judicial process, and to understand that in our government relief is personal. It belongs to the individual and across-the-board decisions affecting great social problems may not be possible or desirable. It would be easier and cheaper and simpler and lots less work but maybe it is not sensible to hope for that sort of thing. We have to work and we have to pay for freedom. (Applause) . . .

Chairman Brown: Next question, please?

Mr. John Williams: I am John Williams of Howard University. I would like to know Mr. Marshall's opinion concerning the statement by Miss McKenzie, that efforts to force the Court to rule on across-the-board segregation were unwise.

Chairman Brown: Did everybody hear the question? The question asked that Mr. Marshall refer to the statement made by Miss McKenzie that the attack on segregation across-the-board is unwise. I did not understand that that was exactly her statement. Is that your statement? I think the young man misquoted Miss McKenzie, or I misquoted you.

However, I do feel—well, Mr. Marshall knows what he means. Mr. Marshall, will you answer the question?

Mr. Marshall: I agree with you that it is not what she said. But let us get just what is meant by "across-the-board segregation." If anybody thinks you are going to get the Supreme Court, in any decision in the foreseeable future, to say that all segregation under any circumstances on any ground is unconstitutional, you are crazy. The most that anyone asks the Supreme Court to rule is in so far as segregation is applied to this phase of what we are talking about, that is unconstitutional. That is what we said on the university and graduate level; that is what we said on the professional level; in the elementary and high school cases we say that the segregation law applied to elementary and high schools is unconstitutional. If the Supreme Court says everything we ask them to say, it will only be that the segregation statutes as applied to elementary and high schools are unconstitutional. It will not touch transportation; it will not touch assembly; it will not touch barbershops; it will not touch bulldogs; it will not touch anything but elementary and high schools.

Don't think about this magic solution of one case. Marjorie did not mean it; I did not mean it; none of us meant that. I hope that no one will get that impression. We are talking about getting a specific ruling on a specific issue, and anyone knows that is all you get decided when you are touching on a very touchy problem.

Chairman [Homer] Brown: President [Martin D.] Jenkins of Morgan College.

Mr. Jenkins: I am trying to get some help. I do not know whether this is a double-barreled question or not. . . . Thurgood Marshall first.

I say that I think the general opinion has been that we can't have racial integration in Mississippi in the foreseeable future regardless of the Supreme Court decision.

Now let us assume that we get a specific kind of Supreme Court decision, which outlaws segregation in elementary education. Do our legal lights then expect that Mississippi, for example, will tomorrow integrate and if not—I assume the answer to that will be "no"—what will be the next step? Will it then be good strategy on our part to compromise, to be selective in the localities in which we attempt to implement the decision of the Court? Is that a clear question?

Chairman Brown: It is directed to Mr. Marshall. We will let him see if he can answer it.

Mr. Marshall: I will give an equally clear answer.

No. 1: I do not know how correct you are about Mississippi. I say that, for you and I both know about what happened. I will ask you; don't you agree that you would not have believed that Arkansas would admit Negroes, to be the first state to admit Negroes? None of us thought that was possible. Arkansas did, and Arkansas is just barely, by the skin of its teeth, above Mississippi.

Now suppose in Clarendon County, or any other place, there is a decision saying that the segregation laws of the State of South Carolina are unconstitutional as applied to elementary and high school education in South Carolina. The answer is that that decision would not only not be binding on Mississippi, it would not bind any county in South Carolina but Clarendon County. It would nevertheless be what is known as a precedent. I believe quite firmly that we will have to go from county to county and from state to state even after we get it, whichever kind of decision we get. Bear in mind in Georgia you have two hundred and some counties.

So I still say there is no shortcut to it. But I think as lawyers at least, the legal staff of NAACP and several of the law schools of the country, we are working on trying to find a shortcut. Yet most of us believe there will be no finding of such a shortcut because we will not have the necessary cooperation from the court for the shortcut. So I think that about answers it.

Now as to carefully planning where you are going to bring lawsuits, we can only bring lawsuits where we find people that want to sue. If we had been asked to file suit against a college, we most likely would have started on the college level right after Sweatt and McLaurin. We have not been asked. We have not filed any suits in Mississippi, because we have not been asked yet except as to teachers' salaries.

We are going to move in Georgia. When you go through all of this careful overall strategy of planning, bear in mind that when you find a group of people in a community that are ready to fight for the rights and privileges of its people, and they say, "We have a plaintiff; we have as much money as we can raise, if you can get some more we can go to court," we cannot turn our backs on them.

Mr. Frank Summers: I am Frank Summers of East St. Louis. I would like to ask Mr. Marshall this question. In our State of Illinois he has had some recent experiences, especially in Cairo. We find that at the college level—that was at the beginning of integration—after the door was opened we did not find students to go, to come into the door. Now that they have opened the door at the grade school and high school level I want to ask you, Mr. Marshall, what means, if any, you think should be taken in order to get the Negroes to come to the integrated schools?

Coming back to the college level, I would like to ask you this also: Is it not a fact that those parents who were able to send their children to these integrated schools, is not it a fact that they seem to be unwilling, and those who are willing seem to be unable?

Mr. Marshall: That gets back to the problem that I think there has been a lot of stress laid on today about its being necessary to have community support for these cases.

As to the university level, I know of states where not one Negro will apply for the state university. And yet in Oklahoma last year they had four hundred-and-some Negro students.

I think the answer is to the community itself. I believe that organizations like the NAACP and the teachers' associations should build up enough support in the communities so that the Negroes would be encouraged to grow.

How do we know that they will go in the elementary and high school level? "Spot" Robinson[34] can guarantee they will go in the Prince Edward case because they went out on strike in the first place. I can guarantee you in Clarendon County everyone will go. That depends on the community. As these cases are pending in court and despite the stress that has resulted by the prolonged period of time that these cases have been pending, to my mind, as long as those cases are pending there is an educational policy going on in the community as a result of the commenting upon the pendency of the cases.

The Sweatt case was in court for four years. As a result of that time period there was no resentment from anybody in Texas about it, except a few diehards. So the mere pendency of the cases themselves educates the people. I would still believe that not only the organization I represent, but the other organizations, the people represented in this room, and even other organizations not represented here—and also I did not mean to leave out the churches—have a responsibility to sell the Negro community on the problem that it is necessary to go to court when necessary, or to picket or do anything else you want to about segregation. And once you establish it, if you have a good enough campaign on that, if you once establish it, then you will not have to worry about the Negroes. They will go. . . .

34. Spottswood William Robinson, III, was former dean of Howard Law School and leading lawyer in Virginia.

The Future Lies with Our Youth

Dr. [Luther] Foster, Faculty, Students and Friends:

I really came down here to meet the publishers, but I am never going to pass up an opportunity to talk with younger people, because the future lies with them.

It is good to be in Tuskegee. Some of you know that I have been here several times. This institution has been out in the forefront in a number of events of extended importance. I remember when, several years ago, the American Teachers' Association, composed of Negro teachers throughout the country, met right here. It was here that we began the fight for equalization of teachers' salaries on a national scale.

I think that the role of the schools is significantly important. When they tell you that they are training you for leadership, I hope they will explain exactly what they mean by it and that you, in your own mind, will understand it.

At the same time, I think, you should be taught the facts of life. For example, when I finished college, the president, who was a pretty broad-minded and fair man, took us aside—I will always remember that—and he said, "Everybody in his commencement speech, that you will hear tomorrow, will tell you this and that. They will tell you that the world is waiting for you with outstretched arms. That is half of the truth. The full truth is that the world is waiting for you with outstretched arms, with a club in each hand, and if you don't look out, it will beat your brains out."

Thurgood Marshall gave this address before the National Newspaper Publishers' Association's Mid-Winter Meeting, at Tuskegee Institute, Tuskegee, Alabama, January 23, 1954. Luther Foster was president of the institute. The meeting was held less than four months before the U.S. Supreme Court decided Brown v. Board of Education, 347 U.S. 483 (1954) (Brown I). Tuskegee Institute (renamed Tuskegee University on June 27, 1985) was founded by Booker T. Washington in 1881. *See Four-Time Governor Wallace Pictorial*, MONTGOMERY ADVERTISER, Sept. 15, 1998, at 4B (regarding date of name change); *Tuskegee Name Change Annoys Some Alumni*, LEXIS, UPI, Aug. 10, 1985. For more information on the founding of Tuskegee Institute, *see* EMMETT J. SCOTT AND LYMAN BEECHER STOWE, BOOKER T. WASHINGTON: BUILDER OF A CIVILIZATION 3–18 (1917); ANN KENDRICK WALKER, TUSKEGEE AND THE BLACK BELT: A PORTRAIT OF RACE (1944).

Those of you who are looking ahead to the future had better look out for those clubs. When you look for those clubs, bear in mind that they are neither white clubs nor black clubs. Everybody will carry one.

The publishers' meeting here this week is an important one. The reason it is important is that too many of us do not understand. We take too many things for granted. Today, too many of us take the Negro press just as much for granted as we take the electric lightbulb for granted. We criticize it and just take it for a matter of course.

Those of us in the struggle, from the NAACP, we know what it means. The biggest job we have is the job of educating the public to their problem—telling them what the score is.

Those of us who happen to be Negroes, while we are interested in what happens in Europe—we are interested in this, and we are interested in that—we are primarily interested in (1) whether it will mean anything that will hurt us, and (2) whether we should have a particular interest in it. There are several ways we might get that. You cannot have it taught to you in schools day in and day out, because you have too many other things to learn. You do not get it enough in the pulpits in the churches, because, in most cases, they are looking out too much for the beyond, instead of what is here.

The NAACP cannot get it to all of its members, because we do not have the facilities to do it. At one time, we had a bulletin which went to its members once a month. It became financially impossible to continue it. The biggest circulation that it gets is that the president of each one of those local units sometimes will read it himself. I emphasize sometimes on that. It is the length and breadth of our educational process.

We have a very small field staff to service 1,500 branches. They cannot do it. The only way the story gets over is through the Negro press, and, as I said before we accept it, look at it, and let it go at that. We do not realize that, when they give up space, they give up money-paying space to us for nothing.

In addition to that, when we filed the cases in the Supreme Court, we had to raise the money. The Negro press came through. They carried ads in those papers. All of them carried ads. They carried them for free, week after week, for thirteen weeks. They were glad to do it. They carried stories. They carried pictures. They carried information to the people. And they not only got the story over to the people as to what was involved in these cases—and what the score happened to be—but they raised the necessary money to get these cases financed. Out of total of some $71,000, the Negro press raised over $17,000, close to $18,000, through the papers themselves—in addition to the ads that they carried and the stories they carried which brought in the other money.

The papers had their own individual fund-raising efforts on their pages. The *Pittsburgh Courier* had "The Double E. Fund." The *Kansas City Call* and the *Cleveland Call and Post* had it. And then we had the one to end all slogans, in Birmingham, Alabama—the fund that was headed: "The Put Up or Shut Up Fund."

Through all those combined efforts, the money came in, and we were able to do a job. We couldn't have done it without the money. We don't believe anymore that this can be done without money.

Ever so often, I hear people of both races engaged in arguments and saying, "Well, if you don't get it done, I'll take you to the Supreme Court!" They don't know a thing in the world about what they are talking. "Every man is entitled to his day in court" is another half-truth. Every man is entitled to his day in court if he has money enough to pay for it. No money, no court.

Let me tell you about these cases—this fight, and let me go back a little, because I think it is interesting to the young people to realize where we stand:

You know, a few years back, when we went to school in a Negro school, we were aiming to be the best Negro in whatever outfit in which we were going—teaching, medicine, law, or whatever else—and we considered our limited scope, ending up by limiting our vision and, ultimately, limiting our training.

If you have to compete with only one or two people, we study just enough to do that. If we have to compete with thousands, we either study a little more or give up, because the odds are too great.

Whether we like it or not, the students in this room today are going to graduate into a community that is becoming more and more integrated. You are going to have to compete with everybody, and you are going to have to measure up. You are not going to be principal of an elementary school by being a better teacher than just those in your school, or a better politician, or a better "Uncle Tom." You are going to get to be a principal of your school in the future because you are better than any other teacher in that system—white or black. That will be the only way you will get the job, and you might as well shape up to it.

Dr. Louis T. Wright, who used to be chairman of our Board of Directors some years back, kept his commission in the U.S. Army, after World War I, and eventually, he took a commission which qualified him to be a Colonel in the Medical Reserve. No Negro had ever been a Colonel, and Dr. Wright had passed way over the top of everybody else. As a matter of fact, when he took the examination, in less than half of the time allowed, he finished it and took his paper into the room of the Surgeon General. The General said, "Dr. Wright, you can't be finished." The answer was "Yes." The General asked, "Is it that you just don't intend to do any more?" The answer was, "No." The Surgeon General then asked, "What do you mean?" Louis said, "I have done enough to pass, and I know I've done enough to pass, because I know more about this than you do, and you are giving the exam." And he did pass.

When all of us were congratulating Louis—I can remember it as if it were yesterday—he said, "I did not deserve any credit for that. I had to be good. I was black."

I have never forgotten that, and you are going to have to bear that in mind. You are not only going to have to be good; you are going to have to be a little better than that. You will have the kind of competition that will make you and that will take you out of the rut of being just a "run of the mill" person.

All of this has been moving along since the early thirties, when these cases were started. As [Carl A.] Murphy said, Charlie Houston, Bill Hastie, and people like that had the necessary vision to see where we are going—not only into these five cases that were argued last year,[1] but with regard to cases that was the result of Charlie Houston's vision when a lot of other people said it could not be done. Whatever any of us do, we all realize that the lawyers who argued these cases in the Supreme Court, with the exception of one, had all been either students of Charlie Houston, or had been, as we say, touched by him.

When these cases started, many people thought we were trying to get separate-but-equal, better schools for Negroes. Back in the good old days, we were shadow boxing, back and forth, because the law was not clear enough for us to know where we could go. Eventually, the law crystallized and became fairly clear, at least, as to where there was an opening here and an opening there.

Then, we had the University of Texas Law School case involving H[eman] Marion Sweatt.[2] We had Ada Lois Sipuel applying to the Law School of the University of Oklahoma,[3] and we had McLaurin going to the University of Oklahoma Graduate School.[4] Those cases were in court over a period of four years, and they all said the same thing. The Dixiecrats[5] and the others said it was horrible. The only thing Negroes were trying to do, they said, was to get social equality. As a matter of fact, there would be intermarriage, they said.

1. See Robert Carter, In Tribute: Charles Hamilton Houston, 111 HARV. L. REV. 2149 (1998); William H. Hastie, Toward an Equalitarian Legal Order, 1930–1950, 407 ANNALS 18 (1973); GILBERT WARE, WILLIAM HASTIE: GRACE UNDER PRESSURE (1985).
2. Sweatt v. Painter, 339 U.S. 629 (1950).
3. See generally ADA LOIS SIPUEL FISHER, A MATTER OF BLACK AND WHITE: THE AUTOBIOGRAPHY OF ADA LOIS SIPUEL FISHER (1996) (discussing case).
4. McLaurin v. Oklahoma State Regents for Higher Ed., 339 U.S. 637 (1950).
5. See, e.g., WILLIAM D. BARNARD, DIXIECRATS AND DEMOCRATS: ALABAMA POLITICS 1942–1950, at 95–124 (1974).

The latter theory was the reason we deliberately chose Professor McLaurin. We had eight people who had applied and who were eligible to be plaintiff, but we deliberately picked Professor McLaurin, because he was sixty-eight years old, and we didn't think he was going to marry or intermarry. As a result, at least, we had one case. They could not bring that one up . . .

Let's not worry about the decisions in these cases, but let us think about what happened. Everything they said in those cases, they are saying now. They said that if Negroes were admitted to the graduate and professional schools, they would wreck the schools, the students would withdraw, and the buildings would fall apart; blood would flow in the streets—everything would happen.

As a result of those decisions, there are Negroes in the graduate and professional schools in twelve of the southern states. There are so many in the University of Oklahoma and Oklahoma A. & N. College that if there were any more in there, it would look like Uncle Tom's cabin.

In Louisiana and Arkansas, let's see what happened. You know what happened? Absolutely nothing. They have been arguing that if we were admitted to white schools, we should have social equality. So, how did the students answer in the University of Texas Law School? At the first meeting of the student body, the first-year class of the Law School elected Sweatt vice-chairman of the social committee. That was the students' answer.

In Oklahoma, they put up signs "Reserved for Colored" and as fast as they put them up, the students tore them down. It got to the point where somebody had to give in. So the trustees gave in and stopped putting up the signs.

The only trouble that we had in Oklahoma during the second year that Negroes attended was that they put four colored, single girls in one of the prefabricated houses outside of the quadrangle that had been formerly set aside for GI married couples. The girls objected to being put out there—to being singled out as Negroes and put in those buildings. And there, we had equalization, but we had equalization down, because they put the four white girls out there. So, what could they do? It was equal. White and colored, both were out there. So, in all of that, we can see that we either get it up, or we get it down.

Now, why do we have the people running around saying that it won't work? If Negroes can attend the University of Arkansas graduate school, law school, and medical school without a lawsuit, they can attend it in any other southern state, including Mississippi, Arkansas, Georgia, South Carolina, and Florida.

We cannot open the law school in the University of South Carolina. We have been unable to do so because we can't get a Negro to apply to it. The reason we can't is because of the level of the law school. No self-respecting Negro will apply to it. The dean of the white law school of the University of South Carolina—the dean, himself—has never been to law school.[6] Yet, he is dean and teaching in that school.

We had a case against Governor Talmadge's University of Georgia Law School, but it was two years before it got up for a hearing. By the time it got up for hearing last September—although two years before the plaintiff could not pass the Army physical, he suddenly passed it with flying colors. So, we lost the lawsuit by losing the plaintiff.

This progress that has been on the graduate and professional level, I tell you, for this reason: because I think it applies to students in all undergraduate colleges throughout the country.

Those of you who are thinking about taking graduate work have yourselves to bear this in mind: that you are not limited to apply to a Negro school for graduate work. You are free to apply to any graduate school you choose. And if they don't let you in, we will find ways and means of getting you in.

Negroes are even attending undergraduate schools, at least one, in Louisiana. One of the publishers who is here, Carter Wesley, of the *Houston Informer*, will tell you that, in his state of Texas, Negroes are attending three junior colleges without any trouble at all. Some one million and three hundred and fifty thousand voted in the last election. Those of you who are so busy studying in schools, who are out of school and are so busy in your own occupations, sometimes fail to realize how fast the change is taking place. Everybody in the Deep South, with whom you talk, from Governor to Attorney General, down to local School Boards, will tell you that segregation is on its way out. When you get out of school, you are going to face that. In some cases, when you go back to your homes in certain areas, you will find that it has already happened. The question is whether or not we can measure up to it. It is a pretty tough job to get something ready and then find that you are not qualified.

You are, nevertheless, about to be living in an integrated South. If we can open up the graduate and professional schools, we can open up the colleges. If we can open the colleges, we can open up all down the line.

To open them up, however, we must have Negroes who are qualified to do so, who are willing to do so, and who are anxious and determined to continue their education in an unsegregated atmosphere; so that when

6. In 1946, Samuel Lander Prince was named dean of the law school. "Prince had never been to law school." GEORGE C. ROGERS, JR., GENERATIONS OF LAWYERS: A HISTORY OF THE SOUTH CAROLINA BAR 196 (1992). In "those days the bar [association] selected the Dean." Apparently, some deans were not lawyers. Telephone discussion with former Associate Dean and Professor Lewis Burke of the University of South Carolina Law School, Nov. 2, 1999.

your education is completed, you will be able to go into your communities and work toward breaking down residential segregation and segregated transportation; to break down Jim Crow in your town. Whether or not you reach the point where you are willing to take the lead in doing those things, I can assure you that you are going to be in the middle of them, because somebody else is going to be doing them. You are going to be drawn into it one way or another, whether you like it or not.

Time is coming when, in every community, you are going to have to stand up and be counted. As my friend, Roy Campanella,[7] said last year, in the hot heat in August—a statement that was by far the most non-original statement ever made, but I remember it because he made it: "This is the time that separates the men from the boys." Oh, it is not original. It had been around ever since we have had a language, perhaps. But this fight for integration will separate the men from the boys.

People have courage about it. We have reached the stage, now, that win, lose, or draw, everybody is talking about it.

The only people that I find now—take the die-hards like Governor Byrnes and Governor Talmadge. They are so sure that they have lost those lawsuits that they are threatening to call out the militia and everything else. They are surely lost.

The Attorney General of Oklahoma, in a public speech, said that he was sure it was lost.

The Attorney General of Georgia, Talmadge's own Attorney General, says, "I am sure the case is lost."

The lawyers whom Governor Byrnes sent up to get a report for him say the same thing.

There are only one people on the face of the globe who don't believe and refuse to believe that segregation is gone—My People!

The other fact we need to face is that this problem will not be solved in any place but in the Deep South. And every time I talk to a northern audience, whether it is a student body, or NAACP meeting, or anything else, I tell them, because I know that I'm correct, that we don't need any of their pity or any of their feeling sorry for us in the South—and I'm from the South. I'm from Up South, in Baltimore, Maryland. Way up South. We don't need the pity that says, "Oh, it's a shame. When segregated schools are broken down, everybody will get hurt. The poor Negroes will. This and that will happen to them."

You and I know that nothing is going to happen. Oh, there might be some scattered stuff here and there. There has been trouble. I was in an all-Negro school, and we had our percentage of fights just the same as we

7. Roy Campanella, the famous catcher for the Brooklyn Dodgers, was the second black player elected to the Baseball Hall of Fame, in 1969.

have anyplace else, because boys are going to fight. It's normal for them to do it. But we are going to solve these problems. We don't need them to worry about it. We can handle it.

Another thing I like to tell them up North is that as soon as we get our problems solved down here, we'll go up there and help them with some of theirs. After all, when you realize it, in southern Illinois discrimination and segregation is so bad that self-respecting Negroes go to Louisville, Kentucky, for some freedom.

We had a case, two years ago, in Cairo, Illinois, to get mixed schools—and the law required no segregation. As a result of the filing of that lawsuit, whites fired into the Negro leader's home with shotguns. They threw a bomb against one Negro home. It just, fortunately, bounced off.[8]

This "Race Problem," of course, is supposed to be in the South; they kick us around, but you won't find any place where the willingness to fight this problem exists like we have it down here.

In South Carolina, where the per capita income of a Negro is so low we are hardly able to count it: they raised $38,000 in nickels and dimes—and a few quarters—for their lawsuit.

In Virginia, where the per capita is a little higher, they raised that much.

In Maryland, from where Mr. [Carl A.] Murphy comes,[9] we are all proud of our state conference. They have had lawsuits in the courts since 1934 and up until the present day. They are straightening out this and that as they go along. Every nickel of their expenses has been paid right there.

The South may be fortunate. The foot has been so heavy on the back of our necks that we have been forced to take courage and fight. We are not worried about the outcome. The only thing we need to do is to clear up our own minds.

When I was in Columbia, South Carolina—and I like to report this—the Reverend Mr. Adams said that we need to feel in our own minds that we are the equals of anybody on the face of the globe. Anybody. The only way to do that is to feel in our own minds that we are not only as good as anybody but that we are better than the average one we pass as we walk down the street. As Reverend Adams says, he likes to think that when the Lord created him, he did not do it on a Saturday when he was tired out and did not have much with which to work. He said he preferred to think that the Lord made him early on Monday morning when he had the best materials to work with and all the energy that he needed.

8. For background on Cairo, Illinois, and race, *see generally* PAUL GOOD, CAIRO, ILLINOIS: RACISM AT FLOOD TIDE (U.S. Commission on Civil Rights, 1973).
9. RICHARD KLUGER, SIMPLE JUSTICE: THE HISTORY OF BROWN v. BOARD OF EDUCATION 183–184, 667 (1975) (Murphy mentioned).

Once he had convinced himself of that, he had no problem knowing, not just thinking, but knowing that he was the equal of anyone else.

As we get ready to go into this integrated society that we all are going into, we must have something that will prevent us from doing what we are now doing. We want to live together. We are always charged with that. As long as we live together in residential areas, voluntarily, we are vulnerable. They will always have a "Jim Crow" school there. We will always have no police protection, and nothing else.

The only salvation is the scatter-group community, and it can be done. We must, however, have the right frame of mind. Let us not do like I see so many people doing in Los Angeles, New York, Chicago, Detroit, Cleveland, and other cities where they have civil rights laws that guarantee that a person can eat wherever he wants to eat. In such place, you will see Negroes, invariably, coming down the street, peering in restaurant windows as they go, until they see one where there is another Negro inside. They won't go in until they see another Negro in there.

Down on Jones Beach, in New York, for an example, there are tens of thousands of people. It is the prettiest beach in the world, I think. Invariably, on Saturday or on a holiday, you will see a Negro come down the boardwalk looking for another Negro, and the first thing you know you are in the middle of a "Jim Crow" community. I did not get out there last summer, because I did not have time. Summer before last, I went out there twice, and on the second Sunday I moved a dozen times from being a part of a "Jim Crow" community.

There is no use in opening up these schools and opening up these colleges; no use in breaking down the restrictions in living where you want to live unless our people are ready for it, determined for it, and will settle for nothing less than that.

That is the responsibility of the young people more than anyone else. So many of the others of us are down in the rut and can't get out of it. There is no excuse under the sun for any young person, today, feeling that there is any ceiling whatsoever on whatever he might do that is based on race or color. There is no reason for it anymore, and it won't do you any good, my friend, to sit there and, in my mind, say, "He sure is right," and then go straight out that door and promptly forget it.

It will do you well if you go home by yourself and analyze your own mind to find out whether or not I am right about you. Then, find out whether or not you need to work on yourself.

It would not be fair if I did not end up by telling you that in our NAACP—and this is especially to our young people who should be in our college chapters of our association—NAACP has a *Fighting Fund for Freedom* going, to raise the money to keep this machine moving.

You know that this association, in going back a few years, did not have money. I remember that in '36 there was around $70,000 in the whole NAACP budget, but $9,000 of that was set aside for the legal department, and that included salaries and everything else.

We have been called on, as we have had to expand our program. Now, the NAACP spends $380,000 a year in the legal department alone. In addition, it spends over $200,000 a year—which totals about $600,000 a year—over a half-million dollars. That doesn't cover the money that the branches spend.

This still is not enough money. The NAACP has decided that on the 100th anniversary of the Emancipation Proclamation, we are going to be free. It has taken a hundred years to get nearly free, and, in this last ten, we are going to get free.

In order to do that, we must make up all those years when we were coasting. In order to do that, it is estimated that it will take a million dollars a year.

You will be called on by your branches, state conferences, youth groups, and everyone else to contribute and help in that Fighting Fund.

As you add up two or three points, to my mind, you should get this:

Progress has been made in getting our civil rights. As the progress has moved along, we have learned lessons here and there. Now, we have reached a point where the real evil, the real stumbling block, the real iron curtain, or whatever you want to call it, is *racial segregation*: and the nub of that is *residential segregation*.

The other point is that we recognize that for over two hundred years our race had been steeped in the belief that, whether we like it or not, we were either slaves or freemen who were second-class citizens. We have to shake every bit of that dust off. Once we do that, we get to the final point:

With careful planning and with the willingness to cooperate; with the willingness of those of us who are college trained to front for and to pro- tect those who are not; and with the willingness of those with money to pull with those who have little; and with the willingness of everybody to bear in mind that maybe other people don't know it, but we, as a racial group, know that the solution of the world problem, today, rests with the darker people of the world;[10] and that the leadership which should be in the hands of the United States is lost because of mistrust of the United States which has been brought about solely because of the way they treat us.

10. In 1936, Dr. Ralph J. Bunche wrote: "The die is cast and racial crisis threat- ens not only the future of the United States but the peace of the world. . . . And so class will some day supplant race in world affairs. Race war then will be merely a side-show to the gigantic class war which will be waged in the big tent we call the world." RALPH J. BUNCHE, A WORLD VIEW OF RACE 97, 98 (1936) (Bronze Booklet No. 4, Published by the Association of Negro Folk Education).

While all the rest of them are around yelping about breaking amendments and treaties, and all that kind of business, we are going to save this country's soul, white or black, whether they like it or not. We are going to do it with courage and determination, and without compromise.

When anybody tells you today that the time is not ripe, tell them that after ninety years most things got ripe. After ninety years, most things become rotten.

If anybody tells you that anything good can be found in separate but equal, you just say, "Point to it."

Whenever anybody tells you that "Jim Crow" cannot be destroyed without great trouble, point out the cases where it has worked.

First of all, work on your own mind. Sell your own self. Then take it upon yourself to go out into the community and sell everybody you can find to sell, regardless of their race.

Segregation and Desegregation

There has been much discussion during recent years concerning the question of the removal in this country of dual citizenship based solely on race and color. The primary emphasis has been on the elimination of racial segregation. No one denies that progress is being made. There are, however, some who say that the progress is too slow and others who say that the progress is too rapid. The important thing to remember is that progress is being made. We are moving ahead. We have passed the crossroads. We are moving toward a completely integrated society, North and South.[1]

Those who doubt this and those who are afraid of complete integration are victims of a background based upon long indoctrination of only one side of the controversy in this country. They know only of one side of the controversy in this country. They know only of one side of slavery. They know only the biased reports about Reconstruction and the long-standing theory which seems to support the "legality" of the separate-but-equal doctrine.

In order to adequately appraise the situation, we must first understand the problem in relation to our history—legal and political. Secondly,

Thurgood Marshall, *Segregation and Desegregation*, 19 THE DILLARD BULLETIN: THE EDWIN R. EMBREE MEMORIAL LECTURES 1953–1954, 33 (Oct. 1954). According to Venola Jones of the Dillard University Library, Marshall delivered the Edwin R. Embree Memorial Lecture at Dillard University, in February 1954. *See Thurgood Marshall Cites Success in Desegregation*, 18 THE DILLARD BULLETIN 1 (Feb. 1954).

1. The Brown decision brought great expectation for the future of the nation. For example, during a meeting at Fisk University in July 1954, one participant stated: "The integration of all citizens of the United States is in the air and both Negroes and whites are ready for it. The recent decision of the wise men of the Supreme Court was a sort of shock treatment for a miserable malady which too long has gnawed at the vitals of our national life. . . . [S]o may we cherish the hope that this momentous decision will make this nation under God—morally and spiritually stronger, and truly a guiding light for the nations of the world. Frayser T. Lane, Meeting the Challenge of Integration Community Responsibility 1, July 5, 1954. On file at Amistad Research Center, Tulane University, B50, F15.

we must give proper weight to progress that has been made with and without legal pressure, and thirdly, we must look to the future.

Our government is based on the principle of the equality of man the individual, not the group. All of us can quote the principle that "All men are created equal." Our basic legal document, the Constitution of the United States, guarantees equal protection of the laws to all of us. Many state constitutions have similar provisions. We even have a "Bill of Rights" in the Constitution of Louisiana. These high-sounding principles we preach and teach. However, in the eyes of the world we stand convicted of violating these principles day in and day out.

Today, one hundred and seventy-seven years after the signing of the Declaration of Independence and eighty-six after the Fourteenth Amendment was adopted, we have a society where, in varying degrees throughout the country, but especially in the South, Negroes, solely because they are Negroes, are segregated, ostracized, and set apart from all other Americans. This discrimination extends from the cradle to the graveyard.[2] (And I emphasize grave*yard*, rather than grave.) Or, to put it even more bluntly, in many areas of this country, a white paroled murderer would be welcome in places which would at the same time exclude such people as Ralph Bunche, Marian Anderson, Jackie Robinson, and many others. Constitutionally protected individual rights have been effectively destroyed by outmoded theories of racial or group inferiority. Why is this true? How long can we afford the luxury of segregation and discrimination?

One reason this condition of dual citizenship exists is because we have been conditioned to an acceptance of this theory as a fact. We are the products of a misunderstanding of history. As a matter of fact, only in recent years have accurate studies of the pre–Civil War period and the Reconstruction period of our history been published.

Our position today is tied up with our past history—at least as far back as the 1820s. At that time the antislavery movement was beginning to take permanent form. It should be borne in mind that those people in New England, Ohio, and other areas who started this movement became dedicated to a principle which has become known as the Judeo-Christian ethic. This principle was carried forth in their determination to remove slavery from our society, and to remove the badges of caste and inferiority whereby an American could be ostracized or set apart

2. The segregation of blacks in southern cemeteries was associated with the Negrophobia of yesteryear. For example, one author quoting the *Richmond* (Ky.) *Register and the Independent,* Aug. 13, 1874, writes: "The graveyards you have selected, beautiful, and adorned as a resting-place of those you have loved must be segregated to satisfy the spite of those liberty lovers, and choice places given to the negro." WILLIAM GILLETTE, RETREAT FROM RECONSTRUCTION, 1869–1879, at 191 (1979).

from fellow Americans solely because of race. Of course, slavery per se was the immediate objective—the abolition of slavery—but the ultimate goal was the same as the unfinished business we have before us today, namely, to remove race and caste from the American life.

These people in the 1820 period—1820 to 1865—sought to translate their moral theories and principles into law. They started by pamphleteering and speechmaking. They recognized that equal protection of the laws must always be, in part, an ethical and moral concept, rather than a law. They sought to constitutionalize this moral argument or ideal. Slavery—with its theories of racial damnation, racial inferiority, and racial discrimination—was inherently repugnant to the American creed and Christian ethics. They sought to support their moral theories by use of the Declaration of Independence and certain sections of the Constitution as it existed at that time. In so far as public meetings were concerned, speakers were barred from such meeting in the South—brutally beaten or killed, and many were run out of similar meetings in Northern cities and towns. It was, therefore, impossible to get behind the original iron curtain to get public support for much of the program.

In their legal attack they were thwarted by the decision of the United States Supreme Court in the Dred Scott case, which held that no person of African descent, slave or free, had any rights that a white man was bound to respect.[3] The important thing to remember throughout this period is that the opponents of slavery were seeking a constitutional basis—a legal platform—for the democratic principle of the equality of man.

After the Emancipation Proclamation was signed, many states passed Black Codes and other infamous statues, effectively returning the emancipated slaves to their inferior status. Consequently, the same people who fought to abolish slavery had to take the lead in Congress in writing the Thirteenth, Fourteenth, and Fifteenth Amendments. This short period of intense legislation was followed by the Reconstruction period. Much of that which we have read concerning this period has emphasized, overstated, and exaggerated the errors of judgment made in trying to work out the "Negro problem"[4] in such fashion as to give real meaning

3. Dred Scott v. Sandford, 60 U.S. (19 How.) 393 (1857).
4. A major concern for southern whites was the "Negro problem" and the solution thereof. *See generally* CARLYLE McKINLEY, AN APPEAL TO PHARAOH (1907). McKinley posed the problem by this question: "Is it probable that the white people of the South, for any reason or motive, under any circumstances that are likely to arise, will ever regard the Negroes among whom they live with much less aversion,—or with more favor, if that term be preferred,—than they now entertain towards them? The answer must be an emphatic, unqualified negative. . . . The removal of the Negro from our country to his own country—from America to Africa—alone will solve it." *Id.* at 91, 123.

to these Civil War amendments[, but these amendments] were actually thwarted by the conspiracy between Northern capitalists and others to bring "harmony" by leaving the Negro and his problem to the tender mercies of the South. This brought about the separate-but-equal pattern, which spread not only throughout the South but extended and now exists in many Northern and Western areas.[5]

Despite the distortion of this historical background, which has become firmly embedded in our minds, is the "understanding" that racial segregation is legal and valid even if in violation of our moral principles. The fallacy of this reasoning is that the equal protection of the laws was intended to be the constitutionalization of the ethic and moral principle of the absolute equality of man—the right of an individual neither to be circumscribed or conditioned by group, race, or color.

It should, therefore, be remembered that our society is the victim of the following periods of history: the period of slavery, when the slaveholders defended slavery by repeating over and over again the myth that slavery was not only a positive good for the nation but was absolutely beneficial and necessary for the Negroes themselves. Consequently, even free Negroes were denied the right of citizenship and subjected to all manner of abuse without legal redress. Immediately following the Civil War, and indeed up to the 1930s, is the period when Negroes were no longer slaves but were certainly not yet full citizens. Having passed through this laissez-faire period[6] insofar as asserting our constitutional rights is concerned, Negroes began in the thirties the all-out fight to secure the right to vote and at the same time to break down discrimination and segregation.

In so far as securing the right to vote, beginning with the registration cases and the white-primary cases and others, much progress has been made to the end that as of the 1948 national elections, at least 1,300,000 Negroes voted in the deep South. We have seen Negroes elected to the city council in Richmond, Virginia, Nashville, Tennessee, and many cities in North Carolina. We have seen Negroes elected to the governing board of the Democratic party in Atlanta, Georgia. We have also seen Negroes elected to school boards in cities such as Atlanta, Georgia, Lynchburg,

---

5. *A Judge Finds New York Schools Separate and Unequal,* U.S. NEWS & WORLD REPORT 82, Jan. 9, 1959. ("A court in New York City now holds that this Northern metropolis is failing to provide for its Negro and Puerto Rican children the 'equal' education that long has been required by the U.S. Supreme Court.") *Id.*
6. During this era the federal courts rejected progressive legislation which diminished the institutional prerogatives of local government, leaving social and protective legislative initiatives benefiting minorities and other poor people beyond the reach of heightened judicial review. This period is often referred to as the Lochner era. *See* Lochner v. New York, 198 U.S. 45 (1905).

Virginia, and Winston-Salem, North Carolina. There are still, however, several small areas in Alabama, Mississippi, and at least four parishes in Louisiana where Negroes are still prevented from registering as qualified voters. (But these are distinctly local problems, which are being attended to and can be pushed aside on that basis.)

In the North we have seen the drive for protection of the right to work without regard to race and color—the drive for FEPC [Fair Employment Practice Commission] legislation. We have seen such legislation passed in at least eight states in the North, leaving forty states and the District of Columbia to go, before we have the necessary safeguards to protect man's right not to be deprived of an opportunity to earn a livelihood because of race, religion, or ancestry.

We have also seen the breaking down of the legal barriers to owning and occupying real property without regard to race or color. Today, as a result of several Supreme Court decisions, any American any place in the United States, regardless of race or color, may own and occupy property wherever he can find a willing seller, has the money to purchase the property and courage to live on it. We still, however, have residential segregation throughout the country, not by law, not by the courts, but by a combination of circumstances, such as, the reactionary policies of mortgage companies and real-estate boards, public-housing agencies, including FHA [Federal Housing Administration], and other governmental agencies. We also find an unwillingness on the part of many Negroes to exercise their rights in this field. In recent years instead of progress toward an integrated community, we find that the Negro ghetto is merely expanding into a larger and more glorified and gilded ghetto. This unwillingness to exercise our own rights is due in part to the long indoctrination that we are different from or inferior to others and therefore should voluntarily segregate ourselves.

As of the present time, the paramount issue in so far as Americanism is concerned is the ending of all racial distinctions in American life. The reasons for this are many. A weighty factor, of course, is the recognition by more and more people in high places that the world situation in regard to the sensitive areas throughout the world depends on how well we can handle our race problem in this country. Our country can no longer tolerate an Achilles heel of discriminatory practices toward its darker citizens. Even more important is the realization that the equality of man as principle and the equal protection of the laws as a Constitutional concept are both based upon the moral principle of individual responsibility rather than racial identity.

Racial segregation in our country is immoral, costly, and damaging to the nation's prestige. Segregation and discrimination violate the Judeo-Christian ethic, and the democratic creed on which our national morality is based is soundly established in the minds of most men. But in addition, it has been shown that the costs of segregation and discrimination to the nation are staggering. Elmo Roper, social scientist and pollster of American public opinion, has stated, "The resultant total of the cost of discrimination comes to roughly $10 out of every $75 paycheck, or, in total, $30 billion lost every year." This figure alone would amount to a cost of $2,000 per year to every individual in America. But perhaps even more damaging to the nation is the current effect of America's racial practices on America's role in international affairs and world leadership. According to a recent statement by our State Department experts, nearly half of the recent Russian propaganda about America has been concentrated on race, linking Communist germ-warfare charges with alleged racial brutality in this country. In addition, Americans returning from abroad consistently report having been questioned over and over about racial problems in this country.

This concern about American racial practices seems especially strong among the two thirds of the world that is darker-skinned. Our former ambassador to India, Chester Bowles, wrote the following statement, after attending an Indian press conference: "As I later discovered is almost invariable the case in any Asian press conference or forum, the Number One question was, 'What about America's treatment of the Negro?'"[7]

Shortly after returning from a tour of Asian and Pacific areas, Vice-President [Richard M.] Nixon made this statement:

Americans must create a better understanding of American ideals abroad by practicing and thinking tolerance and respect for human rights every day of the year. Every act of racial discrimination or prejudice in the United States hurts Americans as much as an espionage agent who turns over a weapon to a foreign enemy.[8]

Historically, we have to ask whether or not, even as we stand today, our country can afford to continue in practicing *not* what they preach. . . .

The harm done to the individual begins with the child's earliest years, when he becomes aware of status differences among groups in society and begins to react to patterns of segregation. Prejudice and discrimination are potentially damaging to the personalities of all children. The children of the majority group are affected differently from those of the minority group. This potential psychological damage is crystallized by segregation practices sanctioned by public law—and it is the

7. *See generally* CHESTER BOWLES, PROMISES TO KEEP: MY YEARS IN PUBLIC LIFE, 1941–1969 (1971). (This particular quote was not found in his autobiography, but the book does treat issues relating to Africa, India and aspects of the civil rights movement.)
8. *Nixon Says, U.S. Must End Bigotry*, BALTIMORE AFRO-AM., Jan. 2, 1954, at A1.

same whether in the North, the East, the West, or the South. Damage to the immediate community is inevitable. This is followed by damage to the state, our federal government and, finally, the world today. The only answer is the complete removal of all racial distinctions that lay at the basis of all this. . . .

While the effects of enforced segregation on majority-group children are more obscure, they are, nevertheless, real. Children who are taught prejudice, directly or indirectly, are also taught to gain and evaluate themselves on a totally unrealistic basis.[9] Perceiving minority-group members as inferior does not permit a member of the majority group to evaluate himself in terms of actual ability or achievement but permits and encourages self-deception—that is, "I am at least better than a Negro."

A culture which permits and encourages enforced segregation motivates feelings of guilt and necessitates an adjustment to protect against recognizing the injustice of racial fears and hatreds. . . .

The results of an effort to get a full picture of desegregation in American communities are now available. And it is hoped that these results can be passed on to every American and to our friends and critics overseas. For these results clearly show that in the past ten years, America has undergone a startling, dramatic, and completely unprecedented change in race relations—and all for the better. Racial desegregation has been attempted successfully in literally hundreds of instances, in all regions, and in all walks of life. In addition to the more noticeable areas of schools and the armed forces, complete success has been reported in desegregating public-housing projects, labor unions, Catholic and Protestant churches, public and private swimming pools, professional organizations, some YMCAs and many YWCAs, Southern industries, notably the Southern plants of International Harvester Company, officers' and enlisted men's clubs, and housing areas on Army posts, hospitals, summer camps, and many other areas—even cemeteries.

An impressive part of these great changes is the way that the "unthinkables" of ten years ago have become the "taken-for-granted" of today. Ten years back, it was unthinkable that Negroes would participate in the white professional baseball leagues. Today, Negroes are on the teams in Dallas, Texas, Atlanta, Georgia, Savannah, Georgia, and other areas.

---

9. Much of this race prejudice was fomented by pamphlets that degraded the Negro. For example, one pamphlet asked the following question: "Has the Negro ever been Constitutionally made a citizen of the United States?" The author's reply was "The Negro has never been Constitutionally made a Citizen of the United States, regardless of how many people think so. What we need today is another ruling by the Supreme Court similar to the Dred Scott decision." Dr. Keen Polk, B.L.D., *The Negro and the Constitution* 1, April 10, 1947 (pamphlet).

During World War II, it was unthinkable that Negro and white children would ever attend the same schools on Southern Army posts. As of 1953, the last federally operated Army school on a Southern military post was desegregated; and a recent announcement from the office of the Secretary of Defense states that segregation will be abolished in all schools of every Southern military post by September 1955, in all states, including Mississippi. Before the war, Negroes traveling by train in Southern regions had great difficulty in getting Pullman berths, and risked embarrassment every time they sought to use the dining car. Since that time, legal action and voluntary adjustments made by some railroads have resulted in a shifting pattern in dining cars in the South—from complete exclusion, to being put behind a curtain, to seating at separate tables without a curtain, and, finally to a completely integrated seating pattern. Interstate travel patterns have been liberalized on railroads, buses, and planes, but this has just barely dented the surface. Southern airports are not progressive.

One of the most impressive signs of change may be seen in the area of schools. In 1943, as far as is known, no Negroes were attending Southern white institutions of higher learning. But today, the Sweatt and McLaurin[10] cases have opened the doors of previously all-white graduate schools in every Southern state except five—Mississippi, Alabama, Georgia, Florida, and South Carolina. It is now estimated that around two thousand Negroes [are] now attending Southern white institutions of higher learning. As of September 1953, Negroes were attending the graduate or professional schools of twenty-three Southern white state-supported institutions, attending the undergraduate levels of ten Southern white state and municipal schools, and attending forty-two Southern white private schools. And, according to the *Journal of Negro Education*, "what is more important, there has not been reported a single untoward incident of any kind as a result of this change."[11] . . .

Perhaps the most noticeable and the most complete example of desegregation involving millions of persons is found in the armed forces. At the beginning of World War II, the Army policy was one of almost complete segregation of Negro troops, the Air Force was just beginning an "experiment" in the training of Negro flyers in the face of a widespread belief that Negroes could not be taught to fly airplanes, the Navy confined Negroes almost exclusively to the Messmen's Branch, and the Marines excluded Negroes entirely. But soon cracks began to appear in the wall. The Army's Officers Candidate School and a few other service

10. Sweatt v. Painter, 339 U.S. 629 (1950); McLaurin v. Oklahoma State Regents of Higher Ed., 339 U.S. 637 (1950).
11. Quotation reference not found.

schools became integrated;[12] the Air Force regarded its experiment with a Negro pursuit squadron as a success and expanded it to a fighter group;[13] the Navy in 1942 allowed Negroes to enlist in branches other than the Messmen's service (although they were still segregated and barred from seagoing vessels); and, in 1942, the Marine Corps admitted its first Negroes, in strictly segregated units, as laborers, antiaircraft gunners, and ammunition handlers.[14]

Subsequently, the pressures for integration increased. The armed forces found that they had serious morale problems in some of the segregated Negro units. They also found that the picture of a segregated American Army of Occupation, attempting to teach democracy to the people of Germany and Japan, was a ridiculous experiment. So, in a series of careful and unpublicized moves, the armed forces began a gradual program of racial desegregation. In 1953, the Secretary of the Army reported that at least 90 percent of the Negroes in the Army were serving in nonsegregated units (the number continues to increase), and added: "The Army policy is one of complete integration, and it is to be accomplished as soon as possible."

In the European Army Command, a battalion commander from the deep South is quoted as saying: "We got the order. We got detailed instructions for carrying it out and a time limit to do it in. And that was it."[15]

And in our armed forces all over the globe, Negro servicemen were brought into previously all-white units rapidly and with no trouble by officers who gave white servicemen such terse instructions as these: "Some Negro men are joining our unit. These men are soldiers. Treat them as such."

This is the problem that everybody says is such a "horrible" thing to face up to.

What is the picture today? According to Lee Nichols's exciting new book *Breakthrough on the Color Front*, the Army reports that less than 10,000 Negroes are still serving in all-Negro units out of some 200,000 Negroes in the Army.[16] Assistant Defense Secretary John A. Hannah

12. *See* W. ALLISON SWEENEY, HISTORY OF THE AMERICAN NEGRO IN THE GREAT WORLD WAR: HIS SPLENDID RECORD IN THE BATTLE ZONES OF EUROPE 119–130 (1919) (roster of Negro officers).
13. LOU POTTER, LIBERATORS: FIGHTING ON TWO FRONTS IN WORLD WAR II 89–91 (1992).
14. *Id.* at 144–145.
15. This exact quotation was not found. However, the order referred to is the President's Executive Order 9981 (13 Fed. Reg. 4313 (1948)), which stated: "It is essential that there be maintained in the armed services of the United States the highest standards of democracy, with equality of treatment and opportunity for all who serve in our country's defense." Quoted in LEE NICHOLS, BREAKTHROUGH ON THE COLOR FRONT 87 (1954).
16. *Id.* at 202 (Lee Nichols).

estimates that by June 1954 there will be no remaining segregated Army units. The Air Force, which had moved more rapidly, stated that Negro servicemen who were in the Air Force in August 1953 had been integrated into all of its units throughout the world. Of the 23,000 Negroes serving in the Navy in 1953, about half were still in the Messmen's or Steward's Branch. The rest were integrated and scattered through nearly every job classification that the Navy has. The Marine Corps, last of all the services to take Negroes, reports that its last two all-Negro units were integrated "some time" before the summer of 1952.

Today, Negro and white draftees from the most poverty-stricken parts of the deep South, as well as the rest of the nation, are inducted into a completely integrated command, and the typical report from commanders who had previously held fears was that "the frictions and antagonisms that lay behind previous race conflicts have been substantially reduced, and that so far there has not been a single major incident traceable to integration."

What about segregation in the nation's capital? Many Americans have expressed disgust, and foreign visitors have stated their amazement, at the fact that public and private facilities in the capital of our democracy were almost completely segregated—restaurants, schools, housing projects, theaters, and so forth. Though there is still much to be done in Washington, there have been several recent examples of progress. On June 3, 1953, the National Capital Housing Authority announced the adoption of a policy of opening all present and future public low-rent housing properties in the District of Columbia to low-income families, without regard to race. Around that same time, the Supreme Court handed down a decision preventing discrimination in Washington restaurants. All the restaurants have abided by the decision, and no incident of any kind has been reported. Hotel accommodations now are available to Negroes in most of the larger hotels, although the policy of many smaller hotels is still uncertain. Negroes are now admitted to the three legitimate theaters of Washington, and to at least four—and probably more—of the downtown movie theaters. The majority of the city's private schools have opened their doors to Negroes, and the Catholic parochial schools have also become integrated. A recent bulletin reports that the nation's capital has even agreed to desegregate the jails. Washington is slowly moving toward a position where it can command the respect of the world where race relations are involved.

Why have people decided to desegregate? Members of American communities have tried to integrate their institutions for an extremely varied number of reasons. The pressure to desegregate have come from several forces—sometimes from an aroused Negro community, sometimes from administrative rulings of local authorities, sometimes from rulings by a national body, sometimes from voluntary decision by a majority of concerned community members. It now appears that the success or failure of the desegregation effort is not related to the reason for desegregating, since the reasons are so varied.

The success of racial desegregation has been shown to be related not so much to the type of community that is involved or the prejudice of its members as to the close adherence to a set of specific principles. We have reached the stage where scientists, sociologists, and others have agreed upon rules which when followed bring about smooth desegregation whether in Illinois or Louisiana. The main point is that once the state law preventing intergroup communication in institutional life is removed, it is then up to the local community to work out its own salvation, with the understanding that it must be done within the American framework.

The accomplishment of effective and efficient desegregation with a minimum of social disturbance depends on the following five things:

1. There must be a clear and unequivocal statement of policy by leaders with prestige, and by authority officials.
2. There must be firm enforcement and persistent execution of the nonsegregation policy in the face of initial resistance.
3. Authorities and law enforcement officials must show a willingness to deal with violations, attempted violations, or incitement to violations, by applying the law and backing it up with strong enforcement action.
4. Authorities must refuse to employ, engage in, or tolerate subterfuges, gerrymandering, or other devices for evading the principle and the fact of desegregation.
5. The accomplishment of desegregation must be accompanied by continual interpretation of the reasons for the action, and appealing to the democratic and moral values of all persons involved.

In conclusion, racial segregation is grounded upon the myth of inherent racial superiority. This myth has been completely exploded by all scientific studies. It now stands exposed as a theory which can only be explained as a vehicle for perpetuating racial prejudice. History reveals that racial segregation is a badge of slavery, is just as unscientifically supported, immoral, and un-American as slavery. Recent history shows that it can be removed, and that it can be done effectively when approached intelligently.

There is no longer any justification for segregation. There is no longer any excuse for it. There is no longer any reason under the sun why intelligent people should continue to find excuses for not ending segregation in their own community, in the South as well as in the North.

Interpretation of Supreme Court Decisions and the NAACP

The May 31 decision combined with the May 17 decision of last year [1954] must be viewed as the latest in a series of steps toward full integration of Negroes into American life. When the NAACP began this campaign it was met with state statutes requiring or permitting segregation in public education. These statutory provisions were a complete block to all voluntary efforts to end segregation.

The first cases destroyed the validity of out-of-state scholarships as an excuse for the exclusion of Negroes from professional schools.[1] This was followed by the cases, which declared unconstitutional provisions for the Jim Crow graduate and professional schools.[2] And then the May 17, 1954, decision declared that segregation in public education was unconstitutional.[3] This was followed by the May 31 [1955] decision that all provisions of federal, state, or local law requiring or permitting segregation in public education must yield to the principle announced in the 1954 decision.[4]

This determination by the Supreme Court clears the way for the school boards to desegregate their systems voluntarily. This is being done in many parts of the South. The opinion also gives us the necessary legal weapons to bring about compliance in areas of the South which openly flout the mandate of the Supreme Court.

The question now before us is: under what conditions and with what directives were the school cases remanded to lower courts? We know that

This article was coauthored by Thurgood Marshall and Roy Wilkins and appeared in 62 Crisis 329 (June–July 1955). For historical commentary on and by Wilkins, the executive secretary of the NAACP, *see* Roy Wilkins, Standing Fast: The Autobiography of Roy Wilkins (1984). The editor wishes to thank The Crisis Publishing Co., Inc., the publisher of the magazine of the National Association for the Advancement of Colored People, for authorizing the use of this work.
1. State *ex rel.* Gaines v. Canada, 113 S. W. 2d. 783, 784–85 (Mo. 1937), *rev'd*, 305 U.S. 337 (1938).
2. *See, e.g.* McLaurin v. Oklahoma State Regents for Higher Educ., 339 U.S. 637 (1950).
3. Brown v. Board of Education, 347 U.S. 483 (1954).
4. Brown v. Board of Education, 349 U.S. 294 (1955) (Brown II).

the highest court did not (a) set a deadline date for either the beginning or the completion of desegregation in the public schools; and (b) outline a definite plan by which desegregation must proceed and by which lower courts might judge the efforts of local school boards toward compliance with the May 17 and May 31 rulings. Not having done this, what did the Court do? What language did it use?

Re-Affirmation of Principle

May 17, 1954 decision re-affirmed. "These cases were decided on May 17, 1954. The opinions of that date, declaring the fundamental principle that racial discrimination in public education is unconstitutional, are incorporated herein by reference."[5]

Last year's opinion, as we all know, declared: "We conclude that in the field of public education the doctrine of 'separate but equal' has no place. Separate educational facilities are inherently unequal."[6] On May 31 the Court said simply, as an introduction to its opinion, that this principle stands and that everything in the May 31 opinion hangs upon it; that the items in the May 31 opinion must be considered at all times and under all circumstances in the light of the clear principle in the 1954 opinion. The Court refers to the 1954 "constitutional principles" a total of six times in its May 31 opinion, once as governing "constitutional principles."[7]

All school segregation laws are invalid: "All provisions of Federal, state or local law requiring or permitting such discrimination must yield to this principle."

This means that all laws, local, state, and federal, requiring or permitting racial segregation in the public schools are now null and void, and that no school or other public official or body is bound by such laws.

Good Faith Required

Local school authorities responsible. "School authorities have the primary responsibility for elucidating, assessing, and solving these problems ("full implementation of these constitutional principles").

This means just what it says. It means further that it is right and proper for citizens and community groups to begin the campaign for desegregation with the local school authorities.

Good faith required: ". . . courts will have to consider whether the action

5. *Id.* at 298 (1955).
6. Brown I, *supra* note 3, at 495.
7. Brown II, *supra* note 4, at 299–301. Subsequent quotations in the essay are to this case.

of school authorities constitutes good-faith implementation of the governing constitutional principles."

The Court is saying here that alleged good faith in carrying out the "governing" constitutional principle of nonsegregation can be brought before a court for determination and need not rest upon mere assertion by school authorities or newspapers or politicians or others.

Interest of the plaintiffs: "At stake is the personal interest of the plaintiffs' admission to the public schools as soon as practicable on a nondiscriminatory basis."

Plaintiffs have a right (as set forth in the May 17, 1954, decision) to admission to public schools on a nondiscriminatory basis "as soon as practicable." The latter phrase must be taken to mean with only such delay as may be permitted by the lower courts in the context of language elsewhere in the May 31 opinion.

Must Start Promptly

Obstacles to be eliminated: "To effectuate this interest may call for elimination of a variety of obstacles in making the transition to school systems operated in accordance with the constitutional principles set forth in the May 17, 1954, decision."

When the Court says, as it does here, that to protect the right of the plaintiffs "may call for elimination of a variety of obstacles," it must be taken to mean that the Court in effect is ordering that such obstacles be removed. By the strongest inference it means that pleas of the existence of such obstacles cannot be considered valid reasons for denying plaintiffs their rights. The defendants are duty bound, if such obstacles exist, to remove them, whatever their nature.

Must start promptly: "While giving weight to these public and private considerations, the courts will require that the defendants make a prompt a reasonable start towards full compliance with our May 17, 1954, ruling."

Here the Court says that even while the lower courts may give due weight to the public interest (of the community at large) and to private considerations (the rights of the plaintiffs) the courts "will require" a prompt and reasonable start toward compliance with our May 17, 1954 ruling. "Will require" is strong, definite, positive language in legal terms, a directive which no lawyer or judge misunderstands or underestimates.

Burden upon Defendants

Disagreement no basis for failure to comply: "Courts of equity may properly take into account the public interest in the elimination of such obstacles in a systematic and effective manner. But it should go without saying that the vitality of these constitutional principles cannot be allowed to yield simply because of disagreement with them."

Very simply this means that just because individual citizens, officials, or groups do not like or do not agree with the May 17, 1954, opinion they may not ignore, evade, or defy it. That is, they may not do so in court in a final determination, no matter how much they talk or write about in disagreement outside of a courtroom showdown.

Burden upon the defendants: "Once such a start has been made, the courts may find that additional time may be necessary to carry out the ruling in an effective manner. The burden rests upon the defendants to establish that such time is necessary in the public interest and is consistent with good-faith compliance at the earliest possible date."

It should be noted that only *after* a start has been made will a request for additional time be considered. Here, as in other phases under the jurisdiction of the courts, we have the privilege of challenging such requests for time in the courts, forcing a hearing and for a determination. We need not depend upon the mere assertion of a school official that more time is necessary.

Administrative Problems

Problems to be considered by courts: "To that end, the courts may consider problems related to revision of administration, arising from the physical condition of the school plant, the school transportation system, personnel. . . ."

Non-racial school districts: ". . . Revision of school districts and attendance areas into compact units to achieve a system of determining admission to the public schools on a non-racial basis. . . ."

Revision of local laws: ". . . and revision of local laws and regulations which may be necessary in solving the foregoing problems."

In all its pleading before the courts, the NAACP has granted that allowance should be made for the solving of administrative problems, but it has insisted that diligent attention to solving these would not require a prolonged period. In its section on administrative problems the Court enumerates those which the courts may consider. The time alleged to be required is subject to the "good faith" and "constitutional principles" stipulations. All proposals are subject to challenges in the courts.

It is significant that whereas the Court merely enumerates other administrative problems, it deals in some detail with the possible revision of school districts and attendance areas, in effect saying these should be made "into compact units to achieve a system of determining admission to the public schools on a [nonracial basis]." This would seem to mean that both school official and the lower courts are warned against attempting the gerrymandering of school districts through use of wandering boundary lines for the purpose of insuring racial schools.

In referring specifically to the revision of the local laws and regulations hitherto requiring racial segregation in the school, it would appear that the Court, not content with repeated citations of the "constitutional principles" involved, or with its declaration that all laws must yield to these principles, has pressed the point once more upon school officials and the lower courts. It says plainly that in solving administrative problems no local law or regulation may bar the transition to a nonsegregated school system.

Adequacy of Plans

Adequacy of plans: "They [the courts] will also consider the adequacy of any plans the defendants may propose to meet the problems and to effectuate a transition to a racially non-discriminatory school system."

After listing administrative problems that may be considered by the courts, the Court includes these and every other item in any plan for transition in this one sentence on adequacy. The test is whether a plan of a given school district satisfies the principle laid down in the May 17, 1954, decision. Here again all such plans are subject to challenge in the courts and the school authorities have the burden of proving adequacy.

Courts retain jurisdiction: "During this period transition, the courts will retain jurisdiction of these cases." Until the transition is complete the cases remain in the courts, subject at all times to its hearings and judgments on matters raised. No new actions need to be commenced and old ground re-covered in fresh proceedings.

The May 31 opinion, technically, applies only to the cases before the Court, but as a matter of fact the ruling rendered will be the pattern for all such cases as may be brought in the future.

In the overwhelming majority of instances it can be expected that compliance without legal action will be the rule, perhaps grudgingly and reluctantly in some areas, but compliance, nevertheless.

Legal Weapons in Hand

Armed with the powers embodied in the language of the Court's opinion, we look confidently toward the future. We stand ready with qualified experts in public education and community organization to cooperate with any and all school boards willing to work toward desegregation.

We always realized that there are those who would drag their feet no matter what language the Supreme Court used. We now have the highest court's affirmation of true American principles. This we shall do. We shall not rest until we have ended second-class education for all Americans.

Three Years After Brown I

Despite what many people might think, there actually has been substantial progress in legal action toward eventual desegregation of all public institutions.[1] While we have heard much about the rebellious action of White Citizens Council groups, Klan groups, and many individuals, the courts have moved steadily toward full implementation of the Supreme Court decisions of 1954 and 1955.

As we move toward the final period of desegregation, we must understand our form of government, our legal procedures, and the duties and responsibilities of government officials and private individuals. When the restrictive covenant cases were decided, many people thought that this was the end of segregated housing. However, the ghettos have become larger, and they are still here. The reason for this not the failure of the courts or the laws of the land but, rather, the inaction of the individuals involved. All the law could do and all the Supreme Court could do was to say that no government agency could prevent a Negro from living in a home that he purchased. Much of the responsibility for the continuation of segregated housing rests on the shoulders of Negroes who for one reason or another are unwilling to make an effort to purchase property in nonsegregated areas. This does not at all relieve the responsibility of other Americans who still refuse to sell property to Negroes in nonsegregated neighborhoods and on the other to convince others that Negroes are just as good neighbors as anyone else—no better and no worse.

In the school desegregation decisions, the Supreme Court decided that segregation in public education was unlawful. That is the law of the

Originally titled "Special Message to the 48th Annual NAACP Convention," 1957. Reprinted from JAMYE COLEMAN WILLIAMS AND McDONALD WILLIAMS, EDS., THE NEGRO SPEAKS: THE RHETORIC OF CONTEMPORARY BLACK LEADERS 127 (1970).
1. For a comprehensive update of desegregation two years after the Brown decision, *see The Year Book, Educational Desegregation*, 1956, 25 J. NEGRO EDUC. 203–368 (Summer 1956) (several articles by African American scholars regarding desegregation in the southern states and the District of Columbia).

land, and the unanimous decisions of the Supreme Court have been implemented by state and federal courts in a steady line of decisions during the past two years. However, the Supreme Court did not and could not arrange to put Negroes into every school situation in every town in the South. All the courts can do is to establish and enforce existing laws.

In a democratic form of government, much is left to the individual involved. So, in this area it remains the responsibility of Negro Americans to seek admission to nonsegregated schools in every county and city in the South. There is the responsibility of other Americans who do not have children to join together to give aid and support to Negro parents wanting nonsegregated education for their children. No court and no arm of government can do for the Negro parents what they must do for themselves.

On the other hand, it is the responsibility of the government to protect Negro parents who are exercising their right to apply for non-segregated education. Many lawsuits since the school desegregation cases have clarified the law to the end that in one case from Hoxie, Arkansas, the federal courts decided that it was the positive duty of a local school board to desegregate its schools. The Hoxie case also decided that individuals threatening and using other tactics to prevent the school board from desegregating its schools could and would be punished by the federal courts for this interference. Only a few weeks ago a federal court of appeals in affirming the contempt citation against John Kasper held that he could be punished and should be punished for inciting the community of Clinton, Tennessee, against the lawful admission of Negroes to the heretofore all-white high school.[2]

So, the federal courts instead of limiting the effect of the school desegregation cases are uniformly implementing those decisions, putting the weight of the federal judiciary behind the law of the land. It is but a matter of time until the legislative and executive arms of government will use their authority to bring about desegregation.

While progress in varying degrees has been made toward southern states, the eight remaining states have reached the stage where they are now in open rebellion against the law of the land. The first phase of the campaign in these eight states was the action of the government, attorneys general, and legislators, both federal and state, who used their political offices as a sounding board for denunciation of the United States

2. Kasper v. D. J. Brittain, 245 F. 2d 92 (1957); Bullock v. United States, 265 F.2d 683 (1959); Goss v. Board of Education of the City of Knoxville, Tn., 186 F. Supp. 559, 568 (E.D. Tenn., N.D. 1960). *See also* JACK GREENBERG, CRUSADERS IN THE COURTS: HOW A DEDICATED BAND OF LAWYERS FOUGHT FOR THE CIVIL RIGHTS REVOLUTION 254 (1954); Herbert Brownell, *Civil Rights in the 1950s*, 69 TUL. L. REV. 781, 789 (1995).

Supreme Court, and the NAACP and anyone else who spoke in favor of desegregation.

During the past year, we have really felt the full weight of the second phase of their program. This has been the utilization of the full weight of the state government through the executive, legislative, and judicial arms to prevent the NAACP and its lawyers from either having the NAACP or its lawyers aid Negro parents seeking desegregation. This phase of the program is even more ruthless than the other phase and, indeed, has the best chance of success but for the determination of Negro parents and the southern membership of the NAACP as well as the courage of the NAACP lawyers throughout the South.

There is not time enough to itemize or catalogue all of the oppressive moves that have been made, but they fall into certain general categories.

First, there is the avowed intimidation of Negroes who are either members of the NAACP or who advocate integration. White Citizens Councils and other groups have established the precedent that wherever such Negroes are discovered, they will feel the full brunt of economic boycott, threats, and other intimidation. Having established this as a fact, they have succeeded in getting the legislatures of their states to pass laws requiring states to end the existing laws as to require the NAACP to submit membership lists or go out of business. All of this is done with the full realization that the NAACP could not expose its members to this unmitigated cowardly pressure during this period of terror in these eight southern states.

Another method has been to circulate throughout the North, as well as the South, libelous, scandalous, unsubstantiated charges against the NAACP and then to have the legislatures of the states pass laws forbidding the NAACP to operate, thereby giving to the people of the nation, as well as the state involved, the impression that the NAACP is some type of subversive organization.

A fourth form of intimidation has been to use existing barratry statutes to declare that is unlawful for the NAACP or its lawyers to represent Negro litigants seeking protection from the unconstitutional oppression of the state involved.

I mention these four types of oppression merely as examples of what is going on, and to state to you briefly the problem that we have considered over and over again during the past year. When the school desegregation cases were decided, there were many in the South, and a few in the North, who suggested that the NAACP "go fishing." Others said the NAACP should move cautiously and slowly. There were others who said the NAACP, having won a victory, should not do anything for several years and let the problem work itself out.

As lawyers, we have taken all of this into consideration and have done so in relation to the oppressive tactics that have been used, and are even now being thought up. The legal staff called in lawyers from all over the country, and the entire situation was canvassed and appraised. Every single statute was studied. Every pending law action was reconsidered, and it was the unanimous conclusion of this group of lawyers that there was not one reason under the sun for the NAACP to change its general overall legal strategy insofar as the program is concerned; and we do not intend to change it.

Let us rid ourselves of confusing words and catch phrases such as "gradual," "moderation," "sympathy for the South," "states' rights," and the like. By now we know what the score is.

What is the NAACP supposed to do? Lower our sights to Mississippi, whose governor this week threatened that "No child born today will ever see racial school integration in Mississippi," or the governor of South Carolina, who says integration will not be possible in less than a thousand years? Or shall we stop our program until some other group takes over? We are not being asked to give up the fight. If this is what is meant by "moderation" or "gradualism," we reject it.

If either moderation or gradualism means what the Supreme Court said in these cases, we accept it. For all of our legal action is controlled by the Supreme Court decision. We have never asked for more. We have never failed to give full consideration to the need for time to bring about integration. We have never failed to give full weight to peculiar local problems. However, we have not, can not and will stand by and see state and local government refuse to start to begin to consider integration at any time in the foreseeable future.

First, efforts to throttle freedom of speech, freedom of assembly, and free access to the courts, if permitted to succeed, would destroy the very basis of our form of government—not for Negroes alone but for the country at large.

On this particular point, it is time that the NAACP made it clear to the nation that, although they still are willing to fight this battle along these lines, they are more convinced than ever that others in the country, regardless of their race, and regardless of where they live, had better begin feeling a part of the responsibility for counteracting such moves.

Second, the present state of the desegregation battle is not a case involving a group of white citizens and state officials against Negroes, but it is the open rebellion of some citizens and state officials against the law of the land. This was made clear in the cases involving Hoxie, Arkansas, and the conviction of John Kasper.

Third, it is high time that people in and out of the South understand that the school desegregation cases and the movement toward integration is not one giant conspiracy of oppression against the South, who has been the victim of every type of oppression known to man, and who is even yet being denied his constitutional right to vote, as well as his right to vote, as well as his right to an integrated education. It is time that the pendulum of public opinion should begin its swing toward our government, toward the federal courts. . . .

Fourth, integration is not an assault upon the South. Integration is a part of the Fourteenth Amendment of the Constitution and that applies to the whole United States. Perhaps the most potent factor that stymied the enforcement of the Fourteenth Amendment and facilitated the establishment of the "separate-but-equal" doctrine was the fact that the North lost the will to enforce the Constitution insofar as Negro rights were concerned. Today, we find that much of the sympathy in the North for the South and the unwillingness to insist upon integration in the South is brought about by the conscientious realization that the same problems of racial discrimination prevalent in the South are often tolerated in the North. For example, in many areas of the North today, despite the realization that racial segregation is the biggest stumbling block to complete integration, we find citizens of both races who excuse away, explain, or just forget about residential segregation. It is not a question of whether or not conditions are better in New York than they are in Atlanta; or better in Memphis; or better in Los Angeles than they are in Jacksonville, Florida. The true measuring rod is whether or not there is as much integration as could be obtained by lawful means in each of these areas, regardless of where they are. The South cannot excuse its failure to integrate on the ground that there is not complete integration in the North. The North cannot excuse its shortcomings by saying that is better than the South. The Fourteenth Amendment and the human rights doctrine inherent in our democracy require the elimination of race and caste as determining factors. [The] simple solution is for the Negro and others who believe in democracy to work out their problem of integration in their own areas and not be satisfied until they themselves know that they have worked it out on a honorable basis in conformity with the Constitution of the United States, their moral teachings, and their own conscience. This is not a time for emotion, and it is not a time to be carried away by any will-of-the-wisp hope that things will work themselves out. It is time for the most careful appraisal and planning. With that in mind, it is our hope that after carefully surveying the whole picture and after having studied the declarations the NAACP made in Atlanta immediately after the Supreme Court decision, we reread those statements of principle.

In summary, we said that the decisions were not victories for the

Negroes or the NAACP but were democracy in action. We urged all of our branches and state units not to act in any fashion other than that of a normal American citizen. We urged our people to petition their school boards, to offer to sit down and reason with the boards, and to work with them as long as there was a possibility of working out a peaceful solution to the problem. We urged our people, back in 1954, to negotiate with the school boards and even to compromise on the question as to when and how desegregation should take place, because that had been decided by the Supreme Court. Our only words of caution were (1) that they should not compromise on principle and (2) that legal action should only be used as a last recourse after all efforts at negotiation had failed. I hope that you will agree with the lawyers and the NAACP itself that, regardless of everything that has happened since the Supreme Court decision, as mean and vicious as our adversaries' tactics have been, as frustrating and discouraging as have been the results of some of our efforts,[3] we will not be provoked to move any faster or in any manner inconsistent with law, and at the same time, we don't intend to slow down, retract, or retreat in this general program. We shall continue along the lawful road—at all times operating within the law, relying upon the law, and with faith in democratic processes because time and right are both on our side.

3. Marshall is likely referring to attacks against the Supreme Court's ruling by critics such as Senator James O. Eastland. A year after the Brown decision was issued, Senator Eastland's opposition to Brown was published in a pamphlet by the U.S. Government Printing Office, "Not at Government Expense." *See* Speech, The Supreme Court's "Modern Scientific Authorities" in the Segregation Cases 1–12, May 26, 1955.

The South on the Run

Reliance on the Courts

Mr. Marshall is realistically aware of the difficulties that lie ahead. At the same time he is serenely confident that integration in the schools will come about, before too many years. His plans?

"In the hard-core States of the Deep South, we've got to keep pushing in the courts, and in the other States keep working with the school boards," he said. "The only thing we can do is rely on the courts—in cases where people won't reason the thing out."

"Do you think the Deep South ever will yield?" he was asked. "Won't integration be prevented by one means or another, including crowds that gather and make things unpleasant for Negro pupils and their parents?"

"That won't last," he replied. "People are not going to allow little children to be the victims of grown folks' hatred.

"Some States will take longer than others. The length of time, I wouldn't predict. Mississippi, Alabama, South Carolina and Georgia will take quite a while. I don't think Virginia will take long. Things are beginning to move here now."

One court suit has been filed in South Carolina, one is about to be filed and three more are almost ready to be filed. No suits yet have been entered in Alabama, Mississippi or Georgia. Virginia's pupil-placement act is nearing a final court test.

"All North Carolina is doing," the attorney declared, "is admitting a few Negroes for the sole purpose of showing that their pupil-placement program is not aimed at maintaining segregation.

"I think, though, that, by opening up the situation a bit in North Carolina, many school boards may be encouraged to go ahead now. North Carolina is in the stage where there should be more negotiating with the school boards. It's a question whether legal moves should be made."

Excerpt from interview: Thurgood Marshall: *Negro Strategist Sees South on the Run*, 43 U.S. NEWS & WORLD REPORT, 64–68 (Sept. 27, 1957). Copyright 1957, U.S. News and World Report.

Segregation in the North

Mr. Marshall turned to situations in which residential patterns make for segregated schools. "You have that in New York, Chicago, Detroit—any of the larger cities," he said. He spoke of one school in Brooklyn where all of the pupils and faculty are white, and another in Harlem where the whole student body is Negro and the faculty is mixed. The way to end this kind of segregation, he said, is to end residential segregation. And he added:

"There has to be freedom to move."

Mr. Marshall spoke without much hope regarding a situation in numerous cities of Northern and Border States, where white residents are moving to the suburbs, leaving Negro sections and all Negro schools behind them.

"Until Negroes are accepted in newly developed areas," he said, "we won't make much headway."

"What about racial troubles in the Northern cities—Chicago, New York, Detroit?" he was asked. "Are they worse than in the South?"

"These are entirely different problems," was the reply. "In those areas [the North] you have state laws and machinery that are available to correct wrongs. Much of the existing problem is brought about by the inertia of the Negroes themselves. Where they work on these problems, they go out and clear them up.

"Even in the North, people are conditioned to believe that the Negro is a second-class citizen, to be considered something different. Once you clean up the situation in the South, the North will be an easy job. But we can't let down the constant pressure on the North. It would be a bad job if the Negro gets his rights in the South and loses them in the North. But much progress has been made in the North."

Mixed Marriages?

The next question was: "The South contends, Mr. Marshall, that the end product of integration will be intermarriage, a mixing of the races. What do you think?" And the reply:

"I think there is no foundation for it at all. On the other hand, I don't think there should be laws against intermarriage. It's a purely personal problem and the State has nothing to do with it.

"This intermarriage thing has been raised in everything we've tried to do."

It was brought up, he said, even in connection with moves to permit Negroes to vote in Southern primary elections—on the ground that standing in line together at the polling places would create acquaintanceships that would culminate in mixed marriages.

"After all, the white person can say 'No,'" he continued. "But in the South it's deep in their minds. . . . I don't see any connection between that and schooling. There aren't any figures to back it up. Even where intermarriage is permitted by law, the number is insignificant."

"What is NAACP's ultimate purpose?" Mr. Marshall was asked.

"To go out of business with a realization that race is no longer a problem," he replied, adding:

"That doesn't mean a man is not to determine who comes into his home, or his country club. There are lots of people I don't want around my house."

A Negro and the Law

Actually, the attorney has lost track of the exact number of cases he has argued before the Supreme Court. It is either twenty or twenty-one, he said.

"I know I lost two of them," he added, laughing and gesturing toward his colleagues in the next room. "Those fellows in there won't let me forget that. I guess that's good for me."

Mr. Marshall was born and reared in Baltimore. His father was the steward of several prominent Baltimore clubs. His mother taught in the Baltimore schools.

The son recalls that his father once told him: "If anyone calls you 'nigger,' you not only got my permission to fight him—you got my *orders* to fight him."

The Living Constitution:
Civil Rights and the Negro

Eric Goldman: The Constitution and Negro rights. Our panelists to discuss this [are] four men who are certain experts in many phases of this. Mr. Jack W. Peltason, professor of political science at the University of Illinois, and Mr. Thurgood Marshall, special counsel of the National Association for the Advancement of Colored People. And may I pause, Mr. Marshall, to congratulate you warmly in your victory before the three-judge panel in New Orleans, certainly a victory for law, for common sense, and for human decency.[1]

Thurgood Marshall: I was just there.

Eric Goldman: Mr. Thomas Emerson, professor of law at Yale University, and Mr. Clement Vose, associate professor of government at Wesleyan University.

Mr. Marshall, having been just there in New Orleans, may I turn to you first and ask you to get us going? In that particular legal battle, interposition has been tried and has been struck down as unconstitutional. As I read my *New York Times*, another possible move is this. Senator Russell Long made a speech to the Louisiana legislature. He said, "There is no hope of undoing the school decision or evading it. The only choice for those who wish to continue segregation at all costs is to abandon public schools and to set up a system of state-aided private schools." What constitutional problems are involved there? I wish you would comment.

Courtesy of Raymond Trent, University of Pennsylvania Law Library. The moderator of this panel discussion, which occurred circa 1959, was Eric F. Goldman, a prolific author and a distinguished professor of history at Princeton University. One of his most important books is RENDEZVOUS OF MODERN AMERICAN REFORM (1952). *See also E. F. Goldman; Presidential Aide, Author*, L.A. TIMES, Feb. 23, 1989, at 30.
1. There were several cases before the Fifth Circuit three-judge panels during 1959 and 1960. However, the one that is likely referred to as relevant to the panel discussion is Louisiana State University v. Fleming, 265 F.2d 736 (5th Cir. 1959) (Chief Judge Hutcheson and Judges Brown and Wisdom). The decision upheld a district court order enjoining the Board of Supervisors of Louisiana State University and Agricultural and Mechanical College from denying Negroes admission.

Thurgood Marshall: Well, in the first place, the proposition begs the question. If they set up private schools and it's impossible for the state to set up private schools, once the state sets them up, they're public schools. The real problem is not a constitutional problem as such. Before we get to that, we get to the basic problem. The important part of the decision in 1954 by the Supreme Court was the recognition that public education is perhaps the most important function of our government in these days.

For years this country struggled to get the public school system it now has, and to abandon it would be a step back into the Dark Ages. I just don't believe the people in Louisiana would be willing to make that step, but we are confident that if the legislature, bullheaded as it appears to be, attempts to set up a private school system, it will be patently a subterfuge and an evasion of the Constitution, the Supreme Court's decision, and the injunction of the federal courts, will be treated as such by the federal courts.

Eric Goldman: Is the feeling shared around the table that no real constitutional problem will be involved in such an effort if Louisiana should make it? Mr. Emerson.

Thomas Emerson: I think there would be a constitutional problem at some point, the answer to which is not entirely clear to me. I agree with Mr. Marshall that if the state participates in a school system to the extent of controlling the teachers or paying teachers pensions or controlling the curriculum, that there would be sufficient state action involved so that it would be unconstitutional.

But I'm not at all so clear about the situation such as exists now in Virginia, as I understand it, where the state simply pays private scholarships to families and they can send their children to any school they wish to. And any school they wish to may include a segregated school. On that proposition, I think there is a constitutional question, which has not yet been ruled upon and would be a somewhat difficult one, I think.

Thurgood Marshall: I agree it hasn't been ruled on. I don't agree it's difficult. I think it would be one thing to consider it in the posture of a state setting up a school system for the first time, starting to get grants in aid, rather than to set up its own system, and so long as they didn't use race or color, I imagine that there would be no real constitutional question involved, would be accepted as such.

But in an area where clearly the purpose is to maintain segregated schools, I think then we have the problem as to whether or not the purpose behind the action—and here I'll have to, Tom, you know: I'll have to take the position that I'm talking about purpose and not motive, and I assume that there is a difference. But if the purpose is to evade a court decision, I think that that act is in a different posture for court consideration from one that is obviously clear-cut.

Eric Goldman: Go ahead, Mr. Peltason.

J. W. Peltason: In order for Louisiana or any other state, it seems to me, to avoid this constitutional [unclear], they would have to really close up completely the public schools all over the state, because it was already established, I think, in the Virginia case and some other cases, and in the Little Rock case, to close just the schools of Orleans Parish or to establish a separate system in that particular city designed to circumvent the judicial decree, would jeopardize their case. So if they want to make the strongest constitutional case, it has to be statewide, which eventually seems to me to be politically and socially and economically impossible.

Thomas Emerson: I agree with that. I do not think they could institute a system, which applied only to one parish or one county, or one school system. They'd have to treat all the same. But the system that I understand prevails in Virginia now is that the public schools do operate and they technically, at least, would be operating on an unsegregated basis. But the state pays a scholarship to families, and they can send their children to any school they want to.

Now, as Mr. Marshall says, if that is done on a sufficiently wide scale, or under such circumstances that it clearly constitutes an evasion of the Supreme Court decision, then I think it will be struck down. But I think it could be done on the fringes, with only certain people taking advantage of it and so forth, and under those circumstances it might present a more difficult constitutional issue.

Thomas Emerson: I would agree. And where the real constitutional problem in Virginia is in Prince Edwards County, where there are no public schools, in my judgment.

Thurgood Marshall: That's back in litigation, so to get back to Tom's point, there is obviously a constitutional question involved.

Eric Goldman: Mr. Vose.

Clement Vose: Yes. Well, I would expect that using the analogies of Supreme Court decisions in other fields, where in voting, for instance, the Supreme Court, first in 1915, outlawed the grandfather clause,[2] in the 1920s they made decisions which forbade outright discrimination by statute, and as time went on, as the South responded to this by discriminating in seven Democratic primaries, the Supreme Court then caught up to this and broadened their interpretation of state action. I'm sure we're all—in the school question, it seems to me that it would be very difficult, considering the trend of decisions in the Supreme Court, for the South to retreat successfully behind a private education system, both

2. Guinn and Beal v. United States, 238 U.S. 347 (1915).

because of this analogy and, because of the analogy, the great difficulty of arguing successfully that a private school system is, in fact, private.

Eric Goldman: Gentlemen, one of the statements frequently made in the literature of this subject is that the reason that Mr. Marshall and the other men fighting this battle have so much trouble is the unfortunate nature of the actual Supreme Court decision itself in 1954 on desegregation. For example, Mr. Edward S. Corwin, a distinguished constitutional lawyer, attacks the decision because of its reliance on the famous footnote number eleven, use of psychological evidence to support the argument that separate schools cannot be equal.

Or the latest book that I've seen on the subject, Mr. Robert Harris' *The Quest for Equality*,[3] goes even further. It says,

Seldom, if ever, has the Supreme Court of the United States reversed an earlier decision without finding either, (1) that the case was erroneously decided . . . or (2) the case has not been followed subsequently and is indeed in conflict with later decisions. It was unnecessary for the court to do what it did. . . . All it had to do was hold that the "equal but separate" formula . . . was not in accord with precedents . . . before and after 1896 . . .[4]

Eric Goldman: The argument being, in short, that the South can make a much better case against this decision as it was rendered, because of its reliance upon psychological materials, than it could have if a decision had been rendered on the basis of precedence.

Thurgood Marshall: Professor Goldman, in the first place, I don't agree with Professor Harris that the *Brown* decision reversed *Plessy against Ferguson*. It didn't. It was actually reversed in the *Bus* case from Montgomery, Alabama, a year or so later.[5]

As to this question about the footnote, that question was just what it was intended to be a footnote. It was not necessary for the opinion itself. But I would have thought that all that was laid to rest in the decision in *Aaron v. Cooper*, which was the Little Rock case in '57 or '58, I think it was, which the Supreme Court went all the way back to the *Peters* case and Chief Justice [John] Marshall as to the supremacy of the United States Constitution over state constitutions, and used the language which I think is very well documented legal language that the legislature and the governor cannot "war against the United States Constitution." That decision was well documented.[6]

3. ROBERT HARRIS, THE QUEST FOR EQUALITY: THE CONSTITUTION, CONGRESS, AND THE SUPREME COURT (1960).
4. *Id.* at 148, 149.
5. It is likely that Marshall is referring to Browder v. Gayle, 142 F. Supp. 707, 716, 718 (M.D. Ala. 1956), *aff'd*, 352 U.S. 903 (956) (without opinion).
6. 358 U.S. 1 (1958); United States v. Peters, 9 U.S. 115, 141 (1809).

Eric Goldman: I think, Mr. Marshall, the argument is not that the Supreme Court has not subsequently taken care of the situation. The argument, as I understand it, is that by relying upon psychological and sociological materials, which the court also did in the decision itself, in addition to the footnote, it weakened the case.

Thurgood Marshall: I don't think it weakened the case at all. It was discussing the "separate but equal" doctrine, which in itself was based on no facts whatsoever, of any kind, except the "separate but equal" theory out of the *Plessy v. Ferguson* case, which was no documentation at all, and anybody who wants to read the briefs can read them, it wasn't briefed, it wasn't argued, and it was not in the court's decision. They just sat as a Supreme Court and decided that "separate but equal" was not a violation. No reasons at all. The language was that if the Negro thinks he is getting unequal treatment, it is because he thinks it.[7]

Eric Goldman: Mr. Emerson.

Thomas Emerson: I would agree with Mr. Marshall. I don't think that the problems that have arisen out of the Supreme Court decision [were] due in any way to the manner in which it was rendered or the reasoning. It would have encountered very severe opposition in any event, but it seems to me the reasoning is perfectly simple and perfectly in accord with methods of constitutional decision.

Once they face the issue of whether or not separate but equal facilities constituted discrimination, then it seems to me the answer is obvious, because anyone who knows the system of segregation knows that it is meant to be discriminatory and operates in that way, and is, therefore, quite clearly a denial of equal protection. The reasons which influenced the court in *Plessy against Ferguson* could not be accepted, namely, that it was only discriminatory because the Negro race thought it to be.

Eric Goldman: Mr. Emerson, would you define *Plessy versus Ferguson* for our audience?

Thomas Emerson: *Plessy against Ferguson* was a case decided in 1896, which first established the doctrine that the requirements of the equal protection clause could be satisfied if the—

Eric Goldman: Equal protection under the Fourteenth Amendment.

Thomas Emerson: Fourteenth Amendment of the Constitution. That clause provides that no state may deny any person equal protection of the laws. The question involved was whether, in the transportation system, by providing separate cause for Negroes and separate cause for whites, and having the facilities in one sense the same, whether that satisfied the requirements of assuring equal protection. The court held that it did,

---

7. *See* Plessy v. Ferguson, 163 U.S. 537, 551 (1896).

and it established the doctrine of separate but equal facilities. That is, it's the facilities for—

J. W. Peltason: I would like to say that, now that we're back to the *Plessy* case, that I think that it's instructive to point out that the *Plessy* doctrine, the decision of the Supreme Court in the *Plessy* case, was not obeyed, and that the difference between the difficulty of implementing the *Brown* decision and the *Plessy* decision is not that *Plessy* was obeyed and the *Brown* isn't, but that in 1896 the forces that were working for the "equal" side of the "separate" were not strong enough even to make much noise about it. Now, today they're strong enough so that we're having this conflict.

Clement Vose: whether or not it was obeyed, the decision established the legal principle that a state could comply with the Fourteenth Amendment if it furnished facilities or if its action was on a basis of equal but separate, namely, segregation.

Eric Goldman: I gather there's no sympathy around the table for this criticism of the court's decision in 1954, even if it were made by my colleague, Mr. Edmund Corrigan.

Thurgood Marshall: If he had written the decision, we would have been in this with the same opposition. If anybody had written it.

J. W. Peltason: I think the weakness of that decision was the ambiguity of the instructions to the district courts, but I can say that only with hindsight.

Eric Goldman: Excuse me. Mr. Vose.

Clement Vose: I'd just like to say, before we leave the *Brown* case, that there are certain strengths in the decision, and one was the unanimity of the court, and for the court, for a unanimous decision, requires certain compromises of language within the court.

Also with respect to footnote eleven,[8] the court had been undermining the strength of the *Plessy* decision for a very long time. Since at least 1915 one can see a clear trend of decision.[9]

Eric Goldman: Pardon me. As I understand Mr. Corwin and Mr. Harris, what they're saying is what you're saying; the court has been undermining the *Plessy* doctrine for a long time. Why not simply base the 1954 decision on the undermined doctrine and leave out the sociological material, leave out the sociological support?

Thurgood Marshall: I, of course, cannot speak to the court, but I think the court reached the point where they thought it was time to face up

8. Here, Clement Vose is referring to footnote 11 in Brown v. Board of Education, 347 U.S. 483, 494 (1954), which cited with approval social science evidence regarding the effects of segregation on black children.
9. Guinn, *supra* note 2.

and make it clear to the entire country what they intended to give as their interpretation of the Fourteenth Amendment.

Eric Goldman: And you don't think—

Thurgood Marshall: They've been giving all these little bits and everybody was ignoring it, but it was their hope that now they would make it crystal clear and that the states who wanted to be law abiding and the state officers who wanted to abide by the oath they took under the Sixth Amendment to support the Constitution of the United States, that this would mean the end of segregation throughout the public school system.

Eric Goldman: And you do not think they could have made it clear without using sociological evidence?

Thurgood Marshall: They did not need the sociological testimony at all.

Eric Goldman: That's what these men are arguing: they didn't need it. You see?

Thurgood Marshall: Well, I mean, if they're arguing that they gave too much, then I think that their argument is baseless. I think the argument would be that if somebody wanted to say the court didn't say enough. But to say court gave too much basis for its decision, to my mind, is a little out of the ordinary.

Eric Goldman: Mr. Peltason.

J. W. Peltason: I can see the point they're making. There might have been a tactical advantage. I don't think it would have made too much difference, but there might have been a tactical advantage if the court had cited, as it did in the Little Rock case later on, the conventional case law and avoided mentioning social scientists, who don't perhaps have as much prestige.

Thurgood Marshall: Frankly, I assume that the court assumed that the lawyers and judges and officials who read it were familiar with Chief Justice Marshall's pronouncements.

J. W. Peltason: But in the appeal for public support, perhaps there might have been a minor tactical advantage.

Clement Vose: It should be remembered and known perhaps better by the public and by lawyers that the Supreme Court has reversed itself something over ninety times in its history, and it has often relied upon writings of persons who are not lawyers. This has been done many times.

Thomas Emerson: I want to put in a word in support of the Supreme Court on this. I think they handled it exactly properly. For one thing, the decision in *Plessy against Ferguson*, which upheld separate but equal facilities, fundamentally assumed certain sociological propositions. It assumed that Negroes, in a system of segregation, did not regard the segregation as discriminatory or harmful or injurious to them. It also assumed that this would work out as the best system, that government shouldn't interfere with this local custom because it would tend to work itself out in a way, which would be best for social adjustment.

Well, the passage of time, the economic changes in the status of the Negro, the sociological, psychological information which we have obtained in the meantime, all indicated that these assumptions were wrong, and I think it was quite proper for the court to point out that the basic common sense judgment that segregation, separate but equal, is discrimination and therefore a violation of the equal protection clause, is confirmed by developments in scientific material. I think that they used the material exactly rightly.

Eric Goldman: Well, having upheld the Supreme Court, gentlemen, may I push us ahead a little bit to another phase of this. You mentioned a moment ago the lower courts in one of your remarks. I know that some of this discussion of the segregation situation runs along the line that we are depending awfully heavily at the present time upon the Supreme Court, that the President is not doing enough, the Congress is not doing enough, and that there is a further problem in dependence upon the Supreme Court, that it throws a burden on the lower courts which they cannot sustain in many cases. This is peculiarly your field, Mr. Peltason. Any comment on that?

J. W. Peltason: I think the southern federal judges, speaking generally, some of them have done what's expected of them and perhaps more. Going back to the point we were discussing earlier, I think the Supreme Court could have helped them by giving them a more precise instruction.[10] What these judges, I think, want and need is not so much of an area of discretion. The judge is in a better position to take the heat than the school board is. The court of appeals is in a better position to take the heat than the poor district judge, and the Supreme Court is in the best position of all to take the heat.

I would have preferred, or would like to see, the Supreme Court firm up its instructions so that these judges will be armed with more precise orders from the Supreme Court. I think this would help them in their very difficult job.

Eric Goldman: I see you stirring unhappily, Mr. Marshall.

Thurgood Marshall: Well, I would add just one point to that. I don't disagree at all, but I just happen to know in several instances of the terrific pressure that the local district judges are under—social ostracism,

---

10. Perhaps a criticism of the "with all deliberate speed" language in Brown II: Brown v. Board of Education, 349 U.S. 294, 301 (1955). *See* Robert Carter, *Equal Education Opportunity for Negroes—Abstractions or Reality*, *in* John H. McCord, With All Deliberate Speed: Civil Rights Theory and Reality 56, 73 (1969).

horrible telephone calls to the judge and his family, etc., etc., etc.[11] And to my mind, it's pretty hard to take, but at the same time that's racy in action. It's the very bitter with the sweet.

But I still believe, to get back to the original part of the answer, that, on a whole, the local federal district judges and the judges of the courts of appeal, I think are doing a tremendous job under tremendous difficulties. As to whether the Supreme Court could hand down something further, as of this day I think that's a wide open, debatable question. I think it's entirely different, and I hope that's what you were driving at. The situation is entirely different today than what it was in '54 and '55, in that there might be, one, enough expertise in the variety of cases that have come up, there is complete frustration in some areas, and on that basis it might be well for a case to be considered by the Supreme Court to set down a more definite rule.

J. W. Peltason: And I was agreeing with you in the tremendous pressure that these district judges are under, and it was my feeling that a more precise order from the Supreme Court, a reformulation in more specific terms, would help these men, as well as prod those who have not gone forward.

Thurgood Marshall: As much as I think of the pressure they're under, I also think of the pressures that the poor Negroes have been under for so long. So you see I have mixed emotions.

Eric Goldman: Mr. Emerson.

Thomas Emerson: I disagree, I think, with a good deal of what you say.

Eric Goldman: With what Mr. Peltason says?

Thomas Emerson: With what Mr. Peltason has said, yes. I agree that the federal judiciary has done an excellent job and deserves real support

---

11. *See, e.g.,* Jack Bass, *Frank Johnson: Legal Giant*, N.Y.L.J., Aug. 16, 1999, at A19; JACK BASS, TAMING THE STORM: THE LIFE AND TIMES OF JUDGE FRANK M. JOHNSON, JR. AND THE SOUTH'S FIGHT OVER CIVIL RIGHTS 469 (1993). Later, a black graduate of Tuskegee Institute wrote: "Judge Johnson represented to me . . . the validation of my beliefs that contrary to how it might seem, not every white person thinks the same when it comes to fairness and justice." Patricia Grace Smith, *Judge Johnson Stood for Fairness and Justice*, MONTGOMERY ADVERTISER, July 21, 1991, at 3D. *See also* Letter to Editor from J. Randall Minchew, WASH. POST, Aug. 26, 1999, at Vo2. Both Bass and Minchew talk about death threats and dangerous circumstances surrounding Judge Johnson, who was often referred to by the Klan as the most dangerous man in Alabama. Other federal judges faced the same threats claiming that these federal judges had turned their backs on the South. *See Judge John Wisdom, Ruled the South*, CHI. TRIB., May 16, 1999, at 8C. Other "unrecognized heroes of the American judiciary were district judges J. Waites Waring, J. Skelly Wright. . . , and federal appeals court judges Elbert Tuttle, Richard Taylor Rives and John R. Brown." PAUL L. BRADY, A CERTAIN BLINDNESS: A BLACK FAMILY'S QUEST FOR THE PROMISE OF AMERICA 220 (1990).

from the country, by and large, but I do not think they could have been helped by a more specific Supreme Court decision.

The Supreme Court, it seems to me, had two alternatives. One was to order immediate entrance of the actual Negro children involved as plaintiffs in the suits before them immediately into the schools and proceed on that basis. That alternative they did not take. They took the alternative of giving back to the district courts the function of formulating general plans of desegregation.

I do not think they could very well have formulated more specific instructions to the district courts at that point. The way the judicial process works is that they give them general principles, and then as the specific problems come up, they pass on them by way of appeal. Now, it may be that they should have, in these cases which have come up since '54, made more specific terms or considered them more, more of them, and handed down more specific terms, but I don't think that that's the real problem in the administration of this.

Thurgood Marshall: As of now?

Thomas Emerson: Certainly as of the beginning and less so as of now because, as I said, I think the court could not take some of these plans that are being proposed and consider them. But I don't think that's the major problem. I think the major problem of administration here was the lack of activity on the part of the executive in supporting the judicial.

Eric Goldman: In this original criticism, there was comment upon what the President and Congress has not done. You put it mainly on what the President has not done?

Thomas Emerson: Well, because the President could have done something. Congress is tied up with the filibuster and it's more difficult.

Eric Goldman: Mr. Vose, were you going to comment?

Clement Vose: I think that Mr. Marshall's work shows the important activities of an organization, the National Association for the Advancement of Colored People, and in a sense, the judicial process works in such a way that the NAACP had to do the work before the decision in 1954. That is, they supported plaintiffs, provided the legal talent and skill and continuity that allowed those Negro plaintiffs to win this important victory in the courts.

But after the decisions of 1954 and '55, it seems to me that from then on, the burden of carrying out what the Supreme Court had said should not have rested so heavily on that organization. It should not have—

J. W. Peltason: Or on the courts either.

Clement Vose: Or on the courts either. It seems to me that it should have been—

Eric Goldman: Where? The President?

Clement Vose: —the job of the executive branch of the government, specifically the Department of Justice.

Eric Goldman: Not Congress? Nobody wants to beat on Congress?

Thurgood Marshall: I'm sitting quietly by, and I have a full-sized baseball bat waiting for the Congress.

Eric Goldman: All right.

Clement Vose: I think that Congress surely could have enacted civil rights acts before they did, and could have made them stronger.

Thomas Emerson: They might have been different kinds of acts.

Clement Vose: But it does seem to me that it is the traditional function of the Justice Department and of the executive branch of the national government to carry out the orders of the judiciary.

Eric Goldman: Mr. Marshall, would you like to raise your baseball bat now?

Thurgood Marshall: Well, so far as I'm concerned, Tom put his finger on it about this threat of a filibuster in the Senate, but basically in Congress the only time we talk about bipartisan support for foreign affairs, that's not 100 percent true. That's true here and there. The only time we have 100 percent bipartisan support in Congress is when some social legislation comes up and on top of that is civil rights. If a bill is put in Congress right now which will give every state in the union ten million dollars per state to do whatever they want with it, if they put a label on it of civil rights, it'll more than likely be defeated. I mean, that's the way that Congress reacts.

I think that Congress has been obliged to put in a strong civil rights bill implementing the court decision in the whole field of civil rights, to have the filibuster and stand there and fight it out. What always happens when the filibuster starts, they bring up some important bill, and then the Negroes are persuaded to step aside for the good of the whole country in general.

Eric Goldman: Wouldn't you fight for changing the filibuster rule first?

Thurgood Marshall: I, of course, favor that, and I believe in working on it. I mean, even if it isn't changed, I wouldn't give up. I would bear in mind that as late as through World War II, the southern influence in government insisted on maintaining rigid segregation in the armed forces, even if it meant losing the war. They considered segregation more important. And I think its high time that the Negroes and other people in this country who believe in right say, "You either pass civil rights legislation or, all right, let's slow the country down." I think we have to face up to it.

And there you have this middle body of people that won't move. They sit there. They're very law-abiding, they're very wonderful people, but they are completely without leadership because they don't get leadership from any place. If Congress would take the leadership, well and good. If Congress won't do it, then it's the President's job to speak out as the moral and spiritual leader of this country, and say, "The Supreme Court's decision in the *Brown* case was not only legally correct and it's the law of the land, but it was morally correct and has my full support, and I urge all good law-abiding Americans to abide with this decision in spirit as well as the letter. I have to advise you that if you don't do it, I will use the full power of my office to see that it is followed." Then this huge group of middle-of-the-road people would have found someplace to go.

Eric Goldman: Mr. Peltason.

J. W. Peltason: In the absence of presidential leadership on this issue, what has happened since '56 is there has been no person of national stature who commands nationwide attention to answer the Faubuses[12] and people who put that position forward. If you turn on the television and look at these things, you can hear the other side, but you don't hear the side supporting the Supreme Court's decision.

Eric Goldman: Now that we've clobbered Congress and the President, let's go back to the Supreme Court a minute. Mr. Marshall, where is the NAACP legal strategy going? I notice in an interview of yours, fall 1959, you say the two big problems now are the stairstep plan,[13] which, of course, involves letting the Negroes in to one grade at a time, and the pupil assignment plan, which permits a child in an integrated class to transfer to a segregated school if he wants to.

The rest of this lengthy and interesting interview, you seem to be disagreeing with or disapproving of both of those things. Now, I'm sure everybody in our audience understands why you disapprove of the pupil assignment plan, but what about the stairstep plan, if you do disapprove of it?

Thurgood Marshall: I most certainly disapprove of the stairstep plan. There are two stairstep plans. One provides that you integrate the twelfth grade this year, the eleventh grade next year, and on down. Twelve years later, you integrate the first grade. The other one is start at the first grade and go up to the twelfth grade.

Well, my disagreement is supported by two particular places. In Little Rock, they had the twelve-year plan coming down. The twelve-year plan was adopted '55 or '56, and there are now about eleven children integrated in that period of years. And in New Orleans, the stairstep plan in

12. Referring to the defiance of Arkansas Governor Orval Faubus to federal court orders to integrate public schools. Muriel Dobbin McClatchy, *Little Rock Nine Return*, ATL. J. CONST., Sept. 26, 1997, at 14A.
13. Stairstep plans were also called grade-per-year plans. Most of these plans were "invalidated and upheld by various courts." GEOFFREY R. STONE, ET AL., CONSTITUTIONAL LAW 534 (1996, 3rd ed.).

New Orleans integrated four Negro children out of a Negro school population of 55,000. There's something wrong with that.

Eric Goldman: Is it the structure of the stairstep plan that you object to or that not enough people are sitting on each stair?

Thurgood Marshall: The trouble is that we are not getting integration. Under both of those plans we've gotten throughout the South 6 percent of the Negroes integrated in six years, and as a young student told me at Fisk University, he did not have to go to a college to find out how long it would take to get 100 percent, if you got 6 percent in six years.

The plan might have merit. Legally I'm opposed to the stairstep plan because the students who filed the lawsuit never get their benefits. They are schoolchildren when they file the suit, and there we have this very interesting anomaly in the law of a court saying that your constitutional rights are satisfied by somebody else getting theirs. From a legal standpoint, I just cannot accept it.

From a sociological standpoint, you have a family of four children, two of them are in integrated classes and two of them are in segregated classes. There's constant discussion as to who's who and what's what and who's going on.

Thirdly, actually administration, what do you do in the schoolyard? You have a little integrated yard and a segregated yard? Who passes down the halls on what lines?

I think that all of those problems are so easily solved by saying, "This is it. This is six years later. Six years since the Supreme Court. It's not tomorrow. This is tomorrow six years later."

Clement Vose: I certainly agree with the stairstep plan which requires either eight years or twelve years and sometimes begins at the top and sometimes begins at the bottom is too long and doesn't embody any consistent principle of operation. However, I do feel that even more important, perhaps, is the requirement that a beginning be made, that some plan be adopted in as many areas as possible, because once the principle is established, once the 100 percent segregation is ended, I think that is a major step.

I would tend to feel that perhaps even more important than fighting the stairstep plan, although I agree that should be resisted at least in its extreme forms, would be some sort of program by which to get some plan adopted in as many areas as possible and as soon as possible.

Eric Goldman: Mr. Peltason.

J. W. Peltason: This goes back to my position of clarification of the decree implementing the decision. I feel that pupil placement plans have been the greatest defeat since 1954.

?: I agree with that.

J. W. Peltason: Because by reducing the possibility of a class suit, by the—well, they introduce into the school system the same delaying tactics that are frequently used by voting registrars when you try to get Negroes registered. I would like to see the Supreme Court at this stage say, "Six years have passed or seven years have passed, and we hereby say that at this stage the judges should be required to require the school boards to at least immediately come forward with a plan." Now, that's a very modest beginning, but it would be a big step beyond the pupil placement what I call a dodge.

Clement Vose: I would agree. In fact, that's exactly what I was suggesting. Let me just say one thing, if I may, about the pupil placement plan. It certainly intended to evade the decision. Otherwise, there's no point in it. These states have never had such plans before. They theoretically assign students on the basis of various factors such as their educational attainments and so forth, but that really isn't the purpose. The purpose is to keep the number of Negroes down to the lowest possible number.

J. W. Peltason: In some states, to prevent any integration.

Clement Vose: Well, that's my point. The pupil placement plan is one step forward in the sense that it does not permit 100 percent segregation. Now, I think it's important that that principle be established. The principle that the presence of one Negro child, a six-year-old girl in school, will contaminate the white community is the emotional basis on which the whole system of educational segregation rests. As soon as that is broken down, I think that a good deal of the fundamental opposition will tend to disappear so that although there's no doubt that the pupil placement plans have delayed the program, I don't think they should be written off entirely.

Thurgood Marshall: What do you do about Little Rock? They put the nine in there. We got over that hurdle. Then they cut it down from nine to six.

Clement Vose: Well, certainly the process is going to be a long and a very difficult one. I think at some point—I don't think you have to go up to 100 percent year by year. At some point, say, when you get to 30 percent students, the rest of the opposition will have to—

Thurgood Marshall: I think you ought to all remember a story I was told as a kid, that it all depends on how hungry you are, but if you're hungry enough, a frankfurter tastes like a T-bone steak.

Eric Goldman: Gentlemen, our time is racing away, and nobody would forgive us unless we got to sit-downs.

Thurgood Marshall: Sit-ins.[14]

14. *See* Thomas R. Brooks, Walls Come Tumbling Down: A History of the Civil Rights Movement 1940–1970, at 146–147 (1974) (stating that "'Over 100 cities in the South and in the border states have had sit-ins or other forms of direct action. . . . An estimated 3, 600 students and supporters—in southern and border states—have been arrested'"). *Id.* at 147.

Eric Goldman: Sit-ins. I beg your pardon, sit-ins. These have come up, of course, in a recent period, and this is the kind of question that people are asking. Mr. Vose, may I direct it to you? In defense of the sit-ins, Judge Harold Stevens, the first Negro to be appointed to the Appellate Division of the New York State Supreme Court,[15] said that they were just like the Boston Tea Party: they may be illegal, it's just something that had to be done. He is defending them on some kind of higher law.

Then there are those people who say they're just plain illegal and that's the end of it, including that gentleman who has some experience in government, if not a legal expert, Mr. Truman, who said, "If anyone comes into my store and tries to stop business, I'd throw him out."

Now, the question I want to put to you is one that keeps getting raised in all these discussions. If Negro leaders like Mr. Stevens defend these sit-ins on the ground that there is a higher law than legal decisions, what is their answer to the Stellis argument that there's a higher law than the Supreme Court decision of 1954?[16]

Clement Vose: Well, it seems to me that the sit-ins have occurred in public places. They've occurred in stores, which are privately owned, to be sure, but which advertise themselves as being open to the public. All of these stores have parts of their business available to the public, as long as it's a standing public, of all races.

Eric Goldman: You don't think they're really illegal, then?

Clement Vose: I don't think that the sit-ins are illegal.

Eric Goldman: You think if the case went to the Supreme Court, the Supreme Court would not rule it would be illegal?

Clement Vose: Well—

Eric Goldman: That's just a guess.

Clement Vose: This would depend very much on what form the action took. It's difficult enough to predict the Supreme Court. When you predict it without a specific case—

Eric Goldman: See, what I'm trying to get it, suppose the Supreme Court did rule them to be illegal. The kind of defense Mr. Stevens is making is that people ought to go ahead and do them anyhow.

Thomas Emerson: I think the point there is this. If you disregard the legal question and assume for the moment that they are illegal, it then becomes a moral question. The only justification for resisting the laws of society is on moral grounds. Now, the moral question is such that I think the segregationists have nothing to stand on. It's the question of comparing the morals of equal protection and full rights of Negroes

---

15. *See* Mireya Navaro, *Judge Harold Stevens, 83, Dies, First Black on Court of Appeals*, N.Y. Times, Nov. 11, 1990, at 40.

16. *Compare* Edward S. Corwin, "The Higher Law": The Background of American Constitutional Law 5 (1955) *with* A Certain Blindness, *supra* note 11, at 317.

against the morals of discrimination. Seems to be quite obvious that in moral or ethical terms, it's perfectly proper, and that doesn't imply that it's proper in moral or ethical terms to continue segregation.

Thurgood Marshall: I would say this. I happen to know Judge Stevens very well, and I don't remember that statement necessarily, but I think there was more to it. I'm quite certain he would never advocate a violation of any law.

Eric Goldman: No, what he said—

Thurgood Marshall: I know him too well for that.

Eric Goldman: Well, I didn't mean to—what he said was that in reply to a question on legality of sit-ins, he cited the Boston Tea Party and the American tendency to overlook its illegality. "It's just something that had to be done," he said, implying that sometimes—

Thurgood Marshall: Well, there's another judge who said that he would rather see young people do wrong than to do nothing. But I think that's a little out of context. The truth of the matter here is that there is no pronouncement that I know of from the Supreme Court that automatically says what are that these young people doing is illegal.

Eric Goldman: No.

Thurgood Marshall: And we're not too far off base, because there's a case on its way from Louisiana to the Supreme Court and it'll be in there in about three or four weeks, and it'll give you an idea.[17] There are some—well, we don't have the actual count of how many we have in the office, but we have in the neighborhood of sixteen to eighteen hundred of these sit-in cases, and they run the whole gamut. Some of them tried to get service in the country courthouse. Well, that's not exactly private. Others tried to get it in public bus terminals that are not exactly private. It ranges from there all the way down to the lunch counters in certain stores in certain towns.

These people, it's not a question so much of the private property. These young people have been arrested by police, and they're not private. And in some instances, we have cases where the Negroes had left the premises, they were ordered to leave and they left, the police still arrested them. In one case in one particular town, the policeman testified, when the lawyer asked all the questions about what were they doing, were they disorderly, etc., etc., he said no. Then he was asked, "Well, assuming that this defendant had been doing exactly the same thing that he did, and if he'd been white, would he have been arrested?" And the

17. *See* Garner v. Louisiana, 368 U.S. 157 (1961) (Chief Justice Earl Warren, writing for the majority of the Court held that the conviction of the sit-in defendants should be reversed on the ground that peaceful sit-ins demonstrations in public facilities violate no law and without evidence of action against them violated the due process clause of the Fourteenth Amendment).

policeman said, "Certainly not." Well, that's not private action; that's action of a policeman.

Eric Goldman: Mr. Peltason.

J. W. Peltason: I think that sometimes the confusion gets into these discussions about legality, because really what people are talking about are city ordinances or state laws, and the question is, are these laws constitutional. Now, the conduct might violate the city ordinance, but the city ordinance might be unconstitutional. You frequently have to have a test case and violate a city ordinance in an orderly fashion, so to speak, in order that its constitutionality may be tested.

Thurgood Marshall: Well, getting back to Mr. Goldman's point, Mr. Goldman says that there are people in the South that say in the same vein we consider the Supreme Court's decision in the school case to be immoral or what have you, and therefore we can violate that.

Eric Goldman: What they're talking about is the kind of debate that's going on between this gentleman, James Kilpatrick, of the *Richmond News Leader,* who seems to be an indefatigable arguer for segregation, and Martin Luther King [Jr.]. King said this is a violation of the city ordinance, which you people are doing—Kilpatrick says. "You're violating a law." King's answer was, "The law is no good. It's an immoral law. Therefore, you don't have to obey it." Now, I'm paraphrasing here, but this is the impression.[18]

?: My answer would be to question is that law constitutional.

Eric Goldman: Well, as our Mr. Marshall says, it has not—it is coming up to the court now, is that correct?

Thurgood Marshall: One from Baton Rouge, Louisiana, is due in the Supreme Court a month from next week.[19]

Clement Vose: And we don't have a declaratory constitution. The question of constitutionality has to be tested. Many local ordinances, many federal statutes, many state statutes have been violated, and this is the way in which courts rule on such questions.

Eric Goldman: The way Mr. Emerson is commenting, do I read you right? Do I understand you right? If the Supreme Court should declare these ordinances constitutional, there is a moral right, in your opinion, for the Negro to continue the sit-in, isn't there?

Thomas Emerson: Well, then my position is then it is a moral question, and I would agree that whether the South should resist the Supreme Court decisions, resort to civil disobedience is a moral question. They

18. Around this period Dr. King stated: "Our world hinges on moral foundations. God has made it so! God has made the universe based on a moral law." CLAYBORNE CARSON, ED., THE PAPERS OF MARTIN LUTHER KING, JR., REDISCOVERING PRECIOUS VALUES, JULY 1951–NOVEMBER 1955, at 248, 251–252 (1994).
19. *Supra* note 17.

have no legal right to do that. Then I say if it's a moral question, the answer is quite clear to me that it is moral and ethnical to maintain equality among citizens, but not moral and ethical to maintain discrimination among citizens.

Eric Goldman: The difficulty was that the moral issue was quite clear to both North and South in 1860. The only difference was that they saw diametrically opposite moral issues.

Thomas Emerson: Well, that's what happens if—

Thurgood Marshall: There is an answer to that. If the Supreme Court should declare that this sit-in is unlawful and a violation of personal rights and indeed a violation of state law and everything else, and if there's going to be a moral question, that's an individual's moral question. Any individual has the right to feel that he considers that to be morally incorrect, and for him to personally obey it would be to interfere with his own morals and his conscience. He has a perfect right to disobey it, and he also has a right to go to jail for disobeying it.

Now, that's my answer to the southerner that says he has a right to oppose the school case. He has a right to oppose it, and he has a right to do any act he cares to do to oppose it, but with the full understanding that he pays the penalty of going to jail for doing it. Not that he does it—

Eric Goldman: I doubt if Mr. Kilpatrick would like that answer.

Thurgood Marshall: Oh, I'm sure he wouldn't. I know him of old.

Thomas Emerson: May I say a word on the legal question? I think there's a very good chance that the Supreme Court would sustain the proposition that the application of state police force and state judicial systems to prosecuting persons for trespass when they enter a dime store and are asked to leave, that that constitutes discriminatory action, and that therefore, to that extent, those trespass laws are unconstitutional.[20]

I think you have to draw the line at some point. I do not think that the use of police force to expel a person who is not wanted from private property, in the sense of a house, would be contrary to the Fourteenth Amendment. I also think that a private club, and I would even say the West Side Tennis Club insofar as it is a private tennis club, has a right to choose its own members, and that if someone it doesn't want to admit comes into the club to play tennis, it can use the police to exclude them.

But I think the line must be drawn at those points where the action is in a more public area, and I think coming into a store which purports to open its facilities to all people except at the lunch counter is quite a different proposition.

Eric Goldman: Well, we'll have to leave that one to the Supreme Court. Let me hurry on here and just touch upon this, the question of housing

20. *Id.*

and constitutional issues. I've been reading your book, Mr. Vose, your very interesting book, *Caucasians Only*,[21] in which you talk about the 1848 and 1853 actions of the Supreme Court in striking down the validity of any restrictive covenants and in implementing them.

I notice this sentence in here in your book, which seems to me to bring up this age-old but fascinating argument. You say, "The fact that racial segregation in the residential areas of America's largest cities has not been altered to any substantial degree by the Supreme Court act suggests the limited potency of court victories in some cases."[22]

Of course, this is the kind of thing that Mr. [Dwight D.] Eisenhower was talking about when he got off that wretched sentence about "You can't change what's in men's hearts by laws," and so forth. How far do you want to push this?

Clement Vose: I'd restrict it first, if I may make a joke about a historian. The decisions were made in this century, 1948 and 1950.

Eric Goldman: Did I say—I'm sorry.

Clement Vose: It seems to me that here the Supreme Court in 1948 made a decision which forbade lower courts to enforce racial restrictive covenants,[23] and no court since that time has enforced racial restrictive covenants in housing. So as far as that matter went, it went a great distance.

Eric Goldman: But you say there hasn't been much desegregation anyhow.

Clement Vose: One of the things that was created by the practice of the existence of racial restrictions and their enforcement before 1948 were segregated cities in the northern part of the United States, and housing patterns are very difficult to alter. They alter, after all, by voluntary action, very largely.

I think the decision was an important one, and it created the opportunity for other people—well, for Negroes—to buy houses in areas which did have restrictions, but which could not be enforced. This has been an important development. There have been also some developments with respect to urban redevelopment, which has led to integrated housing and there's also been some development in that area.

Eric Goldman: I noticed what I took to be in your writings some of this perhaps exaggerated skepticism as to what the courts and law can and cannot do. Am I misreading you?

J. W. Peltason: Well, in this context I would not want to be included with President Eisenhower, because I feel that he confused prejudice

21. CLEMENT VOSE, CAUCASIANS ONLY: THE SUPREME COURT, THE NAACP, AND THE RESTRICTIVE COVENANT CASES (1959).
22. *Id.* at ix.
23. Shelley v. Kraemer, 334 U.S. 1 (1948).

and discrimination. Prejudice is an attitude, and discrimination is overt conduct. There are certain areas in which I think you can control conduct and let the prejudice alone. That is, people change their seats on the bus before they change their minds. You don't have to wait until they're all converted to decide it's all right to sit next to a Negro. But by law you can regulate behavior.

In many areas, the problem is not—we're not worried so much about what a person thinks, as long as he will allow somebody else to have his rights.

Thurgood Marshall: Well, housing shows for the North the same problem we have in the South. You can't expect either the courts or legislature or executive to do the job; the individual's got to do it. In order to have a free sale of a house, you've got to have a willing seller and a willing buyer. And I don't think that we've done enough on either side to get either the willing sellers or the willing buyers. That's a job that should be done. It's a job that needs to be done.

In the North you'll find people that will say, "It's horrible to deny Negroes the right to vote in Mississippi or the right to vote in Alabama or to be lynched in this town or that town. It's a shame what they're doing to the Negroes in New Orleans, what they did to them in Little Rock, Arkansas. Oh, but what was it you said about a Negro living next to me? Well, that's a different problem." Well, it's not a different problem. It's the exact same problem in the North as we have in the South.

Eric Goldman: Mr. Emerson.

Thomas Emerson: I think this situation with respect to housing is perhaps typical of the whole civil rights picture at the present time, in the sense that here again I think we have relied too much on the judicial system and not on other parts of the government. I agree with Mr. Marshall with respect to what individuals should do, but looking at it from the point of what the government should do, our constitutional system supposes both the legislature and an executive, and the tendency to thrust these very difficult problems entirely on the courts, which have a procedure for handling particular cases in accordance with a rather rigid formula, is simply not sufficient.

Now, here again is a good example of an area in which the President can take some very effective action. For instance, federal housing authorities have by no means eliminated segregation or adopted policies, which would eliminate segregation, and they can do that under existing laws. So that the possibility of action at the executive level here again seems to me very important, as it does in all the other areas.

Eric Goldman: May I thank you, Mr. J. W. Peltason, Mr. Thurgood Marshall, Mr. Thomas Emerson, and Mr. Clement Vose.

Judicial Method in Due Process

This afternoon for just a few minutes I want to throw two or three ideas in the hopper for the purpose of discussion; that is, to bring up certain practical matters, nothing of which is new but which I for one believe should be thrown out to be considered in the discussion.

In the first place, I find no disagreement with Judge Hastie's paper at all. And as a matter of fact, some of the matters that are in footnotes in the paper, and some that are not covered there, should be brought out. Those are the real practical matters that come about in the everyday trial of lawsuits. These practical matters, to my mind, give the necessary practical support to the thesis that runs throughout the paper. In the first place, we have the question of judicial self-restraint. And of course, at the very beginning, there is no argument with that. I believe everyone will agree that in this field of due process, at least, there should be judicial restraint. The only problem is how much or how little.[1]

In 1955, a conference at Harvard Law School commemorated the bicentennial of John Marshall, Chief Justice of the U.S. Supreme Court, 1801–1835. Among the distinguished lawyers and judges participating in the conference was Judge William Henry Hastie, a member of the Third Circuit U.S. Court of Appeals, who presented a paper entitled "Judicial Method in Due Process Inquiry." Thurgood Marshall gave this response to Hastie's paper. Marshall's response and other discussion that ensued were published, along with other presenters' papers, in ARTHUR E. SUTHERLAND, ED., GOVERNMENT UNDER LAW 326–347 (Hastie), 347–355 (Marshall) (1956). Reprinted by permission of Harvard University Press, Copyright © 1955, 1956 by the President and Fellows of Harvard College.
1. One author explains, "Twice the Constitution spells out the guarantee that no person shall be deprived of 'life, liberty, or property' by government without 'due process of law.' In these words found in the Fifth and Fourteenth amendments lies the Court's most prolific source of power to strike down national legislation which may be valid under the more specific clauses of the Constitution or state laws enacted to effect policies which the state deems essential for the social and economic well-being of its people. Likewise, here must be found the basis of protection under the national Constitution against state infringement of civil liberties and for the enforcement of the 'rudiments of fair play' in proceedings before governmental agencies of a judicial or quasi-judicial nature . . . But the path of due process protection has not been straight." VIRGINIA WOOD, DUE PROCESS OF LAW: 1932–1949 vii (1972).

Let's start with that basis. In the first place, there is a definite need for certain minimum standards. In order to get to the minimum standards, we have, it seems to me, first to get to what is the general idea of due process. Well, it's a distillation of many theories of fair method and fair trial, as well as ethics and possibly some religious scruples. These all go into the judges' minds on these cases. Of course, they cannot be spelled out in detail. And as a matter of fact it is very often a combination of all of these elements. But underlying all of this is the contrast between one side—the protection of the individual, personal rights—and the other—the actual belief and need of protection of society, whether it be the state or the federal government. Very often state action—legislative, executive or judicial—is dictated by the belief that the end justifies the means. Oftentimes local mores and customs from long usage have completely beclouded the true meaning of clauses of the state and federal constitutions. And then constitutionally protected rights become small "niceties of the law" or "mere legal technicalities to free vicious criminals." There is this constant danger of these local mores and customs in one small community being combined with similar customs in other local communities, with the result, in the end, that the entire state law enforcement machinery is tainted with the belief that it is necessary, for the time being, to step on a little right here, or ignore a little personal right there. So we do need these minimum standards in the regular substantial due process cases involving legislation, executive rules, etc.

The same is true in criminal trials. We need fair and just trials. Everybody will agree on that. Where we have that we can all recognize it; and then everyone, from the individual layman up to the highest court in the land, will become shocked at any other sort of trial because it shocks the very decency of man as well as of the law. Well, there is no trouble with either of those cases. One good—the other bad. But it's that great big 99 $^{44}/_{100}$ percent of cases that lie between those two—that's the group that I'd like to talk about for a minute. And I think all of us in reading or in actual practice have run across this throughout the procedural due process cases so far as criminal trials are concerned.

You look at the average criminal trial, and what do you have? Well, pick one where everybody is actually looking for justice; they all are looking for a fair and just trial. One group of advocates in that trial—the prosecuting attorneys—are constantly seeking evidence and testimony for the sole object of getting all the truth before the court, but in doing that they want all restraints taken off, withdrawn, so that they can get all the "evidence" they can find. On the other hand, there's the other group of advocates—the defense attorneys—also seeking justice and truth, and they are constantly seeking more restraints to protect the defendant from what they consider to be unlawful procedures. As a matter of fact, the defendant legally arrested should be put in jail and allowed to remain there and not be required to talk to anybody under any circumstances, should be left completely alone. We have all heard prosecuting attorneys say that if they are prevented from talking to a defendant they would never be able to get a conviction in many instances. So there we have the two. On one hand, there is the defendant's counsel saying he wants as many safeguards as possible; on the other, the prosecuting attorney is saying he wants as much freedom as possible to get the facts before the court.

But the real evil in all of this is that in many communities and in many areas this practice one way or the other tends to become the accepted law of that community, unwritten if you please, and there is always the danger in these communities of what was just a mere practice, temporary in the first instance, perhaps tolerated in the belief that it could be pushed aside, coming up to the point where on one side one group of lawyers think it can be done, or to put it even more bluntly, that they think they can get away with it.

So to my mind, and I'm sure to the minds of many other advocates, there is a necessity for many safeguards, many lines of attack to protect us against this sort of injustice; for our courts of last resort, if you please, to work this out so that there will be assurance that these rights are not stepped upon.

There is also another conflict; this belief in "substantial justice," that in this particular trial, although some constitutional right was violated, anybody, absolutely anybody, can see that the man would have been convicted anyway. There is too much of the belief that regardless of what happened in the trial the jury can, for some reason I have never been able to understand, cut through and give this "substantial justice." The biggest danger to due process in a criminal trial is the theory of substantial justice. It's obviously impossible to set out detailed rules that you can question a defendant for one hour and fifteen minutes a day but after that it is a violation of due process. Or that you can question him in his cell but you can't question him in a police room. Or that you can question him in the police jail, but you can't take him to another jail. Or that it is perfectly all right to obtain evidence if you only break open one door but if you break open two it is wrong. Obviously, that is not what, I believe, anybody would argue for.

On the other hand, there is the theory that this matter should be left entirely to the state courts—that once the state supreme court passes on it, that's it. In that area, the record will show, I think, that the Supreme Court, the United States Supreme Court, has already used the necessary restraints. If anybody is interested in figures, the number of petitions for certiorari applied for and the number granted will certainly convince you of that. So what do we suggest as a working basis in the everyday practice of the law in conjunction with Judge Hastie's paper?

It seems to me that there must be certain agreements at the outset. There are three points I would like to leave with you. One is that the only possible damper to hold down the possibility of temporary local customs and mores denying fundamental theories of due process that all of us agree on is to have ultimate review in the federal courts, meaning, of course, the United States Supreme Court. And that the only restraint on the right, this goes for substantive as well as procedural due process, is the restraint that the court itself exercises. And third—I for one would like to see less restraint than has been used.

The Rise and Collapse of the White Democratic Primary

Of all the so-called "legal" devices for checking Negro participation in Southern politics perhaps the most effective, and on the surface the most legal was the white Democratic Party primary—the most effective because it disfranchised the Negro by excluding him from participating in the pre-elections which for all practical purposes were the elections in the one-party South, and the most "legal" because the Democratic Party, according to contemporary legal theory, was considered as being a voluntary association of citizens could discriminate on the basis of race and color or along any other line in the conduct of its private affairs without offending the Fourteenth and Fifteenth Amendments.

For these reasons, solely, the rise and collapse of the white Democratic primary is an important and distinct chapter in the story of the Negro's struggle for political equality. But an equally important reason for writing this chapter is its rough analogy to the chapter now being developed with respect to educational equality.

The origins of the white Democratic primary are obscure and not easily traced. Lewinson in his *Race, Class and Party*,[1] however, suggests that its beginnings go back to the color line drawn during Reconstruction days by self-labeled "white man's parties"—first called Conservative and, subsequently, simply Democratic—which opposed Black Republicanism. V. O. Keys's authoritative *Southern Politics*,[2] on the other hand, concludes only that this device originated about as early as the direct primary method of nomination appeared on the Southern scene.

In any event, it can hardly be gainsaid that Negroes were admitted to Democratic and Conservative councils, caucuses or conventions during Reconstruction and the policy of excluding Negroes from the Democratic Party's nominating process was born during that time.

Thurgood Marshall, *The Rise and Collapse of the "White Democratic Primary,"* 26 J. NEGRO EDUC. 249 (1957). Copyright © 1957 by Howard University.
1. PAUL LEWINSON, RACE, CLASS, AND PARTY: A HISTORY OF NEGRO SUFFRAGE AND WHITE POLITICS IN THE SOUTH 46 (1932); DARLENE CLARK HINES, BLACK VICTORY: THE RISE AND FALL OF THE WHITE PRIMARY IN TEXAS (1979).
2. V. O. KEYS, SOUTHERN POLITICS IN STATE AND NATION 8, 541 (1949).

Use of the primary election method of nomination did not enter South-ern politics until after the end of Reconstruction. The earliest primaries were local, informal and unregulated by law. Statutory recognition and regulation first appeared in the mid-1880s when Alabama and South Carolina passed acts providing for mandatory primary elections. There-after, the legally regulated primary slowly spread throughout the South and by the turn of the century every Southern state required or permit-ted its use. During these twenty years, roughly speaking, and, for another twenty years thereafter, exclusion of Negroes from these pre-elections was not written on the law books.

Nevertheless the white primary system flourished. First, by tacit under-standings or gentlemen's agreements between competing factions within state and local Democratic organizations and, later, with formal rules passed pursuant to statutory delegations of the power to prescribe qual-ifications for voting in primaries, the Democratic Party limited partici-pation in them to white voters only, although there were many localities where the formal rule was never adopted and others where it was waived in closely contested elections. But, overall, the system had become so effective that a Southern legislator who opposed another disfranchise-ment device, in a letter published by the *Atlanta Constitution* in 1907, was able to exclaim: "We already had the Negro eliminated from politics by the white primary."[3]

It is one of those little ironies of which Southern politics is full, that the primary movement which is motivated, at least in part, by democra-tic motives and a desire for wider participation in the representative process was turned into a device for eliminating millions of Negroes from participation in government.

It is even more ironical that a petty squabble between the candidates for a minor political office in Texas ended in the enactment of a statute which declared Negroes ineligible to vote in a Democratic primary and touched off the series of lawsuits which brought about the collapse of the white primary system.

This chain of events was set off in 1918 by two candidates for the dis-trict attorneyship of Bexar County, Texas.[4] Both sought the support of Negro voters and both had previously had such support in other local primaries. The unsuccessful candidate this time, however, set out upon a

3. Alexander Keyssar writes: "The white primary, [was] probably the most effica-cious method of denying the vote to African Americans." ALEXANDER KEYSSAR, THE RIGHT TO VOTE: THE CONTESTED HISTORY OF DEMOCRACY IN THE UNITED STATES 249 (2000).

4. Other variations of this story appear in Lewinson, *supra* note 1, at 113; BERNARD H. NELSON, THE FOURTEENTH AMENDMENT AND THE NEGRO SINCE 1920, at 37 (1946).

campaign for legislation which would require exclusion of Negro voters from the Democratic primary and thus undermine the victor's political strength in the country. The campaign attracted little support in the legislature at the outset save from those legislators who were professed Negrophobes. By 1923, however, a number of conservative legislators, who were undoubtedly encouraged by the Supreme Court's ruling in the Newberry case[5] that primaries were not elections within the meaning of the Constitution, furnished in Democratic primaries.

Four years after its enactment this statute was held unconstitutional by the Supreme Court in the First Texas White Primary Case.[6] The suit had been filed in 1924 on behalf of Dr. L. A. Nixon, an El Paso physician, well-known Negro Democrat, who sought to recover damages from the election officials who denied him the right to vote in the primary which nominated the Democratic candidates for seats in the federal Congress and various state offices. Specifically, the complaint alleged that the law which the defendants had enforced against the plaintiff was violative of the Fourteenth and Fifteenth Amendments. The federal district court sitting in El Paso granted defendants' motion to dismiss on the merits and the case then came direct to the Supreme Court. Speaking for a unanimous Court, Justice [Oliver Wendell] Holmes declared: "It seems to us hard to imagine a more direct and obvious infringement of the Fourteenth Amendment." The Court declined to consider the validity of the statute under the Fifteenth Amendment.

Most people, including Justice Holmes,[7] felt that this decision laid the white primary to rest;[8] but succeeding events showed them up as far too optimistic. For the Texas legislature promptly tried again. In 1928 it repealed the 1924 law and enacted another, which empowered the state executive committees of political parties to determine the qualifications of voters in primary elections. And, pursuant thereto, the State Executive Committee of the Democratic Party passed a resolution limiting participation in primaries to white persons. This combination of statutory delegation and formal party rule, as we previously noted, was the means by which Negroes were excluded from Democratic primaries throughout most of the South; and it was also the one which legal scholars deemed immune from the reach of the federal Constitution.

This system did not long remain unchallenged. Following the exclusion of Negroes from the 1928 Democratic primaries, suits challenging it were filed in Arkansas, Florida, Texas, and Virginia. Only one, the

---

5. Newberry v. United States, 256 U.S. 232 (1921).
6. Nixon v. Herndon, 273 U.S. 536 (1927).
7. Note, *Right of Negroes to Vote in State Primaries*, 43 Harv. L. Rev. 467, 469 (1930).
8. *See, e.g.*, N.Y. Times, March 8, 1927, at 24; 34 Crisis 224 (1927); 5 Opportunity 97 (1927).

Second Texas White Primary Case,[9] was brought up to the Supreme Court. Dr. Nixon was again the plaintiff in an action for damages against the election officials who refused to permit him to vote. He contended that the state was a party to the discrimination against him since it had delegated control over the primary to the State Executive Committee of the Democratic Party. Both the federal district court and the Circuit Court of Appeals upheld the challenged device. But the Supreme Court pricked open the private association fiction and reversed in a 5-to-4 decision. The majority, however, gratuitously pointed out a way in which Negroes could be excluded from primaries by remarking that the power to do this lay with the State Democratic Convention and not the State Executive Committee, if any such power existed.

Although most were apprehensive about the Court's gratuitous suggestion, Negroes and their friends generally regarded the decision as the final step in their effort to throw open the white primary. Supporters of the white primary system were also confused, not so much with respect to the course to take but how to navigate it. Within three weeks of decision day however, the confusion was dissipated when the Democratic Party called a state convention and it adopted a resolution restricting membership in the party plus participation in party primaries to white citizens of Texas.

Since 1932 was an election year and the resolution was rigorously enforced a number of cases testing the constitutionality of the convention resolution were filed and lost in lower federal courts. One of them carried up to the Supreme Court and became the Third Texas White Primary Case.[10] R. R. Grovey, a Negro citizen of Houston, was the plaintiff in the case. The pleadings admitted that candidates for federal office were to be nominated at the primary and that nomination in the primary was equivalent to election. Nevertheless, the members of the Court "blinded themselves as judges to what they knew as men" and unanimously held that the Democratic primary was a private matter and that Grovey had not been discriminated against pursuant to any state law nor had he been denied any right guaranteed under the Fourteenth and Fifteenth Amendments.

Thus on April Fool's Day, 1935, the same day on which the second Scottsboro case was handed down, almost a decade of litigation was brought to nought. Dean Williams Pickens, in an article which appeared in the *Norfolk Journal and Guide* on April 13, could not resist commenting upon the coincidence. "If one were suspicious of the Court's motives," he said, "it would look as if they made a trade." Undoubtedly, from a

9. Nixon v. Condon, 286 U.S. 73 (1932).
10. Grovey v. Townsend, 294 U.S. 45 (1935).

purely racial perspective and in view of the Court's disposition of the earlier Primary cases, the decision was a rude jolt to the political aspirations of Negroes.[11] But hope did not die out. P. B. Young, writing for the same issue of the *Journal and Guide* as the one in which Dean Pickens's comment appeared, sensed the hope and boldly predicted that this "barrier will not effective long. The Court in 1935 did not ferret out the trickery behind the statutes. Later, it will go behind the law."

As predicted, Grovey did not remain an effective barrier. In *United States v. Classic*,[12] the Court pierced the façade of legality which had shielded primaries from the reach of federal laws regulating the conduct for decision, unanimously agreed that Congress had the right to regulate primary elections and that the criminal sections of the civil rights law could be involving nominations for federal office. The Court's opinion followed and adopted the very arguments which had been rejected in the Third Texas White Primary Case; and the Court, without a single reference to Grovey, practically overruled it.

Because it was not a white primary case, Classic, of course, did not go behind the law and ferret out the trickery. However, it paved the way to the next milestone on the long road toward political equality—the Fourth Texas White Primary Case.[13]

This will be seen in proper perspective by turning back to 1940. It was the first general election year after *Grovey v. Townsend* and the assault upon the white primary began anew. Most of the cases arose in Texas. None met with any success in the trial courts and few were appealed. Indeed, in one of them, an appeal had been noted just about the time the Classic decision came down. That appeal, however, was withdrawn and a new suit based upon the rationale of the Classic case was filed. This was the Fourth Texas White Primary Case.

It was brought on behalf of Lonnie E. Smith, a Negro citizen of Houston, on behalf of himself and all other Negroes similarly qualified to vote yet denied the right to do so by the election judges. Their action, it was alleged, violated rights secured under the Constitution and laws of the U.S. and for this alleged illegal conduct a declaratory judgement, injunctive relief and monetary damages were sought. Needless to say, the lower courts refused to overrule Grovey.[14]

The Supreme Court, however, looked behind the law and ferreted out

11. *See, e.g.*, Ralph J. Bunche, *Tactics and Problems of Minority Groups*, 4 J. NEGRO EDUC. 308, 319 (1935); E. Franklin Frazer, *The Negro in the American Social Order*, 4 J. NEGRO EDUC., 293, 302 (1935).
12. 313 U.S. 299 (1941).
13. Smith v. Allwright, 321 U.S. 649 (1944).
14. Smith v. Allwright, 131 F.2d 593, 594 (5th Cir. 1942) (*per curiam*), *rev'd*, Smith v. Allwright, 321 U.S. 649 (1944).

the trickery. It concluded that the Democratic Party, after "the fusing by the Classic case of the primary and general elections into a single instrumentality for the choice of officers," had become, under elaborate statutory regulations, "an agency of the state" in determining the participants in primary elections. "The party takes its character as a state agency from the duties imposed upon it by state statute; the duties do not become matters of private law because they were performed by a political party." Thus the Court held that the Democratic Party as such, under the statutes, through whatever agency it acted, can no more discriminate against voters in primary elections than the state itself in general elections without violating the Fifteenth Amendment and the privileges and immunities clause of the Fourteenth Amendment.

This decision, one of the landmarks in constitutional history, leveled the greater barrier to Negro voting in the South. But the Southern ingenuity was not spent and clever stratagems were conceived in a desperate effect to circumvent *Smith v. Allwright* and restore the white democratic primary. In South Carolina, for example, a special session of the legislature was called for the purpose of repealing all laws on its statute books, which dealt with political parties and primaries. By doing this, according to the thinking of the Governor and the legislators, the tie-up between the party and the state would be severed and then like a "private club" the Democratic Party could exclude Negroes from its primaries. In Alabama and Georgia different props to avoid the Fourth Texas Primary Case were thrown up. All were either struck down by lower Federal courts[15] or were not enforced.

Texas, however, was destined to be the scene of the last chapter. There, instead of an attempt to preserve the white Democratic primary, the device involved an all-white "club"—the Jaybird Party or Jaybird Democratic Association—which held its own pre-election some weeks in advance of the Democratic primary regulated by the State. The winners of the Jaybird primary would then enter the Democratic primary, which was open to Negroes as well as whites, and won without opposition in the Democratic primary and the general election that followed. A suit challenging the exclusion of Negroes from the Jaybird primaries was filed after the 1948 elections by John Terry and a group of Negro citizens of Fort Bend County. Like *Smith v. Allwright*, it was a classic suit and the same broad relief was sought. The case eventually came up to the Supreme Court and it held that the discriminatory practices described above

---

15. Elmer v. Rice, 72 F. Supp. 516 (E.D. S.C. 1947), *aff'd* 165 F.2d 387 (C.A. 4th 1947), *cert. denied,* 333 U.S. 875 (1948); Brown, 80 F. Supp. 1017 (E.D. S.C. 1948), *aff'd* 174 F.2d 391 (C.A. 4th 1949); Davis v. School, 81 F. Supp. 872 (S.D. Ala. 1949), *aff'd* U. S. 933 (1949).

were unconstitutional.[16] The collapse of the white Democratic primary, despite fond hopes, has not resulted in full participation by all in the political life of the South. But the story of the struggle to overcome this barrier is particularly meaningful today. For, if nothing else, it indicates the fate which awaits the "legal means" which some of the Southern states have drafted to preserve segregated schools.

16. Terry v. Adams, 345 U.S. 416 (1952).

Summary Justice:
The Negro GI in Korea

Thirty-nine Negro American solders convicted and sentenced by courts-martial held in Korea asked the NAACP to represent them. All, beginning with Lt. Leon A. Gilbert, who received sentence of death on September 6, had pleaded "Not Guilty." When we examined records of the trials, we knew something was very wrong.

These soldiers were members of the 24th Infantry Regiment. This Regiment won the first notable United Nations' victory in retaking the rail and highway city of Yechon on July 28 after a bloody sixteen-hour battle. At Bloody Peak, its Third Battalion fought its way up and down the mountain several times in the face of superior enemy fighting power, with whole companies being wiped out. Despite staggering casualties, these infantrymen fought on until they took Bloody Peak and held it.

And yet, we were faced with a large number of courts-martial cases involving Negroes, with conviction for cowardice, for desertion, for misbehavior in the presence of the enemy, and other serious offenses. It seemed hard to believe that these men could change over from heroes to cowards, all within a few days, even under the violent pressures of warfare.

Letters from the men insisted they had been treated unfairly. In most cases there was no dispute between the prosecution and defense on points of law, but versions of the facts given by witnesses varied widely.

We needed facts. It would do little good to submit appeals for review of these trials unless we found out everything we could about each individual case. And the place to get the facts was across the Pacific. At first, General MacArthur refused permission for me to go to Tokyo, where the prisoners were. He sent a cable which read:

58 CRISIS 297 (1951). The editor wishes to thank The Crisis Publishing Co., Inc., the publisher of the magazine of the National Association for the Advancement of Colored People, for authorizing the use of this work. Thurgood Marshall, special counsel to the NAACP, spent five weeks in Japan and Korea in January and February 1951 investigating circumstances surrounding the court-martial convictions of Negro troops. *See also* BRENDA GALE PLUMMER, RISING WIND: BLACK AMERICANS AND U.S. FOREIGN AFFAIRS, 1935–1960, at 205 (1996) (regarding Marshall's travels to Japan and Korea).

Not the slightest evidence exists here of discrimination as alleged. As I think you know in this command there is no slightest bias of its various members because of race, color or other distinguishing characteristics. Every soldier in this command is measured on a completely uniform basis with the sole criteria his efficiency and his character. Nevertheless, on receipt of your message I at once ordered the Inspector General to make thorough investigation of your charges and will be glad to have you forward here any evidence in your possession bearing upon the matter. In any individual trial a soldier can obtain special counsel to defend him if he so desires. In such individual trial there would of course be no objection to Thurgood Marshall representing the accused and coming to this command for such purpose. You understand of course that courts martial are convened by the Major Subordinate Commander in Korea and the hearings are conducted there.

Decision No Help

This decision of MacArthur was certainly no help to the men who had already been condemned, and we were continuing to receive requests from others who had been convicted under questionable circumstances. We did not hear of these trials until long after they took place, so the General's willingness to have me represent men who might be accused in the future was not encouraging. That same afternoon Walter White, executive secretary of the NAACP, sent another cable to MacArthur, urging reconsideration of its decision, and said: "Examination of courts martial records indicates many convicted under circumstances make impartial justice improbable."

He also forwarded a memorandum of twenty-three cases of individual soldiers, and requested a conference between General MacArthur, the Inspector General, and myself. On December 24, MacArthur cabled that there was "no objection" to such a conference.

Immediately after my arrival in Tokyo on January 14, General MacArthur ordered that I be given the fullest cooperation from everyone under his command. My work was to be carried on through the office of the Inspector General. The most complete cooperation possible was forthcoming throughout my stay. . . .

All the condemned men were confined in a stockade outside Tokyo. I was permitted to see every man I wanted to, as many times as I liked, and with complete privacy. Altogether, I saw about eighty men. I talked to Lt. Gilbert half a dozen times and to some of the others several times. It was possible to hear each man's story, and he wanted to tell it. . . .

Further Investigation

Each day a list of all points which warranted further investigation was submitted to the Inspector General. Inquiry into these detailed points would begin that very day, so that this checking process moved along only a few days behind my questioning.

I then went back and did my own checking on stories that did not quite fit together. . . .

In many cases, charges were made or strengthened by officers whose statements in the records of the trials called for extremely careful checking. It wasn't possible for some of the things they said to be true. And yet, to find out where they now were required use of the Locator File in the huge six-story Dai Ichi building which was MacArthur's Far East Command headquarters. I hate to think how many times it turned out that the officer had been killed in action. Back in August, September, and October of 1950 the casualty rate was horribly high.

After three weeks of this process, I made a preliminary report to General MacArthur and General Hickey, his chief of staff. This was at a conference in the Dai Ichi building at night. I told them what had been found so far in my investigation, what I believed to be the cause of these courts-martial trials, and who in my opinion, was to blame.

Went to Korea

Then I told General MacArthur I wanted to go to Korea, and they made arrangements for the same complete cooperation that had been given to me in Tokyo.

All through my inquiry in Korea I was allowed to see anybody I needed to see. From the beginning to the end of that part of my trip a Deputy Inspector General, Colonel D. D. Martin, accompanied me. With his authority and with my published orders from MacArthur, we could open any door. And we did . . .

What Happened

What actually happened in virtually every case was that a defendant would be confronted by two officers, who told him they were assigned to serve as his counsel. Then, observing the letter of military law, they would tell the prisoner, *"You are allowed to choose your own counsel if there is anyone you prefer."*

"Then I want Captain A," the accused man would say.

They'd be sorry, but Captain A was busy right now in a fire fight with North Korean forces on the Main Line of Resistance. His company needed him.

"What about Lieutenant B?" the prisoner would ask.

It was regrettable, but Lieutenant B was up on a ridge with his platoon and could not possibly be disturbed because the enemy was threatening to engulf the whole situation. While the accused man was assured of counsel of his choice, the court-assigned counsel advised him to choose them. The trial was going to begin very shortly. He's been charged with a serious offense, and he needed counsel, Captain A and Lieutenant B were away, and they—the two assigned counsel—were right there. So was the trial.

In numerous instances the counsel spent no more than fifteen or twenty minutes with the men about to be tried. There were cases when a man was pulled out of his foxhole—told to get out of his blanket, get dressed, and ride to Pusan. He'd arrive in Pusan in the middle of the night, be allowed to go to sleep for a while on the court-room floor, only to wake up for his trial to be held then and there.

Since these officers had no wish to endanger their careers, they certainly were not going to concede that there had been insufficient time to prepare the cases properly. . . .

Officers White

The 24th Regiment was the same kind of Negro regiment the Army has maintained since 1865. All enlisted men were Negroes, but for the most part the officers above the level of lieutenant were white. As was apparent from my visits to the Locator File in Tokyo, the casualty rate for these officers and their replacements was extremely high. Although many of these officers were dead, they and many of their successors were responsible for the facts revealed by a comparative table drawn up to show how differently Negro and white defendants were treated by courts-martial proceedings.

A court-martial begins with a complaint—usually made by an officer. The commanding officer either arrests the man or allows him to go free. An investigation, by another designated officer, ascertains whether the official charges are well founded.

In the 25th Division, between the time of Lt. Gilbert's conviction on September 6 and my visit in late February, there were a total of 118 complaints filed for all types of offenses. Of these, 82 resulted in trials, the rest being either withdrawn or dropped.

Out of the 82 cases which resulted in general court-martial trials, 54 were Negroes, 27 were white, and one was Japanese. In these 82 cases, 66 were investigated by white officers and 16 were investigated by Negro officers.

Most of the charges filed against Negroes—60 of them—were for violation of the 75th Article of War, misbehavior in the presence of the enemy. This means cowardice. In Army life there is no more serious charge.

In the files were complaints against white solders for sleeping on their posts during guard duty, up on the front lines within spitting distance of the enemy. But they were not charged with any violation of the 75th Article of War. They were charged with sleeping on their posts. White boys were charged with leaving a sentry post and sleeping on duty who did not even put up a defense, and they were acquitted. One man was found wrapped up in a blanket sound asleep. In this case, his commanding officer testified, *"I saw him there and he was sleeping."* One witness testified he didn't *think* the man was asleep. Other witnesses took the stand all saying the boy was asleep. One sergeant testified, *"I was right there, I not only saw him but I heard him. If he wasn't sleeping, he was snoring while wide awake."*

The accused soldier was acquitted, found not guilty.

100 Percent White

Was it a coincidence that all the commanding officers who approved charges were white, that the entire staffs of the Inspector General's office, and of the trial Judge Advocate's office were 100 percent white? Was it also purely coincidental that one week before my visit to Korea a Negro was added to each of these two staffs?

Here is a summary of the actual results of courts-martial in Korea for alleged violation of the 75th Article of War:

	Negro	White
Charges withdrawn	23	2
Charges reduced to AWOL	1	0
Acquittals	4	4
Sentenced	32	2
	60	8

These are the sentences given to the defendants:

	Negro	White
Death	1	0
Natural Life	15	0
50 years	1	0
25 years	2	0
20 years	3	0
15 years	1	0
10 years	7	0
5 years	2	1
3 years	0	1
	32	2

The white defendant who got the worst sentence (five years) offered as his defense that he was a chronic drunkard, but this sentence has been since reduced to one year.

The investigation reports, all kept as official records by the Army, revealed that no credence was ever given to the story each individual accused man would tell. The investigating officers totally ignored the statements of the men about to be charged with the worst offenses in the Army code. Scant effort was made to find out what was true and what was not. I had not only talked to these men, but had the benefit of the investigations made by the Judge Advocate's office to check what stories could be proved.

The Men

And what actually had happened? Who were the individuals condemned to serve out their lives in army prisons, or endure terms of ten, fifteen, twenty, twenty-five, and fifty years at hard labor for being cowards?

One boy convicted of cowardice had enlisted when he was fifteen. He remained in that bloody, frozen Korean fighting without telling anybody he was underage, knowing full well that he could at any time be returned to the United States as a hero. This coward remained in the front lines of his own free choice until he was confronted with court-martial charges. We checked, and found he told the truth. His eighteenth birthday occurred eleven days after his court-martial convicted him of being a coward . . .

Quick Justice

In four cases the trials which sentenced men to life imprisonment ran forty-two minutes, forty-four minutes, and the other two for fifty minutes each. This included the entire process of hearing the charges read, swearing in witnesses, examining all the evidence presented, hearing arguments (if any), explaining to the men their rights under the manual of courts-martial, the recess periods, discussion by the court, and pronouncing sentence. Other trials ran hour or an hour and ten minutes. I have seen many miscarriages of justice in my capacity as head of the NAACP legal department. But even in Mississippi a Negro will get a trial longer than forty-two minutes, if he is fortunate enough to be brought to trial.

The men in the stockade had a common feeling of hopelessness. Some men with airtight defense had not presented evidence clearly demonstrating their innocence of the charges. Time and again I would ask them, *"Why didn't you tell your lawyer what really happened? Why didn't you tell the court? Why didn't you tell somebody?"*

Even though each man is an individual in the eyes of God and under our Constitution, these individuals gave me the same answer. *"It wasn't worth trying. We knew when we went in there we were all going to come out the same way. Each one of us hoped and prayed we would only get life. They gave that officer, Lt. Gilbert, death, only because he is a Negro. What did you expect them to give a Negro enlisted man? We know what the score is."*

Such a spirit of hopelessness will strip away from any man the ability to defend himself adequately. One particular sergeant imprisoned in the stockade outside Tokyo was representative of the devotion we have come to associate with our armed forces. Under fire in Korea three of his commanding officers were killed in a period of two days. This man had kept his company together. He did not lose a single wounded man in ninety days. He brought every injured man out, sometimes on his own back. He saw to it that his men received hot food, regularly, which he took up to them at the remoter points along the firing line. One after another he saw his friends killed, but refused to be relieved. Day in and day out, he kept on fighting. Several times in command of the entire company because there weren't officers around. . . .

Officer Behavior

How could officers of our Army behave in such a way? The official records proved that they did, but the explanation for their behavior was still lacking. My last Sunday in Korea was spent at a very forward position of the 24th Infantry Regiment, where I talked to the key man in every company of the regiment and of the 159th Field Artillery battery. These men knew what was behind these courts-martial operations.

The Regiment's forward positions were then moved north of Seoul. They had just taken an airstrip six hours before we got there.

These soldiers were survivors of the action occurring prior to and during the three months of courts-martial. There was one man whose father had been in the regiment for twenty years, and he's been in it for nine. I talked to about seventy of these veterans, asking them to tell me what had been going on last summer and fall.

One after another, they all said the same thing. The regiment's morale had been at a disastrously low ebb. Their white officers were in many instances Southerners who had brought their prejudices with them when assigned to duty with the 24th Infantry.

Time and again these officers told the men whom they were going to order into battle, *"I despise nigger troops. I don't want to command you or any other niggers. This Division is no good, and you are lousy. You don't know how to fight."*

I cannot imagine a worse situation in combat, where a man does not care what happens to those serving under him There is no way to make the soldiers care less what is going to happen to the outcome of the fighting, or to their officers. . . .

Made Report

I now had the information for a complete report to General MacArthur, with recommendations. . . .

But in my report it was necessary to place the ultimate responsibility for these courts-martial squarely upon General Douglas MacArthur. He had both the authority and the responsibility for maintaining or ending racial segregation in the Army's Far East Command. . . .

In every war in which this country has participated, Negro Americans have had to fight for the right to fight. At the start of each war, military leaders have questioned the Negro's abilities and finally accepted Negro participation under the pressure of necessity.

Although 920,000 Negroes served in the Army during the Second World War, the Army didn't take most of them until manpower shortages impelled their acceptance, using them for menial jobs wherever possible. These men were treated as inferiors in southern training camps. The great majority were used for arduous, dirty work overseas, but they covered themselves with glory just the same. . . .

Part II
Solicitor General, Judge, and Supreme Court Justice, 1960s–1990s

4. Marshall's swearing in as Justice of U.S. Supreme Court, 1967. Thurgood Marshall Jr., John William Marshall, Mrs. Thurgood Marshall, President Lyndon B. Johnson, Thurgood Marshall, Justice Hugo Black, Attorney General Nicholas deB. Katzenbach, Justice Tom C. Clark. Library of Congress.

The 1960s:
Transition from
Lawyer to Jurist

The 1960s was a period in American history that tested the soul of the nation. Perhaps the most trying issue was the civil rights revolution led by black and white high school and college students calling for the social and political reconstruction of the United States.[1] This period challenged the American people to support the quests of African Americans to realize the promises of *Brown v. Board of Education* and issues of equality beyond school segregation.[2]

Marshall recognized the desire of African Americans to broaden their demands for better housing, wages, and other opportunities denied on the basis of racial discrimination. The cry of the decade was for freedom and demands to end white violence that killed Emmett Till in Mississippi, Sammy Young (Tuskegee, Alabama), and four black girls attending Sunday school in Birmingham, Alabama.[3] The challenge of the decade was to rid America of elements of an apartheid system.

1. Anthony M. Orum writes: "February 1, 1960, signaled the beginning of a long series of political demonstrations by black high school and college students throughout the United States. The demonstrations were unexpected for in the preceding decade people rarely expressed political opinions, much less political dissent. According to some observers, the 1950s was the end of ideology, and nowhere was the fact more evident than on college campuses all across the nation." Anthony M. Orum, *Black Students in Protest: A Study of the Origins of the Black Student Movement* 1 (1974) (pamphlet).

2. *See* Constance Baker Motley, School Desegregation Cases: The Present Status of the Law in the Fifth Circuit, Speech Before the NAACP Legal Defense and Educational Fund-Lawyers' Conference, June 20, 1960 (discussing cases). *See, e.g.,* James T. Patterson, Brown v. Board of Education: A Civil Rights Milestone and Its Troubled Legacy 118 (2001).

3. Juan Williams, Eyes on the Prize 37–53 (1988) (Till); *see also Birmingham After the Bombing,* U.S. News & World Report 38, Sept. 30, 1963; Lee A. Daniels, *Recalling a Sunday in Birmingham,* Wash. Afro-Am., June 17, 2000, at A5. (The girls killed by the bomb were Denise McNair, age eleven, and Addie Mae Collins, Carole Robertson, and Cynthia Wesley, all fourteen.) Sammy Young, a twenty-one-year-old student leader in the Student Nonviolent Coordinating Committee was shot down by a white man in Tuskegee Alabama, his hometown, for trying to use the "whites only" restroom at a local gas station. *See* James Forman, Sammy

This was the decade that black students risked their lives to eliminate race-based discrimination, particularly in the South. It was the era when a growing population of black and white student leaders declared that it was an insult for blacks to be denied the right to sit down at lunch counters to buy a cup of coffee after spending their money for merchandise in the same store. One sit-in student leader described the protest movement as "commonly known as 'sit-in' demonstrations." He states that the sit-ins "provided his generation with a vehicle which realistically conveys the principle that there is a necessity to break the law in order to make new law."[4] Thurgood Marshall was supportive of youth, stating that "These young people are just simply sick and tired of waiting patiently without protests for the rights they know to be theirs."[5]

Many students were arrested, beaten, and jailed for protesting against white establishments denying blacks the right to equal accommodations. Marshall assured the students and informed the South that the NAACP was prepared to stay in court, in state after state, until the curtain of racism was lifted or torn down.

The 1960s marked Thurgood Marshall's transition from a civil rights lawyer to jurist. During this decade President John F. Kennedy nominated him to the Second Circuit Court of Appeals of New York. President Lyndon B. Johnson nominated Marshall to be Solicitor General and as the first black Justice of the Supreme Court of the United States.[6] During his tenure in each of these posts, Marshall participated in public forums on the law. He explained his views on the law and its application to social policy. Marshall never wavered from his view that much could be learned from history. He reminded America of "the dark past," and the fallacy that "the struggle for equality was over."[7]

YOUNG, JR.: THE FIRST BLACK COLLEGE STUDENT TO DIE IN THE BLACK LIBERATION MOVEMENT 185–196 (1968).

4. Laurence G. Henry, *Forgive Us Our Trespasses*, 3 HOW. U. MAG. 17, Jan. 1961.

5. Thurgood Marshall, *The Cry for Freedom, in* RHETORIC OF RACIAL REVOLT 318, 319 (Roy L. Hill. ed. 1960) (speech before the NAACP Meeting in Charlotte, N.C., March 20, 1960).

6. *See* Letter (enclosure of "my biographical sketch") from Thurgood Marshall to Raymond Trent, July 11, 1989: The United States Senate confirmed Marshall on Sept. 11, 1962. Marshall took the oath of Office as Solicitor General of the United States on Aug. 24, 1965. He took the constitutional oath as Associate Justice of the Supreme Court of the United States on June 13, 1967. *See also* Carroll Kilpatrick, *Marshall Is Nominated Solicitor General of U.S.*, WASH. POST, July 14, 1965, at 1; *Senate Confirms Marshall, 69–11, for High Court*, WASH. POST, Aug. 31, 1967, at 1.

7. The dark past continued. *See, e.g., Mississippi Versus the United States*, NEWSWEEK, Oct. 8, 1962, at 32; *"They'll' Never Forget Meredith at Ole Miss*," OMAHA WORLD HERALD, Jan. 27, 1963, at 14A; *NAACP Leader Dies of Rifle Bullet in Back*, OMAHA WORLD HERALD, June 12, 1963, at 1 (Medgar W. Evers, age 37). March on

While some criticized the role of Federal courts as being concerned with certain basic values,[8] Marshall asserted that the courts had played an important role adjudicating disputes involving American values of equality and justice. When Judge Marshall was elevated to the Federal courts, he brought more than his extensive experience as a civil rights lawyer. He also brought a brilliant mind and the heart and soul of the voices of the downtrodden to the highest offices of the republic that had once enslaved his ancestors.

The speeches from this decade are Marshall's story as advocate for and teacher of his supporters in the movement and the passing of the torch of Charles Hamilton Houston to a new generation of fighters for justice. Marshall reminded his successors that Houston's plan to rid America of Jim Crow would end in "the next ten years or more."

Marshall recalled his relationship with his benefactor, President Lyndon B. Johnson in an interview with T. H. Baker in 1969. This document, which remained sealed until after Johnson died, reveals circumstances that in a decade would elevate Marshall to heights never reached before by an African American lawyer.

Washington: *On The March*, NEWSWEEK, Sept. 2, 1963, at 17; *Biggest Protest March*, EBONY, Nov., 1963, at 29; Dr. Martin Luther King selected as Man of the Year: *Man of the Year*, TIME, Jan. 3, 1964, at 13. *See also Negro Leaders Tell Their Plans for '64*, U.S. NEWS & WORLD REPORT, Feb. 24, 1964, at 56 (interviews of Whitney M. Young, Martin Luther King, Jr., Roy Wilkins, James L. Farmer, James Forman); ". . . *Shall Now also Be Equal. . .* ," NEWSWEEK, July 13, 1964, at 17 ("President Lyndon B. Johnson strode into the chandeliered East Room of the White House at precisely 6:45 p.m., nodded perfunctorily to acknowledge the applause that greeted him, then sat down at a specially installed mahogany desk on which lay the crisp pages of The Civil Rights Act of 1964 . . . Mr. Johnson reached for the first of the 72 pens [signed the Bill into law dated] July 2, 1964—Washington, D.C.").

8. *Is the Supreme Court Reaching for Too Much Power?* U.S. NEWS & WORLD REPORT, Oct. 7, 1963, at 64.

5. Thurgood Marshall meeting with President Lyndon B. Johnson in the Oval Office of the White House, September 26, 1968. LBJ Library. Photograph by Yoichi Okamoto.

The United States as the
Moral Leader of the World

It is an extreme privilege to be permitted to speak to the graduating class of the "Institution of Learning." In speaking to you in 1961, a year which can very well be the year in which the entire world recognized the need for recognition of individual and human dignity as against outmoded systems of colonialism and racial intolerance. As 1961 graduates you enter into the arena where the rising tide of independence for nations in Africa and Asia, along with the many drives toward the removal of racial discrimination in our country, takes second place only to the drive toward outer space.[1]

While the drive toward outer space commands the attention of all,[2] we cannot allow this drive toward outer space to be unmatched by our drive toward control of man's inner mind.[3] While arguments can be made that our country is behind in the drive for outer space and, indeed, arguments can be made that we might not close the gap, no one can possibly make an argument that our country is incapable of taking over the moral leadership of the world. Indeed, the ultimate and lasting peace will only come about once this is established.

It is not only that the darker people of the world form two-thirds to three-fourths of the world population but it is also true that by 1962 the

Commencement address, Kalamazoo College, June 4, 1961.

1. The year 1961 was an important year for the American space program: Alan Shepard became the first American in space on May 5. A month before Justice Marshall presented the Kalamazoo speech, President John F. Kennedy had stated before a joint session of Congress: "I believe this nation should commit itself to achieving the goal, before the decade is out, of landing a man on the moon and returning him safely to earth." 107 CONG. REC. 8877, 8881 (May 25, 1961).

2. *See, e.g., Space: High Polish*, TIME 20, Nov. 28, 1960. This article is an example of some of the developments that were taking place in the "ever-brightening space program" around the time the Thurgood Marshall gave this speech.

3. Here, Marshall's words echo President Kennedy's speech before the joint session of Congress. CONG. REC., *supra* note 1. However, Marshall's context is that the interest of blacks was not at that moment about space, but about the nation's moral responsibility to confront and conquer racial discrimination. It was a "battle for men's minds." *Id.* at 8881.

African-Asia bloc in the United Nations will have a clear majority of votes on any issue facing the world. The emergence of independent African states challenges the imagination of all of us. You cannot possibly get the feeling of this modern trend unless you are fortunate enough to be in Africa and see Ghana become a Republic and Sierre Leone become independent. Then go to Kenya, [and] Tanganyika and watch the Africans working toward independence. The government of Great Britain has for the most part gracefully cooperated with these countries toward a stable independence while Belgium and France have not been graceful as independence has come to their former colonies. Regardless of which country you go through in Africa you find not only the shouting in the streets of the songs all blended around "Freedom Now" but even in the quiet you feel the tense optimism of ultimate freedom. Whether you hear the cry of "Freedom Now" from the Africans or listen to speeches of Prime Minister Macmillan of Great Britain recognizing the "Winds of Change" sweeping over Africa, you come away with the feeling that freedom from racial discrimination is at an end with mere time for formalities. With this background we find that other nations, such as the Soviet Union, feel they have a stake in misleading and attempting to mislead these emerging nations. We find in these nations themselves and in the United Nations the constant political maneuvering based upon the contest of offers of wealth and materials as well as the contest of ideologies. For example, wherever one travels in Africa and Asia and, indeed, in most places in Europe, once it is discovered you are American, you are usually asked the question: "Are you from Little Rock or Big Rock?" While the disgraceful actions in Little Rock can be explained away by the statement that Little Rock was just an isolated incident in a small town in a small state, it becomes very difficult to explain away New Orleans and the disgraceful resentment at four little colored girls going to two previously all white schools. It is even more difficult to explain away the burning bus in Anniston, Alabama,[4] last month or the police dogs turned loose on Negro children in Jackson, Mississippi. As a matter of fact, we are running out of little isolated spots as a defense.

If we are to truly represent democracy for the rest of the world or come up against realities as they exist, first of all college graduates in this year must realize that regardless of the college attended, regardless of the personal sacrifices made, regardless of the cost to the student, each graduate owes a measure of his education to his community, his state, and his government. The training that each graduate has received requires that a portion of that training be dedicated to service to his

4. *See* JOHN LEWIS, WALKING WITH THE WIND: A MEMOIR OF THE MOVEMENT 144–145 (1998) (Anniston).

fellowman. I know that many graduates will take the position that they will do all they can for their fellowman but they will take care of them one at a time and as soon as he gets his security, he will be willing to work for the security of his fellowman. This, of course, will not bring the results we want.

This usually leads to a sincere desire to disengage one's self from controversy. This is true in politics as well in the field of civil rights. There are several dangers inherent in this renunciation of politics. First, if the emerging middle class is unable to fill the role in politics which has been traditionally assigned to it, we will be confronted with a vacuum in political leadership. This void will be most apparent, at the outset, at the state or local level. Certainly this has been the tragedy in the South. The moderate and law-abiding people of Little Rock and similar cities are members of the middle class, and an increasing number of them are corporation employees. Because they want to remain respectable and avoid controversy, because they have no real interest in the outcome of the conflict over segregation, because they are ill-suited to play any role of consequence in party politics they have been unable to exercise an influence for freedom and justice in a critical situation. The same may be said of the North in the area of civil liberties: the middle class, while tolerant in informal social relationships, has not been notable in defending the freedom of the dissident groups and individuals. Such a defense would require political participation and the middle class has forsaken such a commitment.

While many will consider that their scientific training can best be used in the fight for outer space, there must be many more who believe that their training can best be used to making this world a better place to live in by dedicating a portion of this training toward making Democracy work.

Our own basic legal document—the Declaration of Independence— continues to set the framework of this government. The Constitution of the United States, you will remember, was almost immediately amended by the Bill of Rights guaranteeing the people against oppression by the federal government and the denial by it of basic human rights such as freedom of religion, freedom of speech and press, guarantee of a fair trial, to name but a few. While this Constitution not only did not abolish but actually tolerated and gave aid and comfort to the institution of slavery, good people of the country looking to their basic religious principles set out to destroy the practice of one human being setting himself up as master of another human being. . . .

Today in many areas of the South the average person is afraid to even speak out in favor of what he knows is morally right—to follow the law as interpreted by the Supreme Court. Others even join those who seek to continue the immoral practice of perpetuating enforced racial segregation. Many in the North either believe in or are afraid to oppose residential segregation by custom. Both groups refuse or are afraid to follow their religious teachings because of fear of economic or social reprisals from their fellow citizens. This atmosphere forms an effective barrier between principle and practice. The victims of this oppression are powerless to remove this barrier. It can only be done by those who are unwilling to act. The remaining problem between principle and practice must be returned to the high moral plane of the equalitarian principles of our religious teachings.[5]

The first stumbling block to this is the conscience of the individual involved. No one likes to admit even to himself that he has been going wrong in his dealing with his fellowman. Any good citizen knows that it is wrong to hold hatred against a fellowman—that it is immoral to deny human rights or liberties to anyone. This should be our basis for action rather than any motivation brought about by the desire for world leadership. . . .

5. *See* J. Clay Smith, Jr., Thurgood Marshall: Fighting for a Moral Society, Paper before the Annual Meeting of the Association for the Study of African-American Life and History, Inc., Sept. 29, 2000.

No Peace at Any Cost

For some reason, I feel obliged at occasions of this sort (maybe it is because I'm getting old) to reminisce a little. The reason this institute is so important to me and some few of us left around is because it is the brainchild of two Charlies: Charlie Johnson and Charlie Houston.[1] The reason I have to mention that is because so many of us tend to forget. I was impressed about five years ago, talking to some, believe it or not, NAACP people . . . and when I mentioned the name of Charlie H. Houston; they wanted to know who he is. I got news for you. Two months ago I talked to some people and I mentioned the name Walter White[2] and they wanted to know who he is. So, I feel obliged to point out the farsightedness of people of that kind. For example, Charles Johnson thought up this whole institute as a contribution to the overall program that had to be brought forth. Whatever any lawyer does in the field of civil rights, whatever he does up to this year and for the next ten or more years will be the result of Charlie Houston's plan of a legal assault to obtain rights for Negroes through legal action.[3]

So, once again, I have the responsibility of trying to bring you up to date on the legal side at least, what's happened in the past twelve months and the program as it is set up this year is to take into consideration the public affairs, public opinion, in the public realm.

Opening remarks by Thurgood Marshall at the Seventh Annual Institute of Race Relations, Fisk University, Nashville, Tenn., 1961. Reproduced courtesy of the Race Relations Department, United Church Board for Homeland Ministries (UCBHM) Archives, Amistad Research Center, Tulane University.
1. Dr. Charles Johnson was the Dean of the School of Education at Howard University. Dr. Charles Hamilton Houston was the former Dean of the Howard University School of Law. Houston has been referred to as the father of the modern day legal civil rights movement. *See, e.g.*, GENNA RAE MCNEIL, GROUNDWORK: CHARLES HAMILTON HOUSTON AND THE STRUGGLE FOR CIVIL RIGHTS (1983); J. Clay Smith, Jr., *Forgotten Hero*, 98 HARV. L. REV. 482 (1984) (review of GROUNDWORK); GERALDINE R. SEGAL, IN ANY FIGHT SOME FALL 42 (1975).
2. *See generally* WALTER WHITE, A MAN CALLED WHITE: THE AUTOBIOGRAPHY OF WALTER WHITE (1948).
3. GROUNDWORK at 143, *supra* note 1 (McNeil).

I'm impressed with the fact that in the past twelve months, despite all other things that happen, I can find much in the Civil War Centennial believe it or not. I think that it is because every once in a while, I need something to get me mad. That's what it is.

When you look at the project, it was opened with the firing on the Union Ship of the Citadel in South Carolina. It was on television all over the country. It was like something good was being done and I'm impressed with the fact that the Citadel in South Carolina, that the college is as rigidly segregated today as it was one hundred years ago. The only difference is that this year they are getting more federal money to discriminate with. That is the only difference, which is not typical of the South. All the money comes from the federal government, but no response comes in return. Then the firing on Fort Sumter. Then the great demonstration in Montgomery, Alabama, the cradle of the Confederacy; soon thereafter, we have the Freedom Riders coming after them in the same town, Montgomery. I don't believe you can look at this hundred year's centennial unless you look at it as I do. This is, for God's sake, let us win this one, 'cause we didn't win the other one.

Then you look at the North. Nothing is being done in the North. You take the World's Fair which is to come off in New York in two years. The poor southern states are spending ten times as much as New York is spending so they can show their side to the world.

I'm beginning to wonder whether we're winning or losing in this battle for man's mind because while there is this big contest for the outer space, there is the question as to whether we're ahead or the Russians are ahead. There are people who they say that we are behind and indeed there are people who say we'll never catch up. But there is nobody too interested in the struggle for man's mind. If we're going to get peace, we're going to get it out of man's mind. We'll never get it out of the weapons of two super powers, each of which will destroy three-fourths of the other country. I just begin to wonder in this field of civil rights just how far we are getting. I think I'm going to end up tonight with what I started out to say which is, it could be, we're losing.

The research by John Hope Franklin and other expert historians shows that after the Civil War we lost the battle of the Reconstruction because the South gambled that the North had either a guilty conscience of its own or would get tired.[4] Over and over again I urge people to understand this because that might be what is happening now.

In order to see whether or not we are winning, let's go into the several fields of legal action, for example, the school cases. In the past year, we

---

4. *See* John Hope Franklin, From Slavery to Freedom: A History of Negro Americans 331–332 (1967).

saw officially the burying of a massive resistance plan. Everybody gave up; there will be no more of this massive resistance like we had in Virginia, etc. Some get very excited because those who want to do right are so encouraged by so little that they thought this would be the end, not realizing that massive resistance was replaced by token compliance. Token compliance is very interesting. For example, a few months ago, I was in Raleigh, North Carolina. It is not a small city. They had desegregated their schools. Any official in Raleigh will tell you that from the governor of North Carolina on down, that they have desegregated their schools. They desegregated by integrating one whole Negro.

You take New Orleans. They integrated four little Negro girls. The total Negro public school population in New Orleans is 55,000 and they integrated four. I've been going from one end of town to another to find a mathematician who could work out that percentage. I haven't found one yet. Four out of 55,000. Everybody thought that was bad, but let's go along with it. And lo and behold, they have had every kind of reaction you could imagine in New Orleans: rioting, mobs of mothers who took their children out of school; all white children were taken out of school. They paraded the streets, they yelled, they whooped, they carried on. It was almost unbelievable. The Klans took over, the White Citizens Council took over,[5] everybody took over because of four little colored girls, five-year-olds. Now, what could they do? What could they corrupt? What could they damage? What could they upset? Nothing. They even started talking about intermarriage at five. All those women out there parading around and carrying on. You never saw such a group of people in all your life. What the best example of it is you could look at the whole group and you couldn't find a pair of stockings in the whole group. They were parading around about what's going to happen to us if these "Negras" are going to be admitted. So help me, not a one of those four little colored girls wanted any member of that mob as a mother-in-law, so help me they didn't. As a matter of fact, they'd take anybody else for a mother-in-law over them, the people in that group.

But, this is the point I want to stick a pin in. The school board in New Orleans over a period of six years has refused to follow the *Brown* decision.[6] There have been forty-six hearings up and down to the Supreme Court. Eventually Judge [J. Skelly] Wright had these children all alone;

5. Commentators have written that the White Citizens Council is the like the Ku Klux Klan. Jonathan Yardley, *Book World*, WASH. POST, May 16, 1999, at xo2; Colbert I. King, *Lott's Odd Friends*, WASH. POST, Dec. 19, 1998, at A25 (King reports: "In the [1960s] white Citizen Councils members shared the Ku Klux Klan's views on civil rights but tended to speaks and dress better and not slink around after dark in white hoods.") *Id.*
6. Brown v. Board of Education, 347 U.S. 483 (1954) (Brown I).

they wouldn't help them at all. When they did this trick of putting in only four children and deliberately putting them in the white area of town where they knew trouble would break out . . . when the trouble did break out, now the school board members are the heroes of the liberal people. They all feel so sorry for the school board. Now everybody wants token compliance. They even say, well, if we had four last year, we'll take five next year. You see, the public relations image has been developed so that the culprits are not evil. Everybody in New Orleans and people who know about the New Orleans situation, all of the good liberal people, all are either crying in their beer or their milk because the poor school board is so harassed. People telephone and call them dirty names. They threaten them with economic boycotts. It is a shame what they do to those poor school board members.

What about those four little girls and their parents? As I told the people in New Orleans not long ago, I feel very sorry that you get those telephone calls. My heart bleeds for you, but as much as my heart bleeds for you, I can't get Emmett Till's mother's heart to bleed for you, 'cause, you see, whites in Mississippi murdered her son.[7] I can't get the Negro in Mississippi to bleed for you because they suffer every day. What's wrong with telephone calls? You can do one of two things: you can hang up like some people do or you can do like I do, because of all the calls I've ever gotten, I guarantee you that by the time the call is over, I called him a brand new one that he had never had before. I develop new words in my vocabulary over such things. All you have to do is take over and people hang up.

The New Orleans situation I mention in rather great detail because it is typical of what is going on all over the South. There is hardly a city in the South today and I'm talking about the middle power structure, the good people, not the NAACP, not the bad people, but the good people, the liberals, the moderates, the middle-of-the-road people. I challenge you to show me any city in the South today where good people aren't satisfied if they integrate one more Negro. That is all they want—one. Well, we'll fight about two. Everybody has lost the urge to comply with the law. The law never said token. The constitutional rights are present and personal to each person and if I file a lawsuit for my rights, you can't satisfy my rights by giving some other Negro his rights. You've got to give me mine.

Then they say, what are we driving at? I understand this question came up at one of the seminars a couple of afternoons ago. What do the Negroes want? The answer is very simple in—in words—all and

---

7. *See generally* STEPHEN J. WHITFIELD, A DEATH IN THE DELTA: THE STORY OF EMMETT TILL (1988).

now.[8] You see, this gradual approach, this token compliance meant something in 1954 and 1955, but what does it mean in 1961? In 1990 will we say, well, we'll put one more in? My point is that the good people are buying it and I'm afraid that some Negroes are buying it because I know that they are buying it, but I just don't want to believe it. The reason I know it is that under the stairstep plan of one grade a year of the pupil placement plan where if you want to transfer, you have to get a transfer, the responsibility is put on the Negroes to make the move— and the Negroes aren't making the move. I'm guaranteeing you that the general public is not going to—move any faster than the Negroes themselves move. I can bet your bottom dollar on that. The question is whether they move half as fast, but they certainly will move faster. You see, this middle group wants peace at any cost. There are many reasons for it. They don't like violence, bless their souls. So, when they are up against facing violence or sacrificing Negroes' rights, the solution is simple, sacrifice the Negroes' rights. We are told over and over again that when violence breaks loose, then we will settle for almost anything to get peace.

That reminds me of an old story that my father used to tell me, that the only thing it depended upon is how hungry you are. But, if you are hungry enough, a hot dog tastes like a T-bone steak. So, it you are denied your rights long enough and if the opposition is violent enough, you take token compliance and convince yourself that you are protecting constitutional rights when, as a matter of fact, you are sacrificing what you claim you are doing.

A year or so ago you were told to have patience, to hide your faces, take it easy, then we have a change in administration and the new administration tells us we should have a cooling-off period.[9] The Emancipation Proclamation was adopted in 1863; it is now 1961. A cooling-off period? We've been in the deep freeze for ninety-eight years and somebody tells us to cool off. In the segregation problem, we've been cooling off since '54. We have 6 percent of the Negro children in the South integrated. Six percent in six years. Cooling off? We've cooled off. I'm afraid that there are people that don't understand it. I think there are more people

8. A similar question was posed in 1929 by Robert Russia Motion, president of Tuskegee Institute. He wrote: "Meanwhile nothing can contribute more toward the permanent establishment of our national welfare than the continued effort to realize for the humblest in our national life, whether black or white, that full measure of justice and equal opportunity for which America stands as a symbol before all the world." ROBERT RUSSIA MOTION, WHAT THE NEGRO THINKS 266–267 (1929).

9. Michael Lind reports that "When President Kennedy delayed his promise to abolish segregation with the stroke of a pen, for example, liberal critics sent him pens in the mail." Michael Lind, *Dream on, Democrats*, U.S. NEWS & WORLD REPORT, Aug. 4, 1997, at 28.

that have got to realize it. That's all very fine—this cooling-off period and taking it easy. We're not down on our knees begging for a handout or for charity. We're demanding our constitutional rights.

There is no cooling-off period to your rights. You either have them or you don't have them. You either have them now or you never have them. There is no constitutional right that says in the future. There is no constitution that delineated the rights. From the United States Constitution to every state constitution I've read and every law, but every one of them I've ever seen starts off with, We, the People. I have yet to see a constitution that starts off we, the Son of the People. I haven't seen one yet, maybe somebody's got one. These rights are there. We're not asking the President of the U.S., we're not asking the Congress, we're not asking the courts, we're not asking the states for a handout or something that we are not entitled to. We are simply saying that as American citizens, this is our right; we are entitled to it and the right itself says that we are entitled to it now. That means that even if you didn't agree with the decision in 1954,[10] even if you didn't agree with the decision of 1955,[11] certainly by 1961, the poor sharecropper's child in Mississippi is entitled to an integrated education and on the day he asks for it, not some years later. You won't find anybody who will stand up to it. Let's don't rock the boat. Let's don't embarrass the State Department and our statesmen when they negotiate with other countries. Let's don't embarrass the President when he goes to Europe. That came out all during the Freedom Rides.[12]

Honest to goodness. You know that bus, the burning bus in Anniston, Alabama was on the front page of every newspaper in the world.[13] So help me. The Freedom Riders didn't burn that bus, so help me they didn't. Now, who is creating this bad atmosphere overseas? It's not the Negro. So they say, wait a while. Wait how long and for what? Wait to start all over again or wait until the other side decides to do right? If

---

10. Brown I , *supra* note 6.
11. Brown v. Board of Education, 347 U.S. 483 (1955) (Brown II).
12. The Congress of Racial Equality "is a civil rights organization formed in 1942 to desegregate public facilities. Of its most notable demonstration was the 'Freedom Rides' during which two interracial groups of students rode buses together across several states." Brenda D. Di Luigi, *The Notari Alternative: A Better Approach to the Square-Peg-Round-Hole Problem Found in Reverse Discrimination Cases*, 64 BROOK. L. REV. 353, 359 n. 35 (1998). *See also* AUGUST MEIER AND ELLIOT M. RUDWICK, CORE: A STUDY IN THE CIVIL RIGHTS MOVEMENT 1942–1968, 135–145 (1973). The Freedom Rides and other protests "contributed to the collapse of Southern segregation." Harold A. McDougall, *Social Movements, Law, and Implementation: A Clinical Dimension for the New Legal Process*, 75 CORNELL L. REV. 83, 105 (1989).
13. Jerry Brown, *Major Events in the Civil Rights Movement*, ST. LOUIS POST-DISPATCH, May 18, 1997, at 6B.

there is anybody in this audience who can conscientiously say that he or she is willing to wait until Senator [James O.] Eastland decides to give Negroes their rights in Mississippi please stand up. What do you mean wait? Wait for what? Patience for what? I think that we have to take the position that good people in this country have to save the conscience of this country and if the country is embarrassed in the meantime, so what? Nobody thinks any more of this country than the Negroes do. They better. There's no place else for them to go.

I suggest that we have waited long enough. We have been patient long enough. I think that in every town, in every hamlet, in the South, every single person, Negroes in each community between now and September insist that their children be transferred into the new white schools. It should be done in every place. There is no longer any time to wait for voluntary compliance. Voluntary compliance is run out. The only way you can get your rights from here in is to insist upon them. Present it to them and if they refuse, get yourself a lawyer and go to court. I would like to see it done in every town and hamlet because I am firmly convinced that there are people on both sides of the fence, those who believe in segregation and those who want integration and that the great majority of the people in this country today don't believe that Negroes actually want it. There is only one way to show them and that is to present yourself. One word of caution; don't wait until all other Negroes agree to go because you'll never go. Each individual goes. This is a matter of personal conscience. . . .

The Courts

My hope here is to point up some of the ways in which the courts have contributed in the past—and may continue to contribute in the future—to realizing the twin goals of our society: liberty under law and equality before it.

The first point I wish to make, however, is the extent to which the federal courts are not wholly free to engage in the task of molding a freer or more democratic society. In the lower federal courts our task in the overwhelming majority of cases is to give effect to the wishes and intentions of the bodies that enacted the laws we must apply, insofar as we can discern them. Where the question concerns state law, we must look to the state legislatures and the state court decisions construing the acts of these legislatures. Where federal law is involved, we must seek to ascertain what Congress would have us do in the cases where the action involves construction of the statutes, subject of course to the binding interpretations of the Supreme Court on those matters; in cases where even the federal law is primarily judge-made, we are also bound by the Supreme Court decisions.

As my colleague, Judge Henry J. Friendly, pointed out recently, the unsystematized profusion of federal statutes governing a great variety of matters, and the often confusing and imprecise language in which they are framed, create enough problems of interpretation to keep any judge well-occupied, and well-frustrated, without his ever getting a chance to deal with more transcendent matters.[1] I do not minimize the discretionary element involved for judges in any formulation they may make of a rule of law, whether or not it is in the guise of a "statutory interpretation"; to do so would be to ignore what every important legal thinker has

This article appeared in the Center for Study of Democratic Institutions, *The Mazes of Modern Government* 34 (1964). At the time, Marshall was a judge on the U.S. Court of Appeals, Second Circuit.
1. Henry J. Friendly was the Chief Judge of the Second Circuit Court of Appeals for twenty-seven years. *See Tribute to Henry J. Friendly*, 132 CONG. REC. E792 (March 13, 1986); Richard A. Posner, *In Memoriam: Henry J. Friendly*, 99 HARV. L. REV. 1724 (1986).

been saying for the past four decades. The general language in which a statute is usually framed can never be said with absolute certainty to apply to particular cases. Ambiguities are inescapable, and to resolve them the judge must often look to his own values and his own concept of a better society as well as to the manifestations of intent on the part of those who framed the general rule.

My predecessor on the Second Circuit bench, Judge Learned Hand, put matters this way: "When a judge tries to find out what the government would have intended which it did not say, he puts into its mouth things which he thinks it ought to have said, and that is very close to substituting what he himself thinks right. . . . Nobody does this exactly right; great judges do it better than the rest of us. It is necessary that someone shall do it, if we are to realize the hope that we can collectively rule ourselves."[2]

In many instances, the interests that the judge will take into account are included among our democratic concepts, but they are not the only interests to be weighed and they are not always discernible. To take a concrete example, I do not think we can say that the notion of a more equitable distribution of risk of personal harm in industrial operations, which lies at the foundation of the many federal court decisions liberalizing the rules that govern recovery for personal injury, has anything to do with democracy or liberty, though it has much to do with one's concept of a fairer society.

Furthermore, it is important to remember that in all the areas where the courts act, so to speak, as the agent of Congress or of some other body, our determinations, insofar as they constitute rules of law, are subject to reversal by that body. This is obvious when the question is one of statutory interpretation; it is less obvious but equally true in many cases involving constitutional interpretation. For example, a great body of law has grown up under the authority of the commerce clause of the Constitution restricting the powers of the states to regulate business that has interstate characteristics. These cases have often held state laws invalid as an intrusion on reserved federal authority, which is paramount even though there is no applicable federal regulation. Yet Congress could, if it wishes, reject this entire approach simply by passing enabling legislation pursuant to its power under the same clause.

Another example of this are the cases, more famous than numerous, in which the courts have refused to sanction acts done under the express command of the President. The most noteworthy example is *Youngstown Sheet and Tube Co. v. Sawyer*,[3] in which both federal district court and the

2. Learned Hand, The Spirit of Liberty 109–110 (1954).
3. 343 U.S. 579 (1952).

Supreme Court held President Truman's seizure of the steel mills unconstitutional. Had the seizure been authorized by Congressional legislation, there could have been no question of its legality; without such sanction, the President was simply an officer acting without legal authority and, as such, subject to judicial correction under long-established principles.

Having said this, I must of course hastily add that, under the American system of constitutional government, there are areas in which the courts do have an obligation to make an independent, and binding, decision that governmental power may not be exercised in certain cases, regardless of the fact that legislative approval has been given. Here we get into the different problem of *judicial review*, with all it implies as a qualification of the principle that the majority, acting through its elected representatives, ought to be able to effectuate its desire.

I have no desire to enter the debate over the justifications to be found for this peculiarly American institution of judicial review, which has been the subject of discussion in recent years by such giants of the courts as Robert Jackson, Hugo Black, Felix Frankfurter, and Learned Hand and such scholars as Eugene Rostow, Herbert Wechsler, Charles L. Black, and Alexander Bickel, among others. Let me simply say that, like all these men, I believe that the propriety of federal judicial invalidation of state legislation is unassailable as a matter of constitutional logic, textual exegesis, and history. It would be impossible to maintain a system of supreme federal law, demanded by Article VI of the Constitution,[4] without a means of ensuring a uniform interpretation of that law throughout the states. The only practical way of assuring this is by providing access to a federal forum, which can finally resolve questions of interpretation.

It is precisely this aspect of judicial review, which is under attack in the most vocal manner. I find it difficult to believe that any of the opponents have ever given even slight attention to the consequences of their position. If any have, I find it difficult to believe that their arguments are made in good faith. With regard to judicial review of federal enactments, I feel that its legitimacy, if not absolutely assured, is certainly strengthened by the fact that both the original Constitution and the Bill of Rights contain express prohibitions of certain laws. If these are to be regarded as anything more than mere exhortations, the courts have a strong claim to be able to give them the force of law in appropriate instances. This process will inevitably result in some instances of so-called "judicial supremacy," not strictly compatible with the usual pattern of representative government. But where the power is exercised in the name of

4. Article VI, Sec. 2 states: "This Constitution, and the Laws of the United States which shall be made in pursuance thereof . . . shall be the Supreme Law of the Land; and the Judges in every State shall be bound by Oath or Affirmation, to support this Constitution."

personal liberty, the price is not too high to pay. Protection of the great values set down in the Bill of Rights and the Fourteenth Amendment as they have come to be interpreted is a task of sufficient importance in our society that some interference with the will of the legislature, done in a prudent and principled manner, can and should be tolerated and expected.

Thus far, I have been discussing the general question of the role of the courts—important though limited—in affirming, furthering, and promoting the values we most cherish. How is this function exercised in actual cases? As Alexander Bickel remarked in his book, *The Least Dangerous Branch*, the effort to "view the functions as a whole without examining the process . . . is absurd, except as one may find it convenient for analytical purposes."[5] Consequently, I would like now to discuss a few of the specific areas in which the courts, especially the Supreme Court, have been instrumental in recent years in deepening the understanding and promoting the acceptance of values that are of crucial importance in the democratic tradition.

In an article in the *Atlantic*,[6] my colleague, Judge Irving R. Kaufman, identified four of the areas in which recent Supreme Court decisions have had most important influence in this process: the decisions regarding racial segregation, legislative apportionment, religious activity in public schools, and procedural due process in state criminal prosecutions.[7] Add to this list the court's numerous decisions interpreting the First Amendment guarantees of freedom of speech and press and the implicit guarantee of free association, and I suppose we have a fairly complete catalogue of the areas in which judicial decisions have been most influential in the continuing struggle to preserve and promote individual liberty and equality for all under the law.

Judge Kaufman distinguishes the racial equality and reapportionment decisions from the school prayer and criminal law decisions on the ground that, in the first two areas, the Court's decisions might be said to reflect an already existing widespread consensus that something ought to be done that was not being done by any other branch of the government, for various unsatisfactory reasons, whereas, in the second group, the Court's opinions have not been crystallizations of public opinion but rather attempts to guide and mold it; in these, the Court has served as

5. ALEXANDER BICKEL, THE LEAST DANGEROUS BRANCH: THE SUPREME COURT AT THE BAR OF POLITICS 34 (1962). The principle asserted is when the political institution insists upon an unprincipled course of action, the court should not approve it.
6. Irving R. Kaufman, *The Supreme Court and Its Critics*, ATL. MONTHLY 50 (Dec. 1963).
7. *Id.*

a voice not of contemporary opinion but of communal conscience, or, in Chief Justice Hughes; phrase, as "teachers to the citizenry."[8]

I should like to explore in some detail two of these areas: racial equality and state criminal procedures. My reasons for selecting these are, first, I am most familiar with them as the result of my career in practice; second, the standards and approach of the Court are more clearly defined because of the large number of cases it has decided in these fields.

At this time, when much attention is paid—most properly and justly—to what lies ahead in the struggle for *racial equality*, it is helpful to look back to the road already traveled. Just twenty-five years ago, in the states of the union where most Negroes then lived, their lives were constricted by a whole series of state-imposed and state-fostered laws and regulations designed to foreclose them from participation in the political process and to erect high barriers to their attaining any sort of social or economic equality. Since then, the federal courts—and very nearly they alone—have completely removed the legal justification for any form of state-required, state-supported, or state-inspired racial discrimination. The result obtains whether the locus is voting in primary elections, education at any level, interstate or local transportation, public recreational facilities, or facilities on any state property.

To be sure, the illegality of school segregation, to take the most conspicuous and most important example, has not yet led to statistically significant progress toward desegregation in many areas. There are several reasons for this: the necessity of bringing suit before any of the districts in many states will begin desegregation; the room for delay intentionally built into the decree in *Brown v. Board of Education*;[9] the evasive and dilatory, often desperately defiant, tactics adopted by many state officials and local school boards; and a certain reluctance of some Negro citizens to jeopardize their own position by moving vigorously to upset the established social order. This last factor in particular is of rapidly diminishing importance, particularly among the young. In addition, the federal courts in the affected states are becoming less and less tolerant of delay in implementing desegregation. The road ahead is still long and rocky, but there can be no doubt of the ultimate destination.

What is even more important than the specific progress in eradicating the last legal barriers to the achievement of racial and political equality is the impetus the courts have given to the broad-scale assault on all

8. Justices Charles Evans Hughes and Louis D. Brandeis believed that "[b]oth the pettiest details and the broadest concepts of government have come within the judicial ambit. Ideally, the modern judge should be . . . a master of both microscope and telescope." Irving R. Kaufman, *Chilling Judicial Independence*, 88 YALE L.J. 681, 686 and n. 39 (1979).
9. 349 U.S. 294 (1955) (Brown II).

forms of racial discrimination, private as well as public, North as well as South, which is now in progress. It is a commonplace, none the less true for being so, that more progress has been made here in the less than ten years since the *Brown* decision than in the entire century before.[10] What makes one uneasy, of course, is the truly awesome magnitude of what has yet to be done. It would be erroneous to claim that the progress is wholly the result of the stronger meaning that the federal courts have given to the equal protection clause. As Judge Kaufman pointed out, a broadly based consensus has existed for some time that the amelioration of the condition of Negroes and other minority groups is one of the great unfinished pieces of social business for Americans.[11] However, it remains true that in a society where the language of a written Constitution enjoys such overwhelming dignity the impetus that the courts have given to transforming a moral duty into a constitutional imperative is of great importance and value.

With regard to *de facto* segregation, and the function that litigation in the federal courts may have in combating it, I will point out only that it is rooted in widespread habits and attitudes which cannot be overturned by judicial decree as readily as the naked language of statutes and ordinances. The problem is obviously far less susceptible to legal correction than was legally enforced segregation. This is especially true as a federal constitutional matter, for the Fourteenth Amendment pertains only to action by the states. On the other hand, in a great many areas, segregation policies can be enforced only with the help of legal protections extended by the state; in other areas, persons who discriminate have received state-conferred benefits.

Under the extended view of "state action" suggested by *Shelley v. Kraemer,*[12] and applied in such more recent cases as *Burton v. Wilmington Parking Authority*[13] and *Peterson v. City of Greenville,*[14] which prohibits the employment of state power to sanction private acts of discrimination, a considerable segment of private activity may be encompassed within the Fourteenth Amendment prohibition. And if the Supreme Court reverses the convictions in the sit-in cases now pending before it, on the constitutional grounds argued by the petitioners, the range of the Fourteenth Amendment would be broader still.[15] The usefulness of litigation founded on the Constitution has not been exhausted by its victories so far, though

10. 347 U.S. 483 (1954) (Brown I).
11. *Supra* note 6.
12. 334 U.S. 1 (1948).
13. 365 U.S. 715 (1961).
14. 373 U.S. 244 (1963).
15. *See* Peterson v. City of Greenville, 373 U.S. 244 (1963); Lombard v. Louisiana, 373 U.S. 267 (1963); Robinson v. Florida, 378 U.S. 153 (1964).

there is no gainsaying the fact that a far larger role must now be played by legislation, executive action, and public persuasion if the injustice and social waste inherent in racial discrimination are to be eliminated.

Comparison of the work of the federal courts in fostering the fair conduct of *state criminal proceedings* with their work in forging the equal protection clause into a meaningful weapon in the struggle against racial inequality involves a number of similarities and a number of important differences. Among the similarities is the far from accidental circumstance that both are largely a product of the modern era in constitutional adjudication, when emphasis has shifted dramatically from the protection of business enterprise against governmental restriction to the protection of what are usually termed "human rights." Again, in both cases, the courts have been asked to weigh claims put forward in the name of the constitution by litigants whose strength in the popular, political arena has usually been weak. The meaning of this is obvious in the case of racial segregation; in the criminal area, I do not mean to suggest that a trial is in any way a political function but simply to point out that the federal courts, in exercising a continuing scrutiny over the processes of state justice, will generally be involved in a publicly thankless task.

This suggests, however, a point of important difference between the two areas. There is nothing inherent, especially in the American system, that demands the permanent exclusion of Negroes or any other group from political power, and indeed we see today a steadily increasing trend toward their full participation in the rights and duties of citizenship. On the other hand, the cause of persons accused of crime, however much protection it may receive in legal theory, is inherently one that is unattractive to the popular mind, and the rights they receive are in constant danger of erosion. This is particularly true in the United States, where a pattern of public tolerance of brutal police practices, mob violence, and grossly unfair trial procedure has existed in many places, as a sort of dark underside to the noble pronouncements of the Bill of Rights. And yet I think there are few who would deny that an impeccably fair process of criminal justice is one of the values that lies closest to the core of any free society, simply because the power asserted by government against a convicted criminal is so great as to dwarf any others it exercises.

Chief Justice [Earl] Warren put the matter well in *Coppedge v. United States*,[16] when he said: "When society acts to deprive one of its members of his life, liberty or property, it takes its most awesome steps. No general respect for, nor adherence to, the law as a whole can well be expected without judicial recognition of the paramount need for prompt, eminently fair and sober criminal law procedures. The methods we employ

16. 369 U.S. 438 (1961).

in the enforcement of our criminal law have aptly been called the measures by which the quality of our civilization may be judged."[17]

Furthermore, if the words "nor shall any state deprive any person of life, liberty or property, without due process of law"[18] mean anything, they would surely seem to refer at least to criminal trials and demand the formulation of federal standards of "due process." It is not much of a distance from this to the idea, now firmly fixed in our law, that "due process" means "fundamental fairness," at every stage of a criminal proceeding. Influenced by these circumstances, and by the idea that certain provisions of the Bill of Rights are themselves declaratory of and inherent in the notion of fundamental fairness, the federal courts in the past three decades, again following the Supreme Court, have fashioned an impressive structure of protections to which an accused in any court is entitled, whatever his offense.

Among the most important principles are that an accused may not be convicted through the use of a confession found to be involuntary, or through the use of evidence obtained through illegal, unreasonable search and seizure; and that a conviction based on knowingly perjured testimony or false testimony not corrected at the trial, or a conviction where the prosecution has suppressed material evidence favorable to an accused, may not stand. Nor, of course, is a conviction constitutionally valid where racial discrimination has influenced the composition of either the grand or petit jury. Under the important *Gideon* case[19] decided last term, an indigent person must be provided trial counsel unless he affirmatively and intelligently waives the right after being apprised of it.

We have also had indications from the Supreme Court that in some cases at least, where important federal rights are claimed, questions of whether there is evidence to support a verdict and whether error in the admission of evidence may be deemed harmless are federal questions. In addition to the formulation of standards of fair play under the due process clause, the judiciary has been concerned to assure an opportunity for indigent defendants to obtain the same measure of justice in such matters as appeal and state post-conviction remedies as those who are able to pay the fees normally required.

Paralleling this development of a defendant's constitutional rights at the trial and appeal stages has come an expansion of the way in which federal questions may be raised. The chief instrumentality is the writ of *habeas corpus*, which by statute may be sought by persons alleging that they are in custody in violation of the constitution or laws of the United

17. *Id.* at 449.
18. *See* Fifth Amendment of the Bill of Rights, U.S. Constitution.
19. Gideon v. Wainwright, 372 U.S. 335 (1963).

States. It has been clear for about a decade that the federal courts on a writ of *habeas corpus* may consider federal questions even if the state courts have considered them at the trial, in order to determine the correctness of the legal standard used in passing on the claim and the application of that standard to the facts on which the claim is based.

Two Supreme Court decisions last term have gone further in assuring access to a federal forum for a prisoner with a constitutional claim. In one, it was held that the rule that state remedies must be exhausted before federal *habeas corpus* is permitted does not require dismissal of a petition even if a state remedy that had once been available was lost through lapse of time or otherwise.[20] As an example, the failure to take an appeal from a judgment of conviction will not necessarily bar a prisoner in custody from applying for *habeas corpus*, although the failure may be considered by the federal court in passing on the merits of the petition. In the other case, the Court spelled out fairly specific guides for federal district court judges to follow in deciding whether to grant a hearing on a petition for *habeas corpus* rather than dismiss it summarily.[21] The effect of the decision will be to require hearings in more cases than has previously been common.

Both these decisions represent a judgment that, in the words of the *Harvard Law Review*, "the interest in achieving finality in criminal proceedings is to be valued less highly than the interest in assuring that no individual is deprived of life or liberty in violation of the Constitution."[22] Reasonable men certainly can and do differ over the correctness of a decision, say, that a particular confession was obtained under circumstances amounting to mental or psychological coercion, and, indeed, over the general advisability of a system that seems to set up two almost independent systems of review of constitutional claims. Ideally, of course, the state courts themselves should have the primary responsibility of insuring that criminal defendants receive treatment in accordance with federal constitutional standards. However, as long as this is not always so—and I intend no disrespect to the many state court judges who are conscientiously striving to dispense the full measure of justice to which criminal defendants are entitled—I believe that the balance between finality and justice has been properly struck. Personal liberty is too vital a thing to be subject to deprivation save in accordance with the highest standards of fairness and decency.

The record of the federal judiciary in the area of criminal law enforcement, both federal and state, is the most striking example of its greatest

20. *See* Fay v. Noia, 372 U.S. 391, 415–420 (1963).
21. *See* Townsend v. Sain, 372 U.S. 293, 312–318 (1963).
22. Note, *The Supreme Court 1962 Term*, 77 HARV. L. REV. 62, 140 (1963).

function, which is the protection of individual liberties against the encroachments of governmental power. One of our highest achievements is surely that we have seen fit to establish and further this institution of deliberate self-restraint within the governmental process. It is most important for the courts to continue this work in an era when, both at home and abroad; individual freedoms are placed in increasing jeopardy by the pressures of a mass society.

Let me end with the words of Mr. Justice Brandeis, dissenting in *Olmstead v. United States*:[23] "Decency, security, and liberty alike demand that government officials shall be subjected to the same rules of conduct that are commands to the citizen. In a government of laws, existence of the government will be imperilled if it fails to observe the law scrupulously. Our government is the potent, the omnipresent, teacher. For good or for ill, it teaches the whole people by its example. Crime is contagious. If the government becomes a law-breaker, it breeds contempt for law; it invites every man to become a law unto him; it invites anarchy. To declare that in the administration of the criminal law the end justifies the means—to declare that the government may commit crimes in order to secure the conviction of a private criminal—would bring terrible retribution."[24]

23. 277 U.S. 438 (1928).
24. *Id.* at 485.

The Impact of the Constitution
and Panel Discussion

Thank you, Mr. Steinberg, Ladies, and Gentlemen.

I was just sitting here, wondering whom you were talking about. I notice you mentioned Ralph Bunche and Martin Luther King, along with me. There's a slight difference. Both of them have received Nobel Peace Prizes totaling $56,000 apiece, and I'll be very glad to show you my income tax return.

Thurgood Marshall Collection, Library of Congress, Box 3, Folder 8, Miscellan. "G." Before the Greater Hartford Forum, Fall 1964. Introduction by Joseph L. Steinberg: "When the West was settled, they said the great American frontier had closed. And with it, they said, we had completed the inventory of all out nation's great resources. Quietly, the men who opened those new frontiers, Fremont, Lewis, and Clark, disappeared from the scene, hailed as the last of a pioneering breed. Yet it was during our decade that a new frontier was opened. Such men as Roy Wilkins, Martin Luther King, and Whitney Young took on the pioneer's mantle, took on a new crusade to liberate a dormant national resource. Gems had been uncovered and hailed as precious national treasures, such as Ralph Bunche and Robert Weaver. But a much greater field of treasures lay locked below the surface, imprisoned by tradition, stifled by fear. Some crusaders proposed blasting the impediments to free the assets. But the pioneers, forsaking force, turned to a legal engineer—a man of singular skill. And in a series of maneuvers, each carefully calculated to undermine that suffocating tradition, their legal engineer peacefully procured expanded voting powers, transportation rights, and housing privileges. Then, on May 14, 1954, the Supreme Court of the United States, in answer to a brief prepared under his direction, and in response to his brilliant oral presentation, decreed that racial segregation in public schools was unconstitutional. A new frontier! Assets beyond our nation's dreams had been uncovered. The children of 25 million people were free of the stifling discrimination that denied our country the power of their potential. And by dedicating his ability to his people's aspirations and his nation's needs, by exposing that ability to the flames of intense controversy, his skills crystallized . . . and the battle itself produced still another national gem. An honor graduate of Baltimore's Douglass High School, a *cum laude* graduate of Pennsylvania's Lincoln University, and a magna cum laude graduate of the Howard University School of Law, our guest now sits as a member of one of the highest courts and most universally respected." Judge Steinberg sat on the Middlesex County Superior Court in Middlesex, Hartford, Connecticut. See Marlene Clark, *Middletown Judge Has Masterful Approach to Mediating Custody Disputes,* HARTFORD COURANT, May 19, 1997, at B1.

I am thoroughly appreciative of the nice things you said about me, but I've never been able to take things without putting them into complete perspective, and I'll take the fine things you've said about me along with what was said during the eleven months while my nomination was pending in the Senate by some of the southern Senators, and I'll put them in the scales and weigh them, half and half, and the odds are I'll come out just exactly who I am and where I stand.

Seriously, though, what we have to talk about tonight, in the past ten years, or so, I've been traveling to Africa, Europe, Asia, etc., and I've tried to figure just what our government had to be proud of in the field of civil rights and civil liberties. And what I have to say tonight is my most recent evaluation of just what we have to be proud of. I start with our government, and I'm going to put emphasis on the courts.

The Supreme Court has always played a paramount role in deepening the understanding and promoting the acceptance of values that are of critical importance to our society. The Court's special concern and focus has shifted throughout our constitutional history; and each Court has found itself, either through accident or deliberate choice, identified with safeguarding and protecting and promoting certain basic values. Chief Justice [John] Marshall, for example, conceived of the mission of his Court as consolidating the growth of the federal power and establishing the constitutional foundations of American federalism. And it seems to me that the Supreme Court of our generation, roughly delineated in time by the appointment of Chief Justice [Charles Evans] Hughes and then of Chief Justice [Earl] Warren. That court has also emerged with a special mission—the protection of human rights, or more particularly the fulfillment of the constitutional promise of equality and the correction of federal and state criminal proceedings to assure that no individual is deprived of life or liberty in violation of the Constitution.

The Supreme Court's first major effort to fulfill the promise of equality consisted of the response to the struggle for racial equality. Just twenty-five years ago, in the states of the nation where most Negroes then lived, their lives were constricted by a whole series of state-imposed and state-fostered laws and regulations designed to foreclose them from participation in the political process and to erect high barriers to their attaining any sort of social or economic equality. Since then, the Supreme Court has completely removed the legal justification for any form of state-required, state-supported, or state-inspired racial discrimination. The same result obtains whether the locus is voting in primary elections, registration, education at any level, interstate or local transportation, public recreational facilities, or facilities on any state property.

To be sure, the illegality of school segregation, to take the most conspicuous and most important example, has not yet led to statistically significant progress towards desegregation in many areas. There are several reasons for this: The necessity of bringing suit before any of the districts in many states will begin desegregation; the room for delay intentionally built into the decree of the Supreme Court in those cases (*Brown v. Board of Education*);[1] the evasive and dilatory, often desperately defiant, tactics adopted by many state officials and local school boards; and a certain reluctance of some Negro citizens to jeopardize their own security by moving vigorously to upset the established social order in their community. This last factor in particular is of rapidly diminishing importance, particularly among the young. In addition, the federal courts in the affected states are becoming less and less tolerant of delay in implementing desegregation. The road ahead is still long and rocky, but there can be no doubt of the ultimate destination.

The Supreme Court has also sought to fulfill the constitutional promise of equality in the reapportionment cases (I understand you have some problems with this in Connecticut). The equality that emerged from these cases could be deemed a political equality. I read these cases as standing for the proposition that in the most important processes in a democracy, elections, the political power that all men must be equal, that each is entitled to the same political power, one vote. This proposition can be derived from the equalitarian premises underlying the Fourteenth and Fifteenth Amendments, or from the fundamental tenets of a political democracy. The difficulty with the reapportionment cases stems not from a refusal to embrace the goal of political equality, but rather from the embarrassing fact that we have become so accustomed to settling for half, malapportionment has become woven into the pattern of the familiar. The Supreme Court found itself as the institution most capable of fulfilling the promise of political equality, and it took the necessary and far-reaching steps.

Racial equality and political equality have been the two most pronounced themes in the Supreme Court's efforts to fulfill the constitutional promise of equality. I now want to turn to a third dimension of this equality, and that, in my opinion, represents a "new frontier" in constitutional law—economic equality. The philosophic roots of this aspect of equality have best been expressed by the late Justice [Robert H.] Jackson in his separate concurrence in Edwards v. California[2], where the Court was confronted with a state law prohibited the "bringing" or transportation of indigent persons into California. The majority held the law unconstitutional as a violation of the commerce clause, but Justice Jackson, although reaching the same result, saw the problem in a

1. Brown v. Board of Education, 347 U.S. 483 (1954).
2. Edwards v. California, 314 U.S. 160 (1941).

different light. He wrote: "Does 'indigence' as defined by the application of the California statute constitute a basis for restricting the freedom of a citizen, as crime or contagion warrants its restriction? We should say now, and in no uncertain terms, that a man's mere property status, without more, cannot be used by a state to test, qualify, or limit his rights as a citizen of the United States. 'Indigence' in itself is neither a source of rights nor a basis for denying them. The mere state of being without funds is a neutral fact—constitutionally an irrelevance, like race, creed, or color."[3]

There are, of course, difficulties of working with this unrefined principle. First, indigence may in some circumstances be within the control of the individual to eliminate or to correct; the peculiar ugliness of racial discrimination stems in part from the fact that an individual is being judged on the basis of qualities over which he has no control. However, as Justice Jackson so correctly perceived, there are many situations where the economic status of being an indigent is as far beyond the control or free choice of an individual as being white or Negro, or being born of Jewish or Protestant parents.

The second difficulty of working with Justice Jackson's unrefined principle of economic equality stems from the fact that few laws explicitly limit or restrict the liberties and privileges of the indigent, although in fact they may place this unequal burden on the indigent. For example, a state may require of all persons seeking an appeal in a criminal cases that a transcript of the proceedings below be docketed; for the indigent the cost involved in preparing and docketing the transcript may work to deprive him, but not the rich man, of his right to review. In 1956, in *Griffin v. Illinois*,[4] the Supreme Court faced this very situation and ultimately realized the irony in the reflection that "The law in all its majesty treats the rich and poor alike; both are forbidden to sleep on the park benches."[5]

Although Justice Jackson may have been the first to articulate this dimension of economic equality, and he did so in 1941, the principle remained dormant for some time, and it is only within recent years that the principle has begun to flourish. So far, the concern has been almost exclusively with the rights of the indigents in the criminal process, and understandably so. It should have been added years ago, when the statement was made, that every man had his day in court, "He's entitled to his day in court, if he can afford it." For it is in these processes that the full force of governmental power comes to be applied to an individual in the

3. *Id.* at 184 (Douglas, J., concurring).
4. Griffin v. Illinois, 351 U.S. 12 (1956).
5. *Id.* at 23 (Frankfurter, J., concurring).

most direct fashion. The concern today is to employ legal tools other than the equal protection clause, such as the due process clause and the panoply of rights incorporated into that clause. For example, in *Gideon v. Wainwright*,[6] the Supreme Court saw the accused's constitutional right to counsel as the basis for requiring states to furnish the indigent accused the assistance of appointed counsel.[7] In so doing, the Supreme Court removed one of the most basic inequalities that an indigent must suffer. The notion of economic equality is still germinating; but in a short time many of the traditional institutions, such as bail, will have to be reexamined in terms of whether it falls short of constitutional promise of economic equality.

I have briefly outlined the contours of the problem of realizing the basic equalitiarian goal of our society and suggested that the three principal areas have been racial equality, political equality, and economic equality. But for the most part, it seems to me that the Supreme Court has been the institution most responsible for realizing this constitutional promise, and I think that the time has been reached when this responsibility must be shared by other American institutions. The Supreme Court has been forced into "the center of the storm" partly because few other institutions have made the Supreme Court's "special mission" their mission.

First, it would seem that the lower federal courts and all the state courts must make some affirmative responses to the guidelines established by the Supreme Court. Often some of these other courts have persistently dragged their feet, and have taken appropriate action only after the Supreme Court has specifically reversed them. This only makes the Supreme Court's task more difficult, it has impaired the smooth functioning of our judicial system, and it has resulted in waste of intellectual and economic resources. Of course, there are exceptions. In some areas of the United States, the lower federal courts and state courts have done their part, and it could be said in most parts of the country that the courts have responded affirmatively to the mandate of the reapportionment cases. It would not be too much to hope for a similar response in the areas of racial equality and economic equality.

Secondly, it seems enormously important that governmental institutions other than the courts become engaged in the task of fulfilling the constitutional promise of equality. I am particularly addressing myself to the state and federal legislatures, supposedly the most representative and democratic of all our political institutions. I consider it as one of the great tragedies of our political history that it was the courts and not

6. Gideon v. Wainwright, 372 U.S. 335 (1963).
7. *Id.* at 344.

these more representative institutions that had to take the initial and most important step towards the realization of constitutional equality. It must be remembered that legislators, as well as judges, take an oath to uphold and support the Constitution. The value of having these representative institutions becoming involved in the achievement of equality cannot be overestimated: The solution worked out by a legislature has the appeal inherent in any negotiated or consensual solution of a problem; the solution is likely to have deeper and more widespread roots in the community; and the legislature has a greater spectrum of remedies available to it, and these remedies are likely to be more imaginative, more flexible, and more effective. One can understand why a legislature that itself suffers from malapportionment is not likely to initiate the reform; it may well put some of the legislators out of a job. However, I have less sympathy with legislature inertia and paralysis in the fields of racial equality and economic equality. To be sure, Congress' effort in the Civil Rights Act of 1964, and the Criminal Justice Act, providing for the appointment of counsel for indigents being tried in federal courts, cannot and should not be belittled. However, this action was long overdue, and so much remains to be done, that I am sure that it would not be inappropriate for me to challenge to the legislatures to now become the paramount "teachers of citizenry."

Thirdly, it seems to me that, even if the courts and legislatures become deeply involved in the achievement of equality in America, they can make but a small contribution toward that ultimate goal. The courts are principally restricted to the interpretation and application of statutes and the Constitution, and there is a limit to what can be done by the executive and legislative branches of government. A great unfinished job will always remain if we come to rely exclusively on the agencies of government. It is imperative that what has become the special mission the Supreme Court—the fulfillment of the promise of equality—become the special mission of every American as a citizen, as a member of a trade union, or a corporate executive, as a member of a parent-teachers association, as a parent, or as an individual. There may be little to what can be done in achieving racial equality and economic equality. The courts have given an impetus to be a broadscale assault on all forms of discrimination, private as well as public, North as well as South, that is now in progress. And it is commonplace that more progress has been made in the achievement of equality in the ten years since the Brown decision than in the entire century before. What makes one uneasy, however, is the truly awesome magnitude of what has yet to be done.

I would now like to turn to another aspect of the Supreme Court's effort to protect basic human rights: Seeing that the human rights guaranteed by the Constitution are not violated in a criminal proceeding.

The causes of persons accused of crime, however much protection it may receive in legal theory, is inherently one that is unattractive to the popular mind, and the rights they receive are in constant danger of erosion. This is particularly true in the United States where a pattern of public tolerance of brutal police practices, mob violence, and grossly unfair trial procedure has existed in many places, as a sort of dark underside of the noble pronouncements of the Bill of Rights. And yet I think there are few who would deny that an impeccably fair process of criminal justice is one of the values that lies closest to the core of any free society, simply because the power asserted by government against a convicted criminal is so great as to dwarf any others it exercises.

Chief Justice Warren put the matter well in *Coppedge v. United States*[8] when he said: "When Society acts to deprive one of its members of his life, liberty, or property, it takes its most awesome steps. No general respect for, nor adherence to, the law as a whole can well be expected without judicial recognition of the paramount need for prompt, eminently fair and sober criminal law procedures. The methods we employ in the enforcement of our criminal law have aptly been called the measures by which the quality of our civilization may be judged."[9]

Furthermore, if the words "nor shall any state deprive any person of life, liberty or property, without due process of law" means anything, they would surely seem to refer at least to criminal trails and demand the formulation of federal standards of "due process." It is not much of a distance from this to the idea, now firmly fixed in our law, that "due process" means "fundamental fairness," at every stage of a criminal proceeding. Influenced by these circumstances, and by the idea that certain provisions of the Bill of Rights are themselves declaratory of and inherent in the notion of fundamental fairness, the federal courts in the past three decades, again following the Supreme Court, have fashioned an impressive structure of protections to which an accused in any court is entitled, whatever his offense.

Among the most important principles are that an accused may not be convicted through the use of a confession found to be involuntary, or through the use of evidence obtained through illegal, unreasonable search and seizure; and that a conviction based on knowingly perjured testimony or false testimony not corrected at the trial, or a conviction where the prosecution has suppressed material evidence favorable to an accused, may not stand. Nor, of course, is a conviction constitutionally valid where racial discrimination has influenced the composition of either the grand or petit jury.

8. Coppedge v. United States, 369 U.S. 438 (1962).
9. *Id.* at 449.

We have also had indications from the Supreme Court that in some cases at least, where important federal rights are claimed, questions of whether there is evidence to support a verdict and whether error in the admission of evidence may be deemed harmless are federal questions. In *Gideon v. Wainwright*[10] the Supreme Court emphasized the need for counsel to insure fairness in a criminal proceeding, and last term, in *Escobedo v. Illinois*,[11] the Court extended this protection by holding that . . . "Where, . . . the investigation is no longer a general inquiry into an unsolved crime but has begun to focus on a particular suspect, the suspect has been taken into police custody, the police carry out a process of interrogations that lends itself to eliciting incriminating statements, the suspect has requested and been denied an opportunity to consult with his lawyer, and the police have not effectively warned him of his absolute constitutional right to remain silent, the accused has been denied 'the Assistance of Counsel' . . . and . . . no statement elicited by the police during the interrogation may be used against him at a criminal trial."[12]

The record of the federal judiciary in the area of criminal law enforcement, both federal and state, is one of the most striking examples of its greatest function, which is the protection of human rights against the encroachments of governmental power. One of our highest achievements is surely that we have seen fit to establish and further this institution of deliberate self-restraint within the governmental process. The public interest requires that the courts continue this work in an era when, both at home and abroad, human rights are placed in increasing jeopardy by the pressures of a mass society. This was expressed by Mr. Justice Brandeis dissenting in *Olmstead v. United States*,[13] and I would like to end with his words: "Decency, security, and liberty alike demand that government officials shall be subjected to the same rules of conduct that are commands to the citizen. In a government of laws, existence of the government will be imperiled if it fails to observe the law scrupulously. Our government is the potent, the omnipresent, teacher. For good or for ill, it teaches the whole people by its example. Crime is contagious. If the government becomes a lawbreaker, it breeds contempt for law; it invites every man to become a law unto himself; it invites anarchy. To declare that in the administration of the criminal law the end justifies the means—to declare that the government may commit crimes in order to secure the conviction of a private criminal—would bring terrible retribution."[14]

10. Gideon, *supra* note 6.
11. Escobedo v. Illinois, 378 U.S. 478, 490–91 (1964).
12. *Id.*
13. Olmstead v. United States, 277 U.S. 438 (1928).
14. *Id.* 485.

Panel Discussion After Judge Marshall's Speech

Panelists: Judge Thurgood Marshall; John Hamilton King, Chief Justice, Connecticut Supreme Court of Error; Robert Lucas, Editor, *Hartford Times*

Robert Lucas: Judge Marshall, you've taken note, and certainly it has been driven home to the people of this country in recent years, almost in recent months, that the trend of court decisions, Supreme Court decisions and subsequently, and obviously, the lower courts, toward renewed attention toward the rights of the accused. And in your very eloquent paper you made mention of the increased jeopardy of individual rights in our mass society. I'd like to ask you why, in your judgment, this increased attention to the rights of the accused, interwoven with the economic rights of the poor man in court, for example, and to be specific, why is this only but recently coming into focus? What took it so long to germinate?

Judge Marshall: Well, I think my own personal view would be on one particular matter—the use of illegally seized evidence in a trial. There were three or four cases that reached Supreme Court on that matter, before the *Mapp v. Ohio* decision,[15] and if you read those decisions carefully, you'll see that the Supreme Court with increasingly forceful language, told the States that "you should clean this up yourself," and only after the State failed to clean it up, over a period of some forty years, the Supreme Court decided, "Well, we'll just have to take it over." I think that the Supreme Court has consistently hoped that the States would give the type of due process that the Constitution requires. I think that's what has been holding it up.

Joseph L. Steinberg: Judge, I think that one of the primary questions, and certainly one that has been raised by the two speakers who preceded you, had to do with the balance that exists between the liberty of the individual and the needs of the community. I think the audience would appreciate having your opinion on whether or not the recent decisions of the Supreme Court of the United States have set this delicate balance into imbalance.

Judge Marshall: I don't know that there's too much to be balanced between the community and the individual. The constitution was set up to protect the individual rights. The old Bill of Rights was to protect the individual from the federal government. The Fourteenth Amendment was to protect the individual from oppressive state action. I believe that if we consider the rights of the individual to be tempered by the wishes of the immediate community, we destroy the effect of the Constitution.

Joseph L. Steinberg: Commissioner [Patrick] Murphy [of the New

15. Mapp v. Ohio, 367 U.S. 643 (1961).

York Police Department] said he used wire-tapping warrants issued by the New York Supreme Court, and that they could not be in conflict with Federal Communications Act or they would have been restricted. Are these warrants, in fact, in defiance of the Federal Communications Act, and if so, why has nothing been done to stop them?

Judge Marshall: I'm not in the enforcement end. I'm a judge. If such a case is presented to me, I'll apply the law to the facts, and then I'll make a decision.

Justice King: One of the problems, Judge Marshall, that flows from these new concepts, and I think you'll agree with Mr. Lucas that they are new, with the present group of members of the Supreme Court, in the matter of applying the right to counsel. Now, Connecticut is the fore-runner of our whole country in public defense. We have always allowed the public defender to use judgment in what appeals he should take and what he shouldn't. Now, of course this hasn't crystallized, but we're faced with the problem that the claim is made, and with some support, that under the theory of the Supreme Court of the United States, any appeal, however frivolous, however ill-founded, must be financed by the State (and when I say "financed," I'm not talking merely about the small cost of providing legal counsel—that's a few hundred dollars, by tying up court rooms, tying up judges), on the type of the thing doomed to failure before you start, because if you don't let the fellow do that, then in a sense you are censoring him, and controlling him, and it's as bad as it is for me to censor Mr. Lucas' newspaper, because my views are more or less going to be unconsciously imposed upon him.

Judge Marshall: Well, Judge, the only answer I can give: that's been the rule in the federal courts for quite a few years, and we've managed to live with it.

Justice King: Then you've had more luck than we, so far, in control-ling it through the right of withdrawal, haven't you?

Judge Marshall: No, in speaking just for the Second Circuit, which covers the states of New York, Connecticut, and Vermont, the Legal Aid Society will take any case on appeal that any convicted man asks to be taken up.

Justice King: Even though it's worthless.

Judge Marshall: Yes—you mean, in their opinion it's worthless.

Justice King: Well, nobody knows what a court will do.

Judge Marshall: The theory is, that if a person is completely and legally convicted, and he has money enough to hire a lawyer, he can appeal.

Justice King: The difference is, that while we get an equality of wealth, we don't get an equality in poverty. The man of means, it is true, can take a groundless appeal. But he isn't likely to do it, because he will have to pay through the nose to do it. But if he has nothing, and he's drawing a blank check on the taxpayers for the trip, he will be able to take ground-less appeal, and be glad to do it. There is no longer this equality. He is in the ascendancy. He's getting a free ride.

Judge Marshall: It's the same taxpayers who insisted upon putting him in jail.

Justice King: Of course, that presupposes that he didn't belong there.

Judge Marshall: Under our Constitution, he doesn't belong there until the last court has an opportunity to pass on it.

Justice King: I hadn't thought of it that way. I'd thought of it, after conviction. At the trial court level, if he were presumed guilty, unless and until that was changed, to carry it right through to the end.

Judge Marshall: We can't. We're required to judge with the evidence most favorable to the defendant.

Justice King: The judges, yes. But we're talking some other way tonight.

Judge Marshall: The only answer we can give is that statement I quoted tonight, about the equality between the wealthy man and the poor man being that neither are allowed to sleep on the park bench.

Robert Lucas: May I ask you a question? This question has come up several times in the two previous seminars, and I'm obviously sensitive to it, because I'm involved. I'd like to ask you, Judge, has it been [your] experience that pretrial publicity, by newspaper, radio, and television, has raised doubt in given instances of a defendant's ability to receive a fair trial? If that is the case, in your experience, or from your knowl-edge, what would you suggest by way of correction or mitigation or that situation?

Judge Marshall: I participated in an opinion last term which said just about what you said, and there was a retrial, and there was a change of venue, and the man was convicted. The answer would be somewhere between the British system and ours. The British system was exemplified by a case I ran across while I was there in 1960, of a newspaper (and hold on, because you're going to shudder when I get through with this one) in Scotland that was fined a total of approximately $25,000, and the opinion pointed out that the only reason the editor was not a defendant in this action was because he was not only sick in bed in a hospital, he was unable to communicate with anybody. Because, under their law, the editor is responsible for every word in the newspaper. Imagine, the *Sunday Times*! The charge against the newspaper was this: A man had been arrested for burglary, and newspaper published a picture of the arrest with the man's picture. That's all. And the basis of the complaint against the newspaper was that the man's defense was going to "mistaken identity." Two—some prospective juror might have seen that picture, and therefore that man would not be able to get a fair trial. Now, I would say my suggestion would be some place between that and what we have on the other hand. I recognize the problem that the newspaper has. It would be all right if there were one newspaper in a town. But there is competition now between the newspapers and radio and television, and it's very hard to get the self-restraint that we would prefer. Now you will remember a case down in New Jersey about a week ago, where the lawyers involved were threatened. The courts can discipline the lawyers, but they expressly said they would not make any threat as to the news media, with the hope that they would discipline themselves. Well, you couldn't publish it if the officials didn't give it to you, or the defense counsel. And in some of these cases the defense counsel is involved, too.

Robert Lucas: I won't shudder at that illustration as long as the First Amendment stays in the Constitution, and as long as you stay on the Second Circuit Court of Appeals.

Judge Marshall: Well, you know, incidentally, Mr. Justice Black of the Supreme Court is directly contrary. He goes so far as to advocate no libel or slander actions—just absolutely complete freedom or speech.

Joseph L. Steinberg: Here's a question that I think is running through the minds of many people in the audience. Judge Marshall, under the *Escobedo* case[16] which you quoted, should it be required that an accused specifically request counsel when he becomes a prime suspect, in order to properly claim his constitutional rights. Doesn't this in effect favor the more sophisticated.

Judge Marshall: Before you go any further, we have two cases on it on a panel where I am now sitting, and I couldn't comment on it.

Robert Lucas: Could I ask for you comments on the proposed Constitutional amendment that would create a Supreme, Supreme Court composed of the Chief Justice of the fifty states.

Judge Marshall: I'm against it, and I'm against it personally; and I am against it because I don't know of a single judicial body who is for it.

Justice King: There isn't any, that I know of.

Judge Marshall: It would be a marvelous meeting, though, and just imaging a 26–24 opinion. That would really be something.

Joseph L. Steinberg: Judge Marshall, I have a question here that reads, "In Connecticut we have a coroner's warrant which permits the coroner to hold an accused man without counsel or bail until twenty-four hours after the inquest has been completed. Do you feel this is consistent with due process?

Judge Marshall: I wouldn't comment on that.

Robert Lucas: Judge, I have a question that is carried over from one of your previous meetings. I don't suppose either of our distinguished judges would comment. But I have a reporter working on a story for our

16. *Escobedo, supra* note 11.

paper on the unanswered questions that were produced by this audience. It makes a very good story. One of the questions that you rushed over to me to be included in this story . . . was this "Police Commissioner Murphy indicates that more agreement in these awkward situations can often be reached over a glass of beer. Why doesn't Joe Steinberg serve beer next year?"

Judge Marshall: Well? Ask for it.

Joseph L. Steinberg: Another question, Judge Marshall. I recall at the Episcopal Church Convention you supported a resolution which in effect advocated civil disobedience to the law. How can you, a United States Judge, take such a position?

Judge Marshall: Now, let's get the record straight. The record didn't advocate disobedience. The record gave everyone the right, if they wanted to disobey a law, which they considered against their conscience, after five or six restraints. One was to make up your mind; Two was to pray; Three was to go talk to the Minister; Four was to consider the things and all; and after you did all that and were willing to go to jail, you had the right to disobey it. I was not there to judge. I was there as a discipline of the Episcopal Church, and I seem to remember some place in the Bible where Jesus grabbed some moneychangers and kicked the living daylights out of them, which I assume was against the law. I did not support that resolution officially, because I didn't get an opportunity to speak on it. And number two, it wasn't my turn to vote for my delegation. But I did leave the convention. I left the convention because of that, and they wouldn't let the women in, either. And I told them I supported the resolution to let the women in, and they wanted to know why. I said I was there under instructions. And they said instructions of the Bishop. I said no. Of your diocese? I said no. Of your conscience? I said no. Of who? I said, "My wife, are you kidding?" But they didn't let them in.

Robert Lucas: Judge Marshall, what do you believe to be the effect of the type of criticisms of the judiciary that arose during the recent political campaign, when one of the candidates said that, in his opinion, he would like to have the opportunity to appoint judges of his persuasion. And more recently a high official of the government of this country in the Department of Justice made the statement that he thinks the courts are too soft on criminals.

Judge Marshall: Well, as far back as we've had a court, we've had members of the executive and legislative branches of government that periodically assert their right guaranteed by the Constitution, the right of freedom of speech, to say what they want to say, and it's nothing new in my book, nothing new at all. The only problem is that the court is in a very tough proposition in not being able to engage in controversy.

That's the only comment I could make on it. I don't think the Supreme Court needs any defense. I never did, even when they've voted against me.

Joseph L. Steinberg: Judge Marshall, a question from the audience reads, "The suggestion has been made that the interest of the community would be better served in cases involving the uses of the rights of an accused, by punishing the policeman, rather than by excluding evidence which would otherwise be valid. What do you think of this idea?"

Judge Marshall: The answer is very simple. There's not a single state that I know of that does not have criminal laws to protect the citizens from the police. And the federal laws specifically say that anybody acting under court or state laws that denies anyone his rights under the protection of the Constitution has committed a federal crime. Number one, the complaints are not usually made. Number two, very seldom do you see convictions. There have been quite a few convictions in the south, starting with the case in Georgia, *Screws, Williams*, and a few down south.[17] But I don't remember having seen any in the North. Once the court finds that a policeman had beaten up a prisoner, he's violated a law, both state and federal.

Robert Lucas: Judge, since I'm bracketed by the chief judicial officer of the state and by the chief executive, I'd like to ask this question of one or both. If Judge Marshall will excuse me? What is the responsibility of either the state Supreme Court or the governor and/or the legislature, by way of implementing the Supreme Court's decision on a required system of subsidized public defense for indigent criminals of the courts of this state?

Justice King: I am not bragging, Mr. Lucas, but we have a system that is the pioneer in the United States. It started in 1919, as a public defender system. The federal government doesn't come into it for some forty years later. Under our system the only point now that remains debatable is whether or not the public defender comes in early enough, in other words, as far as the main trial is concerned, it's all been taken care of right along. Now that was the point that Judge Marshall brought up—drawing the distinction between a general investigation into crime, while you are looking around, the Supreme Court says you can ask people about that, if you're a policeman, but the moment you get really hot and you think this is the fellow, probably, and you start to ask him, not to get general information as to who did it, but to see whether he did it—then, don't you think, Judge Marshall—you're getting on tender ground if you don't give him an attorney?

Judge Marshall: Now, at that point, if he gets an attorney, not direct from the mental institution, he will be told not to talk, so the investigation will stop right there. The only point, Mr. Lucas, that I could see

17. *See* Screws v. United States, 325 U.S. 91 (1945).

where there would be any argument at all in Connecticut is in that little narrow area. We've got—actually, and it's a fact, that the fellow without means in Connecticut, now and for many years, has had better representation than all but the extremely wealthy, because you have to pay an awful lot of money to get a lawyer who can stand an experience in criminal practice equal to a fellow like Cosgrove[18] in Hartford of the public defenders elsewhere. Those fellows know their book, and they are dedicated and they work.

Judge Marshall: For a little while, and then he became state's attorney.

Robert Lucas: Do I understand that you say Connecticut was literally the pioneer in this, of all the states?

Justice King: I think that we go back the farthest of them all. We are very close to it, if we aren't literally there—1919 was when we started. We've been pretty much the model all around on this system, because prior to that (my father was a young fellow, and afterwards) they tapped a lawyer, as the federal courts did for a long time. And he did it as a public service. But the difficulty with that system made you not always sure whom you were getting. You may have a fine person. Although I tapped a couple youngsters down in the court when I needed a lawyer very fast, years ago, and asked them if they were lawyers. They said they were. They looked like it to me, but I wanted to be sure. And I said, "Now do you understand that law is a profession, or do you think it's the same as the junk business." They said, "We understand it is a profession." I said, "All right. Now I don't think this girl should plead guilty without checking. Will you take her into the conference room and talk to her, and come back and tell me whether I should accept this plea of guilty or not." I said, "You're not going to get a dime for this, and if you don't want to do it, say so. Then I'll know that you should have been in the junk business." So then they did it, and came back in an hour and a half (she was a kind of a pretty girl, but there were two of them, so I wasn't worried), and they said, "We don't know whether she should or not." I said, "If you two, in an hour and a half, can't tell, and certainly she can't, I'm going to put the case over." The interesting thing was, in the fall session, three or four months later, she was acquitted. She came up there to plead guilty, but I wouldn't take the plea, because it was conspiracy, and I didn't think she knew what it meant. I'd asked her, and she couldn't define it, so I caught it that way.

Robert Lucas: Are these two young lawyers now in the junk business, or on the bench?

Justice King: You know, the interesting thing is, I never knew who they were. They might even be in the audience tonight. I've never seen them since.

18. James D. Cosgrove was the Public Defender in Hartford, Connecticut.

Judge Marshall: In New York we get a very high caliber lawyer, and we appoint on these pauper cases. Indeed, when we checked, last term . . . we were surprised that one of the very responsible firms had seventeen pauper cases. One firm had seventeen! Seven in our court, and ten over at the State Court. They give us top-flight lawyers.

Justice King: That's one of the sad things about this. I'm in favor of our system, but what we do lose, when you pay everybody, even though you don't pay them very well, you lost the spirit of the profession. Of course if you've got a lot of youngsters to feed, maybe you can't afford to bother with this too much. It is a loss.

Joseph L. Steinberg: Judge Marshall, would you comment for us on your own opinion about the impact of the recent Supreme Court decisions in so far as they affect the ability of the police to be competent—the ability of the police to procure the convictions, which they feel is their reason for being.

Judge Marshall: I don't see anything wrong with requiring the police to follow the law, and I think that police who abide by the law are not restricted. I think that it is very dangerous to say that the police are restricted, which infers the police are a group of people who run around violating people's rights. I would much rather say that the police now are able to justifiably follow the law. Of course, as I've said before, there are some people who take the flat position that if you and I know that Joe around the corner is violating the law, and you and I tell the policeman all that is necessary is for him to go arrest him and put him in the penitentiary. . . . Our government is just not built that way. We're supposed to give the guilty man a fair trial.

Joseph L. Steinberg: Moving along in this area, and taking the other side of the coin, there's a question that reads, "Do not the police often gather enough legitimate evidence to convict, and then find, because one of their men was too exuberant, that the entire case was lost, whereas the illegal police action was totally unnecessary?"

Judge Marshall: It happens every day. Prosecutors throughout the country constantly urge the police, "Stop fouling up my records of convictions."

Justice King: Don't you think, Judge Marshall, that one of the things that has to be done to avoid this very point, somehow or other police have got to be given instruction in the rudiments of the new technique—enough so that they won't be doing that, because this is not a concept that was generally accepted ten years ago. It's something new, and it involves a complete change of all of their prior procedures.

Judge Marshall: I would think that the best process would be for each individual community to have the prosecutor take the policemen to school. I don't know of a better person to do it.

Justice King: Except that I'd like to see the public defender there, too. And then I'd be more sure that we'd get a balanced education.

Judge Marshall: I'd be very worried about the policeman and the public defender, because I think they'd consider him to be a spy.

Justice King: Let them!

Judge Marshall: No, I think that is absolutely necessary and should be done. In a space like New York it would be very difficult because of the number of policemen.

Justice King: It would be difficult everywhere.

Judge Marshall: But it wouldn't be impossible for them to get the captains and lieutenants.

Justice King: It is difficult to get down to the street, the fellow who is doing the things that make work for you and for me.

Joseph L. Steinberg: If it's of any comfort to you gentlemen, I can tell you that when this program was announced, I received phone calls from the chiefs of police of a good twenty communities, as well as from the staff of the Connecticut State Police, so I think this shows an awareness of the need in that area, and the willingness to accept information and education in that area.

Judge Marshall: I've said for years, and I've attended two or three national meetings of state police chiefs of different levels, and I know their problems about as well as they do; and while I sympathize with them, the way they look at it, I still believe that the Constitution means the same thing to the triple-murderer that it means to the person who spits on the sidewalk, as it means to the man who doesn't commit any crime.

Justice King: That's right, except that the Constitution's meaning has been changed in the areas in which we've been talking, within the last ten years.

Judge Marshall: That's what everybody is so worried about.

Justice King: Oh, I'm not worried about it. I mean, it's a fact. It has been discovered to have a meaning that it was never discovered to have had before.

Joseph L. Steinberg: Judge Marshall, a number of questions, and I'll try to paraphrase them, are trying to put you on the horns of a dilemma here.

Judge Marshall: They'll never make it.

Joseph L. Steinberg: They discuss the court's strong concern for the rights of the individual, and the feeling on the questioner's part is that this encourages the criminal element, and they point on the other hand to the crime rate which is rising, they seem to feel, at the same time the court's concern for the criminals grows. Do you see a relationship?

Judge Marshall: I don't know. We're getting over into psychology now, that I know nothing about. But from my experience as defense counsel for quite a few years, and in the NAACP for quite a few years, and on the court for a tiny number of years, I work on the theory that criminals don't need encouragement. That's my answer to the question. They don't need it. I mean, just like a deterring effect, how in the world anybody in his right mind would rob a national bank! And yet they do it every day. If deterrents don't help, why would charges that things are loose help? In England, when they made pickpocketing a hanging offense, you know what happened at the first hanging? People's pockets got picked. I think the lack of deterrent is just the same as this. I don't believe that. The average real criminal is convinced that his particular lawyers—or first, he doesn't think he'll get caught, and secondly, he believed, before these decisions, just the same as he believes now, and with no more belief, that his lawyer is a smart enough operator to find some way to get him out of it. I could be wrong, but we're over in psychology now.

Robert Lucas: Judge Marshall, you're not saying there's no relationship between the incidence of crime and the range of punishment?

Judge Marshall: I could argue that, but I wouldn't do it, because I am not an expert, but I've heard it argued both ways.

Robert Lucas: It's certainly been argued in the case of capital punishment, hasn't it?

Judge Marshall: Oh, surely it has. I listened to it all Sunday night on some television program. They really fouled it up good.

Robert Lucas: I'd be interested in Justice King's comment on that same subject. What do you feel about the relationship between punishment and the incidence of crime?

Justice King: Well, I used to ask the accused, when I was on the trial court, in the plea, and I said, "Do you know what the maximum permissible punishment is for the crime for which you have just been found guilty, or pleaded guilty?" I found that they didn't know. The only ones who knew were the ones whose lawyers knew I had the idiosyncrasy and primed them in advance. And I said, well, would you sit into a poker game if you didn't know what the chips mean? Why didn't you, before you went in this thing, why didn't you figure what it would cost you if you miscalculated? Well, they never did. So I don't believe, Mr. Lucas, on the basis of that, that this thing amounts to much. They don't figure it out in a businesslike way.

Robert Lucas: I wish, somehow, you could formalize those views so that we could run a lot more people through our penitentiary in a big hurry that way, and build a lot less penitentiaries. I'm inclined to agree with you, myself.

Justice King: On capital punishment, of course, I am opposed to it and always have been, anyway, so I don't think I ought to talk about it, not on moral grounds, because I'm not satisfied that the truth-finding of our system is sufficiently accurate so that I'd want to snuff out a life and betting on it. Otherwise, if I were sure, I wouldn't mind, but I'm sure, therefore I do mind. One thing I do think is dreadful, in criminal procedures, and that is making an example of somebody; that is, take a person and give a terrific sentence, in order to deter some other fellow whom this criminal has never seen nor heard of. He shouldn't be used for that purpose. The purpose of punishment is rehabilitation and every sentence or punishment should be tailor-made, with no readymade goods at all. You study the individual, and you give him as much of a punishment, and no more than you think will succeed in rehabilitating him. By no means should it be to make an example or to terrify some other person with whom he had no connection. I guess that's about all I have to say on that question.

Joseph L. Steinberg: Judge Marshall, I have a number of questions on an issue that has followed each of our speakers on "Law Enforcement and the Rights of the Accused," and it has to do with civilian review boards. Do you have an opinion on the value of civilian review boards.

Judge Marshall: I have been, all along, in favor of civilian review boards, provided they are boards equivalent to the type of people you would put on a court—I mean people who are completely removed from community pressure, political pressure, and any other kind of pressure. The real difficulty would be to get the proper board. I do not like the civilian boards that the police department in most of the cities get up. The only thing they mean by "civilian" is that they don't have a uniform on. But they're employed by the police department. I don't know why if everyone else can get reviewed, why they can't. I don't see anything wrong with it. In New York, for example, it's a very hot subject. I know my good friend, Commissioner Murphy, is opposed to it, and I've heard all of his reasons, and I'm still not convinced. I still would rather a civilian review board.

Joseph L. Steinberg: Could you comment, too, on another item that was discussed by our two previous speakers on "suspicion arrests." We were told that there were 93,000 of them in 1963.

Judge Marshall: No, I wouldn't care to comment on that, because I know that's coming up in court.

Joseph L. Steinberg: Judge Marshall, and members of the panel, Judge King, Mr. Lucas, on behalf of our audience and the Greater Hartford Forum, I'd like to thank you for your participation in what has proved to be a most invigorating evening.

Civil Rights in the United States

I want to talk to you this morning about the result of commuting back and forth to Africa from 1959 until around 1964 and in different areas around the world. I would like to share with you some of the questions I have gotten and the answers you can give.

The biggest problem wherever you go away from this country is to explain to people of different governments and different cultures the delicate relationship between our federal government and our state governments. They find it very difficult to understand and you must be very careful in your own understanding of it.

I noticed, for example, in helping to draft the constitution of Kenya—I represented the fourteen African republics in London and was their quote constitutional adviser unquote—that my main task was to draft a "shedule" of rights.[1] "Shedule" of rights because, after all, I was in London and could not quite understand the "shedule" business. It was explained to me that, after all, this was the Mother tongue. The Mother said it was "shedule" and the child shouldn't question it. I remember distinctly discussing this with the Colonial Secretary and some faculty member from Oxford that if the correct pronunciation of that word was "schedule," how were their children doing in "shool" today?

But I did prepare this schedule of rights and my only purpose was to draft a law, a constitution that would protect the average Negro in Mississippi. Because after the takeover the white man in Kenya was going to be far in the minority, and he would need some real good protection and, indeed, it did give just that protection.

I mention this because despite the fact you have heard of people who have left Kenya, many have remained. When I was there in 1964 at their final freedom ceremony,[2] I saw a huge fellow, believe it or not, born and

---

Civil Rights and Race Relations: A Seminar 17 (1966) (Department of State Publication 8157; Department and Foreign Service Series 135).

1. *U.S. Negro Leader Arrives in Kenya*, N.Y. TIMES, Jan. 11, 1960, at 5.

2. "The first amendment of the Constitution in 1964 severed the colonial link to make Kenya a republic." Abdullahi A. An-Na'im, *The Contingent Universality of Human Rights*, 11 EMORY INT'L L. REV. 19, 56 (1997) (Jomo Kenyatta became president).

raised in South Africa, quite white and quite blond with a big handlebar mustache, and he had made it quite clear in London before freedom that he was not going to leave and there was nothing the Africans could do to make him leave because he had too much invested there. This man is my example of the type of a member of a minority group, if you please, who did stay and now is not only in the legislature, but he is a minister. He is about number three or four from the top. If that can be done in Kenya, it can be done all over.

Civil Rights in Perspective

I give you this example as a prelude to looking at our government in relation to what is going on in the world today, and I have to revert immediately to some history for a moment of how our country got where it is today.

You see, when you read about protests, and so forth, people ask, are you in favor of protest? Are you in favor of peaceful demonstrations? And the answer is that this government was founded on protest. A quantity of teas in a harbor in Boston is closely related to a protest in my book, and I am not too sure how peaceful it was. We see this again when you go back to the Romans' protection of the Roman citizen; when you go to Runnymede and the Magna Carta, you find great protection for individual rights.[3]

But you also must remember that the individuals they were talking about were a very small group—the citizens of Rome; it was the British citizen in the Magna Carta. Therefore, when our Constitution was drafted it was a revolutionary constitution. Many people who drafted it and many people who agreed to it did not expect it to last so long. It was too far-reaching.

Even though people like Jefferson and Adams and a few others were bitterly opposed to slavery, then lost the battle and our Constitution, our basic document specifically recognized slavery as being valid. When our Constitution was written it said, "We, the people." It actually meant, We the some of the people.

And then we had this horrible fuss back and forth through the anti-slavery movement when justification had to be put up for the maintenance of slavery and it had to be built up. There we were aided by "scholars" with all of these theories about the inherent inferiority of a Negro slave. But once they established the inherent inferiority of the Negro it had to rub off on the Negro freedom, too, because they were the same people.

3. *See generally* A. E. Dick Howard, Magna Carta: Text and Commentary (1964).

This lasted until, I think, around 1920 when certain "scholars" who were constantly measuring the brains from the cadavers of white and Negro people invariably found the Negro's brain was smaller. I think it was around 1920 that the head of a particular laboratory said, let's put numbers on the specimens instead of race and let's see how they add up. And they averaged out. They took race off of them.

Getting back to the slavery movement, it ended with the Dred Scott case in the Supreme Court. The Supreme Court said neither the Negro slave nor the freedman had any rights which the white man was bound to respect because he was not a citizen and if he were not a citizen he had no rights.[4]

And then we had a little war. After that came the First Amendment— the Thirteenth, Fourteenth, and Fifteenth Amendments. Of course, the Emancipation Proclamation had no legal value as such because it had no enforcement power. The Thirteenth Amendment abolished slavery but it was the Fourteenth Amendment, which said that everybody born or naturalized in the United States was a citizen of the United States and in the state where he resided. Believe it or not, that is the first law of the United States that gave anybody United States citizenship. So for once the Negro started on an equal footing with everybody else. Everybody got their citizenship from the first section of the Fourteenth Amendment.

Then we had the civil rights law, and so forth. Our government and the officials in our government were so busy in getting to the West Coast and seeing who could cheat whom out of getting the railroads and every thing else that the stalwart antislavery bloc got tired, and then they had a little compromise in which everybody in government said we will leave all of this to the tender mercies of the several states.[5] In 1896 the Supreme the Supreme Court in the case of *Plessy v. Ferguson* said separate but equal did not violate the Constitution of the United States.[6] And then everybody started passing laws, North as well as South.

The Negro by law was segregated from before birth until after death. If you doubt this, there was not a hospital in the South that would accept a Negro expectant mother. That was before birth, and after you died you couldn't be buried in any graveyard except the Negro cemetery. That is before birth until after death. Indeed it went so far we found it impossible to get a Negro's pet buried where pets owned by white people were buried.

4. Dred Scott v. Sandford, 60 U.S. 393 (1857).
5. *See generally* Henry Kisor, *Working on the Railroad*, N.Y. TIMES BOOK REV., Sept. 17, 2000 (reviewing STEPHEN E. AMBROSE, NOTHING LIKE IT IN THE WORLD: THE MEN WHO BUILT THE TRANSCONTINENTAL RAILROAD, 1863–1869 (2000)).
6. Plessy v. Ferguson, 163 U.S. 537 (1896).

In this town of Washington, D.C., back in either the late twenties or early thirties, a wealthy doctor had a dog, which died. He tried to put it in a high-powered pet cemetery. They told him they were very sorry. The end of the story. I know the man. I knew the dog. The dog was a pure white Spitz but he had made the mistake of having a black owner.

For years, until the late thirties, the federal government was out of the civil rights business. Neither the executive, the judicial, nor the legislative arm of the government was interested at all in living up to the basic principles of our Constitution.

Then cases began to be filed in the courts by private organizations with money solicited from private people, running up into the hundreds of thousands of dollars. After a series of cases in the Supreme Court, starting with the Roosevelt Court, the Court began to whittle away at the rights of a state to put its mores and customs above the Constitution of the United States, especially the Fourteenth Amendment. During this period nobody was moving but the courts. And it was not until the Truman Administration that the executive arm of the government began to work. President Truman established a Committee on Civil Rights. His Committee on Segregation in the Armed Services ended segregation completely. Then we came through the Kennedy and Johnson Administrations when Congress began to pass its first civil rights bills in over eighty years.

I mention all of this so that you can understand our present civil rights problems in this country. I give you this history not to show how far we have come but rather to indicate that the Government is actually moving.

The Federal Role in Civil Rights

President Johnson has made it clear over and over again that the federal government is in the civil rights business and that the full force of the federal government is behind this movement. Now we have the executive, the legislative, and the judicial branches all operating toward that end. But the problem is still here; and make no mistake; you cannot sweep it under the rug.

I found great difficulty in Africa in explaining the big picture of the Birmingham policeman with a police dog biting a Negro. It was on the front page of almost every European and African paper, I constantly got the question—"Is that unlawful?" I said certainly it is unlawful for a policeman to turn a dog on a citizen, especially a police dog.[7]

7. Attorney General of the United States Nicholas de B. Katzenbach predicted that African nations would be interested in race relations in 1965. He makes this

Before I left I told a government official who asked that question, there is only one way I can explain that picture away and that is to say that it was a lousy photograph and the animal was actually a rabbit; it wasn't a dog. I am certainly not going to do that.

Once you explain that we do not have a federal police force—and indeed we do not want a federal police force—and that normal crimes are the concern of the local police force, one might ask: Okay, what about the local police?

One youngster in Tanganyika—and I will never forget this—said: "By the way isn't the mayor of Birmingham the same party as the governor?" I said, "Yes." [He said]: "And the governor is the same party as the President?" I said, "yes." [He said:] "And nobody can do anything?" [I said:] "it is up to the city, it is up to the state, and that is the way our government is organized."

After explaining that over and over again, I got the same question: "Well, assume that you have separation of power and assume there is federal, state, and local authority and assume that somebody has authority, is that policeman in jail or not." And the answer is he has never been arrested. Now that is no reason to panic. The reason we do not panic is that there is still much to be done. The job is not over.

And that brings me to what I think can very well wind up most of this. Our local governments in many areas of the country have not yet reached the point where they are willing to recognize that they, as well as the federal government, have initial responsibility to remove segregation and discrimination on the local level.

Where the federal government has moved in has been restricted to instances where the local governments failed to act. We still insist on retaining this relationship between federal and state governments.

When these different forms of government develop mutual respect for each other, we believe they will eventually reach the point where our democratic heritage can be reached.

_____

point in a Memorandum to President Lyndon B. Johnson, which states: "As you know, I had planned to head the United States Delegation to the Crime Conference in Stockholm this coming week. I feel, however, that with the passage of the voting legislation this week I should forego my Swedish trip in order to oversee the litigating and other decisions on implementation, which should follow immediately upon the Act becoming law. I am afraid that the civil rights groups might misunderstand any other course. With the concurrence of the State Department I have asked Thurgood Marshall to head the United States Delegation. I think this is a particularly happy choice because inevitably much of the discussion will be concerned with racial problems, and I think judge Marshall will be a particularly effective spokesman for the United States." President Lyndon B. Johnson Lib., (National Archives and Records Administration), Exe. FG135, Aug. 4, 1965.

Progress in Civil Rights

Bear in mind that as of today, when you see the marchers walking through Mississippi, the state and local police are there. As to what they are doing—what they should be doing—everybody is free to make his own judgement. Nevertheless the federal government is there. John Doar, who is head of the Civil Rights Division of the Justice Department, is there. I am not at liberty to say how many of his staff is there, except to say there are staff members there in addition to John Doar. There are FBI agents there, and I am not at liberty to say how many of them are there as of today.

Marches that could not possibly have occurred ten years ago are occurring, and they are being given protection. It is a question as to whether it is enough or not—you can make up your own minds on that.

I think you will find that today there are Negroes voting in every area of this country. There are Negroes voting who have never been able to vote before.

I say that with the new civil rights bill that will pass Congress there will be reason to believe that the final roadblock in fair trials will be eliminated, that is, to have a jury, which is not prejudiced. The housing section of that bill will go a long way toward achieving and understanding that the ghetto does not have to continue to exist.

When you go out, you should remember—and take it from me, please— we have nothing to sweep under the rug: that is the worst thing that you can do. We can explain the problem by saying it cannot be solved by a dictator sitting up in Washington and waving his big stick. We would prefer our government to operate as it is operating. But don't try to cover up, for the simple reason you cannot. Everything that is done in this country is broadcast as widely as possible.

You will get the problem I got in Uganda where a young student said: "Judge, when you go back to the United States, I insist that you deliver a message to the Supreme Court." I said, you did say the Supreme Court? "Yes, the Supreme Court." I said—well, you cannot send a message to the Supreme Court because only members of the bar of the Supreme Court can talk to the Court. He said—"I insist that you tell the Supreme Court they have to do more for the Negro in the United States." I said— you did single out the Supreme Court? He said, "Yes."

Then I took off my State Department hat and invited him some place. He didn't go. I believe you have to watch for unreasonable criticism, but bear in mind that much can be done, and with this I am through.

For years I spoke to foreign students who came to the *Herald Tribune* Forum. I did this until I went on the bench. Then I was precluded from doing it. In two years running the student from the Union of South

Africa, with that millstone [of apartheid] around his neck, ended up the best-liked member of the group because he faced up to the problem, explained the problem, and asked for an understanding of the problem.

That is all I have to say on that point because I assume there are going to be some questions. The only question which I will not answer is if anybody wants to know why I am not at the march in Mississippi. The answer is—I have been down there.

Remembering Lyndon B. Johnson and the Civil Rights Struggle

T. H. Baker: This is the interview with Thurgood Marshall. Sir, to begin in the beginning, did you have knowledge of Mr. Johnson back when he was a congressman or senator?

Justice Thurgood Marshall: I knew of him when he was a congressman, and I knew of him directly through Aubrey Williams and people like that in the Youth Administration. The first I became interested was when we ran for the Senate.

T. H. Baker: Was this in the '48—?

Justice Marshall: Yes, in Texas. I was in Texas working on the primary cases, and all of our people of the NAACP in that area were enthusiastically behind him.

T. H. Baker: Excuse me, sir, this must have been in '41 then, when Mr. Johnson first ran for the Senate and didn't get elected.

Justice Marshall: It was '41 when he first ran. It was '41, because that's when the primary cases started. If I remember correctly, in the runoff the labor support dwindled away but the Negro support stuck with him. But when he became a senator, he was not among the liberals.

T. H. Baker: I was going to ask you about that. You said that the NAACP people in Texas were favorably inclined toward Mr. Johnson in those days?

Justice Marshall: Solidly. So was the national office.

T. H. Baker: Did they have any real basis for this?

Justice Marshall: Yes. Well, they knew him. The Negroes down there, they know each other pretty well. They were a pretty hard bunch. We followed their judgment. I didn't know him. But we couldn't engage in politics. All we could do was to talk about it. But Walter White,[1] the head of the NAACP, did meet with him, as I remember, and did say that he was all right.

Gift of Personal Statement by Justice Thurgood Marshall to the Lyndon Baines Johnson Library, Jan. 1, 1976. Interviewer T. H. Baker (July 10, 1969).
1. *See generally* Walter White's autobiography: WALTER WHITE, A MAN NAMED WHITE (1948).

T. H. Baker: Did Mr. Johnson have any direct connection with what became the primary cases?

Justice Marshall: No, none at all. He had no connection with them one way or the other. I never saw him, so he could not have any connection. I ran the case and I didn't—

T. H. Baker: You certainly would have seen him.

Justice Marshall: I would have known it, yes.

T. H. Baker: Then after 1948—after he became a senator—was there any change in this feeling?

Justice Marshall: Well, Walter White, who handled the legislative matters in Congress, got very angry with him and stayed angry until he died, as a matter of fact.

T. H. Baker: On what basis?

Justice Marshall: He just wouldn't support any of the legislation the NAACP was after. Walter White chalked it up to his great admiration for Sam Rayburn.[2] He thought Sam Rayburn was calling the turn. Now whether that's true or not I don't know. But on our records he was not a liberal senator.

T. H. Baker: Incidentally, did Mr. Johnson have any connection with your other Texas case in the fifties?

Justice Marshall: None.

T. H. Baker: *Sweatt versus Painter*[3] at the University—?

Justice Marshall: None. Not one way or the other. We never knew what happened.

T. H. Baker: How about, I guess what is *the* case, the school integration case—*Brown versus the Board of Education*?[4]

Justice Marshall: Nothing. He had nothing to do with it at all.

T. H. Baker: This attitude you mentioned that Walter White had—did Mr. Johnson's activity in connection with the '57 civil rights bill change that any?

Justice Marshall: Walter was dead in 1957; Walter died in '55.

T. H. Baker: That's right. Roy Wilkins—

Justice Marshall: Roy Wilkins[5] took over [then]. No. Roy did not have the same opinion of him. Roy had a better opinion of him. He felt that he was the type of man in the Senate who could get things done, but he didn't. He could have. He just chalked it up to politics. But he didn't

2. Sam Rayburn served as Speaker of the House in the U.S. Congress from 1940 to 1961, except for two terms. He died in Bonham, Texas in 1961. *People*, DALLAS MORNING NEWS, Nov. 16, 1998, at 2A.
3. 339 U.S. 629 (1950).
4. 349 U.S. 294 (1955) (Brown II).
5. *See generally* ROY WILKINS, STANDING FAST: THE AUTOBIOGRAPHY OF ROY WILKINS (1982).

have any—. As a matter of fact, Roy had very good thoughts about him. I know that as then and as of now.

T. H. Baker: What was the general opinion among civil rights leaders like yourself, of the '57 bill? Did you feel it was progress?

Justice Marshall: Nothing. It wasn't doing any good. It was just barely progress because it had been a hundred years—eighty years—since we'd had one. The smallest slice was good rather than the whole loaf of bread. But it was understandable in my book because it was strictly a political move of getting something done. But when we'd been fighting since 1909 for something . . . good. Then when we looked at it, we had a different feeling.

T. H. Baker: Mostly I guess because of the elimination of Part 3 divisions?[6]

Justice Marshall: Sure. Oh, yes, we fought to the bitter end on that. Yet as you look back, it was great progress, it seems to me, to get them to move at all. I don't know, and I guess nobody would know, just what was sold in there and how it was sold. Whether we could have gotten more or not, I don't know. Nobody will know except—well, Lyndon Johnson would know and those people that were running that inner corps of the Senate in those days.

You see, as I looked at him as a senator and leader, they always said he was a great compromiser, but I've always thought that he had the compromise in his pocket when the thing started each time. He just waited for the right time to take it out.

T. H. Baker: You mean he had already figured out what was going to happen?

Justice Marshall: Sure. He always won. Well, that all changed when he became President, anyhow.

---

6. Thurgood Marshall's response to the interviewer's question may simply have been that the civil rights bill that passed was better than nothing. In 1957 Lyndon B. Johnson, Majority Leader of the U.S. Senate, pledged to pass a civil rights law under pressure from the NAACP and other groups. The NAACP, led by Roy Wilkins, believed that the heart of the bill was part 3, which allowed the Attorney General to bring suits in a variety of areas, such as segregation of schools and in public places, including swimming pools, hotels, motels, theaters, and restaurants. But part 3 was bitterly opposed by Democrats, in particular, who wanted to pass a bill without any teeth. To undermine its most essential part, Johnson supported a provision that made it a crime to violate certain terms of the bill, expecting no white juries in the South to convict a person for violating part 3. Johnson was caught between his promises to the civil rights groups and his promises to the southern block to water down the bill; in the end, the Civil Rights Act of 1957 was passed without the part 3 division. See WILKINS, STANDING FAST *supra* note 5, 243–246; ROBERT A. CARO, THE YEARS OF LYNDON JOHNSON: MASTER OF THE SENATE 870–872, 910–922 (2002).

T. H. Baker: In those years before Mr. Johnson left the Senate, did you ever talk to him about this problem of compliance with the '54 decision?[7]

Justice Marshall: I never talked to him. I don't remember having ever talked to him until I came down as Solicitor General; I don't believe. I might have, but I don't remember.

T. H. Baker: Incidentally, I would like to ask one question here that's not directly related to Mr. Johnson. What happened in '55 that caused the NAACP Legal Defense Fund and the NAACP to end their directorate connection—to split almost entirely?

Justice Marshall: The United States Treasury Department, specifically the Internal Revenue Service—they decided that they were going to take away the exemption of the Legal Defense Fund.

T. H. Baker: Because the directorate was—?

Justice Marshall: No, no. They then got reasons afterwards. But as soon as the Eisenhower Administration took over, they came after us. I think they're still under investigation. We've been under investigation all the way up to the Kennedy Administration. We found out that if they took away our tax exemption, it would be two years before we could litigate it—complete the litigation. With a reserve fund of about twenty or thirty thousand dollars, we couldn't take that chance. So we ended up with three or four specific things. One was the board of directors had to be entirely separate. The staff had to be entirely separate. The books were always separate. The staff had to be entirely separate. . . . And the fourth one was we had to take NAACP out of the name.

Well, we agreed to the first two and we had already agreed to the third. We refused to take the name out; that's why we split. That's the only reason we split it—to save it.

T. H. Baker: Was that a general tone of the Eisenhower Administration, or was there any one particular—?

Justice Marshall: Well, it just happened at that time. I don't blame anybody. It could be efficiency. Up until that time the charitable organizations group was run by very inefficient bureaucrats. The reason was it meant nothing to the government because if you knock out the exemption of one charity, the people will give it to another charity. The government doesn't make any money out of it. And the Eisenhower Administration, bent on efficiency it could be that. But I do also know the Internal Revenue and the Secretary of Treasury got repeated letters from the southern Senators and Congressmen, "How come they're tax exempt?" What did it I don't know. But I do know we were under—. I know of one time when they had two men in my office and two men in

---

7. Brown v. Board of Education, 347 U.S. 483 (1954) (Brown I).

the NAACP office for six months, going through every single check, trying to find something. Well, they didn't find anything.

T. H. Baker: Actually the two have been practically separate for a good many years.

Justice Marshall: We only had the interlocking board; that's all we had. We have separate buildings; separate bank accounts; separate books; and we were very careful about it.

T. H. Baker: To get back to Mr. Johnson, was there any dismay among civil rights leaders like yourself when he showed up on the '60 ticket for the Democratic party?

Justice Marshall: It wasn't dismay; it was great surprise! If I remember correctly, some of them were dismayed. I was not. I have a funny feeling of giving the people a chance. And I remember before Averell Harriman[8] went to the convention, in his house he talked to me about Johnson being Vice President and was positive he was going to be, and asked me what was my impression.

T. H. Baker: Harriman must have been one of the very few people who was seriously considering that.

Justice Marshall: Before the convention. I told him I thought there was no problem at all. I said, "Because in my book Texas is not South; it's Southwest," and that his record wasn't that bad. But I do remember that other people in NAACP hit the ceiling.

T. H. Baker: Surely not Mr. Wilkins himself?

Justice Marshall: Yeah, oh he did hit the ceiling! He bounced off the ceiling.

T. H. Baker: But I believe he calmed down or endorsed—

Justice Marshall: Very shortly thereafter—it wasn't long.

T. H. Baker: Did anyone have to talk to him to—?

Justice Marshall: At that stage they were all talking to the Kennedys. I don't know how many times Roy must have been in there with the Kennedys. Once I talked to Bobby [Kennedy]—that's all—just once. Roy ran the show, I mean. Being in Legal Defense I had to stay out of anything that looked like politics, so I did. But once I talked . . . had a very unsatisfactory conference with Bobby about the civil rights movement.

T. H. Baker: When was that?

Justice Marshall: Shortly after they took over—about the first of the year, I guess.

8. W. Averell Harriman was an "American diplomat and administrator, who served in key diplomatic posts from 1941 through the administration of President Lyndon B. Johnson." 13 ENCYCLOPEDIA AMERICANA 811 (1977). At this time he was ambassador-at-large; in this capacity he conducted the peace negotiations with North Vietnam.

T. H. Baker: After President Kennedy was inaugurated?

Justice Marshall: Yes.

T. H. Baker: It was an unsatisfactory conference?

Justice Marshall: Yes.

T. H. Baker: In what way?

Justice Marshall: He spent all this time telling us what we should do.

T. H. Baker: What sort of suggestions did he have for you?

Justice Marshall: Well, that we ought to concentrate on this and concentrate on that and what have you. I told him that so far as I was concerned we had been in the civil rights business since 1909, and he'd been in the President business a year. Well, I mean, that's the way—. But Roy used to have many conferences with the President, very rewarding ones.

T. H. Baker: People have said that the intensity of the civil rights movement kind of caught the Kennedy Administration by surprise when they came in.

Justice Marshall: [It] should have. I don't know. I did have a conference with the President about three months before he announced his candidacy, when he was a senator, about just what was cooking. I'm sure I didn't pull any punches with him. I don't remember. It was a lunch and we spent about two hours together. But he got the story. He knew what it was. But I don't think the President realized the urgency of it.

T. H. Baker: You're referring to President Kennedy now?

Justice Marshall: Yes. I don't think he realized.

T. H. Baker: Then in that first year President Kennedy appointed you to the circuit judgeship.

Justice Marshall: Yes. That was when—'61. Congress held it up for a year—eleven months.

T. H. Baker: Did you have any doubts about leaving your work with the Legal and Defense Fund to—?

Justice Marshall: No. I thought it was time for younger people to take over, as a matter of fact. It was a good possibility I might have gone into private practice in about five years from then. I mean, I had to look forward to taking care of a family.

T. H. Baker: You mean you had been contemplating retirement?

Justice Marshall: Yes.

T. H. Baker: Incidentally, sir, at that time in '61, was there any serious debate about you being replaced by a white man?

Justice Marshall: No. It was strict seniority.

T. H. Baker: Mr. Greenberg was just next in line?[9]

Justice Marshall: By, believe it or not, it was only a month or so over

---

9. *See* Jack Greenberg, Crusaders in the Courts: How a Dedicated Band of Lawyers Fought for the Civil Rights Revolution xviii (1994).

Connie Motley.[10] I called Connie in and told her that this was the score. She said, "Of course." If there was anything she was for, it was the seniority. She just didn't like that two months' business because it was sort of a gamble one way or the other. Then I got them both together, and that's all there was to it. But I thought we'd reached the stage where it was unimportant. But this Black Power business and all now—

T. H. Baker: That's why I asked. Probably now it would be a real issue.

Justice Marshall: No, Connie Motley would be just as rough as anybody else—or rougher. She doesn't believe in that stuff.

T. H. Baker: That's why I asked. Probably now it would be a real issue.

Justice Marshall: No way, not until he called. That's the first time I knew about it.

T. H. Baker: That would be in '65 when he called you about the—

Justice Marshall: '61.

T. H. Baker: I'm talking about Mr. Johnson now.

Justice Marshall: That's right, '65.

T. H. Baker: When he called you about the Solicitor Generalship.

Justice Marshall: He called one day, around this time [July] I think, and I was up in the judges' dining room at the courthouse. My bailiff came up and tapped me on the shoulder. I said, "Fred, what in the world is wrong?" I mean, he's not supposed to bother us at lunch. He was as mad as a beet. I said, "what's wrong, Fred?" . . . He said, "the President wants to speak to you. He's on the phone!" I said, "The President of what?" "The President of the United States!" So he held an elevator, and I went down. Sure enough he was on there. We chatted for about two or three minutes, and he said, "I want you to be my Solicitor General." I said, "Sir." We chatted about it, and I said, "Well, Mr. President, I'll have to think this over." He said, "Well, go ahead, but don't tell a living soul." I said, "I assume that means nobody but my wife?" He said, "Yes, that's what I mean by nobody." He said, "Take all the time you want." I said, "Very well, sir." He hung up, and I hung up.

I went home and talked to my wife and we discussed the problems, because one was a lifetime job to trade in for a job at the beckoning of one person. Secondly, it was a $4,500 cut in salary. Third, the living expenses in Washington would be twice what I was paying in New York. So she said okay. We kept thinking about it, and the next day the phone rang. He was on the phone again. I said, "Well, Mr. President, you said I had all the time I needed." He said, "You had it." I said, "Okay."

I went down the next morning, and I started telling him these things. He said, "You don't have to tell me. I can tell you everything including

10. Constance Baker Motley, Equal Justice Under Law: An Autobiography 151 (1998).

what you've got in your bank account. I'm still asking you to make the sacrifice." We talked for quite a while, and I said, "Okay with me."

T. H. Baker: Did he explain to you why he wants you as opposed to just somebody else?

Justice Marshall: He said he wanted, number one, he wanted me in his Administration. Number two, he wanted me in that spot for two reasons. One, he thought I could handle it. Secondly, he wanted people—young people—of both races to come into the Supreme Court Room, as they all do by the hundreds and thousands, and somebody to say, "Who is that man up there with that swallow tail coat arguing," and somebody to say, "He's the Solicitor General of the United States." Somebody will say, "But he's a Negro!" He wanted that image, number one.

Number two, he thought that he would like to have me as his representative before the Court. The other thing which goes through every conversation we had from then on—he would say at least three or four times, "You know this had nothing to with any Supreme Court appointment. I want that distinctly understood. There's no quid pro quo here at all. You do your job. If you don't do it, you go out. If you do it, you stay here. And that's all there is to it."

T. H. Baker: He made it clear this did not mean that you would eventually get a Supreme Court appointment?

Justice Marshall: Over and over again. He made the announcement in the East Room, and it was very funny when I went in. The press knew nothing about any of this. When I went in he first said that I would come behind Mrs. Johnson, and then he said, "You come and go in right side-by-side with me at the door." We went in together. A murmur went around the press boys, and I found out afterwards that the question they were asking was, "Who has resigned from the Supreme Court?" He made the announcement and then we had the swearing in, and that was that.

T. H. Baker: During those conversations, did either of you discuss what would happen before Congress with your confirmation?

Justice Marshall: No, he said he could take care of that—that it would be hard, would be tough. He said, "If you can stand the gaff, I can." That time and every other time I've talked to him, the thing I was impressed with was what he intended to do with this country.

T. H. Baker: Could you elaborate on that, sir?

Justice Marshall: Well, he intended to wipe as much of it out as he could.

T. H. Baker: You mean white discrimination?

Justice Marshall: He intended to be to this century what Abraham Lincoln was to the last century, and he was going to do it. I frankly believe if he had had four more years, he just about would have done it. I mean, he rebelled at the discrimination against women—women judges.

He always did. He said he wanted to leave the presidency in a position that there was no government job with a race tag on it—none! That's what he was driving at. He would constantly say, "If you've got any ideas, let me have them. If you don't want to bother with me, give them to Ramsey or Nick[11] or somebody like that. But if there's any way we can break through, let me know."

T. H. Baker: Did you do that, sir?

Justice Marshall: Only once or twice. I couldn't give him any ideas. I mean, he had most of them himself. And then he was pushing them like mad.

T. H. Baker: While you were Solicitor General, did you, in addition to work of the Solicitor Generalship itself, serve Mr. Johnson or the White House as an advisor on civil rights generally or appointments or things?

Justice Marshall: No, sir. Any ideas I'd have I would funnel them through the Attorney General which I thought was proper. It was particularly true, because I knew they got through. I mean, I know both Nick Katzenbach and Ramsey. I know if I made a suggestion they would pass it on.

He didn't welcome too much suggestion. If he wanted your advice, he would ask for it. On some occasions he did, and I always gave it to him. I would go up there sometimes, especially on Saturday afternoon. It was the best time to get in that joint, and not be seen going in, because everybody was gone on Saturday afternoon.

T. H. Baker: What kind of things would he ask your advice on?

Justice Marshall: It was just problems about the [Justice] Department, or my job, or the whole race problem, in general. But in absolute general terms, nothing specific. Then when I came on the Court, that was cut off completely. I didn't have to worry about it. He said the same thing, so that was cut off.

T. H. Baker: Within the Justice Department in those years, were there any serious debates over the speed of prosecution, particularly in the civil rights area?

Justice Marshall: Oh, yes, we didn't have to worry too much in the civil rights area because John Doar,[12] who was running it, he was about as dedicated as anybody in government. We would sit down. We had these Wednesday night meetings with all department heads, but we'd have earlier ones with John and people like that. The whole trouble in those

11. Ramsey Clark served as Attorney General under President Johnson. Nicholas deB. Katzenbach served as Under Secretary of State and Attorney General under President Johnson.

12. *See* TAYLOR BRANCH, PARTING THE WATERS; AMERICA IN THE KING YEARS 1954–63, 331–33, 778 (1988); Book Review: William H. Chafe, *Parting the Waters in the King Years, 1954–1963*, 248, THE NATION 277 (1989).

days was it was just completely understaffed. He just didn't have the staff, and he would say that the entire Department of Justice had been geared to it. They could get preference over any other department. But it was tough.

T. H. Baker: Did you ever think in those days about moving efforts into the North as opposed to the southern small towns?

Justice Marshall: We've always been looking at the North. We were always looking at the North. But you couldn't get any complaints. Nobody would complain.

T. H. Baker: Surely the Urban League or the NAACP could have lent a hand there.

Justice Marshall: Only on labor cases. That's all they seemed to be interested in. They didn't do it. I think that after—well, from after '55 on, I think we sort of laid down a little.

T. H. Baker: You mean after '65 on—after the passage of the voting laws? Or were you referring to the NAACP?

Justice Marshall: No, I'm talking about '65. I think we thought that was the sine qua non. That was it—we're here! You see, we tended to do that in '55. Then we got out of that with Martin Luther King, etc. Then '65, I think, it moved in again. You know, everybody fighting in the civil rights fight has always been a little inclined to just sit down and take a breather. We found out you can't take a breather. If you do, that other guy will run you ragged.

Let me tell you about my appointment to the Supreme Court. I was sitting in my office, and it was about, I guess, ten o'clock in the morning. Ramsey Clark called Mrs. Lavery, who is the same secretary I have with me now, and said, "Is the Judge in? She said, "Yes." "Well, I've got to go up to the White House and talk to some students," one of these student groups, I've forgotten what it was, maybe with the Fellows, I don't know, "over in the Executive Building." He said, "What time are you due up there?" I said, "Well, I know Mrs. Lavery well enough to be sure she's called for a car, and there'll be a car down there waiting for me." He said, "Well, instead of getting there at eleven, you get there at a quarter of eleven. Instead of going over across the street, you go in the main—. The boss wants to see you." I said, "About what?" He said, "I don't know." Ramsey, I mean, he won't tell you anything about anybody anyhow. I kept trying. He said, "I actually don't know." So I said, "Well, which way shall I go in?" There are three different ways you can go in without being seen. And he told me which way to go, and I went up there and went in and waited a few minutes. Marvin Watson[13] came out and

13. At the time, Marvin Watson was Chief of Staff in the White House and later served as Postmaster General during the Johnson Administration. See James R. Jones, *Behind L.B.J.'s Decision Not to Run in '68*, N.Y. TIMES, April 16, 1998, at 31.

said, "Come in." And I went in and we chatted—the President and I. He said, "You know something, Thurgood, I'm going to put you on the Supreme Court." I said, "Well, thank you, sir." We talked a little while. We went out to the press and he announced it. We came back in the room and I said, "Now, Mr. President, if it's all right with you I'd like to call my wife. It would be better than for her to hear it on the radio." He said, "You mean you haven't called Cissy yet?"[14] I said, "No, how could I? I've been talking to you!" So we got her on the phone and I told her to sit down. She said, "Well, I'm standing." I said, "Well, sit down." She sat down and he said, "Cissy—Lyndon Johnson." She said, "Yes, Mr. President." "I've just put your husband on the Supreme Court." She said, "I'm sure glad I'm sitting down."

T. H. Baker: Didn't you have a little bit of a suspicion that it might be coming?

Justice Marshall: I had a hope. Any lawyer has a hope, but no suspicion. We had a party the night before for Tom Clark[15] because he resigned that day. All of us were chatting around, and nobody suspected—and nobody said a word to me. A lot of people think it was discussed. I didn't know about it. I imagine it was. I know Clark must have known, and I know Ramsey knew. But they just don't pass out any information.

T. H. Baker: Did Mr. Johnson ever, then or later before you were actually on the bench, talk to you about what he thought a Supreme Court Justice ought to be?

Justice Marshall: Yes, his own man, and I told him that. He said, "Like what?" I said, "Just like the steel decision.[16] When President Truman's, one of his very closest friends, Justice Tom C. Clark, not only voted against him but wrote the opinion against him." He said, "You mean you'd do that to me?" I said, "Exactly." He said, "Well, that's the kind I'm looking for." No, he dwelled on independence. The same way with Solicitor General. He said, "If you and Katzenbach can't make a decision, come up here and I'll make it for you. But you are your own boss." But he insisted on that. I found with him that, while I was Solicitor General, several times I didn't agree fully with the Attorney General. He had no trouble with me. I didn't win every time.

T. H. Baker: What sort of disagreements would you have?

Justice Marshall: About technical things.

T. H. Baker: Tactics in a case?

14. Mrs. Thurgood Marshall.
15. Justice Tom Clark served on the United States Supreme Court from 1949 to 1967. Martin Well, *Former Court Justice Clark Dies at 77*, WASH. POST, June 14, 1977, at C6.
16. Youngstown Sheet & Tube Co. v. Sawyer, 343 U.S. 579 (1952) (referred to as the Steel Seizure Case).

Justice Marshall: No, about whether we should take a case or not or what have you—certain things in there which I wouldn't discuss because that story won't be told, I'm sure, by anybody.

T. H. Baker: Well that's the problem. If you don't tell it here, it won't be, except when you write your memoirs.

Justice Marshall: I can guarantee you that the three people involved, not a one of them is going to tell it. I'll bet you money on it.

T. H. Baker: I guess we'll leave it at that. In that case, that's a story that's lost. Did you also discuss with the President whether or not you would have trouble with Congress this time?

Justice Marshall: No, he said he would get it through. I remember the day that it cleared the Senate. I got a call in the afternoon shortly after it cleared, and he was upstairs in his living quarters. He said, "Well, you made it." I said, "Yes, sir. Thank you again," etc., etc. He said, "You know, you sure got me into a lot of trouble." I said, "Who got who into it? You did it, I didn't do it. I didn't do it." He just laughed! But I still don't see how he got it through, but he did.

You also realize that when he took me off the Court of Appeals he put Connie Motley on the district court. Everybody was saying, "The first Negro woman!" To me that wasn't important! She was the first woman on the Second Circuit District Court. She was the first woman, not the first Negro woman—the first woman! He had that in his mind for quite awhile.

T. H. Baker: And you did have a rough time before the committee.

Justice Marshall: Oh, that first one. Well, the second one, I knew what was coming because Senator [Strom] Thurmond [of South Carolina] had as his advisor a lawyer who is a law professor now down at Memphis Law School. He writes articles on the Fourteenth Amendment, and law schools won't publish them. When I saw him advising him, I said, "Well, I don't have too much to worry about." The questions he asked I expected. I wasn't going to answer them in the first place, because he wanted to know what was in the minds of the committee that drafted the Fourteenth Amendment. I don't know how you're going to find that out. I said I didn't know, because I'm not a person that goes around lying. But you see I had already been through eleven months before, so I mean this few days—

T. H. Baker: You mentioned this earlier, but I think it would be appropriate to repeat it. After the accession to the bench here, no more contact with Mr. Johnson?

Justice Marshall: Except at dinners and receptions—that's all.

T. H. Baker: Did he ever try to seek your advice?

Justice Marshall: No. A couple of times I wanted to volunteer, but I decided not—and I didn't.

T. H. Baker: In that regard, sir, did the disturbance over Mr. Justice Fortas—the two disturbances—hurt the Court very badly?[17]

Justice Marshall: I think so. I think it hurt it to this extent. We felt it on the Court very badly because this—despite what anybody might say is about as close a knit family as you can find. And both my wife and I— we really had it, just like it was a real blood brother.

I had been in New Orleans, and then I was up at the Seventh Circuit the next day it broke. I was on my way. The press people were just unbe- lievable—I found out they had been working on my secretary and my wife, and they'll tell you nothing in plain English. The press people met me at the airport, every place I moved. Then when I finished the Judicial Conference, which is the circuit that I'm over, and I have to hold this conference once a year, and I agreed to stay over for a moot court at Northwestern. All three news agencies called Northwestern and asked how much I was being paid for a moot court. I never heard of anybody getting paid for a moot court—don't even get expenses. One guy was particularly obnoxious. He kept running around behind me in the lobby of the hotel out there and eventually I said, "Well, look, I see I cannot get away from you. You're just too persistent, and I have to give in. I will answer your questions." He says, "Are you being paid for this moot court tomorrow?" I said, "Yes." "Who's paying it?" "Northwestern is paying it." "And how much are you being paid?" I said, "25,000 [dollars]." So he ran out with that information. The Chief Judge of the circuit court out there said to me, "Why would you tell a barefaced lie like that?" I replied, "If he prints it, he's going to be fired sure as shooting—I mean if he hasn't got any better sense than to print that."

T. H. Baker: Was all this at the time of Mr. Fortas' nomination for Chief Justice or later on this year?

Justice Marshall: No.

T. H. Baker: This year at the time of the *Life* magazine story.

Justice Marshall: This year. Anything hurts the Court. Everybody else can do whatever they want, but the Court—we can't. I mean, I can't even violate the speed laws. I can't even do anything.

T. H. Baker: Another thing. The court you joined I suppose will always be called "Warren Court." Was Chief Justice Warren really the leader of the Court, or does your group have a leader in that sense?

Justice Marshall: Yes, he was the leader. Well, he's just one of the great- est people who ever lived, and I think history will record when both of us are long since dead that he is probably the greatest Chief Justice who ever lived. He had the opportunity. He grasped it. He didn't duck

---

17. *See generally* BRUCE A. MURPHY, FORTAS: THE RISE AND RUIN OF A SUPREME COURT JUSTICE (1988).

it, and I think he did extremely well with it. But, in addition, he had warmth like—I'm right next to his chambers. When he would want anything, he would come in here. I always—over and over again—I said, "Look, Chief, number one, you are the Chief Justice. Number two, I'm the low man on the totem pole. I just got here. Number three, I'm a tiny bit younger than you are. Why don't you have Mrs. McHugh call and I'll be in there by the time she hangs the phone up." Each time he'd very simply say, "I don't operate that way." Well, that kind of a feeling—but when we would go in the conference room on Fridays and vote on these cases, he only has one vote. He had the same vote the others had.

T. H. Baker: That's really the gravamen of the question I was asking. Does this kind of personality exert an influence over—?

Justice Marshall: When you get in that conference room, his power of persuasion is great. There is a little something that goes along with the Chief Justice. But he has got to back up with cases, just like each one of us has to. If I, as the junior Justice, get more cases on my side and argue them, he's in trouble. It's he who has got there the mostest is the man who wins the argument.

T. H. Baker: So, in addition to his warm personality, Chief Justice Warren must have a pretty strong intellectual force behind him, too.

Justice Marshall: And he digs. He takes that briefcase. You should see that briefcase he takes home at night! I don't see how he goes to all these affairs. He must stay up all night—is the only way I can figure it out. But I think the Chief Justice does have an effect on the Court. That goes all the way back to [Chief Justice John] Marshall.[18] Back in those days the Chief Justice just ran the joint. But I think in the present time, you do down the line from Hughes, Stone, etc.—they left their print on their Court.[19] I think all of them did. But he's a great man.

The new Chief Justice [Warren E. Burger] I think is going to be just as great.[20] There are a lot of things they have in common. They're very interesting. We've been watching them.

T. H. Baker: Oh really?

Justice Marshall: Yes. You know, [they] let you go, you know. Listen.

T. H. Baker: I imagine you've been kind of watching the new Chief Justice like schoolboys with a new headmaster.

18. *See John Marshall, in* George Van Santvoord, Lives of the Chief-Justices of the Supreme Court of the United States 295 (1854); John P. Roche, ed., John Marshall: Major Opinions and Other Writings (1967).

19. *See generally* Samuel Hendel, Charles Evans Hughes and the Supreme Court (1951); Merlo J. Pusey, Charles Evans Hughes (1951), and Alpheus T. Mason, Harlan Fiske Stone: Pillar of the Law (1955).

20. In 1969, President Nixon appointed Warren E. Burger to replace Earl Warren as Chief Justice. *See* Henry J. Reske, The Diverse Legacy of Warren Burger, 81 A.B.A.J., Aug. 1995, at 36.

Justice Marshall: Yes, it won't help you.

T. H. Baker: I know you've got another appointment coming up here. Is there anything else you would like to add?

Justice Marshall: No, I just think Lyndon Johnson, insofar as minorities, civil rights, people in general, the inherent dignity of the individual human being—I don't believe there has ever been a President to equal Lyndon Johnson—bar none!

T. H. Baker: That's high praise indeed, sir. Do you see any faults—?

Justice Marshall: Well, Lincoln, for example—Lincoln had a lot of politics involved with what he was doing.

T. H. Baker: There are those who would say, "So does Lyndon Johnson!"

Justice Marshall: I don't think so. That's the difference when you talk to him man-to-man. He's talking from his heart. When he does things, it doesn't seem so, but when you actually talk to him, the basic instincts that come out, I mean, he has no reason to persuade me about it—no. I've got one solid vote. That's all I've got. I don't even control my wife's vote. A guy tends to let it out. He had just gotten frustrated at times. But, of course, he had to use his political acumen to get these things through Congress. There is no other way to do it. I don't know how he got my nomination through. I don't know until this day. It took some doing, I'm sure.

T. H. Baker: It must have.

Justice Marshall: I'm sure it took some doing.

T. H. Baker: All that's high praise, sir. Do you see any faults—any bad side to the man?

Justice Marshall: I don't. I don't even think he was intemperate. I don't think he shot from the hip ever. I don't think he did. I think he gave the impression of shooting from the hip after planning six months where to shoot.

T. H. Baker: These frustrations you mention, would these be frustrations over the progress of civil rights and anti-discrimination?

Justice Marshall: Yes.

T. H. Baker: Is there anything else you would like to add?

Justice Marshall: No that's about it.

T. H. Baker: Thank you very much, sir.

Group Action in the Pursuit of Justice

I am deeply honored to have the privilege of delivering this tenth annual lecture in the James Madison series. I am particularly pleased to have been invited to participate in the third cycle of these lectures, which is devoted to the broad, and yet vital, theme of "justice." The previous two cycles of lectures dealt with the great rights guaranteed by our Constitution. Justice [Hugo] Black spoke on the Bill of Rights and the federal government; Justice [William] Brennan spoke of the application of these rights to the states; Chief Justice [Earl] Warren dealt with the relationship of the Bill of Rights to the military; and Justice [William O.] Douglas concluded the first series of lectures with a plea for a judiciary committed to the goal of maintaining the guarantees of the Bill of Rights. The second cycle of lectures, delivered by Justices [Arthur] Goldberg and [Abe] Fortas and Circuit Judges [Elbert] Tuttle and [J. Skelly] Wright, was devoted to the concept of equality. Justice [Tom] Clark, who preceded me both on the Supreme Court and in this forum, began the third cycle with a call for improvements in the administration of justice in our courts. I propose to deal with the topic of "Group Action in the Pursuit of Justice." I hope to explain to you tonight why I believe that organized groups are becoming increasingly necessary in the pursuit of justice. I will also explore the implications that this new development has for the legal profession.

This theme would seem to call, first, for a definition of those rights and liberties, which are encompassed by the term justice. I do not intend to dwell on this point, however, for those who have preceded me in this forum have covered the subject well. They have eloquently expounded upon those rights and liberties guaranteed by our great Bill of Rights, and reaffirmed and expanded by the Thirteenth, Fourteenth, and Fifteenth amendments. These great constitutional declarations remain as expressions of the ideals of our society, ideals that unfortunately have only infrequently been realized throughout the history of our nation. Of

Thurgood Marshall, *Group Action in the Pursuit of Justice*, 44 N.Y.U. L. Rev. 661 (1969). Marshall delivered the 1969 James Madison lecture at New York University School of Law. (Numbered footnotes in original.)

course, even these grand words fail to tell the whole world story. For me at least, justice means more than the traditional concepts embodied in the amendments to our Constitution. True justice requires that the ideals expressed in those amendments be translated into economic and social progress for all of our people.

But we must not let definitional problems detain us here. For there can be no justice—justice in the true sense of the word—until the Bill of Rights and the Civil War amendments, together with the broader ideals they embody, become more than mere abstract expressions. From the perspective of history, we can see that the crucial task is not so much to define our rights and liberties, but to establish institutions which can make the principles embodied in our Constitution meaningful in the lives of ordinary citizens. Only in this way can the solemn declarations embodied in that document be translated into justice. Justice Douglas spoke to the point in the title of his address in this forum: "The Bill of Rights is Not Enough."

In last year's address, Justice Clark spoke to you of one of the most basic institutions for the attainment of justice—the courts. I speak to you tonight of another institution essential to the attainment of justice, an institution perhaps even more basic. No matter how solemn and profound the declarations of principle contained in our charter of government, no matter how dedicated and independent our judiciary, true justice can only be obtained through the actions of committed individuals, individuals acting both independently and through organized groups.

In the past several decades, committed members of the bar have played a decisive role in reviving the concepts of justice embodied in the Bill of Rights and in our other constitutional guarantees. We shall have occasion to refer to some of their efforts in a moment. Although their efforts were a significant factor in promoting the cause of justice, my message tonight is that committed action on the part of individual members of the bar will not be enough to consolidate the gains of the past or to accomplish the role formerly filled for the most part by individuals will have to be filled to an increasingly large degree by organized group practice. If we are to move from a declaration of rights to their implementation, especially with regard to the politically and economically underprivileged, large numbers of lawyers are needed at the working level. This need for lawyers and supporting personnel cannot be met by individual effort; the task is simply too great. The need can be met only in an organized way.

My message can be aptly illustrated by the history of the Civil War amendments, a history in which I was in recent years fortunate enough to have played a small part. That history demonstrates that mere declarations of rights have not been sufficient to secure justice. It further illustrates that true progress can only be made by organized effort. The rights guaranteed by our Constitution are not self-enforcing; they can be made meaningful only by legislative or judicial action. As we shall see, legislation does not pass itself and the courts cannot act in the absence of a controversy. Organized, committed effort is necessary to promote legislation and institute legal action on any significant scale.

The fourteenth amendment, like the Bill of Rights, was a declaration of principle. It enshrined into national law the principles of freedom and equality, which an earlier generation had announced in more abstract form in the Declaration of Independence. The framers of the fourteenth amendment set their sights high. They spoke during the ratification debates in broad, general terms.[1] The nation was to be given the power to make certain that the fundamental rights of all individuals were respected. It was not a time for defining those rights with any precision; it was a time for creating institutions, which would guarantee their maintenance. Without the power to enforce basic human rights, they would become mere paper promises. But the terms of the amendment, however powerful they may seem, could mean little without activism in the pursuit of justice. Each of the two most important sections of the amendment[2] shared the same deceptive positivism; both seemed to solve problems, which they actually only provided tools for the proper solutions.

Section one sets forth the basic ideals of 1868 in positive form. It is self-executing on its face and declaratory in language. Various phrases were used to describe, in their different and overlapping aspects, the fundamental rights which were to be guaranteed to all men—privileges and immunities of citizens of the United States; life, liberty, and property; equal protection of the law. As Senator Howard of Michigan put it during the ratification debates, the language of the amendment establishes equality before the law, and it gives to the humbled, the poorest, the most despised of the race the same rights and the same protection before the law as it gives to the most powerful, the most wealthy, or the most haughty.[3]

This self-executing language is, however, deceiving. Its positive form does not guarantee automatic enforcement. The courts, naturally enough, exercise the power in cases brought before them to decree when the rights guaranteed by the amendment have been infringed. But these rights cannot be enforced unless those who possess them know they exist and are given the legal means to vindicate them. Without the commitment of

1. *See generally* HORACE EDGAR FLACK, THE ADOPTION OF THE FOURTEENTH AMENDMENT 55–139 (1908); J. B. J. BLISS JAMES, THE FRAMING OF THE FOURTEENTH AMENDMENT 182–202 (1956); J. TEN BROEK, EQUAL UNDER LAW 201–233 (1956).
2. U.S. CONST. amend. XIV, § 1, 5.
3. CONG. GLOBE, 39th Cong., 1st Sess. 2766 (1866).

the bar, those protected by the amendment will ordinarily possess neither the knowledge nor the skills needed to make the promises of the
amendment meaningful. Without the commitment of large numbers of
lawyers, of "private attorneys-general"[4] if you will, the amendment will
mean nothing.

Section five of the Fourteenth Amendment is even more dependent for
its enforcement upon the active, dedicated work of committed individuals and groups. All it does is grant legislative power. The grant is broad,
and the power potentially of great importance.[5] Although the courts were
left as the last resort for individuals who felt their individual rights were
being infringed, only the legislature could act more generally. The final
protection of the basic rights granted by the amendment was, in effect, to
be democracy itself; through participation in democracy, those formerly
deprived of their rights would help insure their own future equality.

But the hopes of the framers were soon dashed. From the 1870s to the
1950s not a single civil rights measure was placed on the statute books.
Without active support for the promises of 1868, the rights granted by
the amendment fell from sight and became historical anachronisms. Section five, its promises and its power for good, was forgotten. A quick
glance through the history of the century, which separates us from 1868,
confirms this view. Although three constitutional amendments and four
important civil rights bills were passed in the decade following the Civil
War, the postwar radical fervor soon died. The judicial decisions of the
era only reflected social attitudes as they evidenced the rapid decline of
the fourteenth amendment as a declaration of justice and equality.

In the *Slaughterhouse Cases*,[6] decided in 1873, the Court echoed the
framers and read the amendment as a declaration of "the freedom of the
slave race, the security and firm establishment of that freedom, and the
protection of the newly-made freeman and citizen from the oppressions
of those who had formerly exercised unlimited dominion over him."[7] So
sure was the Court of the great purposes for which the amendment
spoke to any problem but racial discrimination.[8] Only the dissents fore-
shadowed what was too soon to come-the incorporation of laissez-faire
economics into the Fourteenth Amendment.[9] For a while, it seemed that

---

4. *See* Note, *Private Attorneys-General: Group Action in the Fight for Civil Liberties*, 58
YALE L.J. 574 (1949).
5. United States v. Guest, 383 U.S. 745, 784 (1966) (Brennan, J., concurring and
dissenting in part).
6. 83 U.S. (16 Wall.) 36 (1873).
7. *Id.* at 71.
8. *Id.* at 81.
9. *See id.*, at 83 (Field, J., dissenting); at 111 (Bradley, J., dissenting); at 124
(Swayne, J., dissenting).

the Court meant what it had said in the *Slaughterhouse Cases.* In 1880, a series of state jury laws was found in conflict with the Civil Rights Act of 1875.[10] The language of the Court in these decisions was broad enough to encompass any kind of racial discrimination.[11] But Reconstruction, already moribund, died with the Compromise of 1877.[12] The attention of both Republicans and Democrats turned to the dominant themes of the day—economic expansion and the nation's surge westward. Negroes could no longer seek help through the political process—all eyes were turned elsewhere. It was thus no surprise in 1883 when the Supreme Court voided the public accommodation sections of the Civil Rights Act of 1875 in an opinion, which spelled an end to the great promises of the Fourteenth Amendment.[13] Only the first Justice Harlan foresaw the future, as he warned that "the recent amendments [will become] splendid baubles, thrown out to delude . . . the nation."[14] But the nation was not listening. While the attention of the nation was directed elsewhere, the South was undergoing a minor revolution of its own. The political structure, thrown into disarray by Reconstruction and its rather abrupt end, was stabilizing in favor of white supremacy. The Southern states were seemingly unaware of the Civil War amendments and sought to ensure the perpetuation of that supremacy through legislation—the infamous "Jim Crow laws." The laws seemed blatant violations of the fourteenth amendment, and they called out for challenge—a challenge that was not long in coming. But the result of that challenge dealt the basic principles of the fourteenth amendment a staggering blow—a blow from which it took sixty years to recover fully.

The state legislature which enacted the segregation statute challenged in 1896 in *Plessy v. Ferguson*[15] ironically included a number of Negroes.[16] In addition, the challenge was at least partially motivated by economic reasons—the railroad found the cost of separate "Jim Crow" cars unduly high. The challenge was in vain. The Court was simply not interested—equal meant equal—it did not mean together. Again, only Justice Harlan called for an application of the spirit of the Fourteenth Amendment.[17]

The states took their cue from *Plessy.* Separation of races soon became

10. *Ex parte* Virginia, 100 U.S. 339 (1880); Virginia v. Rives, 100 U.S. 313 (1880); Strauder v. West Virginia, 100 U.S. 303 (1880).
11. *See, e.g.,* Strauder v. West Virginia, 100 U.S. 303, 307–308 (1880).
12. *See* JOHN HOPE FRANKLIN, RECONSTRUCTION: AFTER THE CIVIL WAR 212–217 (1961).
13. Civil Rights Cases, 109 U.S. 3 (1883).
14. *Id.* at 48 (dissenting opinion).
15. 163 U.S. 537 (1896).
16. *See* THE CONSTITUTION AND THE SUPREME COURT 247–57 (L. Pollak ed. 1966).
17. 163 U.S. at 552 (dissenting opinion).

firmly entrenched in the South, and elsewhere for that matter. "Jim Crow" pervaded every aspect of life—even homes for the blind were segregated. Challenges were few and sporadic; and when they succeeded, the states reenacted the same scheme in different forms. Their ingenuity was certainly not taxed. Again, through the first two and a half decades of the [twentieth] century, the minds of the nation and nation's lawyers and legislators were largely elsewhere, although the next two decades did see a weak but steady legal attack on racial discrimination. The situation was such that in the 1940s one commentator said: "There is no power in the world—not even in all the mechanized armies of the earth . . . which could not force Southern white people to the abandonment of the principle of social segregation."[18]

And yet, segregation and its incidents, while still with us, are rapidly becoming a thing of the past. What happened? Mechanized armies did not impose the change. It was not even prompted by the states or by federal legislation. It came from the private citizen, the citizen who believed that equal protection meant just that—the citizen who, with the assistance of those lawyers who still believed in the promise of justice and equality never gave up the fight against the relics of slavery. The fight has been long, and the targets many. The turning point was of course *Brown v. Board of Education*, whose story is familiar.[19] During this period since 1954, law after law has been struck down and the tactics of delay are now being met head-on. New life has been breathed into the Civil War amendments and enactments.[20] The fight to reestablish the self-executing sections of the Fourteenth Amendment reawakened the legislatures to their powers, under both the Civil War amendments and other parts of the Constitution as well, to establish racial justice in the land. The acts are familiar, from the Civil Rights Acts of 1957 through the Open Housing Act of 1968.

The spirit of justice was not limited to racial discrimination. The germ planted was infectious and has spread. It is certainly not an exaggeration to say that the concern for the rights of the criminally accused and for the economically disadvantaged has to come in part from the lessons learned in the fight against discrimination. Today, the legislatures, the courts, the bar, and the people of this country are demonstrating a concern for fairness and justice unparalleled in the history of our nation.

The history of the Civil War amendments demonstrates quite clearly, I think, the necessity for committed action. It also demonstrates the

18. Mark Ethridge, *quoted in* C. Vann Woodward, The Strange Career of Jim Crow 120 (2d ed. 1966).
19. 347 U.S. 483 (1954). [*See* Richard Kluger, Simple Justice: The History of Brown v. Board of Education (1976)—ed.].
20. *See, e.g.,* Jones v. Alfred H. Mayer Co., 392 U.S. 409 (1968).

second, and more important aspect of my message—that individual effort is not enough to secure justice. Today, even more than in the past, only organized action can hope to that the concept of justice remains meaningful to all of our people.

Until only a few decades ago, the efforts to enforce the guarantees of the fourteenth amendment and the other post–Civil War enactments were sporadic and largely defensive in nature. It was not until the rudiments of organization were applied to the problem that significant progress was made. Much of that progress was made by the NAACP, an organization I had the honor of being associated with for many years. Its example can be instructive.

During the early period of its existence, the NAACP participated in several cases that resulted in striking down discriminatory legislation. However, it was not until the 1930s that the seeds of significant progress were sown. At that time, the organization developed a conscious program of legal action designed to eliminate discrimination and inequality. The financial and human resources that were funneled into this program were in large part responsible for recent successes in striking down discriminatory laws and practices. Similar examples could be multiplied. But whichever group you examine, one thing becomes evident: the organized and committed effort of groups of this sort has been of immeasurable importance in making our constitutional guarantees meaningful.

The concept of justice is, however, not a static one. Our tactics must be revised to suit the times. The needs are many and obvious. In traditional terms, there are of course the continuing problems of criminal and racial justice. Perhaps more significant, however, are the problems peculiar to the economically and socially disadvantaged. Lawyers have long spoken for the other segments of our society, both in court and in legislatures. But now who is to speak for the poor, the disadvantaged, and these days, for the ordinary consumer?

I think the thrust of my remarks thus far makes the answer clear. The goals of economic and social justice, like the goal of racial justice, can only be achieved through committed effort. All segments of society are, of course, essential to this effort, but one of the most effective contributions will be that made by lawyers. The brief history I have outlined for you makes another thing clear. Effective response to the problems facing our society today requires that the contribution of the bar be in terms of organized and focused effort. Individual action was, as we have seen, not sufficient to meet the more simple and identifiable problems of the past. Racial discrimination was effectively attacked only through effort. Certainly no less is necessary to meet the complex and pervading problems of today, particularly those problems that do not admit of solutions wholly legal. The role of the legal lawyer remains a necessary ingredient, but he simply cannot do enough to make more than a dent in the complex set of problems facing segments of today's society. The individual lawyer could, and did, secure justice for the criminally accused. But can one man, no matter how dedicated and talented, protect the consumer from the predatory commercial practices so common in many of our cities? Can he secure meaningful compliance with the Supreme Court's desegregation decisions? Clearly, he cannot. Solutions to these problems demand human and financial resources that can be focused on a problem only through organization.

We come then, as always, to the inevitable problem of remedies. If, as I have attempted to show, there are grave inadequacies in the traditional system of individual attorneys protecting particular individual rights, what is to take its place? Of course the traditional system remains perfectly adequate in many traditional contexts. But in the new problem areas, where a new institutional framework is necessary, what approach should we take? What implications will such an approach have for the legal profession?

Although in the final analysis this difficult policy question must be resolved by bar associations and legislative bodies, there are vital constitutional considerations lurking in the background.[21] As a series of recent Supreme Court decisions has made clear, the First and Fourteenth Amendments forbid state interference with certain forms of group legal practice. These decisions rest on a basic assumption about the nature of litigation. As the Court said in *NAACP v. Button*, litigation is often "a form of political expression. Groups which find themselves unable to achieve their objectives through the ballot frequently turn to the courts. . . . And under the conditions of modern government, litigation may well be the sole practicable avenue open to a minority to petition for redress of grievances."[22]

Litigation, the Court has thus held, is a protected mode of group expression. Persons may join together to pursue joint ends through the courts, just as they do through the legislature. And this First Amendment right extends beyond traditional "political" contexts. As we held last term in the United Mine Workers case, "the First Amendment does not protect speech and assembly only to the extent it can be characterized as political."[23] We therefore held that union members have a constitutional right to join together and hire attorneys to represent them in workmen's compensation cases. The union members, although actually

21. *See* Peter L. Zimroth, *Group Legal Services and the Constitution* 76 YALE L.J. 966 (1967); Note, *Group Legal Services*, 79 HARV. L. REV. 416 (1965).
22. 371 U.S. at 429–430 (1963).
23. Mine Workers v. Illinois Bar Assn., 389 U.S. 217, 223 (1967).

seeking only money damages, were engaged in a group activity entitled to First Amendment protection.

These cases make it clear that the states are not free to prohibit all forms of group practice. Of course, as the Court has continually stressed, the states do have interests in regulating the practice of law.[24] But the Constitution protects certain kinds of group activities, and to the extent it does, the states must satisfy their legitimate concerns in other ways. The old concept that each lawyer must be an individual practitioner, hired and paid only by individual clients, and associated with other attorneys only through partnership arrangements, must yield to modern realities.

It is obvious, therefore, that the bar must face up to some basic structural questions. Changes must be made, partially because there are severe constitutional problems associated with many of the old rules of champerty and maintenance and the old prohibitions against group practice, but more importantly because the old structure is no longer completely responsive to present needs. The needs of the poor, of minorities, of indigent criminal defendants—these needs can only be met through forms of group practice. If the bar is to live up to its social responsibilities, it cannot let the narrow interests of a few practitioners stand in the way.

We have seen a number of important developments already. The federal government has financed endeavors which have also made important contributions. Legal aid and public defender organizations have grown, often with the support of the large reservoir of talent, which can be provided by law schools. The law schools themselves have recognized the changed scope of their responsibilities to society and have instituted programs and curriculum changes more responsive to the needs of today. Thus, we have seen active participation in legal aid and similar programs and more emphasis on courses in criminal law and procedure, social welfare, and the like.

But the basic decisions have not yet been made. The bar has not yet acted definitively to bring its structure into line with current needs. In the process, certain important values must be kept in mind. On one side, we have the clear need for that kind of group practice which brings legal representation to those persons who have previously been left entirely outside the system. On the other, we have the traditional values of professional responsibility, which must not be impaired. We have assumed in the past that the fidelity of the lawyer to his client's interest can be strengthened by the financial bond between them. The client pays the bill, and he ultimately will call the tune. The lawyer, while maintaining proper ethical standards, represents only the interests of the person supplying the retainer. In group practice, the old financial tie is broken.

24. *See, e.g.,* Sperry v. Florida ex rel. Florida Bar, 373 U.S. 379, 383 (1963).

The client no longer pays the bill. And yet, the lawyer's ultimate responsibility must still be to his client. The financial link with an intermediary must not be allowed to warp his responsibility.

This is the problem. The solution, however, is not to fall back on the old theory that only the financial tie between lawyer and client can guarantee professional fidelity. Group legal services must be organized in ways, which insulate the lawyer-client relationship, which protect it from influences. Our ingenuity may be challenged in this endeavor. But we must never forget the ultimate goal—making the law a reality for those to whom it is now largely meaningless.

The American Bar Association has taken the first step toward bringing its Canons of Ethics into line with current day realities. The Special Committee on Evaluation of Ethical Standards has proposed a new Code of Professional Responsibility. This August, it will be presented to the House of Delegates for action. The preliminary draft recently circulated contains some promising steps forward. It would allow lawyers to be furnished and paid by approved legal aid offices, professional and trade associations, or labor unions. More importantly, similar rights are extended to all bona fide, nonprofit organizations which, as an incident to their primary activities, pay for legal services furnished to members or beneficiaries. Under this provision all sorts of community organizations presumably could be established and provided with counsel; lawyers employed by these groups could then represent their members, or others who would benefit from organization programs. Moreover, the definition of legal aid offices includes programs operated by "bona fide, non-profit community organization[s]."*

These provisions of the new code would certainly be a great step forward. Of course other changes would still have to be made; state statutes regulating the practice of law have to be made; state statutes regulating the practice of law also have to be updated, and even federal procedure—especially administrative procedure—could warrant some reform. But

---

* [Editor's note: Three months after Justice Marshall's address, the ABA House of Delegates unanimously adopted the new Code of Professional Responsibility proposed by the Special Committee on Evaluation of Ethical Standards, to become effective January 1, 1970. The *American Bar News* commented on the action: "The issue of group legal services brought the only controversy over the code on the House floor. The Special Committee on Availability of Legal Services proposed an amendment that would have approved and regulated extension of group service arrangements such as those provided by a union for its individual members. This proposal was defeated by a voice vote. The code as adopted limits group service to nonprofit organizations whose group plans have been upheld as constitutional by court decisions." 14 AMERICAN BAR NEWS 9 (1969).]

the goal is clear. The structure of the bar must be redesigned to meet the responsibilities faced by a new generation.

I need not dwell here on the mechanical details. What is important is the commitment of men dedicated to the ideals of justice. Change will not be easy. The narrow interests of the few often carry disproportionate weight. But without both structural reform and the commitment of large numbers of men, our grand ideals will speak nothing more than paper promises. The lesson of the past century is clear. The battle will not win itself. If the bar does not move forward decisively, the nation that looks to it for leadership will soon forget the lessons of the past one hundred years. Elihu Root spoke to the point in 1904. His words still hold true:

"[The] lawyer's profession demands of him something more than the ordinary public service of citizenship. He has a duty to the law. In the cause of peace and order and human rights against all injustice and wrong, he is the advocate of all men, present and to come."[25]

25. Whitney North Seymour, Jr., The Obligations of the Lawyer to His Profession 12 (1968).

THE 1970s

During the 1970s Justice Marshall, long recognized for his role in the civil rights movement, also became known for his concerns for humanity and efforts to move the people of America toward a common goal of unity. As a member of the U.S. Supreme Court, Marshall effectively used his position to extend the equal protection clause of the Fourteenth Amendment of the Constitution to all.

During the 1970s, Marshall urged judges to consider themselves as agents "bound together in a common endeavor with a common purpose,"[1] a theme that Charles Hamilton Houston had sounded in his efforts to tear down the apartheid-like system in America. Marshall encouraged judges and the nation to come together in reconciliation. He believed the courts could play a role as liberals and conservatives faced off on civil rights issues.

To harmonize differences in the nation, Marshall made a distinction between positive law and its application to "humans." Marshall's speeches viewed the law as abstractions, projection, and conjecture. He reminded lawyers and judges to never forget that law "deals in a world of individuals."[2]

As part of his call for common unity, Marshall was a critic of black separatist ideas. He viewed separatism as "anarchy" and lent his voice to the view that "black is beautiful, but so are people of other colors." Thus, Marshall's call for a more perfect union was intended not only as a functional application of law, but also as an appeal for social respect. Marshall's philosophy was consistent with his exhortation to judges and prosecutors to live up to the letter of the constitution by applying equal justice for all.[3]

During the 1970s Justice Marshall remained concerned by the lack of access to the courts by the poor for competent lawyers on their side. His elevation to the U.S. Supreme Court did not blind him to his early years

1. Thurgood Marshall, The Law Deals with a World of Individuals (1970), *infra*, at p. 226.
2. *Id.*
3. *Id.*

as a lawyer in the local courts in Baltimore and other courts in the nation where he had witnessed poor defendants without lawyers facing well-staffed government lawyers. Justice Marshall spoke out against systems that stigmatized the poor and made them outcasts of the legal system, asserting that the legitimacy of the judicial system required "that all persons and groups should be able to receive competent representation in the legal process."[4]

Justice Marshall's first visit to Africa in 1960 broadened his perspective of the need of more understanding among all races. This trip no doubt reaffirmed his belief in the meaning of equal justice for all. Six years after the Court's decision in *Brown v. Board of Education*, Marshall was a special adviser to the African delegation to the Kenya constitutional conference. His appointment was a strategic one by the U.S. government, as Marshall was known all over the world as a man of fairness and justice. Marshall stated that his reason for accepting the appointment was that Africans were aware of the plight of blacks in America, and among other things, that he hoped to provide dialogue for the expansion and international contacts for Negro businessmen.[5]

Marshall's travels to Africa may have influenced his participation in the World Peace Through Law Conferences in 1973 in the Ivory Coast and in 1977 in Manila, where he delivered a speech calling on the world to give peace a chance through the respect for law.[6]

Near the end of the decade, Marshall was honored by the state of Texas when Texas Southern University School of Law was renamed the Thurgood Marshall School of Law. In his speech during the ceremony, Marshall named and praised the men and women involved in *Sweatt v. Painter*, the case that in 1950 had struck down separate-but-equal higher education in Texas. He spoke about the traditions of law schools and reminded the students that "bricks and mortar do not a law school make."[7] Marshall used this opportunity to quote Charles Hamilton Houston's expectations of the entering law class of 1930 at Howard University School of Law: "I'm not training lawyers; I am not training members of the bar. I am training social engineers."[8]

---

4. Thurgood Marshall, Financing Public Law Practice: The Role of the Organized Bar (1975), *infra*, p. 242.
5. *Negroes' Lawyer on World Stage*, N.Y. TIMES, Jan. 22, 1960, at 2. Marshall also met with the Asian community in Nairobi relative to African agitation against them. *U.S. Negro Leader Arrives in Kenya*, N.Y. TIMES, Jan. 11, 1960, at 5.
6. *See, e.g.*, Thurgood Marshall, World Peace Through Law: An Urgent Task, *infra*, p. 236.
7. Thurgood Marshall, Building a Tradition of Public Service (1976), *infra*, at p. 232.
8. *Id.*, at 233.

In 1978, Marshall returned to Howard Law School to honor the elevation of his friend, Wiley Austin Branton, the new law dean. His speech was lively, as Marshall was at home and with his closest friends. Marshall sternly recalled, however, that under the tutelage of Charles Houston and the law faculty, he was one of a handful of students who made it through the rigor of Howard's law school. Marshall's speech gives insight about the discipline of his teachers, who expected him to survive as a lawyer in the real world.

The Law Deals with a
World of Individuals

It is a great honor to be here this evening. It is also an opportunity for the kind of informal communication between bench and bar which is so important and all too rare. We are, after all, lawyers and judges alike, bound together in a common endeavor with a common purpose. Our common mission is nothing less than doing justice; our common charge, the responsibility for the legal system which binds together the social fabric of our troubled nation.

Together we daily strive toward our common goals in courtrooms across the nation as we deal with people and their individual problems on a case-by-case basis. Our daily encounters are, without doubt, the very heart of our system of justice. They are what give uniqueness and strength to the judicial branch of government. And whether in the chambers of a judge on the city's Family Court or in the marbled courtroom of the Supreme Court of the United States, we who serve the law serve a common master, and in so doing sit astride the nexus between the people and their government.

Our legislatures pass laws in the abstract; they deal in a world of statistics and projections, of compromises and conjecture. The executive enforces the law on a broad scale; his concern is also with the greatest good for the greatest number.

We, however, deal in a world of individuals, whether they be the clients we serve or the litigants who appear before us. In our courtrooms, the statistics come alive, as the general rule must be applied to the specific case. The legislature's carefully prescribed criteria for release on bail must be applied to a flesh and blood man, with real problems and re-sponsibilities. Landlord-tenant laws must be applied to a real dispute between a landlord trying to maintain a crumbling ghetto building with far too little income and the tenant with little money and no place else to go. Our job is at once the most difficult and, in many ways, the most important in the process of government. And our courtrooms are

On the occasion of Justice Marshall's acceptance of an honorary membership in the Association of the Bar of New York, Nov. 20, 1973, in 29 RECORD 15 (1974).

perhaps the most accurate barometers of the extent to which we have succeeded in building a just society.

We are today being overwhelmed with cries for greater efficiency in our courts and for more rapid disposition of cases. But in our hurrying to erect a more efficient system of justice, we must not forget that our system derives its strength from the fact that it deals with individuals. To mechanize the system, to make it lose its human element, to forget that in every case we are dealing with a human being who, before the law, deserves to be treated as an equal of any other man, is to lose that which gives any judicial system its very life.

But while the courtroom is and will ever remain in the heart of our system of justice, it is sometimes an inadequate forum for the bench and bar to engage in the crucial exchange of ideas and insights into what can be done to make further progress in building a better legal system and a better society. I have sometimes wondered how many lawyers have left the Supreme Court after participating in oral argument with [an] uneasy, queasy feeling that somehow, they never really got a chance to say what they wanted to say.

As frustrating as the courtroom must be for some lawyers, it is positively incomprehensible to the laymen who come before the court seeking justice. The formalism, the ritual, the arcane attributes of the law no doubt make those few feet between the judge's bench and the counsel's table seem an inestimable chasm to the uneducated laymen whom the system serves. The law exists for the people; the courts to dispense to their needs, and the lawyer to plead their cases. The people are the consumers of the law, and I believe we owe it to them to make that law understandable to them.

That particular task is one we all too often fail to achieve. We are accused, and often rightfully, of having a narrow and technical view of justice. Criminal law is a prime example. Ask any criminal lawyer what are the prerequisites of a fair criminal justice system and he will most likely give a laundry list of constitutionally guaranteed rights—trial by jury, assistance of counsel, cross-examination of witnesses, privilege against self-incrimination, and so forth down the line.

Now these constitutionally guaranteed rights are a mainstay of our system, and we have come a long way toward construing them liberally and enforcing them carefully so as to provide a rough measure of justice. But we sometimes tend to forget that the Constitution is more than a legal document—it should mean more to us than a list of rights.

In my opinion, our fellow citizens may have an understanding of the Constitution at once less technical, but deeper and more profound than what we were all taught in law school. The Constitution embodies not just a series of legal precepts, but the very spirit of democratic government.

And that notion of our Constitution might well teach us a little about our own profession.

What kind of government does the Constitution require? What is the spirit of the Constitution as understood by the people of this nation? It is, first, that our government is a government of laws, and not of men. The Constitution does not say so, in so many words, but that principle is inherent in its system of checks and balances. It is rooted in the very history of our nation—a history of revolution against the rule of one man. It is reflected in the words carved into the marble over the front of the Supreme Court building in Washington: Equal Justice *Under* Law. In the final analysis, it is grounded in the very fact that we, the people, have established a written Constitution which sets down rules that no men can ignore, no matter how powerful, no matter how great in number.

I submit that we will not achieve true justice in our society simply by ensuring the observance of enumerated constitutional rights. It is not enough that we provide due process in our courtrooms. We cannot stop there. Our system of justice must not only live up to the letter of the Constitution, but also to its spirit—the spirit of a government of laws, not of men; a government which provides equal justice, *under law.*

How close are we today to achieving that goal? Do we have a system of law, rather than men? Two aspects of our criminal justice system immediately come to mind as falling far short of that goal.

Let us look first at the way in which our system of justice initiates criminal cases. It is a process, I submit, of virtually unbridled discretion, the discretion of the prosecutor. For the most part, he alone decides whether to charge an offense or to let a given matter drop. He must decide whether the state will grant immunity from prosecution in return for cooperation in achieving the conviction of another. If a decision is made to proceed with criminal charges, he alone must choose which of several possible offenses to charge, he alone must choose which of several [counts], he alone must decide whether or not the state will accept a guilty plea to a lesser offense in return for dropping the more serious charges.

Whether a suspected shoplifter will be prosecuted or sent home with a warning; whether an alleged drunk driver should only be prosecuted for speeding; whether an alleged armed robber should be permitted to plead to unlawful possession of a firearm; all of the above are typical decisions relying on the decision of the prosecutor.

We must not forget that for a vast majority of our criminal defendants, plea-bargaining is the only trial of their case they receive. To my mind, that imposes on the prosecutor and the defense attorney a grave responsibility. It is to them that the defendant must look for fair treatment and the sometimes ephemeral quality of justice we call due process. But, too often, I fear, copping a plea is bargain basement justice, looked upon by prosecutor and defense attorney alike as a sale more than as a determination of a human being's future. In our headlong rush for efficiency and rapid processing of criminal court caseloads we must not forget that we are dealing with people's lives and futures. The individual orientation and humane character of the judicial system are its greatest strengths. To lose those qualities for the sake of efficiency is to strike a very bad bargain indeed. I do not condemn plea-bargaining, but I think it must be rationalized and humanized as a system. A plea bargain should be premised not on expedience but on genuine concerns for the rights and needs of the defendant. We settle civil cases only after careful thought and thorough research; cases in which a man's life and liberty are at stake certainly deserve no less.

Let us examine another part of our criminal system: the sentencing process. Here too we confront a system of unbridled discretion. Although virtually all of a judge's rulings at trial are controlled by elaborate codes of procedure and evidence, and are subject to review by an appellate court for failure to comply with those rules, ironically, perhaps the most important decision a judge makes in a given case is left for the most part to his unregulated and unreviewable discretion.

The problems of our present sentencing system have already received the careful, and characteristically thoughtful, consideration of a distinguished member of the bench here in the Southern District. And I will not pretend to have given the matter more thought than he has. Judge [Marvin E.] Frankel has expressed what to some may seem a harsh, but what I deem totally apt, characterization of the present system. If I may be permitted to crib part of my speech from his excellent book on the subject: "The almost wholly unchecked and sweeping powers we give to judges in the fashioning of sentences are terrifying and intolerable to a society that professes devotion to the rule of law."[1]

The people of this country must find it very peculiar that our legal system would reverse a conviction for possession of marijuana because of a minor imperfection in a jury instruction relating to whether or not the defendant knew the marijuana was illegally imported, yet the very same system provides no remedy whatsoever for the lawfully convicted defendant who receives a twenty-five-year sentence for possession of an ounce of marijuana when his best friend was let off by the D.A.'s office with a warning not to get caught again, and when most other offenders receive a small fine and a short jail sentence. And should we in the legal profession be any less disturbed?

1. MARVIN E. FRANKEL, CRIMINAL SENTENCES 5 (1973). *See also* Marvin E. Frankel, *Lawlessness in Sentencing*, 41 U. CIN. L. REV. 1 (1972).

By picking out these two areas of our criminal justice system, I do not in any sense mean to condemn our prosecutors or our judges. Indeed, the fact that our system operates on the whole as fairly as it does is a tribute to their concerned professionalism. That professionalism goes a long way in building equity into a system characterized by discretion.

Nor do I wish to suggest that we should substitute for our traditional prosecutorial and sentencing procedures a system which provides no room at all for discretion. In law, as in life, people and cases come in all shapes and sizes. Only a nation of robots could be content with a system of justice with no room for adjustments to meet the particular needs of individual cases and individual defendants.

Some degree of discretion is no doubt inevitable and in fact desirable in any system of justice. But discretion is subject to abuse. Powers given for certain proper purposes all too often can be perverted towards illegitimate ends. In my view we must attempt to strike a new balance between the competing goals of individualized justice and the rule of law. Discretion, where it exists and where it is necessary to ensure that justice retain its human element, should rationalized and controlled.

Reform in this area may not easily come within the traditional case-by-case judicial process. As Judge Frankel has pointed out in his lecture on sentencing discretion, for example, review of sentences by appellate courts on a case-by-case basis is only one of several possible approaches to the problem of limiting discretion and channeling it toward proper purposes. And appellate review of sentences would be a solution fraught with great problems of its own. Other, in my view, more promising solutions would entail more innovative reforms—sentencing councils, better statutory definition of sentencing ranges, and better education of judges in sentencing matters—all are promising avenues of reform.

In the area of prosecutorial discretion as well, the future is cloudy for hoping to solve abuses of discretion through the ordinary judicial process. Discretionary prosecutorial decisions are virtually unreviewable by the courts, and for good reason. For such review would ultimately entwine the judicial and executive functions, and would be inconsistent with the neutrality of the courts vis-à-vis the executive branch of government. Solutions to the problems of unchecked discretion must come, if they are to come at all, in advances in administrative techniques for ensuring equity within a given prosecutorial system, or in better training of prosecutors as to the proper and improper uses of discretion.

But simply because problems cannot be solved within the traditional case-by-case judicial process does not mean that they are not deserving of our attention. Just the opposite is true. Our common mission of providing a fair system of justice requires that each of us be willing to step outside our traditional courtroom roles on occasion and work together in other forums for developing solutions to these problems.

The systematic problems of our judicial system are not confined to the area of criminal justice. Perhaps the most unsettling area of our law today is the problem of access to the courts by the vast majority of our citizenry. The judicial system does not exist as an end in itself. It does not exist to serve lawyers and judges, but to serve the public, our own constituency. Access to the courts, and access to the legal profession, must be preserved not only for our great corporations, not only for the victims of accidents, but for our entire citizenry, whose daily lives more today than ever before are touched by the law in its myriad forms.

One critic has labeled the judiciary the least dangerous branch of our government.[2] In many ways, it is true; we are the least powerful branch. The judiciary cannot by the stroke of a pen conscript a million men, nor can we tax and appropriate the billions of dollars that makes our government move. The only tool at our command is moral suasion. But that doesn't mean that we are without influence at all. We have a rough bargain with our own constituency. As recent events have shown, although we lack power in our own right, we gain strength by virtue of the power of the constituency we serve, the people of our nation. But that power will exist only so long as each person in this country can continue to believe that the courts and the law are available to him on an equal basis. That power will exist only if each person can trust that he will stand before the court, as an individual and as an equal in the eyes of the law to any other litigant.

We whose profession it is to ensure that the game is played according to the rules, have an overriding professional responsibility of ensuring that the game itself is fair for all. Our citizenry expect a system of justice that not only lives up to the letter of the Constitution, but one that also abides by its spirit. They deserve the best efforts of all of us toward meeting the need.

In our day-to-day work we must continue to realize that we are dealing with individuals—not statistics. Sure, we might be overworked. At the same time, while we are looking for more efficient ways to deal with growing backlogs of cases and appeals, we must not allow ourselves to lose our perspective of full justice in order to alleviate the pressure on us.

2. ALEXANDER BICKEL, THE LEAST DANGEROUS BRANCH (1965).

Building a Tradition of Public Service

[This] is a real honor, but it is an honor for quite a few people. You know Texas is a big state, and we got a lot of people involved in all of this. It just did not happen last night. I had trouble explaining to my teen-age sons that these things did not happen last night, and I have been unable to persuade them.

But, first of all, you recognize Lonnie Smith and Heman Sweatt. And, as a lawyer—to those of you in the law school and on the faculty: They were two real good clients. You did not have to worry about them. As a matter of fact, the only problem was in explaining to newspaper people around the country that his name really wasn't "Herman." That is the only problem I had.

Then, I remember people like Maceo Smith and Anne Robinson, Reverend Lucas, Lula White, Carter Wesley, W. J. Durham[1] and the other lawyers who worked on these cases. Their contributions were unbelievably high. They not only contributed their money—and they did; Negroes in Texas paid for all of these cases, every red cent—but they went further. In those days, we didn't stay in big hotels; we stayed in these private homes, and we consumed considerable food—and Coca Cola—and all of that was a legitimate contribution.

I say all of this because this is what I consider to be a great day as an honor to the people of Texas. You know, I am just about a Texan, I guess. Some years ago in this city, Lula White made me an honorary Texan.

In 1976, Thurgood Marshall spoke at the Texas Southern School of Law on the dedication and renaming of the Law School in Marshall's honor. See Address by the Honorable Thurgood Marshall, 4 TEXAS So. U.L. REV. 191 (1976–1977). *See also* Todd Ackerman, *Giant Legacy of Marshall Lives at TSU*, HOUSTON CHRONICLE, Jan. 26, 1993, at 17 (Two-Star Edition).
1. *See* MARK V. TUSHNET, MAKING CIVIL RIGHTS LAW: THURGOOD MARSHALL AND THE SUPREME COURT, *1956–1961*, 102, 128, 158 (1994) (Maceo Smith); 101–102, 128, 133, 273 (Carter Wesley). *See* J. CLAY SMITH, JR., REBELS IN LAW: VOICES IN HISTORY OF BLACK WOMEN LAWYERS 18 (1998) (possibly Ann Robinson, a lawyer in New York City); JUAN WILLIAMS, THURGOOD MARSHALL: AMERICAN REVOLUTIONARY 175 (1998) (Lula White, Texas NAACP, and W. J. Durham, Texas lawyer).

And, guess who put me on the Supreme Court? A Texan [President Lyndon B. Johnson]. And so I am.

This is a great occasion, but we must look to the future. The past is just prologue. It is not how far we came, but how far we go. It is not just, are we better off, but are we better off than what, comparatively speaking? This law school, from all I can hear, is a great building, extremely well equipped, ready to do the job. But, somebody years ago, you remember, said, "Bricks and mortar do not a school make."

What you need is a tradition, and every reputable law school in this country that I know of has a tradition. Unfortunately, most of [these traditions] are in words only. First of all, I say: this law school has to have a tradition, but in addition, it needs to have more than just words. [It has to have] something to build on. There is no place in this world for just another law school. That won't do us any good. This must become a different and, more importantly, a superior law school. And there is a big gap. Legal education is crying for just such a law school, and I say to the faculty and students: Don't try to be the greatest commercial law school in the country; we have got too many that have carved out that spot. Don't try to be the greatest criminal law school in the country; there are others who have carved that out. . . . But I think that the aim and tradition that we must establish in this law school is not just to say it—But to meaningfully do what must be done, and that is very simple: Serve the people. Serve the individual.

I think that you have to do what Charlie Houston started in the law school where I came from at Howard [University]. He started out—and he was quite frank about it—"I am not training lawyers; I am not training members of the bar. I am training social engineers who will go out and do things for the people." Charlie did not live to see it, but I was moved at the argument on the school segregation cases—*Brown* and the other cases—and I looked around at the lawyers here on our side, and everyone with one exception had been touched by Charlie Houston. That is the kind of a tradition that you leave behind. That is the kind of tradition you move for.

Secondly, he taught us that you will get no favors, and I emphasize that. He used to tell us in our first year of law school, "every one of you look at the man on your right; now look at the man on your left: This time next year two of you won't be here." About excellence, that it gave him no pleasure at all to "punch" a student and to fail a student who was stupid or was just an average student. Those that he enjoyed flunking were the ones that had Phi Beta Kappa keys and those that were so great—he enjoyed "punching them out."

What you have got to bear in mind in the practice of law: Many of you have read in recent years about the great favors being done Negro lawyers because they are Negroes—don't rely on it. You don't deserve it, and you are not going to get it. You are going to get it in the marketplace of the law according to how much law you can personally lay on the judge and the jury. You are not going to win your cases by going before a judge or jury and saying, "I'm a poor Negro, and my people have been oppressed all their lives." That [will not] help you. You have got to find the law; you have got to out-study the other fellow: If he burns the gas fourteen hours a day or the electricity fourteen hours a day, you have got to burn it fifteen.

I remember way back: Dr. Louis Wright, former chairman of the board of the NAACP. He was a very great doctor. Back in the late thirties or early forties, he had to take an examination for promotion in the Medical Reserve of the United States Army. He took it, and they said had had to take another one, because his was too perfect. You know, he cheated. So he said to the man:

"Are you the one who gives the exam?" "Yes," the man answered. "Well," Wright asked, "Why don't you give me one of the old ones?"
"What will that do?" the man asked.
"Well," said Wright, "I'll do it right here in your presence."
The examiner agreed, and so Wright took the exam questions and went over into another area of the room on the side, and he worked on it, and finished it in half the time. He brought it back and said to the examiner, "This is it."
The guy said, "Well, you didn't use up all your time."
Wright answered, "That's all right."
The man said, "You don't have a perfect paper, I'm sure."
"No," Wright replied, "But I've got enough to pass."
"Well, how do you know you have enough to pass?" the man asked.
Wright said, "Because you wrote the exam, and I know more medicine than you do."
Later I asked him, "Louis, how can you take that arrogant type of position?"
Heck, he said, "I'm black. I've got to."

Now I hope you understand what I mean: Use your talents for your people. You know, we can give the poor ghetto people better legal service than the wealthy people have—if we get in a storefront, open it up, and let them come in and talk their problems over. You know, the biggest trouble doesn't come before you sign that installment contract: It comes after. And, you can give that kind of help. You can help in the criminal law: volunteer your services.

Finally on that line, the only thing I say is, don't go as far as I did in Baltimore when I was practicing there. A lady came in one day and said that she would like for me to handle her case.

I said, "Do you have any money?"

"No," she said, "But down in South Carolina where I came from, when I get in legal trouble, I go to the judge and he helps me out. So I went here to the courthouse, and I went in to see the judge, and he said they couldn't do that here: I'd have to get a private lawyer. We'll I told him, 'I don't have any money.' The judge said, well, that's a real problem: You go down to 40 East Redwood down there, and you look for a lawyer named Thurgood Marshall. He's freeby lawyer."

Now, I don't suggest that you go that far, because it is awfully difficult to eat.

I think that each one of you has to set your own tradition. That is how the tradition of a law school is made—and that is, that the equity of law is guaranteed by the Constitution. It is not here; it is not automatic, and the only way to get it is in the courts. That is as true today as it was forty or fifty years ago. It is just that a varied type of action is needed.

Build the tradition of public service, of service to the public and service to the individual, and you can make this law school the law school that will go down in history as having done what some of the other law schools promised to do, and others never had the slightest idea of doing.

World Peace Through Law: An Urgent Task

It is truly a humbling experience to stand before hundreds of lawyers and judges from more than a hundred nations around the globe. Among us, we represent all of the great legal systems and traditions of the world. We are gathered, of course, to join in rededicating ourselves to the noble quest of our profession—the peaceful resolution of disputes through the carefully developed processes of the law.

Our task is becoming more urgent. The recent years have been turbulent ones, both internationally and within many of our nations. Grave problems continue to cry for solution. Overpopulation, starvation, poor housing and health care, unequal educational opportunity, and the threat of war and civil unrest, to name but a few, plague many millions of the world's citizens. We can rejoice that bombs no longer fall on innocent people in Indochina, and there are some hopeful signs of international cooperation in the Middle East. But new threats to peace have arisen in areas long neglected by the world community, such as Southern Africa.[1] More and more the emphasis has been on human rights. More is needed.

Many of the most serious problems facing humanity are, of course, beyond the competence of the judicial process to solve. Indeed, courts are usually unable to address these great dilemmas in any but the most limited fashion. Lawyers are fortunate, however, that they have the unusual professional option to step into many government and private sector positions. There, as executive and legislative officers, they are often able to have a more direct impact on meeting human needs.

There are some who have criticized this trend as a "plague of lawyers"

Address by Associate Justice Thurgood Marshall United States Supreme Court at the Eighth Conference on the Law of the World Peace Through Law Center, Manila, Philippines, Aug. 23, 1977.
1. The period referred to is likely the Soweto crisis in 1976 and the savage murder of Steve Biko while in police custody in 1977. *See* CHESTER A. CROCKER, HIGH NOON IN SOUTHERN AFRICA: MAKING PEACE IN A ROUGH NEIGHBORHOOD 21 (1992); MARTIN MEREDITH, NELSON MANDELA: A BIOGRAPHY 329 (Soweto revolt and murder of Steve Biko).

infesting many of the world's public and private institutions. They see our governments, legislatures, and corporations as overburdened with lawyers in policy-making positions. While there is perhaps some truth to these fears, it seems to me that the trend is not sinister. Rather, it reflects for procedure, its disciplined analysis of problems, and its unremitting search for their fundamental sources, the law provides a unique background for public service.

Too often, perhaps, lawyers working in positions of public or private trust use their training as no more than a tool to ensure their own personal success. If so, the critics have good cause for complaint. I believe that those trained in the law have a higher obligation. Executive and legislative officials with legal backgrounds must seek not merely personal aggrandizement, but must strive over the long haul to improve the lives of all people whom they serve.

Those who choose to remain within the narrower traditional confines of the legal profession also have a vital task to perform. In a very real sense, the bench and bar might be called the glue that holds our societies together. We are, in many ways, the most potent social force against terror and revolution.

The bench and bar are often accused of being a reactionary element in society. There is some truth to this charge. Courts unfortunately may become instruments of repression. They may be used to prosecute minority groups, to enjoin free speech and peaceful assembly practiced by those with unpopular views, to enforce the property rights of the rich against those too poor to resist. Some lawyers, too, may often seek to preserve the status quo—in court and out—for the benefit of wealthy and powerful clients. These tendencies are, I am afraid, to some degree inevitable in any legal system.

But in the best functioning systems, they are strongly tempered by the role of bench and bar as the hands guiding and molding social and political change. A strong, active and independent legal system often is the key element making it possible for a society to weather the storms of change sweeping the world today. The ship of a state having such a legal system will survive the tempest, perhaps battered around the waterline and with sails torn, yet proceeding resolutely on course. But lacking a dynamic legal system, a state risks breaking up on the shoals of internal strife and civil conflict.

This point is illustrated by events across the world during the last four years. In my own country, the bench and bar played a key part in preserving democratic institutions that were badly shaken by repeated illegal acts committed by high government officials. The Watergate years subjected my country's Constitution to its greatest crisis in decades, yet ultimately, public confidence was restored and I believe that the U.S. emerged stronger than it had been for many years.[2]

It was shortly after our Abidjan Conference in 1973[3] that the Vice President of the United States [Spiro Agnew] was charged with serious criminal acts predating his term of office. Diligent investigation by prosecutorial forces undaunted by the power and importance of the defendant led to the charges. Through our independent judicial process, they were resolved, on the whole, I think, fairly to all concerned.

The Vice President, having admitted his guilt in court, resigned his public office, and he was quickly replaced in accordance with the procedure laid down in our Constitution. The crisis had, however, only begun. As Americans watched in horror, it slowly became apparent that far more serious crimes had been committed at the highest levels of government, indeed, by the President [Richard M. Nixon] himself. Numbered among those who pierced through the web of perjury and deceit were determined judiciary and fearless prosecution staff, responsible legislative committees and a dedicated free press. I might add that in this monumental venture, as in many others, the dedication and freedom of the press did not always insure accuracy, but I believe that the value of a free press was never more strongly felt or needed than in the years of Watergate.

While it is impossible to measure the contributions made by any one of the institutions involved in uncovering and punishing the Watergate crimes, lawyers and judges were high among those most prominent in the process. For example, all the members of the Judiciary Committee of the House of Representatives conducting the impeachment proceedings were lawyers. Regrettably, persons trained in the law, including the President, were also unduly among the guilty. Their presence should serve as a reminder that constant vigilance is required lest we allow training to become a force for evil.

When the President did resign [1974], under threat of almost impeachment procedures, peacefully and in strict accordance with the rule of law. The great lesson of Watergate, I think, was that it served to remind us of the inestimable strength and resiliency of a democratic society operating under well defined principles of law. It was, in many ways, a triumph of law over lawless behavior; a triumph of the democratic process over those who sought to subvert it to serve their selfish hunger for power.

2. Testimony of George Beall, Federal News Service, Inc., March 3, 1999, LEXIS-NEXIS (on Watergate issues, including reference to public confidence and the resignation of Vice President Spiro Agnew).

3. *See World Peace Through Law Center Holds Tenth Anniversary Conference in the Ivory Coast*, 59 A.B.A.J. 1289 (Nov. 1973). For more on World Peace Through Law Conferences and its history, *see* CHARLES S. RHYNE, WORKING FOR JUSTICE IN AMERICA AND JUSTICE IN THE WORLD 663 (1995).

Some may argue that in the Watergate crisis, judges took an inappropriately active role in the political process. The order to President Nixon to release the White House tapes, for example, certainly precipitated a major political crisis. But it seems to me that the actions of the courts were proper precisely because of their impact on the political sphere. What made them acceptable in a democratic society was the fact that the judges scrupulously respected the limits on their role. They acted in accordance with all the procedural regularities of the judicial branch. The decisions that were reached were right because they were based upon application of the principles of the law to concrete cases at hand.[4]

While no judge deciding such a case can—or should—fail to be aware of the enormous political repercussions that it may generate, strict adherence to the principles and procedures of the law give the judge enormous moral authority in a crisis. There have been reports that President Nixon considered defying the court order to turn over his tape recordings. I submit that such a course would have been futile. In a battle for moral authority, the allegiance of the people will lie with the courts, as long as the judicial branch acts responsibly under the law. I am less sanguine about our performance of our everyday duties. For our real contribution is measured not in dramatic deeds, but in our daily dispensation of advice and justice to hundreds of thousands of individuals experiencing some sort of difficulty in their relationships with others.

When I last spoke to this conference, I suggested that the governing principle of a humane society and a good legal system could be summed up in the simple phrase "People are people." It seems to me that the phrase not only states a universal rule of substantive law, but that it is equally opposite as guiding principle for the way courts and lawyers should conduct their daily business—a procedural maxim, if you will. If bench and bar are to perform successfully their role in civilized society, they must recognize the worth and importance of every person coming before them.

Perhaps the most basic function performed by our legal systems is the ordering of social relationships. A legal system substitutes the rule of law for the violent self-help to which people would otherwise be forced to turn to defend their possessions, their lives, and their human dignity. Courts are an important part of this system, for they are the ultimate arbiters in a peaceful society in preventing violent confrontation if they perform their duties fairly and impartially.

And while equal justice for all is a goal to which all decent legal systems must aspire, it is not enough if only we judges and lawyers know that it

4. *See* Cases and Materials on this point, *in* GEOFFREY R. STONE, et al., CONSTITUTIONAL LAW 412–423 (3rd ed. 1996).

has been reached. In order to displace the use of violence, a legal system must also be perceived by all the people as providing equal justice. If the system is not believed to be fair, it will be a failure, for its effectiveness depends almost entirely on its public appearance.

I would not presume to tell those of you engaged in the business of judging how to decide particular issues that might come before you. Different nations have different needs and traditions that may require varied solutions to similar problems. But I know that whatever the solution a court imposes, it will not be effective in convincing the parties and the society that justice has been done unless all people coming before it are treated as equally important people. I think there are a number of steps that we can take to serve this principle.

First, access to justice must never depend on the wealth or position of the litigant. Justice must be available to men and women struggling in abject poverty just as it is to the owners of great mansions.

When courts—consciously or unconsciously—make decisions that have the appearance of rewarding the wealthy and powerful and harming and unprivileged, they lose some of the credibility that makes them a viable alternative to violence. For decisions that are based on such factors have nothing to do with the merits of the dispute that is being settled. They are no more related to who owns a cow or a piece of land, or to whether a homicide was justifiable, than does the fact that one of the parties is a boxing champion or has a large family that will fight to defend him. In the courts, might—be it fiscal or physical—must never make right.

I am reminded of my early practice of law, during the Depression of the 1930s in the city of Baltimore, Maryland. The highest court of the state had an interesting rule at that time. All briefs, and the complete record, including the transcript of the trial, had to be printed for the court, or an appeal could not be brought before it. This was not a serious barrier for the banks and large businesses represented by prominent law firms in the city. But often it was an insurmountable obstacle for poor criminal defendants and struggling shopkeepers, the sort of clients that I represented. Nowadays, appellate printing costs in the U.S. are generally borne by the state. But that was decades away during the Depression. Once I complained to a clerk in the state's highest court that this was not fair to my impoverished Negro clients. His reply was simple: "Every man has his day in court—if he can pay." Happy we are that we have changed to equal justice for all—regardless of ability to pay.

I submit that in a just society, the clerk's attitude is intolerable. If justice is a scarce commodity, rationed like diamonds only to those who can afford to buy it, unrest and even revolution are inevitable. Only a society that is stabilized by brute force can long survive with an inequitable legal system. Courts can serve their role of holding society together only if they make justice freely available, whatever the wealth, social or political position of the litigants. As my Court said years ago, "there can be no equal justice where the kind of trial that a man gets depends on the amount of money that he has."[5]

Perhaps the single most significant equalizing factor on the scales of justice is the lawyer. I believe that it is the duty of the legal profession to strive to provide lawyers to all persons in need of their assistance. The ever-growing body of laws affecting more and more aspects of everyday life makes this an imperative.

There are many ways to provide legal service for all. In some places, the government may provide lawyers for the poor or pay for their services. Unions and trade associations have experimented with plans to hire lawyers to help their members. The increased use of nonlawyers trained to perform routine services in much the same way as medical paraprofessionals has met with success. But so much more remains to be done, even in the most economically advantaged nations. It is, I think, the duty of our profession to explore every possible means of making the legal system serve all of our fellow human beings with maximum effectiveness.

In the meantime, courts should be readily accessible even to those who proceed without lawyers. Judges and opposing counsel should treat litigants who are unable or unwilling to obtain an attorney with respect, courtesy, and sympathy. The ways of the law are often mysterious, even to lawyers, and justifiable disgust with the system will quickly mount in the face of unnecessary dismissals on technical points, overly strict reliance on minor procedural rules, and similar pettiness. Judges have a particular responsibility, I think, to make sure that their clerks and other staff members do not lose sight, in piles of technical paperwork, of their primary duty to make justice available to all.

It is no less important for judges themselves to act in a way that maximizes their credibility as settlers of social disputes. There is nothing more disturbing for a litigant than to appear in court and receive the unmistakable impression that he has already lost his case . . .

World peace through law is a magnificent goal. Perhaps it can never be achieved. At least we have at these conferences made a modest beginning. More and more lawyers and judges from around the world have joined us. When I think back on my own life, the changes I have seen, a few perhaps that I helped to cause, there is reason to hope. But there is so much more to be done if justice and peace are to become a way of life for every person on earth. That is, I think, the message of this conference. I hope it will become a call to action for every one of us.

5. Griffin v. Illinois, 351 U.S. 12, 19 (1956).

Financing Public Interest Law Practice: The Role of the Organized Bar

One of the most important ideals of the legal profession is that all persons and groups should be able to receive competent representation in the legal process. The time has come for the organized bar to direct more of its energy and resources in this direction. I have some suggestions about the steps that bar associations might consider taking.

My views have developed from basic perceptions about our legal system, which, whether in courts, legislatures, or administrative agencies, is largely an adversary process. Decision-makers generally rely on facts and arguments presented to them by outside parties whose interests often conflict. The presentation of these contending viewpoints makes it possible, in theory at least, for the decision-maker to arrive at a good decision and for wise law to develop.

The theory is flawed in practice. There is often an imbalance in the legal process. Not all viewpoints are equally represented before most decision-makers. For obvious reasons, lawyers generally represent clients who can afford to pay them. As a result, many persons and groups fail to receive adequate legal representation. The effect is that the decision-making process itself is skewed, and the premises of the adversary system and of the lawyer's role in the legal process are questioned.

Neither the problems nor the calls for their solution are new. What is new is that over the last decade or so more and more lawyers have sought to dedicate their professional lives to providing representation to under-represented interests in all facets of the legal process . . .

Public interest law practice is necessary to create a balance in the legal system, to assure that all interests get a fair chance to be heard with the help of a lawyer. The basic point was perfectly put by Justice Hugo Black in *Gideon v. Wainwright*: "That government hires lawyers to prosecute and defendants who have the money hire lawyers to defend are the strongest indications of the widespread belief that lawyers . . . are necessities, not luxuries."[1] To paraphrase Justice Black, if government and industry need

61 A.B.A.J. 1487 (Dec. 1975). Reprinted by permission of the *ABA Journal.*
1. 372 U.S. 335, 344 (1963).

high-quality lawyers to represent their interests in our complex society, less well-organized or less powerful interests also need to have access to high-quality legal representation.

Adversary System Needs Diversity of Viewpoint

We condemn the adversary system to one-sided justice if we deprive the legal process of the benefit of differing viewpoints and perspectives on a given problem. This is not to say that the viewpoint of the under-represented must or should always prevail. I mean no such implication. Rather, I strongly contend that the decision-maker should have the opportunity to assess the impact of any given administrative, legislative, or judicial decision in terms of all the people that it will affect. This cannot be accomplished without a public interest presence whose function is to advocate, in the true sense, the needs and desires of the underrepresented segments of society . . .

Less activity has taken place on the legislative front, largely because private nonprofit organizations and their lawyers may not lobby if they wish to keep their tax-exempt status. This may be one reason that courts are asked to deal with so many large social policy issues. Perhaps the time has come to permit greater lobbying by public interest lawyers.

Public interest lawyers also have played a significant educational and research role, with direct and indirect effects on all of us.

In spite of these successes, public interest law practice has had one major problem: funding. Almost by definition, public interest lawyers represent persons or groups who cannot compete in the ordinary market for legal services. Often the cost of public interest lawyering exceeds the *economic* benefit to the *individual* client. In these circumstances, the funding of public interest law is a problem without an easy solution . . .

In view of the obligation of lawyers for the proper functioning of the adversary system and their monopolistic hold over the role of representation, each member of the profession, in my opinion, must assume a special responsibility to assure fairness in the adversary process. Toward this end several bar associations have initiated pilot funding programs to support the local public interest practice. I salute these efforts and concur in the recommendation of the recent American Assembly that called for an "increase of funding of public interest legal services by lawyers, bar associations and individuals and organizations concerned with social justice."[2] . . .

2. Dwight D. Eisenhower established the American Assembly, a nonpartisan group that asserts opinon on various public policy issues, at Columbia University in 1950. *See Book Review*, 90 Am. J. Int'l Law 344 (April 1996).

While the organized bar has philosophically accepted the idea of its responsibilities in securing adequate representation for all persons, it has yet to come to grips with its responsibility for enforcing this obligation. The American Bar Association and some local bar associations have taken initial steps in exploring new avenues for funding public interest law. The creation of the Council for Public Interest Law is an exciting new development. Through the joint efforts of the American Bar Endowment, the Ford Foundation, and others, it seeks to harness new methods of financing public interest law on a more permanent basis. The first steps by the American Bar Association at a national level are worthy of emulation, but they represent only a beginning . . .

As our society moves toward realization of full representation for all citizens, the permanent funding of public interest law practice by the organized bar offers an administratively feasible and financially reasonable means of demonstrating in tangible form a commitment to equal justice under law. While I recognize that some difficult problems of implementation remain, I see no reason to delay making a special commitment to the public interest practice by offering direct support from the bar associations. With this in mind, I challenge lawyers and the leaders of the state and local bar associations to work toward this end and to encourage the bar to take bold and effective steps in this direction.[3]

3. *But see* Greg Winter, *Legal Firms Cutting Back on Free Services for Poor,* N.Y. TIMES, Aug. 17, 2000, at 1.

Who Is Best Qualified to Be a Judge?

I am delighted to be with you in this beautiful setting for the spring meeting of the American College of Trial Lawyers. (I would have been even more delighted to have been here for the winter meeting. This past winter, faced with the challenge of coping with snow, Washington proved once again that it is truly a city of southern efficiency and northern hospitality.) I would like to speak today about a topic of current interest to members of the bar, and the public generally: the selection of judges.

As you may know, exactly one month ago President [Jimmy] Carter issued an executive order creating a new mechanism for selecting federal appellate judges.[1] Under this order, each time a vacancy on a court of appeals occurs, a panel will be activated to report to the President the names of the five persons considered "best qualified" to fill the vacancy. These panels will consist of approximately equal numbers of lawyers and nonlawyers and will be drawn, in part, from the circuit in which the vacancy occurs. Presumably, the President will make every effort to select his nominees from these lists, as he did while governor of Georgia.

The president's plan, you will note, to a large degree follows the so-called "merit plan" or "Missouri Plan" for selecting judges. This plan, first proposed by Dean [Albert] Kales of Northwestern Law School in 1914,[2] has spread rapidly in recent years; since the 1970 the number of states using it has more than doubled, and almost half the states presently

Address before the spring meeting of the American College of Trial Lawyers in Coronado, California, March 14, 1977.

1. E.O. No. 11,972, 42 Fed. Reg. 9659 (1977), superseded by E.O. No. 12,059, 43 Fed. Reg. 20,949 (1978). The executive orders were issued by the President to ensure that the appointment of circuit judges would be based on merit, without discrimination on the basis of race or gender. Larry C. Berkson and Susan B. Carlson, *The United States Circuit Judge Nominating Commission: Its Members, Procedures and Candidates*, AMERICAN JUDICATURE SOCIETY 24–25 (1980).

2. Glenn R. Winters, *The Merit Plan for Judicial Selection and Tenure—Its Historical Development*, 7 DUQ. L. REV. 61 (1968); Steven P. Croley, *The Majoritarian Difficulty: Elected Judiciaries and the Rule of Law*, 62 U. CHI. L. REV. 689, 724 (1995) (discussing Dean Kale). *See generally* Jack Peltason, *The Missouri Plan for the Selection of Judges*, 20 U. MO. STUD. 1 (1945).

select some or all of their judges under the merit system. My aim, today, is to raise some questions—and express some reservations—about this system.

Of course, no one opposes selecting judges on merit; the alternative, after all, is a meritless selection system, hardly an appealing prospect. Nor can one quarrel with the goal, perhaps first voiced in this country by George Washington, of choosing "the fittest characters to expound the laws and dispense justice": again what types of persons make "the fittest" judges, and by what process are they elevated to the bench.

In theory, at least, the Missouri plan speaks only to the second question—the question of process. Its answer is that "the fittest"—however defined—are best selected by creating a commission of lawyers and laymen to submit a small list of names to the executive from which he must choose judges. My concern, as I shall explain, is that this process will subtly influence the definition of "fitness," by giving preeminent weight to technical or professional selection criteria.

Insofar as the merit plan is designed simply to put an end to cronyism and patronage in judicial appointments, no one can quarrel with it. I can think of no task that judges are properly called upon to perform that requires prior experience as a friend or backer of the appointing officials (or his party). I might add, however, that the one major study that has been done of the first twenty years of the merit plan in Missouri gives substantial reason to question whether the plan can remove friendship with the executive as a criterion for judicial selection.

But questions of effectiveness aside, creating an elaborate set of commissions with broad powers seems unnecessary simply to eliminate cronyism; I cannot help believing that there is an easier way. Perhaps for this reason, proponents of the merit plan never rest their defense on this limited, essentially negative ground. Rather, they contend that it is affirmatively desirable to have a group of lawyers and laypersons assigned the tasks of ferreting out candidates for judgeships, developing information about the candidates, and determining who is best qualified.

I see no basis for objecting to commissions which perform the first two tasks. But I know of no one who suggests that the commissions should simply gather names and information for use by the executive. The crux of the merit system, in the eyes of its advocates, is the selection function of the commissions.

It is this crux that I find troubling. That is not just because I come from Washington, where skepticism about committees is almost as prevalent as committees; indeed in Washington it is said that "nothing is impossible—until you assign it to a committee." I am troubled by judicial selection by committee because it seems to me that two biases, or risks or biases, inhere in the process: (1) objective criteria will be given undue weight; and (2) to the extent subjective factors are considered, they will be value-free or technical ones.

The temptation for committees to rely on objective criteria is obvious. Such criteria simplify the task of paring down long lists of names to manageable numbers. Moreover, they can avoid endless debates as to which candidates have demonstrated the best knowledge of the law, for example, by providing seemingly clear measurements.

Perhaps the clearest example of the over-emphasis on objective factors is the weight nominating committees have assigned to prior judicial experience. A national study of members of such commissions found that after mental and physical health, this was the background factor the commissioners considered most important. Similarly, the twenty-year study in Missouri found that 57 percent of the intermediate court judges and 70 percent of the Supreme Court judges appointed under the merit plan had prior judicial experience. Yet I know of no evidence indicating that appellate judges with prior experience make better judges than those lacking such experience; to the contrary, evaluations of Supreme Court Justices demonstrate, as Felix Frankfurter put it, that at least with respect to my court, "the correlation between prior judicial experience and fitness—is zero."

Much the same may be true of two other objective criteria on which many place great weight: the requirement that nominees have (1) "at least fifteen years significant legal experience," and (2) for trial judges, that the nominees have had "substantial experience in the adversary system." The first of these requirements effectively excludes all lawyers under the age of forty and many lawyer-politicians; the second excludes from the trial bench the overwhelming majority of lawyers. It is clear to me, however, that at the very least some of those disqualified for lack of experience—[Judge] Learned Hand,[3] for one—should not be excluded from consideration. Persons like Judge Hand either already have acquired or could readily acquire the knowledge that experience is thought to guarantee. On the other hand, some who are included by virtue of their experience actually should be disqualified on this basis. These persons have spent too many years learning undesirable practices or approaches. In fact, I know of no empirical evidence to justify either experience requirement. The study of Supreme Court Justices to which I earlier referred found that more of those appointed at a young age (in this context, under fifty-three) went on to greatness—including Justice Joseph Story, appointed at age thirty-two.[4]

---

3. *See generally* GERALD GUNTER, LEARNED HAND, THE MAN AND THE JUDGE (1994).
4. *See generally Biography of Justice Joseph Story, in* GEOFFREY R. STONE, ET AL., CONSTITUTIONAL LAW xci (3rd edition 1995).

But what troubles me most about the merit system is not that it precludes the appointment of some well-qualified persons who don't meet more or less arbitrary standards. I am more concerned that he merit plan may compel or induce the appointment of judges simply because they are technically well qualified, without regard to their basic values, philosophy, or life experience.

It is to be expected that nominating commissions will tend to ignore value-related considerations. We live in an age in which values are viewed as subjective. Unless a nominating committee happens to be homogeneous, therefore, it is unlikely to agree on the values that judges should hold. Moreover, even if the committee could agree, it would be improper for it to impose its values on the selection process. These committees typically are neither representative nor accountable bodies. The national study of state nominating committees found, for example, that 98 percent of the committee members are white, 90 percent are male, and that the lay members are largely businessmen and bankers.

Rather than looking to the values of would-be-nominees, then, nominating committees may be expected to look exclusively to the nominees' professional abilities: their knowledge of the law, proficiency at writing, and ability to "think like a lawyer." As my late friend and colleague Judge Charles Clark put it with characteristic grace, such committees look "to the head exclusively and not to the heart."[5] But as Charlie Clark also insisted, judging is more than just an exercise in technique or craft; it calls for value judgments. This is true of the trial judge required to decide, for example, whether the risk of prejudice outweighs the probative value of a piece of evidence, or whether the risk that an offender will commit more [crimes] outweighs the offender's interest in retaining his liberty before trial or pending appeal. It is equally true of the appellate judge, required to resolve conflicting claims between liberty and order, equality and efficiency, states rights and federal power. Indeed studies of judicial behavior have uniformly found clear voting patterns traceable to the attitudes or values of the judges. Thus, as Judge Clark said, "it is of truly vital importance that the inner convictions as bias of candidates for judicial appointment be appraised."

Of course, nothing in the merit system necessarily disables the appointing official—who *is* popularly elected—from considering "inner convictions or bias" in making his selections. But it is at least possible that, by excluding values from their inquiry, nominating committees inadvertedly will develop lists of ideologically similar persons. It is also possible that the members of the nominating committee will all agree as to the

5. *See generally* Gordon Hunter, *Chief Fifth Circuit Judge Ending Ten-Year Reign*, Tex. Lawyer, July 15, 1991, at 4.

values that judges should hold, and will make their selections accordingly. In either event, the executive could be precluded from appointing judges who share his—and presumably his constituency's—basic philosophical orientation. And even when nominating committees produce ideologically diverse lists, the thrust of merit selection may persuade some appointing officials that it is somehow illegitimate for them to consider the attitudes or experiences of potential nominees. This, I submit, would be tragic. It is not just legitimate but altogether proper for a popularly elected executive to seek to place on the bench persons who share his fundamental values.

This is not to say that the merit plan is wholly meritless or evil. As I said at the outset, I intend only to raise questions and concerns—not to pass definitive judgments. And since I earlier referred to President Carter's executive order, I should note that it may avoid many of the problems I have noted, since it first guarantees women and minority groups representation on the nominating panels; second, requires the panels to recommend only those who have demonstrated "commitment to equal justice under law:" and third, does not oblige the President to accept every panel's choices.[6] Nevertheless, I am *not* persuaded that it is either necessary or desirable to give any nominating panel the power to choose the three or five most qualified persons; it seems to me sufficient to allow the panels to search for candidates, generate information, and perhaps make evaluations. But whatever one's ultimate views on the merit system I think it essential that the biases and risks inherent in the process be carefully exposed so that those involved in making selections can be attentive to them.[7]

---

6. *Supra* note 1.
7. *See, e.g.*, Charles Ogletree, *Why Has the G.O.P. Kept Blacks Off Federal Courts?* N.Y. Times, Aug. 18, 2000, at A27.

Equality Before the Law:
The Cardinal Principle of the Constitution

The University of Virginia is . . . one of the outstanding universities of this country. It was conceived in grandeur, and has, more than most institutions, fulfilled the ambitions and ideals of its founder, Thomas Jefferson. . . .

The democratizing aspects of the Constitution cannot be overstated. For me, its cardinal principle is that all persons stand in a position of equality before the law. The Constitution gives to each and every one of you an equal right to your own opinions and to participate in the process of your own governance. These are precious rights that we must continually strive to preserve, and whose promise we must seek to attain. There are still far too many persons in this country who cannot participate as equals in the processes of government—persons too poor, too ignorant, persons discriminated against by other people for no good reason. But our ideal, the ideal of our Constitution, is to eliminate these barriers to the aspirations of all Americans to participate fully in our government and society. We have realized it far better than most countries, but we still have a long way to travel and we must continue to strive in their direction.

As I said a moment ago . . . there *is* something "higher" than the Constitution—that is, quite simply, the people. I do not mean that "the people" are not bound to live under our system of laws—any other proposition could lead to violence and from there to anarchy. But what I do mean is what Thomas Jefferson said in the Declaration of our Independence—that just governments derive their authority from the consent of the governed. And because of this, you have not only a right but also a responsibility to the government of this country.

Let me elaborate. Governments derive their power from many sources—the military or police are instruments of *power* and may in the short run enforce the government's directives against an unwilling people. But *authority* is a different question—and no government can govern long, or well, without the authority that comes from a shared consensus

Commencement address, University of Virginia, May 21, 1978.

among the governed. They must believe that theirs is a rightful, and lawful, and just government.

But in order to preserve this power in the people—the power of defining and limiting the authority of their government—it is first and foremost essential that the people be well informed. Jefferson's commitment to this University was only part of a larger commitment to the value of public education. That vision accounts for the primacy of public schools in the American community, for it was Jefferson's guiding hand that helped draft the Northwest Ordinance, which resulted in public lands being dedicated across the new territories for public schools. Today, however, just as in Jefferson's times, we still see students of less privileged backgrounds than your own, or people who are just less lucky, being denied quality education at all levels. Voters turn down school financing referenda, legislatures oppose integration of school systems. There is appalling ignorance even among some of the supposedly well-educated youth of our country, and the extent of illiteracy remains staggering. Education toward the goal of an informed citizenry requires all of the qualities that Jefferson embodied: commitment to difficult projects, confidence in the soundness of one's own vision, and perseverance in working through a problem.

As the areas of human knowledge have expanded, so have the aspirations of the American people. It is vitally important that the aspirations of our government keep pace with the knowledge and expectations of our people. With the explosion in human knowledge and expertise, it sometimes seems very difficult to understand what the government is doing, to understand what our problems are, and to keep up. Yet the duty to keep up, to be informed, to be knowledgeable in some area of human endeavor, is an essential one, not only for the continued survival of our government but in the long run for our civilization. It is hard work being well informed; but it is essential work for the citizens of a democracy.

It is a work, moreover, for which people in your position have been specially prepared. The privilege of attending so fine a university as this one must bear with it an unceasing responsibility to use your knowledge and training for improving the lives of others. Whether you pursue this as a lawyer dedicated to the public interest; a doctor serving those in pain and sickness; a scholar adding to the store of human knowledge and sharing that knowledge with others; an engineer applying new technologies to serve human needs; an artist improving the quality of life by creative efforts; or just by seeking to be a good person who values helping others—matters not. What matters is to remember always the obligation you bear to the society that has placed you in a position where you could afford to spend four years of your lives—and for many of you, there have been and will be several more—in an institution of learning.

I said at the beginning of my talk that there were several reasons why I was truly honored to be here today. I have already mentioned the first—that this University represents something special in the American tradition. The second one is because you are young; you are a new generation just starting out. Those of us who are a bit older (like myself— and I said, just a bit), no matter how hard we may have worked to serve humanity—our time is coming to a close. I don't for a moment mean our *lives*, since I for one intend to keep on plugging at my present job for many years to come. But I recall to you now Thomas Jefferson's answer to the pleas of a friend in 1814. His friend begged Jefferson to take a stand then and there as a leader in the fight against slavery. Jefferson's answer, though hardly commendable, shows a human truth; he said, "No, I have outlived the generation with which mutual labors and perils beget mutual confidence and influence. This enterprise is for the young—for those who can follow it up, and bear it through to its consummation."[1]

You people here today, about to use your degrees, it is for you now to undertake the projects of this age—in Jefferson's words, to follow them up and bear them through. It is not for me to tell you what these are— each generation must find its own calling. But you have the energies of youth—and while you have them, use them, that you may look back on your lives with as much of a sense of accomplishment as Jefferson no doubt did.

This is a great country, but fortunately for you it is not perfect. There is much to be done to bring about complete equality. Remove hunger. Bring reality closer to theory and democratic principles.

Each of you as an individual must pick your own goals. Listen to others but do not become a blind follower. Do not wait for others to move out— move out yourself—where you see wrong or inequality or injustice speak out, because this is your country. This is your democracy—make it— protect it—pass it on. You are ready. Go to it.

---

1. *See* Aaron Schwaback, *Jefferson and Slavery*, 19 T. JEFFERSON L. REV. 6, 68, n.43 (1997) (quoting Jefferson in part).

The Fulcrum of Pressure

Mr. Chief Justice, Mr. President, My friends. . . . It is a great day. We are all here because it is a great day. I am particularly happy that people like the Chief Justice of the United States [Warren E. Burger] is here; and other Chief Judges. [Applause.] I want to confess, I begged him not to come; because I know how many different outfits in this country, which he has to go to. And then he has to preside over some five hundred federal judges, each of whom is an individual prima donna. [Laughter.] And with all of that, he shouldn't find time to come to something like this. But, he insisted. To him, it was that important; and to me that truly demonstrates how important it is.

I would like to start off by having a couple of true stories on the record. I do not have a written speech. I have gotten away from written speeches since I heard about that legislator who had a speech committee in his office . . . and he wouldn't even look at them before he delivered them. He just read them off. And this day he said, "Look! Next Monday night I am speaking for Senator Johnson; and I want a speech, twenty minutes [long]; and I want it on energy." And they said, "What are . . . ?" And he said, "That's it. Just go do it." And they did. And on Monday they gave him the speech and he went out, got in his car, got in the place, got there, got in another car, went there. When he was called on to speak, he opened up his speech, and on the first page he went on telling stories like this . . . [Laughter.] Except mine is true. [Laughter.] Then he went on talking in general about the energy problem. And then he said, "he has an airtight program for taking care of the entire energy program. It was very elaborate; and it was set up in five different phases, all five of which, I shall set forth before you tonight." And he turned over the page and to his utter surprise, he saw, "Now, you sucker, you are on your own." [Laughter and applause.] I have given up that idea . . . [Laughter.]

Justice Marshall gave this speech at Howard Law School on November 18, 1978, at the formal installation of Wiley Austin Branton, a close friend, as Dean. Several dignitaries were in attendance including Chief Justice Warren E. Burger and Dr. James Cheek, President of Howard University. The speech was published in the student newspaper. *See* THE BARRISTER (vol. 8, no. 2), 3–4, Nov. 18, 1978.

. . . I am not too much in the line of notes. But the one that really is what I am going to talk about today is a Las Vegas story.

This guy went out from California to Las Vegas and did what all others do. He lost his money. [Laughter.] All of it, including his fare home. And he was commiserating with himself; and as sometimes happens, he had to go. And when he went to the toilet room [bathroom], . . . he found out, that they had no nickel or dime: they had quarter ones. [Laughter] And just then a gentleman came by and he told the gentleman his problem. . . . The guy said, "I will give you a quarter." And the guy said, "Well look, you don't know me. . . . I don't care if you give it back to me or not. You are no problem. Here's a quarter." He took the quarter and went in the room there, and just as he was about to put the quarter in the slot to open the door, the door had been left open for somebody. So he put the quarter in the slot machine. And it wouldn't be any story if he didn't hit the jackpot. [Laughter.] Then he hit the bigger jackpot . . . and he went to the craps table; he went to the roulette table. He ended up with about ten or fifteen thousand dollars worth.

He went back to Los Angeles invested in the right stock. He got the right business together. And in pretty short order, about fifteen years, he became the second wealthiest man in the world. And on television, they asked him about it; and he said he would like to tell the story. And he told the story. And he said, "I am so indebted to that benefactor of mine. That man who made all of this possible. And if he comes forth and proves it; that he was the man, I will give him half of my wealth i-n c-a-s-h." [Laughter.] So a man came forth. . . . They had all the elaborate . . . private detective investigation; and sure enough, "That was the man." . . . The guy said, "Well look. Are you sure you are the one I am looking for?" He said, "Who are you?" He said, "I am the man that gave you that quarter." He said, "Heck, I'm not looking for him. I am looking for the man who left the door open, I would have had to put the quarter in the slot." [Laughter.]

I figure at a stage like this in our development of our law school, we have to be sure we know just what we are after.

Why do we have occasions like this? Well, I will tell you why. Everything in any question of education depends on the reputation of the school. And a part of the reputation of the school, is the reputation of the dean. And being so old as I am, you almost scared me to death, Wiley, talking about the oldest graduate was here. [Laughter.]

. . . In order to find out just where we stand, and to be in a room like this, and on campus like this, I had to go back . . . But you know, it's an awful long way from Fifth Street;[1] which incidentally, I went by not too

1. When Marshall attended Howard Law School, it was located at 420 Fifth Street, N.W., Washington, D.C.

long ago. Those of you that hadn't been by, it's gone. They have torn it down. It was a marvelous place when it was there.

But today, you know, we have reached the place where people say, "We've come a long way. But so [have] other people come a long way. And so have other schools come a long way. Has the gap been getting smaller? It's getting bigger. Everybody's been doing better.

And so, as you look at the law school today, and that's what you have to look at. You look back, and people say we are better off today. Better than what?

You know, I used to be amazed at people who would say that, "The poorest Negro kid in the South was better off than the kid in South Africa." So what! We are not in South Africa. [Applause.] We are here. [Applause.] "You ought to go around the country and show yourself to Negroes; and give them inspiration." "For what? These Negro kids are not fools. They know to tell them there is a possibility that someday you'll have a chance to be the o-n-l-y Negro on the Supreme Court, those odds aren't too good." [Applause.]

When I do get around the country like recently, I have been to places like . . . unfortunately for funerals; like New Orleans, Houston, Dallas, etc. When I get out and talk with the people in the street, I still get the same problems. "You know, like years ago, you told us things were going to get better. But they are not a darn bit better for me. I am still having trouble getting to work. I have trouble eating." And guess what I am getting now? " . . . You not only told me that; you told my father that. And he's no better off; and neither am I. And you can tell me my children will be better off." Well, all I am trying to tell you . . . there's a lot more to be done. Now, think of those good old days. We started at Howard with Charlie Houston as dean . . . [Charles H. Houston, Dean of Howard University Law School, 1930–1935]. . . . The school had several things that they did not have. . . . They did not have a reputation, and they did not have any accreditation; and they did not have anything, "it looked to me."

Charlie Houston took over and in two or three years got full accreditation: American Bar Association, Association of American Law Schools, etc. He did it the hard way.

And for any students that might be interested, for those of you came to this school later, and had complaints, "you should have been there when I was there."

We named Charlie the only repeatable names I could give him as "Iron Shoes and Cement Pants." [Laughter.] We had a lot of others, but . . . [Laughter.]

He even installed the cutback system that would keep you on the books all the time. And that was that, a professor could take five points off your mark for no reason at all. So the only way you could really make it is to get around 95 . . . .

He gave an examination in evidence in our second year that started at nine o'clock in the morning and ended at five in the afternoon. One subject.

In our first year he told us, "Look at the man on your right, look at the man on your left, and at this time next year, two of you won't be here." [Laughter] . . . .

I know my class started, as I remember, it was around thirty; and it ended up with six . . . . He brought in people not on the faculty; but who were coming by Washington. And because of his reputation and background he could get them.

And the people I would list. Every time they came to Washington, they would come by; and we would close up the school and listen to them, in our moot courtroom, which held about fifteen.

For example, a man by the name of Roscoe Pound who just happened to be Dean of Harvard Law School would talk and lecture to us on the common law.

And it just happened that at that time he was the greatest authority in the world . . . . Then he had Bill Lewis, a Negro lawyer from Boston, Massachusetts, who had the distinction of being Assistant Attorney General, a little while back, under Theodore Roosevelt.[2] He would tell us about how to try a lawsuit; and how to argue with the judges; because he was a master of it. And we would run to the Supreme Court and hear him argue.

Then [Arthur] Garfield Hayes would drop by from the American Civil Liberties Union.[3] The first time, I was very impressed with the fact; he was en route from Birmingham, Alabama, where he had defended a poor Negro. He was then en route to Boston, Massachusetts, to defend the Ku Klux Klan. . . . He explained to me about the constitution being color-blind.

Then you had people like Clarence Darrow who told us the importance of sociology and other studies rather than law—which he considered to be unimportant.[4] As witness one time, he was trying a case in North Carolina. A Negro beating up a white man. And his whole argument . . . to the jury was [he had never touched the facts of the

2. See J. CLAY SMITH, JR., EMANCIPATION: THE MAKING OF THE BLACK LAWYER, 1844–1944 (1993), at 106–107 (regarding William Henry Lewis, Sr.).

3. Hayes was the general counsel of the American Civil Liberties Union.

4. Darrow lectured at Howard Law School when Marshall was a law student. See J. Clay Smith, Jr., The Early Days of the Howard Law Alumni Assocation, 1 THE JURIST: HOWARD UNIVERSITY SCHOOL OF LAW ALUMNI NEWS JOURNAL 7, 9 (Dec. 1986) (listing lectures).

case], . . . that this was a waste of time for him to stand up there and argue to this all white Southern prejudiced jury; that no way in the world they could give this Negro a chance. They just couldn't do it because they were out and came back and proved to him that they weren't prejudiced. [Laughter.] And they turned the man loose. [Laughter.]

We had Vaughn S. Cooke, a great expert on conflict of law. People like that because the emphasis was not theory. The emphasis in this school was on practice. How to get it done.

Harvard was training people to join big Wall Street firms. Howard was teaching lawyers to go out and go in court. Charlie's phrase was "social engineer."[5] To be a part of the community. And have the lawyer to take over the leadership in the community.

And we used to hold fort in our little library down there, after school, at night. And start out on research problems sometimes sponsored by him and sometimes on our own.

Indeed, I remember one time, one night. One guy, I believe it was Oliver Hill.[6] . . . He got to work on something, we all joined in. And we found out that in codifying the Code of the District of Columbia, they had just left out the . . . civil rights statute. So, since it didn't apply to anybody but us, they left it out. We eventually got through in court and got that straightened out. And we got to work on segregation. What are we going to do about that?

I for one was very interested in it because I couldn't go the University of Maryland. I had to ride the train every day, twice a day. Back and forth. I didn't like that . . . .

Well, it ended up Bill Hastie [William H. Hastie, Dean of Howard University Law School, 1939–1946] went down to North Carolina and filed our first university case, which we lost on a technicality. But Hastie laid the groundwork for the future.[7]

Then we had a criminal case dealing with a man named George Crawford.[8] We did more litigating, I guess, than any school ever did.

---

5. *See* Genna Rae McNeil, Groundwork: Charles Hamilton Houston and the Struggle for Civil Rights 84, 85 (1983).
6. Years later, Oliver W. Hill, a distinguished civil rights lawyer and a key lawyer in *Brown v. Board of Education*, received the Presidential Medal of Freedom from President Bill Clinton, the highest award bestowed on private citizens in the United States. Michael Paul Williams, *Hill Rises to Occasion; Wheelchair-Sitting Activist Stands Up to Receive Medal*, Richmond Times Dispatch, Aug. 12, 1999, at A-1. *See also*, Oliver W. Hill (with) Jonathan K. Stubbs, The Life Story of Oliver Hill (1997).
7. See *generally* Gilbert Ware, William Hastie, Grace Under Pressure (1984).
8. J. Clay Smith, Jr., Emancipation: The Making of the Black Lawyer, 1844–1944, at 234–235 (1993) (discussing case).

But I emphasize that it was aimed at working in the community. The other thing that Charlie beat in our heads. . . . I think that it is very important. He says, "You know when a doctor makes a mistake, he buries his mistake. When a lawyer makes a mistake, he makes it in front of God and everybody else." [Laughter.]

When you get in the courtroom you can't say, please, Mr. Court, have mercy on me because I am a Negro. You are in competition with a well-trained white lawyer and you better be at least as good as he, and if you expect to win, you better be better. [Applause.] If I give you five cases to read overnight, you read eight. And when I say eight, you read ten. You go that step further; and you might make it. And then you had all these other people, Charles H. Houston, William H. Hastie, George E. C. Hayes, Leon A. Ransom, Edward P. Lovett, James [Madison] Nabrit, [Jr.], Spottswood W[illiam] Robinson, III.[9]

Then later you had Robert L. Carter, Constance Baker Motley, A. T. Walden in Atlanta, Arthur Shores in Birmingham, A. P. Tureaud, Sr., in New Orleans.[10]

Then on the other side you had a very good group of professors from other schools. Charles Black,[11] . . . and others.

Then we had a certain wild guy over there in Arkansas. [Laughter.] I would just like to mention it at this point, because it is very important, I think, to realize that in those days, "it was rough." And I think Wiley [Wiley A. Branton, Dean of Howard University School of Law] is an example of one part of it. I got the credit mostly. But I would go to those places, and I would get out on the fastest damn thing that moved. [Laughter.] I couldn't wait for the plane. And then I couldn't wait for the jet. [Laughter]. . . . He stayed there, and made them take it and like it. I mentioned that because it seems to me, that while we had this whole movement going along, we were beginning to touch it.

Then we had those dry runs that Damon [Damon J. Keith, Judge, U.S. Court of Appeals for the Sixth Circuit] was talking about.[12] We would have both of the lawyers who were going to argue tomorrow's case before the Supreme Court, to come before a panel of judges in our old moot courtroom, when we were in the library down there on the campus. This went on all during the 1940s. The faculty members who set as members of the Court were deliberately urged to be rougher and excuse

9. *See generally* RICHARD KLUGER, SIMPLE JUSTICE (1977).
10. *Id.* (and regarding A. T. Walden) *see* Smith, EMANCIPATION, *supra* note 8, at 198–201.
11. *See* THE ASSOCIATION OF AMERICAN LAW SCHOOLS DIRECTORY OF LAW TEACHERS 1995–96, at 242 (for biographical information on Professor Black).
12. Judge Keith is a 1949 graduate of Howard Law School. HOWARD UNIVERSITY SCHOOL OF LAW 1999 ALUMNI DIRECTORY 34 (1999).

me, "nastier than the judges would be." And you know, it worked well; because once you got through with that slugging match with them, you didn't worry about anything the next day. It was like going to an ice cream party . . . because the members of the court were so polite and nice to you. Well, I keep reminding you that this was done at Howard; all of it. How much it was necessary to the success of those cases, is left to anybody. And finally on that point, I want you to know, that starting with that research in the library of finding the civil rights statute, through all these cases in the Supreme Court, clear up to the present time, in the Bakke case, I will tell anybody, and I will dispute anybody who does not agree, that the [*amicus*] brief filed by Herb Reid [Herbert O. Reid, Sr., Charles Hamilton Houston, Distinguished Professor of Law at Howard University] was one of the best briefs.[13] [Standing ovation.] He didn't pay me a nickel for it. [Laughter.]

Now, you know, Wiley integrated the University of Arkansas. He went back down in there; and cases that were mentioned, I know several other criminal cases that were just unbelievable. He went from there to Atlanta; and up here to Washington. I hate to get down into the gutter; but "Wiley" stands for "brains and guts." I know both of them; I have seen him in action. It seems to me, that what are you going to do now, other than, all of us to give our blessings to what I consider a perfect marriage; Branton and the Howard Law School. [Applause.]

That's not enough because we have got to look to the future. They are still laying traps for us.

I have just requested a book which I heard about. Believe it or not, somebody found out the Klan is still around. I could have told them that. [Laughter.] The Klan never died. They just stopped wearing the sheets, because the sheets cost too much. [Laughter.] When I say they, I think we all know whom they would include. We have them in every phase of American life. And as we dedicate this courtroom, as we launch Wiley on his road, we just have to continue that basic theory of practice; and not just theory. With these clinics that have been set up, you note we can give the poor people in the ghettos for peanuts better legal protection than the millionaires get. If, we could just get them to bring their legal problems to the lawyer, before they sign them. That's how to stay out of trouble. And that can be done with clinics. And I think this law school has to insist on that. And here I have a note, which says all of this has to be done and it has to be done together.

There are people that tell us today, and there are movements that tell us, tell Negroes, "Take it easy man. You made it. No more to worry about.

13. *See* J. Clay Smith, Jr., *Retirement of Herbert Ordre Reid, Sr.,* 3 JURIST 18 (Summer 1989).

Everything is easy." Again, I remind you about what Charlie Houston said, "You have got to be better, boy. You better move better."

Be careful of these people who say, "You have made it. Take it easy; you don't need any more help." . . . I would like to read . . . for these people who tell you, "to take it easy. Don't worry, etc." "The great enemy of truth—very often is not the lie; deliberate, contrived and dishonest; but the myth persistent, persuasive, and unrealistic"—John F. Kennedy.[14]

Be aware of that myth, that everything is going to be all right. Don't give in. I add that, because it seems to me, that what we need to do today is to re-focus. Back in the thirties and forties, we could go no place but to court. We knew them, the court was not the final solution. Many of us knew the final solution would have to be politics, if for no other reason, politics is cheaper than lawsuits. So now we have both. We have our legal arm, and we have our political arm. Let's use them both. And don't listen to this myth that it can be solved by either or that is has already been solved. Take it from me, it has not been solved.

I will conclude, if I may, with a conclusion from another great American. The late Chief Justice [Earl] Warren in his one book. And this is the conclusion of his book. And more important and as we move more in what I consider to be this new phase. He says, "Those who won our independence believed that the greatest menace to freedom is an inert people. That public discussion is a political duty. That this should be a fundamental principle of the American government. They eschewed silence coerced by law."[15]

And then again, Chief Justice Warren, "No, the democratic way of life is not easy. It conveys great privileges with constant vigilance—needed to preserve them. This vigilance must be maintained by those responsible for the government. And in our country those responsible are, we the people, no one else. Responsible citizenship is therefore the . . . anchor of our republic. With it we can withstand the storm. Without it, we are helplessly at sea."[16]

It is beyond question . . .

. . . Benjamin Franklin had it in mind when he said, "A republic if you can keep it."[17]

To me, that means much. It's not a republic if we keep it. With me, it's

14. John F. Kennedy, *Commencement Speech at Yale, in* THE GREAT THOUGHTS 226, 226 (George Seldes, ed., 1985).

15. EARL WARREN, A REPUBLIC IF YOU CAN KEEP IT 169 (1972).

16. *Id.* at 169–170.

17. *Id.* at 170; 2 THE RECORDS by James McHenry in his diary and published in 11 AM. HISTORICAL REV. 618 (1906), reprinted *in* JOHN BARTLETT, FAMILIAR QUOTATIONS 348 (5th ed., 1980).

a democracy, if we can keep it. And in order to keep it, you can't stand still. You must move, and if you don't move, they will run over you.

This law school has been in the front. It's been the bellwether. It's been the fulcrum of pressure.

In driving on, I am just as certain as I have ever been in my life, that under the leadership of Wiley Branton, it will not only continue: it will broaden, increase and continue to be the bulwark that we all can be proud of.

This is a great day. We are entering a great era. And let's do as many of us did back home. You know some people have been going home with the Roots business and all that.[18] [Laughter.] I have been going over these since the late fifties. When Kenya got its independence in 1963, and to see all those hundreds of thousands of people. When freedom was declared, . . . in unison yelled, "Harambee." [Meaning] "Pull Together."

We could, and with Wiley and this school, we will continue to do it. Anything I can do to help, I will do, "that is except raise money." Because there are a couple of committees of the judiciary that say, "No." [Standing Ovation.]

18. Referring to ALEX HALEY, ROOTS: THE SAGA OF AN AMERICAN FAMILY (1974).

THE 1980s

During the 1980s Justice Marshall's speeches focused on four subjects: the Constitution as a living document, the death penalty, right to counsel, and pre-trial detention and civil rights. In 1987, Marshall gave one of his most noted speeches during the bicentennial of the Constitution. Marshall reminded the nation that the Constitution was not "fixed" at the Constitutional Convention in Philadelphia in 1787.

Marshall chided the Framers for what he called their defective belief that "We the people" excluded "Negro slaves" and reminded the nation that black people fought in the American Revolution for its freedom and had earned the right to be counted within the term "We the people." Marshall urged Americans to celebrate the Constitution as a living document, one capable of adaptation to modern eras.

Marshall voiced strong opposition to the death penalty throughout his career; indeed, during his tenure on the Supreme Court he was the only Justice to have defended a person charged in a death penalty case himself. Marshall had heard Clarence Darrow address the subject at Howard Law School during his first year at the invitation of Charles Hamilton Houston.[1] We can surmise the direction of Darrow's comments from his article two years later in the *Forum*: "The plea that capital punishment acts as a deterrent to crime will not stand. The real reason why this barbarous practice persists in a so-called civilized world is that people still hold the primitive belief that the taking of one human life can be atoned for by taking another. It is an age-obsession with punishment that keeps official heads-man busy plying his trade."[2]

Marshall's speeches also imply that the death penalty is a barbarous practice because the penalty is often applied in an unfair manner.[3]

1. *See* J. Clay Smith, Jr., *The Early Days of the Howard Law Alumni Association*, 1 JURIST 7, 9 (Fall–Winter, Dec. 1986).
2. Clarence Darrow, *The Futility of the Death Penalty*, 80 FORUM 327, 329–330 (Sept. 1928).
3. The debate on the death penalty in America, largely led by Justice Thurgood Marshall, Justice William Brennan, and others, would later find the ear of the nation. *See, e.g.*, Sara Rimer, *Florida Legislature Deals with Death*, N.Y. TIMES, Jan.

Death penalty jurisprudence is flawed, in Marshall's view, because capital defendants are denied fair opportunities to defend their lives in the courtroom. This, said Marshall, is due to procedural limitations of judicial review of death sentences, inadequate representation by their counsels and scant resources available to indigent defendants. He urged lawyers and judges not to rush to judgment in death penalty cases, fearing that innocent people would be put to death. Marshall maintained that the right to counsel meant more than a lawyer's presence in the courtroom; that lawyer needed to be prepared to apply every technical skill and available defense tactic to assure that no person is sent to death because of procedural errors or incompetence.

In a speech before the Annual Judicial Conference of the Second Circuit, Marshall praised Charles Hamilton Houston as being responsible for the modern civil rights movement. Marshall's stories about the struggles black lawyers confronted while litigating cases in the South—even facing death for doing so—is a tribute to lawyers like Houston. Marshall, who had a keen sense of history, wanted these lawyers to be remembered and revered.[4]

In Marshall's speeches during the 1980s, he observes a more aggressive conservative Supreme Court drifting to narrow interpretations relating to anti-discrimination laws, affirmative action, as well as criminal law jurisprudence. Marshall to urge civil rights groups to "broaden [their] perspective and target other governmental bodies as well as the

---

6, 2000, at A18 (state legislators in Florida meet to consider replacing execution by lethal injection); Dirk Johnson, *Illinois, Citing Faulty Verdicts, Bars Executions,* N.Y. TIMES, Feb. 1, 2000, at 1 (citing shameful record of convicting innocent people); Sara Rimer, *Questions of Death Row Justice For Poor People in Alabama,* N.Y. TIMES, March 1, 2000, at 1 (citing the severe short comings of lawyers defending death cases); Paul Duggan, *Attorneys' Ineptitude Doesn't Halt Executions,* WASH. POST, May 12, 2000, at 1 (defendants die because they cannot afford lawyers who are experts in criminal defense work); Linda Greenhouse, *Weighing '96 Law, Justices Overturn 2 Death Sentences,* N.Y. TIMES, Apr. 19, 2000, at 1 (holding that the federal courts have a role to play in reviewing the quality of justice administered by the states). Linda Greenhouse, *Justices Chide South Carolina in a Death Sentence, Again,* N.Y. TIMES, Jan. 10, 2002; *The Death Penalty Re-Examined,* N.Y. TIMES, Feb. 23, 2002, at A30.

4. These remarks were actually in a paper in which Marshall addressed the subject of preventive detention, a statutory method of incarcerating criminals without bail where prosecutors assert that the accused is likely to commit future crimes, even if unrelated to the pending charges. Marshall objected to preventive pre-trial detention because he adhered to the principle that a person is innocent until proven guilty. *See* Remarks by Justice Marshall Before the Annual Judicial Conference, Second Circuit, Oct. 15, 1987, 120 F.R.D. 141 (1987).

traditional protector of our liberties."[5] Marshall further encouraged civil rights groups to take the offensive against unfair application of the criminal laws and to realize that a colorblind society remained an aspiration in the 1990s.

5. Thurgood Marshall, New Challenges Facing the Civil Rights Community (1989), *infra*, at 296, 299.

Judicial Power and
Respect for the People

The task of interpretation is the cornerstone of the judicial process. As we undertake it, we must strive for neutrality. None of us is perfect and I recognize that neutrality is more ideal than real. Each of us brings along to the judicial role certain preconceived biases. It is, I suppose, impossible to make a decision totally uninfluenced by them. But we as judges must try to do so to the extent we possibly can.

This ideal of neutrality is particularly hard to maintain in times such as these, when our society faces major unsolved problems. Indeed, we judges are frequently criticized these days for our neutrality. For example, some members of our society argue that the judiciary had not taken an active enough role in combating crime. It is urged that we as judges should take sides, that we should stand shoulder-to-shoulder with the police and prosecutors. Convictions should be easier, appellate review more rapid and resort to habeas corpus—what the founders of this republic called the Great Writ—drastically curtailed. All of this frightens me, because when I was in law school, I was taught not that judges were there to see the defendant convicted and punished in every case but that they were there to see justice done in every case. Of course the state had to carry a heavy burden to obtain conviction. Of course appellate judges would weigh each case carefully. Of course an individual, once convicted, could attack his sentence later. This, so I was taught, was not to coddle the guilty but to protect the innocent. I was raised in the days when the prevailing maxim was "It is better that a thousand guilty people go free than that one innocent person suffers unjustly."[1]

Well, that's just what I was taught, and maybe I was taught wrong. But

These remarks appear in 93 F.R.D. 673, 675 (1981) (Proceedings of the Annual Judicial Conference Second Circuit).

1. This Statement is attributed to Sir William Blackstone. *See* Robert J. Boeckkmann and Tom R. Tyler, *Commonsense Justice and Inclusion*, 3 PSYCHOL. PUB. POL. & L. 362, 366 (1997). Charles Dickens voiced the same ideal, stating, "Better that hundreds of guilty persons escape scot-free . . . than that one innocent person should suffer." DAVID PARIOISSIEN, ED., SELECTED LETTERS OF CHARLES DICKENS 215 (1985).

the suggestion that we as judges take sides frightens me for another, more fundamental reason as well. As I have said, judges are required in our system to be as neutral as they possibly can, to stand above the political questions in which the other branches of government are necessarily entangled. The Constitution established a legislative branch to make the laws and an executive branch to enforce them. Both branches are elected and are designed to respond to ever-changing public concern and problems. Indeed, as we were reminded just last November, the failure of either branch to respond to the will of the majority can quickly be remedied at the polls.

But the framers of the Constitution recognized that responsiveness to the will of the majority might, if unchecked, become a tyranny of the majority.[2] They therefore created a third branch—the judiciary—to check the actions of the legislature and the executive. In order to fulfill this function, the judiciary was intentionally isolated from the political process and purposely spared the task of dealing with changing public concerns and problems. Article III judges are guaranteed lifetime tenure. Similarly, their compensation cannot be decreased during their term in office- a provision, as we have recently seen, that certainly has its tangible benefits. Finally, the constitutional task we are assigned as judges is a very narrow one. We cannot make laws, and it is not our duty to see that they are enforced. We merely interpret them through the painstaking process of adjudicating actual "case or controversies" that come before us.

We have seen what happens when the courts have permitted themselves to be moved by prevailing political pressures and have deferred to the mob rather than interpret the Constitution. Dred Scott, Plessy, Korematsu, and the trial proceedings in *Moore v. Dempsey*, come readily to mind as unfortunate examples.[3] They are decisions of which the entire judicial community, even after all these years, should be ashamed. There have also been times when the courts have stood proudly as a bulwark against what was politically expedient but also unconstitutional. One need only recall the school desegregation cases to understand why this ability to stand above the fray is so important.

2. *See* THE FEDERALIST No. 47, at 321, 322(James Madison, 1788, rprt. 1945) (supporting the view of Montesquieu's admonition that tyranny results when power is concentrated in any branch of government). *See generally* LANI GUINIER, THE TYRANNY OF THE MAJORITY: FUNDAMENTAL FAIRNESS IN REPRESENTATIVE DEMOCRACY (1994); Whitney v. California, 274 U.S. 357, 376 (1927) (referring to "the occasional tyrannies of governing majorities").
3. Dred Scott v. Sanford, 60 U.S. (19 How.) 393 (1857); Plessy v. Ferguson, 163 U.S. 537 (1896); Korematsu v. United States, 323 U.S. 214 (1944); Moore v. Dempsey, 261 U.S. 86 (1923). These cases can be found in DERRICK BELL, RACE, RACISM, AND AMERICAN LAW (1973 ed.).

We must never forget that the only real source of power that we as judges can tap is the respect of the people.[4] We will command that respect only as long as we strive for neutrality. If we are perceived as campaigning for particular policies, as joining with other branches of government in resolving questions not committed to us by the Constitution, we may gain some public acclaims in the short run. In the long run, however, we will cease to be perceived as neutral arbiters, and we will lose that public respect so vital to our function.

I do not suggest that we as judges should not be concerned about the problem of crime. Every thinking American is worried about it. And just about all of us have lurking somewhere in the back of our minds what we consider the ideal solution.

But when we accepted the judicial mantle, we yielded our right to advocate publicly our favored solutions for society's problems. The tools for solving these problems are in the hands of the other branches of government because that is where the Constitution has placed them. That is also where we should leave them. I therefore urge that you politely disregard any suggestion that you give up the robe for the sword.[5]

4. Authors have suggested that the countermajoritarian difficulty which teaches judicial restraint also has escape routes, that is, "A separate effort to respond to the contermajoritarian difficulty suggests that in reality, there is no such difficulty, since the role of the court is to promote, rather than to undermine, democracy, properly understood." GEOFFREY R. STONE et al., CONSTITUTIONAL LAW 45 (1996).

5. See F. FORD, ROBE AND SWORD: THE REGROUPING OF THE FRENCH ARISTOCRACY AFTER LOUIS XIV 105–23, 232 (1953).

Violations of the Constitution Require Corrective Relief

The cases of *Schall v. Martin* and *Heckler v. Day* give me grave concern.[1] Together with a number of other cases from last term, they illustrate a very disturbing pattern. And it's a pattern that has become more and more common. The Court seems to concede in each case that important federal rights are at issue and that they may have been violated. It then denies the victims the only effective remedies to those violations. Almost as an afterthought, it sometimes suggests that the victims pursue other remedies, and it then offers ones that will have little or no effect.

Before I go on, let me state a general principle that I thought was firmly entrenched in our legal culture and central to our system of protection of individual liberties. The principle is that when rights are violated, the court should craft remedies that attempt to make the victims whole and deter future violations. Decisions that do not conform to that principle will erode the faith in the law of those who rely on the law's protections. Where no remedies are offered, or where the only ones offered could accomplish little, those who need protection will have reason to turn away from the legal system. They will be convinced that their rights are being trivialized more than they are being protected.

Schall v. Martin serves as a good starting point. It was a class action challenge to New York's preventive detention scheme for juveniles. Let me describe the scheme briefly. It allows a Family Court judge the discretion to order that a child be "detained" for up to seventeen days between that child's arrest and the adjudication of his or her guilt. The judge simply has to make a conclusory finding that there is a "serious risk." This decision is made in a proceeding that lasts about ten minutes and the law gives no explicit guidance to the judge's discretion. And let me make one thing very clear. "Detention" may mean something very close to imprisonment.

Now let's turn to the challenge to this scheme. All would seem to agree

Remarks before the Annual Judicial Conference, Second Circuit of the United States, Hartford, Connecticut, September 13, 1984, *in* 106 F.R.D. 103, 118 (1984).
1. Schall v. Martin, 467 U.S. 253 (1984); Heckler v. Day, 467 U.S. 104 (1984).

that arbitrary or punitive detention prior to an adjudication of guilt is a very serious violation of the Constitution. I would think that we would also agree that where a person's very liberty is made to rest on someone's unbridled discretion, we must guard against abuse. Here the discretion was very broad and the plaintiff's showed that the results seemed very arbitrary.

Judge Robert Carter declared the law unconstitutional in an opinion that included extensive findings concerning how the system actually operated.[2] The Second Circuit affirmed without dissent.[3] Opinions by Ralph Winter and Jon O. Newman separately and persuasively bolstered the district court's conclusions. The Supreme Court reversed, but clearly did not have the better case.

The court upheld as a whole with the extraordinary conclusion that preventive detention made sense as a *benefit for the children*. Like a parent, the state is seeking to protect its children from their own propensity to stray. That's some case to make in the face of a record that showed prison-like conditions, commingling of those awaiting trial and those awaiting trial and those in long-term custody, and violence—even sexual assault. But at least the court did concede that arbitrary or punitive detention would be unconstitutional. Given that concession, I find it shocking that rather than make an assessment of how likely those evils were under the New York system, it instead validated the scheme as a whole and offered a hollow remedy for any individual abuses. In the court's view, case-by-case adjudication would be a sufficient remedy.

Such reasoning illustrates the point of this talk. Individual actions under this scheme would be almost meaningless. The first problem is practical: Any child's detention would be over prior to the adjudication of his claim.

Leaving aside such issues as mootness, I would note that an unconstitutional detention is hardly a minimal violation of rights, even if short in duration. The second problem is at least as bad. The statute allows detention to be imposed at a very short hearing prior to any fact-finding and to be based on a vague and purely subjective assessment of the child's probable future behavior.

Now, imagine the burden of arguing that you were improperly detained under that statute. Just as the difficulty of making such an argument is frightening, so is the prospect of evaluating it as a judge. All in all, this was a sad decision. . . .

2. United States v. Strasburg, 513 F. Supp. 691 (S.D.N.Y. 1981). Judge Carter was the lead signatory on the Brown v. Board of Education brief in 1954.
3. Martin v. Strasburg, 689 F.2d 365 (2d. Cir. 1982).

Moral and Fair Representation Issues in Death Penalty Cases

What I plan to discuss today . . . is a fact of judicial life that the Second Circuit has been fortunate enough to escape in recent years. These remarks will focus on the death penalty—an element of our criminal justice system about which I have thought and agonized a great deal during my career as an advocate and a judge. I do not want to talk about the theory of the Eighth Amendment, or about the intricacies of death penalty jurisprudence. Instead I want to focus on the practicalities of the administration of the death penalty as it is going on in this country.

My goal is to share with you some of the reasons for my belief that capital defendants do not have a fair opportunity to defend their lives in the courtroom today. I hope that calling attention to this extraordinary unfairness that now surrounds the administration of the death penalty will spur us as lawyers and members of the judiciary and public officials to begin to right that wrong.

I believe we all can agree, and we can agree on one basic proposition; that is, the unique finality of a capital sentence obliges society to assure that capital defendants receive a fair chance to present all available defenses, and that they have at least the same opportunities for acquittal as non-capital defendants.

The system now in place, however, at times affords capital defendants a lesser opportunity to present their cases than virtually any other litigant. Recent decisions of the Supreme Court have taken their special toll on capital defendants, and deny, rather than assure, that these defendants will have an adequate opportunity to present their defenses.

Two aspects of capital case litigation create this problem. The first derives from changes in substantive law and procedural rules that have made collateral review an empty promise for a large group of capital defendants.

Remarks by Justice Marshall September 5, 1985. *See Annual Judicial Conference, Second Judicial Circuit of the United States,* Hershey, Pennsylvania. Judge Wilfred Feinberg, Chief Judge, Presiding, 109 F.R.D. 441 (1986).

The second results from the haste with which capital defendants' claims are reviewed once an execution date is set.

I will discuss each in turn. First, capital defendants frequently suffer the consequences of having trial counsel who are ill equipped to handle capital cases. Death penalty litigation has become a specialized field of practice, and expensive. And even the most well-intentioned attorneys often are unable to recognize, preserve, and defend their clients' rights. Often trial counsel simply is unfamiliar with the special rules that apply in capital cases.

Counsel, whether appointed or retained, often are handling their first criminal cases, or their first murder cases. When confronted with this, the prospect of a death penalty is ominous.

Though acting in good faith, they often make serious mistakes. Thus, in capital cases I have read, counsel have simply been unaware that certain death penalty issues are pending before the appellate courts and that the claims should be preserved; that certain findings by a jury might preclude imposition of a death penalty; or that a separate sentencing procedure or phases of the litigation must follow a conviction. The federal reports are filled with stories of counsel who presented no evidence in mitigation of their clients' sentences, simply because they did not know what to offer or how to offer it, or had not read the state sentencing statute.

I kid you not. Precisely that has happened time and again.

As one commentator noted a few years ago: "It is not enough that inmates have been represented before trial and on the first appeal. Before the imposition of sentence, the case is not really a capital one. So many defendants theoretically face the death penalty but relatively few are actually sentenced to death. For that reason, among others, relatively young and inexperienced attorneys, without investigative sources and with no real expectation that the defendant may actually face execution often defend capital trials."[1]

Trial counsel's lack of expertise takes a heavy toll. A capital defendant seeking postconviction relief is, today, caught up in an increasing pernicious visegrip. Pressing against him from one side is the Supreme Court's continual restriction of what federal courts can remedy on

---

1. *See* Alan N. Dershowitz, Gideon's Trumpet Is But Faintly Heard on Death Row (speech before the American Bar Association), Aug. 1, 1983, reprinted in *Death Row Inmates Need Lawyers More Than Ever*, L.A. DAILY J., Sept. 12, 1983, at 4. Sometimes, defendants facing death sentences are represented by lawyers who want them dead. *See, e.g.*, Matt Fleischer, *His Defense Attorney Wanted Him Dead*, NAT'L L.J., Nov. 20, 2000, at 1.

postconviction review. It has accomplished this by expanding the "presumption of correctness" afforded state court findings, and also by imposing rigid doctrines of procedural default that often turn on technical pleading rules, and, at times, sacrifice fundamental fairness.

The problem is even more acute for capital defendants. The court purports to have created a host of rights that protect the capital defendant at the sentencing phase of a proceeding, but at the same time it has limited appellate and collateral review of those rights, and of the correctness of the sentencer's decision. These rules of limitation often deny capital defendants the kind of personalized inquiry to which they have an indisputable right. Thus, errors of sentencing are often irremediable.

Pressing against the capital defendant from the other side is the Supreme Court's restrictive definition of what constitutes unconstitutional ineffective assistance of counsel at trial. The severe rules the Court has adopted to assure that the trial is the "main event" have been unaccompanied by measures to ensure the fairness and accuracy of that event. The Court has not yet recognized that the right of effective assistance must encompass a right to counsel familiar with death penalty jurisprudence at the trial stage. Instead, in all but the most egregious cases, a court cannot or will not make a finding of ineffective assistance of counsel because counsel has met what the Supreme Court has defined as a minimal standard of competence for criminal lawyers.

As a consequence, many capital defendants find that errors by their lawyers preclude presentation of substantial constitutional claims, but that such errors—with the resulting forfeitures of rights—are not enough in themselves to constitute ineffective assistance.

To quote a recent commentary, "There is little the experienced lawyer can do but regret the failure to preserve rights and to go through the paces of yet another futile round of litigation."[2]

These developments in the substantive law and procedural rules make it imperative for the death penalty bar to reconsider its priorities; it must readjust its thinking on how best to assist capital defendants in receiving a fair hearing. For years, private death penalty counsel has focused their attention on the collateral review phase of litigation. At the trial phase and on direct, nondiscretionary appeal, the Constitution requires that a state provide indigent defendants with counsel; that fact leaves most capital cases in the hands of state-appointed counsel through direct review. Only after direct review is complete, when the states no longer must supply counsel, have private counsel entered these cases.

2. American Bar Association Criminal Justice Section: Report to the House of Delegates, 40 Am. U. L. Rev. 9, 65, n. 139 (1990).

In the changed legal environment death penalty lawyers now face, this assistance—laudable and valuable as it is—often comes too late to help a convicted defendant. Counsel on collateral review is boxed in by any mistakes or inadequacies of trial counsel. In these circumstances, entrance at the habeas corpus stage simply cannot guarantee the defendant the opportunity to vindicate his constitutional rights.

The only way out of the visegrip is for the death penalty bar to adjust decisively to the reality that many errors of constitutional magnitude at trial will be uncorrectable. In order to take advantage of collateral review, competent trial counsel is a necessity. The bar must focus on improving the quality of trial counsel in capital cases, and must find resources to establish training and assistance for local attorneys appointed to handle capital cases. Experienced counsel able to assist at the trial level should be made aware of pending trials through regional or nationwide information centers.

Resources are scant and the time between arrest and trial is short. Nevertheless, there are things that can be done. If resources could be found, regional or national clearinghouses might gather information on capital cases and capital defendants; they also might provide advice on relevant case law, data, or issues for writing briefs. It is now difficult to determine how many capital trials are going on, or to find and match willing counsel with needy clients. Local counsel often is on their own to gain experience—at the expense of their indigent clients facing death. The lack of experience and expertise demonstrated by counsel who act in good faith but are unable to perform as they ought leaves too many defendants without adequate assistance.

Whatever your views about the death penalty, we simply cannot accept this state of affairs. We must do something to improve the quality of representation at the trial stage. Only then can we begin to assure that persons convicted of capital crimes have a fair opportunity to present a defense. Unless there is a change in legal doctrine that would assure retrials until adequate representation is had, the burden will fall on the legal profession to do what it can.

The second problem relates closely to the first. It involves what I have called the rush to judgment—that is, the willingness of the courts and the state governments to expedite proceedings in order to bring about speedy executions. I would have thought that cases involving the death penalty might receive especially cautious handling and attention to minimize errors. The reality, however, is exactly the opposite. The Supreme Court has endorsed, and the states and courts have implemented, a scheme in which capital defendants receive less time to present their cases to the courts than noncapital defendants.

As a result, courts must rule on the cases in a chaotic atmosphere. The tragic result is to turn fairness and logic on their heads and to deprive those capital defendants of the attention and rights accorded other criminal defendants, for whom the penalty for conviction is so substantially less severe.

Contrary to popular perceptions, all capital defendants have not spent years filing frivolous claims in federal courts. Many of these defendants have not yet filed any federal claims when their execution dates are set. We simply cannot allow this inaccurate view to blind us to reality, or to accept the hasty review process on the ground that defendants already have had the benefits of an untruncated review process.

The mechanics of this problem are as follows: Execution dates generally are set about one month before the execution date. Indigent prisoners, who have no constitutional right to the assistance of counsel for habeas, often have had to get counsel for collateral review at this time. Until the execution date is set, and the situation becomes urgent, capital defendants simply have been unable to secure counsel.

A recent committee report of the New York City Bar Association summed it up as follows:

The post-conviction capital defendant who cannot afford a lawyer is left to the mercy of volunteer lawyers. If voluntary representation is not available, the defendant must act pro se or accept death without attempting habeas proceedings. The shortage of volunteer attorneys and the ever-growing death row population raises the specter of *pro se* defendants lacking adequate skill to present the issues in habeas proceedings; or worse, executions of defendants unable ever to marshall such an effort.[3]

This lack of counsel should remove from these defendants any blame for the failure to file petitions prior to the scheduling of their executions. But the courts do not always view the issue in that way.

Once the execution date is set, the race is on. Prisoners who have not yet sought state or federal habeas corpus relief have roughly one month to do so. In a recent case, a capital defendant named Kevin Scott Roscoe filed a *pro se* petition for habeas corpus relief after his execution date was set, and before he could obtain counsel. In the same week, another defendant was still seeking counsel a week before his scheduled execution date. Generally by that time, though, counsel is found to represent the defendant, and indeed Kevin Roscoe's new counsel thereafter filed an amended petition. But the new attorney often has no knowledge of

3. *Committee on Civil Rights, The Death Penalty,* 39 Rec. A.B. City N.Y. 419, 425 (1984).

the record, has not met the client, and has only a few days to read hundreds of pages of transcripts and prepare a petition. This petition, hastily prepared, must include all claims that the defendant might raise because subsequent petitions will likely be declared abusive of the process. The petition must be presented first to the state courts if they entertain collateral attacks. Only then will the federal court hear the case. All the while, the clock runs. State courts often wait until two to three days before the execution date to rule. Thereafter, if the federal court finds that the petition has possible merit, the court might stay the execution. Even then, the defendant has been injured, perhaps fatally; his most important filing has been prepared in necessary but inevitable harmful haste.

In other cases, the district court will expedite its proceedings in order to get the case through the system before the execution date. If the district court denies the writ but grants a certificate of probable cause, the court of appeals then must rule on the merits of the claim. The Supreme Court has authorized the reviewing courts to put these proceedings on fast-forward. The normal contracts claimant has the opportunity to study the district court opinion at length, to research responses to its points, to hone down arguments, and to sharpen the debate. He in effect has the chance to rebut the lower court judge. The same process of evaluation and consideration takes place in petitions for certiorari filed in the Supreme Court; civil litigants have ninety days in which to file a petition for review.

For the capital defendant whose execution looms, the story differs. When the process speeds up, the opportunity for deliberation, consideration, and rebuttal vanishes. The proceedings collapse into each other, and the appellate process loses its vitality.

Courts forgo the input of the party most concerned with the outcome. Yet, the Supreme Court has allowed this process, which usually takes months to years, to occur in a matter of hours.

It has taken from the capital defendant, whose life is on the line, the basic right granted to parties in run-of-the-mill civil litigation. Thus, the result of expedited proceedings is more than the patent indignity of rushing those claimants for whom the proceedings are of unique import. The process also takes its toll on the litigant's ability to present his claims. As an example, last term the Court allowed one defendant to die on a 4–4 vote, and permitted the execution of another defendant although he had presented a substantial federal claim then pending in the lower federal courts in another case.

It may well be that successive habeas petitions that amount to abuses of the writ require a certain watchfulness to prevent blatant tactics, dilatory tactics. But when the petition is a first one or raises new arguments, this unnecessary haste robs the process and robs the thought of all concerned. It denies the defendant's crucial opportunity to participate.

This situation is remediable. First, other federal circuits could join the Court of Appeals for the Eleventh Circuit in establishing rules staying executions. They could then address, in a more considered and coherent fashion, all first habeas petitions in which certificates of probable cause have been or should have been granted. This rule could be extended to subsequent habeas petitions that raise substantial questions. Similarly, circuit and district court rules could place these petitions on the normal track earlier, at the district court stage. The result would be to remove from district judges the pressure to expedite proceedings, and to encourage development of a solid and complete hearing record.

Second, as long as the courts continue to rush these cases along, counsel should alter their approach. Attorneys could begin preparing for collateral review as soon as a capital defendant's sentence is affirmed in the direct state proceedings. The collateral process then could get underway before an execution is inevitable and scheduled.

I note with a degree of hope the recent establishment in Florida of an Office of the Capital Collateral Representative. This state-appointed and financed public defender will represent indigent capital defendants. Representation begins on termination of direct appellate proceedings, and state public defenders are required to notify the representative of the termination. If the legislation creating this office is implemented seriously, the result could be positive.

In those death penalty states in which such public assistance is not available, members of the private bar must attempt to fill the same role.

Third, states could take steps to slow the process. For example, states could set the execution date farther in advance of the execution. This would permit considered judicial proceedings—at least when collateral review has not yet occurred even once.

State statutes that set the maximum period an execution might be set in advance perhaps were passed to prevent a lengthy and agonizing wait for death; but the result is to deprive the prisoner of perhaps his only chance to avoid death.

I do not mean to suggest that these changes would solve the problems inherent in the death penalty. I continue to oppose that sentence under any and all circumstances. But as long as our nation permits executions, lawyers, judges, and public officials have a duty. They must assure that people who face the ultimate sentence receive the same opportunity to present their best case to the court that noncapital defendants receive. Not necessarily more but at least as much.

Until the Supreme Court will make that guarantee, others must work within the existing system to provide that opportunity. The task might be formidable; but the consequences of any failure to undertake it are unacceptably severe.[4]

4. The concerns raised by Marshall continue today. However, some judges are now paying closer attention to his concerns. *See generally*, Richard A. Oppel, Jr., *Death Penalty in Texas Case Is Overturned Citing Lawyer*, N.Y. TIMES, Aug. 31, 2000, at A12 ("a federal judge has overturned the death sentence of a Texas man convicted of killing a sixteen-year-old boy, citing the 'dismal' performance of the convicted man's lawyers during his trial"). Raymond Bonner and Ford Fessenden, *States with No Death Penalty Share Lower Homicide Rates*, N.Y. TIMES, Sept. 22, 2000, at 1; Jim Yardly, *Lawyers Call for Changes in Death Penalty in Texas*, N.Y. TIMES, Oct. 16, 2000, at A16, states: "In a broad critique of capital punishment in Texas, a new report concludes that the State's death penalty system is in dire need of change.... One of the report's central contentions ... is that the appeals process is too cursory," *id.*; Sara Rimer, *Support for a Moratorium in Executions Gets Stronger*, N.Y. TIMES, Oct. 31, 2000, at A16. The new frontier in death penalty cases is its current reach to juvenile criminals. *See Meting Death to Juvenile Criminals*, WASH. POST, Dec. 8, 2000 at A54.

Charles Hamilton Houston

In modest seriousness, I do confess that Ralph [K. Winter, Jr.][1] was my first law clerk and we learned a lot of things together . . .

He mentioned my work before I went on the Court, and I just have to, every time it is mentioned, mention the name of a guy by the name of Charlie Houston who started all of this, and I doubt anybody in this room remembers him. He has been dead quite a while, but he started it all. He raised his students in the 1930s, he trained them not to be lawyers but to be "social engineers," and there is not a movement that I have come across in civil rights or civil liberties that Charlie Houston didn't have a hand in back in those days when it was rough.[2]

When we had to travel in the south in his car—[Houston] had a big, old Grand Paige—there was no place to eat, no place to sleep. We slept in the car and we ate fruit. And one place in Mississippi we were eating, talking to people, and a little kid, I guess twelve, fourteen, a little bright-eyed boy—I was eating an orange, and he was just looking at me. I said, "You want one of these?" He said, "Yes." So I gave him one, and he just bit into it, didn't peel it.

You know why? That was the first time he had ever seen an orange. And that would give you what we had in those days.

Well, enough of that. The sun didn't move and now this is my twentieth year and I just hope that each one of you here is fortunate enough to be with me on my next twentieth year. [Applause.]

That's if you're lucky, because my wife is going to kill me for language

Remarks by Justice Marshall Oct. 15, 1987. *See Annual Judicial Conference, Second Circuit of the United States,* Hershey, Pennsylvania. Judge Wilfred Feinberg, Chief Judge, Presiding. 120 F.R.D. 141, 203 (1987).
1. In 2000 Judge Winter, Chief Judge of the Second Judicial Circuit, reminded an interviewer that Justice Marshall was more than a historic figure, "he was also a lawyer's lawyer." *From Academics to the Bench, It's Another Side of the Law,* 32 THIRD BRANCH 10, 11, July 2000.
2. *See* generally *In Tribute: Charles Hamilton Houston,* 111 HARV. L. REV. 2149 (1998); J. Clay Smith, Jr., and E. Desmond Hogan, *Remembered Hero, Forgotten Contribution: Charles Hamilton Houston, Legal Realism, and Labor Law,* 14 HARV. BLACKLETTER L.J. 1 (1998).

problems, but one old politician years ago, and I can't remember who it was, that they tried to burn off over and over again and he made the statement that I repeat for myself: For all those people who wish very dearly for me to give up and quit and what-have-you, and all these beautiful letters I get, including one that I thought was very good, the last line was, "And another thing, you suffer from complete constipation of the brain."

I thought that was original and good. [Laughter.]

But this statement, I hope you will pardon me for saying it, but it's, "Don't worry, I'm going to outlive those bastards." [Applause.] . . .

The Constitution:
A Living Document

This year marks the two hundredth anniversary of the United States Constitution. A commission has been established to coordinate the celebration. The official meetings, essay contests, and festivities have begun.

The planned commemoration will span three years, and I am told 1987 is "dedicated to the memory of the Founders and the document they drafted in Philadelphia." We are to "recall the achievements of our Founders and the knowledge and experience that inspired them, the nature of the government they established, its origins, its character, and its ends, and the rights and privileges of citizenship, as well as its attendant responsibilities."[1]

Like many anniversary celebrations, the plan for 1987 takes particular events and holds them up as the source of all the very best that has followed. Patriotic feelings will surely swell, prompting proud proclamations of the wisdom, foresight, and sense of justice shared by the Framers and reflected in a written document now yellowed with age. This is unfortunate—not the patriotism itself, but the tendency for the celebration to oversimplify, and overlook the many other event that have been instrumental to our achievements as a nation. The focus of this celebration invites a complacent belief that the vision of those who debated and comprised in Philadelphia yielded the "more perfect Union" it is said we now enjoy.

I cannot accept this invitation, for I do not believe that the meaning of the Constitution was forever "fixed" at the Philadelphia Convention. Nor do I find the wisdom, foresight, and sense of justice exhibited by the Framers particularly profound. To the contrary, the government they devised was defective from the start, requiring several amendments, a civil war, and momentous social transformation to attain the system of

Remarks of Thurgood Marshall at the Annual Seminar of the San Francisco Patent and Trademark Law Conference in Maui, Hawaii, May 6, 1987. Reprinted in Thurgood Marshall, *The Constitution: A Living Document*, 30 How. L.J. 624 (1987).
1. Commission on the Bicentennial of the United States Constitution, First Report at 6 (Sept. 1985).

constitutional government, and its respect for the individual freedoms and human rights, we hold as fundamental today. When contemporary Americans cite "The Constitution," they invoke a concept that is vastly different from what the Framers barely began to construct two centuries ago.

For a sense of the evolving nature of the Constitution we need look no further than the first three words of the document's preamble: *We the people*. When the Founding Fathers used this phrase in 1787, they did not have in mind the majority of America's citizens. *We the people* included, in the words of the Framers, "the whole Number of free Persons."[2] On a matter so basic as the right to vote, for example, Negro slaves were excluded, although they were counted for representational purposes—at three-fifths each. Women did not gain the right to vote for over a hundred and thirty years.

These omissions were intentional. The record of the Framers' debates on the slave question is especially clear: The Southern states acceded to the demanded of the New England states for giving Congress broad power to regulate commerce, in exchange for the right to continue the slave trade. The perpetuation of slavery ensured the primary source of wealth in Southern states.

Despite this clear understanding of the role slavery would play in the new republic, use of the words "slaves" and "slavery" was carefully avoided in the original document. Political representations in the Lower House of Congress was to be based on the population of "'free Persons' in each State, plus three-fifths of all 'other Persons.'" Moral principles against slavery, for those who had them, were compromised, with no explanation of the conflicting principles for which the American Revolutionary War had ostensibly been fought: the self-evident truths "that all men are created equal, that they are endowed by their Creator with certain inalienable Rights, that among these are Life, Liberty and the pursuit of Happiness."

It was not the first such compromise. Even these ringing phrases from the Declaration of Independence are filled with irony, for an early draft of what became that Declaration assailed the king of England for suppressing legislative attempts to end the slave trade and for encouraging slave rebellions. The final draft adopted in 1776 did not contain this criticism. And so again at the Constitutional Convention eloquent objections to the institution of slavery went unheeded, and its opponent eventually consented to a document which laid a foundation for the tragic events that were to follow.

2. U.S. Const. Art. I, §2. Editor: Joe H. Stroud writes, "The Founding Fathers were wrong in thinking we could avoid addressing what it means to be a nation half free and half slave." Joe H. Stroud, *Overcome Race, or It Will Overcome Us*, DETROIT FREE PRESS, March 28, 2001, at 11A.

Pennsylvania's Gouverneur Morris provides an example. He opposed slavery and the counting of slaves in determining the basis for representation in Congress. At the Convention he objected "that the inhabitant of Georgia [or] South Carolina who goes to the Coast of Africa, and in defiance of the most sacred laws of humanity tears away his fellow creatures from their dearest connections and damns them to the most cruel bondages, shall have more votes in a Government instituted for protection of the rights of mankind, than the Citizen of a practice Pennsylvania or New Jersey who views with a laudable horror, so nefarious." And yet Gouverneur Morris eventually accepted the three-fifths accommodation. In fact, he wrote the final draft of the Constitution, the very document the bicentennial will commemorate.

As a result of compromise, the right of the Southern states to continue importing slaves was extended, officially, at least until 1808. We know that it actually lasted a good deal longer, as the Framers possessed no monopoly on the ability to trade moral principles for self-interest. But they nevertheless set an unfortunate example. Slaves could be imported, if the commercial interests of the North were protected. To make the compromise even more palatable, customs duties would be imposed at up to ten dollars per slave as a means of raising public revenues.

No doubt it will be said, when the unpleasant truth of the history of slavery in America is mentioned during this bicentennial year, that the Constitution was a product of its times, and embodied a compromise which, under other circumstances, would not have been made. But the effects of the Framers' compromise have remained for generations. They arose from the contradiction between guaranteeing liberty and justice to all, denying both to Negroes.

The original intent of the phrase, *We the people*, was far too clear too clear any ameliorating construction. Writing for the Supreme Court in 1857, Chief Justice Taney penned the following passage in the *Dred Scott* case, on the issue whether, in the eyes of the Framers, slaves were "constituent member of the sovereignty," and were to be included among *We the people*:

We think they are not, and that they are not included, and were not intended to be included. . . . They had for more than a century before been regarded as associated with the white race . . . ; and so far inferior, that they had nor rights which the white man was bound to respect; and that the Negro might justly and lawfully be reduced to slavery for his benefit. . . . [A]ccordingly, a Negro of the African race was regarded . . . as an article of property, and held, and bought and sold as such. . . . [N]o one seems to have doubted the correctness of the prevailing opinion of the time.[3]

3. Dred Scott v. Sanford, 60 U.S. (19 How.) 393, 407–408 (1857).

And so, nearly seven decades after the Constitutional Convention, the Supreme Court reaffirmed the prevailing opinion of the Framers regarding the rights of Negroes in America. It took a bloody civil war before the Thirteenth Amendment could be adopted to abolish slavery, though not the consequences slavery would have for future Americans.

While the Union survived the Civil War, the Constitution did not. In its place arose a new, more promising basis for justice and equality, the Fourteenth Amendment, ensuring protection of the life, liberty, and property of *all* persons against deprivations without due process, and guaranteeing equal protection of the laws. And yet almost another century would pass before any significant recognition was obtained of the rights of Black Americans to share equally even in such basic opportunity as education, housing and employment, and to have their votes counted, and counted equally. In the meantime, Blacks joined America's military to fight its wars and invested untold hours working in its factories and on its farms, contributing to the development of this country's magnificent wealth and waiting to share its prosperity.

What is striking is the role legal principles have played throughout America's history in determining the condition of Negroes. They were enslaved by law, emancipated by law, disenfranchised and segregated by law; and, finally, they have begun to win equality by law. Along the way, new constitutional principles have emerged to meet the challenges of a changing society. The progress has been dramatic, and it will continue.

The men who gathered in Philadelphia in 1787 could not have envisioned these changes. They could not have imagined, nor would they have accepted, that the document they were drafting would one day be construed by a Supreme Court to which have been appointed a woman and the descendant of an African slave. *We the People* are no longer enslaved, but the credit does not belong to the Framers. It belongs to those who refused to acquiesce in outdated notions of "liberty," "justice," and "equality," and who strived to better them.

And so we must be careful, when focusing on the events which took place in Philadelphia two centuries ago, that we not overlook the momentous events which followed, and thereby lose our proper sense of perspective. Otherwise, the odds are that for many Americans the bicentennial celebration will be little more than a blind pilgrimage to the shrine of the original document now stored in a vault in the National Archives. If we seek, instead, a sensitive understanding of the Constitution's inherent defects and its promising evolution through two hundred years of history, the celebration of the "Miracle at Philadelphia" will, in my view, be a far more meaningful and humbling experience. We will see that the true miracle was not the birth of the Constitution, but its life, a life nurtured through two turbulent centuries of our own making, and a life embodying much good fortune that was not.

Thus, in this bicentennial year, we may not all participate in the festivities with flag-waving fervor. Some may more quietly commemorate the suffering, struggle, and sacrifice that have triumphed over much of what was wrong with the original document, and observe the anniversary with hopes not realized and promises not fulfilled. I plan to celebrate the bicentennial of the Constitution as a living document, including the Bill of Rights and the other amendments protecting individual freedoms and human rights.

A Colorblind Society
Remains an Aspiration

Chief Judge [Wilfred] Feinberg [of the U.S. Court of Appeals, Second Circuit] and friends: As you know, it is wonderful to come up here and, I am one of the Justices on this Court who appreciates the circuit, because I don't have much trouble with it. I sit there at times and listen to the bandying back and forth about all the problems they have in this Circuit and that Circuit, and every now and then somebody asks me, "What about your circuit?" I say, "It runs itself."

What I have to say this morning is, I hope, of interest . . .

I would like to speak today about an issue much discussed in recent months, in part because of cases which came to our Court from this Circuit last year. I refer to the Sheet Metal Workers case,[1] in which our Court affirmed the excellent decision by Judge Pratt, and to the question of affirmative action. Much has been said lately about the scope of permissible remedies, both voluntary and mandatory, in cases of employment discrimination. The decisions of our Court in this past term suggest to me that there is still a basic agreement among a majority of the Justices that the commands of Title VII and the equal protection clause should be implemented, where necessary, through broad-based relief including the imposition of affirmative duties to eradicate the effects of past discrimination. But because statements in sharp opposition to the use of affirmative remedies have recently been heard with increasing frequency, I think it is appropriate to share with you some general thoughts about why affirmative action is necessary, and on the role which it plays in our law despite many people in high offices trying to explain away our decision. We will explain it.

I believe all of the participants in the current debate about affirmative action agree that the ultimate goal is the creation of a colorblind society. From this common premise, however, two very different conclusions have apparently been drawn: The first is that race-conscious remedies may not be used to eliminate the effects of past discrimination against

Address before Annual Judicial Conference, Second Judicial Circuit, 115 F.R.D. 349 (Oct.15, 1987).
1. Sheet Metal Workers v. E.E.O.C., 478 U.S. 421 (1986).

Negroes and other minority groups in American society. This conclusion has been expanded into the proposition that courts and parties entering into consent decrees are limited to remedies, which provide relief to identified individual victims of discrimination only. But the second conclusion, which may be drawn from our common preference for a colorblind society, is that the vestiges of racial bias in America are so pernicious, and so difficult to remove, that we must take advantage of all the remedial measures at our disposal. The difference between these views may be accounted for, at least in part, by difference of opinion as to how close we presently are to the "colorblind society" about which everybody talks. I believe that, given the position from which America began, we still have a very long way to go. The Framers of our Constitution labored "In order to form a more perfect union, establish justice . . . and secure the blessings of liberty."[2] These were beautiful words, but at the same time a Negro slave was but three-fifths of a man in the same Constitution. Negroes who, finding themselves purportedly the property of white men, attempted to secure the blessings of liberty by voting with their feet and running away, were to be captured and returned to slavery pursuant to that same document.

The decisions of the Supreme Court in *Prigg v. Pennsylvania* and *Ableman v. Booth*[3] demonstrated just how strong the assertion of federal power on behalf of the slaveholder could be. There was undeniable historical truth in Chief Justice Taney's statement in Dred Scott that at the time of adoption of the Constitution Negroes "had for more than a century before been regarded as being of an inferior order, and altogether unfit to associate with the white race, either in social or political relations," et cetera, et cetera, et cetera.[4]

Our constitutional jurisprudence at that time rested upon this premise and it continued so for a century. So many have forgotten.

Justice Harlan, as you remember, dissenting in *Plessy v. Ferguson*, gave the first expression to the judicial principle that our constitution is colorblind and neither knows nor tolerates classes among citizens.[5] If Justice Harlan's views had prevailed, and *Plessy* been decided upon the principle of race neutrality, our situation now, ninety years later, would be far different than it is. Affirmative action is an issue today precisely needed because our constitution was not colorblind in the sixty years which intervened between *Plessy* and *Brown*.[6]

2. *See* Preamble to the United States Constitution.
3. Prigg v. Pennsylvania, 41 U.S. 539 (1842); Ableman v. Booth, 62 U.S. 506 (1858).
4. Dred Scott v. Sandford, 60 U.S. 393, 406–407(1857).
5. Plessy v. Ferguson, 163 U.S. 537 (1896).
6. *Id.* (Plessy); Brown v. Board of Education, 347 U.S. 483 (1954) (Brown I).

Obviously, I too believe in a colorblind society; but it has been and remains an aspiration. It is a goal toward which our society has progressed uncertainly, bearing as it does the enormous burden of incalculable injuries inflicted by race prejudice and other bigotry, which the law once sanctioned, and even encouraged. Not having attained our goal, we must face the simple fact that there are groups in every community, which are daily paying the cost of the history of American injustice. The argument against affirmative action is but an argument in favor of leaving that cost to lie where it falls. Our fundamental sense of fairness, particularly as it is embodied in the guarantee of equal protection under the law, requires us to make an effort to see that those costs are shared equitably while we continue to work for the eradication of the consequences of discrimination. Otherwise, we must admit to ourselves that so long as the lingering effects of inequality are with us, the burden will be borne by those who are least able to pay.

For this reason, the argument that equitable remedies should be restricted to redressing the grievances of individual victims of discrimination completely misses the point. The point is that our government has a compelling interest in dealing with all the harm caused by discrimination against racial and other minorities, not merely with the harm immediately occasioned when somebody is denied a job, or a promotion, by reason of the color of his skin.

It has been argued that the use of affirmative race-conscious remedies inflicts an immediate harm on some, in the hope of ameliorating the more remote harm done to others. This, it is said, is as abhorrent as the original discrimination itself. Some have compared the use of such race-conscious remedies to using alcohol to get beyond alcoholism or drugs to overcome a drug addiction, or a few more cigarettes a day to break the smoking habit. I think the comparison is inappropriate and abhorrent. Affirmative action is not, as the analogies often imply, a symptom of lack of societal willpower; when judiciously employed, it is instead an instrument for sharing the burdens, which our history imposes upon all of us.

This is not to say, of course, that affirmative remedies such as the establishment of goals, timetables, and all of that, in hiring, in promotion, or for protection of recently hired minority workers from the disproportionate effects of layoffs, are always necessary or appropriate. Where there is no admission or proof of past discriminatory conduct, or where those individuals whose existing interests may be adversely affected by the remedy have not had an opportunity to participate, serious questions arise which must be carefully scrutinized in the courts. Like all classifications which condition governmental behavior upon considerations of race, affirmative remedies for employment discrimination must overcome the stringent presumption in favor of neutrality, which the equal protection clause embodies. To undertake such remedies except in furtherance of the most important of governmental purposes, and without substantial assurance that narrower alternatives would not achieve the goal, is wrong. But what the recent statements in opposition to affirmative action do not consider, in my judgment, is the fundamental importance of eradicating the consequences of discrimination which are so visible throughout our society, and the basic injustice which is done by imposing all the costs of those lingering consequences upon those who have traditionally been the victims.

In this connection, it is especially important to reflect upon the role which affirmative relief plays when embodied in consent judgments. Last term, in *Local 93, International Association of Firefighters v. City of Cleveland,* the Court held that Title VII does not preclude the ordering of affirmative race-conscious relief in a consent decree entered in settlement of litigation brought under the Act.[7] Six justices agreed that the scope of remedy available in a consent decree under Title VII is at least as broad as that available in judgment after trial on the merits, and may include provisions for race-conscious relief. In my view, this holding is of great significance. We are all aware of the burden and expense which litigation, of whatever size and complexity, imposes on the litigant. Chief Judge Learned Hand surely did not exaggerate in saying that the citizen may do well to fear litigation beyond almost anything short of sickness and death.[8] Where large-scale employment discrimination litigation is concerned, the effects are many times greater. The availability of broad voluntary remedies affords parties the opportunity to settle their differences without the expense and disruption necessitated by trial on the merits, and allows employers, public and private, to correct injustices without being compelled publicly to defend the indefensible. By encouraging parties to enter into such voluntary relief, the Court's decision ensures greater flexibility in the search for workable solutions to the problem of inequality in America.

And this, finally, I believe will be the most important function of affirmative action. The problem of discrimination and prejudice in America is too deep-rooted and too widespread to be solved only in the courts, or only through the intervention of federal authority to convince the recalcitrant that justice cannot be indefinitely delayed.

---

7. 478 U.S. 501 (1986).
8. *See* Address by Judge Learned Hand, *The Deficiencies of Trials to Reach the Heart of the Matter,* before the Assocation of the Bar of the City of New York, Nov. 17, 1921, *reprinted in* 3 Ass'n. B. City of N.Y., Lectures on Legal Topics 1921–22, at 87, 105 (1926). For more on Judge Hand, see Gerald Gunther, Learned Hand: The Man and the Judge 121–123, 452–453 (1994).

Securing equality requires the attention, the energy, and the sense of justice possessed by all the well-intentioned citizens of this society. They need to be assured that the government, the law, and the courts stand behind their efforts to overcome the harm bequeathed to them by the past. They need to know that encouragement and support, not criticism and prohibition are available from those who are sworn to uphold the law. Courts must offer guidance, to the best of our ability, to the attempts by individuals and institutions to rectify the injustices of the past. We must labor to provide examples of solutions that may work, and approaches that may be tried. If we fail, then we delay or postpone altogether the era in which, for the first time, we may say with firm conviction that we have built a society in keeping with our fundamental belief that all people are created equal.

If any one of you is worried about what I mean by the goal of a democracy such as ours, I have often said, and I repeat here, that the goal of a true democracy such as ours, explained simply, is that any baby born in these United States, even if he is born to the blackest, most illiterate, most unprivileged Negro in Mississippi, is, merely by being born and drawing his first breath in this democracy, endowed with the exact same rights as a child born to a Rockefeller.

Of course it's not true. Of course it never will be true. But I challenge anybody to tell me that it isn't the type of goal we should try to get to as fast as we can.

Thank you. (A standing ovation was accorded the Justice.)

Right to Counsel

Today I would like to talk about the right to counsel, which I think is still important. I can remember way back in the good old days when people used to say every man is entitled to his day in court, and they left off the rest of that sentence—if he had the money. We have come a long way from that. But I still don't feel we have come far enough. Although the text of the Sixth Amendment merely refers to the "assistance of counsel," it seems to me that for over fifty years our Supreme Court has recognized that the Constitution guarantees effective assistance. It will not do, then, for the accused's counsel simply to sit idly by. Rather, "an accused is entitled to be assisted by an attorney, whether retained or appointed, who plays the role necessary to insure that the trial is fair."[1]

Defining the different attributes for counsel's necessary role in a particular case is difficult, especially for appellate courts, which are typically called on to address the question on a cold record by a convicted defendant who claims he received ineffective assistance at trial. And most defendants who end up convicted say they had ineffective counsel, not that they were guilty.

The prevailing wisdom from our Supreme Court as to what constitutes ineffective assistance of counsel is contained in the 1984 case of *Strickland v. Washington.* The Strickland case holds that a convicted defendant is entitled to a reversal if he can show, first, "that counsel's performance was deficient]"[2] and, second, "that the deficient performance prejudiced the defense."

Well, how under the sun can a deficient performance not register in the defense? The Court deliberately declined to say what it meant by "deficient," because, it said, any specific guidelines would restrict the wide latitude counsel must have in making "tactical decisions." Beautiful words.

Remarks by Justice Marshall before the Annual Judicial Conference, Second Judicial Circuit, Sept. 9, 1988, Hershey Pennsylvania. *See Annual Judicial Conference, Second Circuit of the United States,* Judge Wilfred Feinberg, Chief Judge, Presiding. 125 F.R.D. 197 (1989).
1. Strickland v. Washington, 466 U.S. 668, 685 (1984).
2. *Id.* at 687.

The majority's standard, therefore, was intentionally and infinitely malleable. In a lone dissent I set forth that that standard told lawyers and the lower courts "almost nothing," nothing about how to evaluate the effectiveness of counsel, or what guidelines should we have. I believed then, and I believe now, that many basic aspects of criminal defense lend themselves to uniform standards whose infringement cannot qualify as a "tactical decision," or maybe I should say excused by those two words. By "refusing to address the merits of [proposals for particularized standards], and indeed [by] suggesting that no such effort [wa]s worthwhile, the opinion of the court, I fear[ed would] stunt the development of constitutional doctrine in the area of counsel representation."[3]

My fears when I wrote that dissent in *Strickland* appear today, if anything, to have underestimated the mischief that has resulted from that decision. The development of constitutional doctrine in the area of effective assistance since *Strickland* has not been very good. Indeed it has not been stunted, but completely ignored. Not once, in the more than four years since that case was decided has the Court found that a petitioner had received ineffective counsel. Not once. And I think everybody in this courtroom can point to at least one case where counsel was ineffective. I know the case here, when I was on the Second Circuit, where the lawyer never heard of the Jencks Act. And that still happens. The district courts and courts of appeal have routinely denied Strickland claims, almost automatically, excusing the most inexcusable lawyering under the all-purpose banner of "strategic decisions."

I can say with confidence that the explanation for this lassitude is not that *Strickland* ushered in a golden new age of uniformly competent assistance. Hardly a week goes by that we aren't required to review a case of a colorable ineffective assistance claim. And the Supreme Court still has "never identified an instance of attorney dereliction that meets the stringent standard."[4] Consider just a few cases which have come up recently.

Number one, a capital case, the petitioner's lawyer called no witnesses and presented no mitigating evidence at the trial and the proceedings. He made no inquiries into the client's educational, medical, or psychological history. He made no attempt to interview any of the many potential mitigating witnesses. His sole effort was to advance a far-fetched unfounded and unsuccessful technical objection to the state's evidence.[5]

The district court and the court of appeals both concluded that counsel's actions could be excused as a tactical decision to preempt rebuttal evidence.

3. *Id.* at 687 (Justice Marshall dissenting).
4. Mitchell v. Kemp, 483 U.S. 1026 (1987) (Justices Marshall, Brennan, and Blackmun dissenting from application for stay of denial of certiorari).
5. *Id.* at 1050.

In the second case, a very recent case, the petitioner's lawyer undertook even fewer efforts. He devoted six hours to preparing for the case, a total of six hours. This is a capital case. He presented no closing argument in the guilt phase of the trial and in the sentencing phase he offered no expanded argument, no opening argument incidentally, no evidence, and no closing argument as I mentioned. The state court of appeals refused petitioner's claim for ineffective assistance of counsel. If it wasn't ineffective, I wonder what it was.

In refusing it, the court said, "Defense counsel deliberately limited his participation to the sentencing stage as a matter of trial strategy."

In yet another capital case, the petitioner's lawyer made no opening statement, put on no case in chief. He performed only cursory cross-examination and did not object to anything. His brief summation emphasized the "horror of the case." In his summation during the sentencing phase he did not give the jury a single reason why they should spare the petitioner's life. He did not inform the jury that petitioner had no prior criminal history, had been steadily employed, had an honorable military record, had been a regular churchgoer and had cooperated with the police. No mention of those. The magistrate, the only fact-finder that considered the question, concluded that counsel's performance at the sentencing phase was "outside the wide range of professionally competent assistance." If you get a chance, tell me what that means. This is a magistrate. The district court, though, concluded that petitioner had not proven any prejudice and the court of appeals held that counsel's performance was not "constitutionally deficient." That phrase just pops up in all of them.

Moving from nonfeasance to actual active malfeasance, the Court recently denied certiorari in a case in which the petitioner's counsel may have been petitioner's most virulent adversary. The lawyer repeatedly demeaned his own client, the petitioner, and on direct examination characterized him as, among other things, "a leech on society." That's his client.

You know, in cases like this you never find any misdeeds on the part of the prosecutor because he doesn't have to do anything. (Laughter.)

In his closing argument the counsel urged the jury to carefully go over what he considered the atrocities involved that his client had committed and "the fear and anguish visited on the victims." This is his counsel. He urged the jury to punish his client, saying, "he ought to be off the streets, he ought to go, he deserves to go, he deserves to do hard time working in the fields." That's his defense counsel. The jury agreed and sentenced the petitioner to a maximum of two life sentences on two counts of robbery.

The district court found that petitioner's counsel was ineffective because "he became the second prosecutor on the case." That's what the district court said. But he never won. The court of appeals reversed, concluding that counsel "employed a strategy in a professionally reasonable manner." That was the sole basis for affirming the conviction.

Well, I could go on with these forever, but I think these cases are aberrations. Certainly the overwhelming majority of defense counsel, paid and appointed, discharge their duties with competence and integrity. Often claims of ineffective assistance focus on the efforts of public defenders that are overworked and understaffed. Too often the combination of a crushing caseload and inadequate resources requires care to be sacrificed in favor of speed. I cannot say, nor is it my purpose to say, that the conclusion of the court of appeals in each of these cases was wrong. Moreover, even if constitutionally deficient, this assistance was provided in each of these instances, and I recognize that our Supreme Court is not a "court of errors." We lack the resources to correct every faulty application of well-settled law. Rather, our docket is reserved for cases of broad national significance. Maybe that's the reason. I don't know.

So why do I, at this late date, vote to grant review in these cases? To help out, in some way, to guarantee effective assistance of counsel? Because, in my opinion, the near-complete stagnation of effective-assistance law in the wake of the *Strickland* case is an issue to me of broad national significance. The short shrift given to claims of ineffective assistance look closely, with an unjaundiced eye, at the many cases that present barely colorable claims of counsel.

Appellate review of Strickland claims is especially important in light of the significant institutional pressures that push against reversing a conviction on grounds of ineffective assistance. Such a reversal means erasing a successful verdict for the state, branding as inadequate defense counsel who probably was court-appointed and working for little money. Such a reversal means wasting the significant judicial and administrative resources that is required whenever the government gears up to prosecute an accused. All this in the service of a defendant whom the court may well believe is guilty and raising a procedural "technicality" as a last-ditch effort to forestall rather than prevent a conviction.

These considerations provide a strong inducement for courts to dispose of ineffective counsel claims by labeling as "strategic" assistance that which is truly substandard. Our Court and the appellate court's practice of not second-guessing these judgments reinforce such summary treatment.

But it is a measure of the seriousness with which we take a fundamental constitutional right that we are willing to honor it even at a significant practical cost. It is the responsibility of the state supreme courts and the courts of appeal of our federal courts to see to its enforcement even when inertia and institutional forces make it unattractive. This is a responsibility the judicial branch has largely forsaken since the Strickland case, permitting all manner of negligence, ineptitude and even callous disregard for the client to be brushed off as "tactical decisions," insulated from constitutional review.

The Sixth Amendment is the poorer for our inattention and, to me, it will stay in that category until we accord greater dignity to that provision of the Constitution that actually guarantees the accused the constitutional guarantee of effective assistance of counsel.

Maybe I am just crying in the wilderness, but as long as I have breath in me I am going to cry.

New Challenges Facing
the Civil Rights Community

Let me review the Circuit's record before the Supreme Court in the term just completed. Twelve cases from the Second Circuit came before the Court during the 1988 term; the Circuit was affirmed in seven cases and was reversed in just five. In a thirteenth case, *United States v. Halper*,[1] a district court in the Southern District of New York was substantially affirmed on direct appeal. On the whole, then, it was a relatively successful term.

That's not what I want to talk about today. I would like to talk about some of the other things that happened in the Supreme Court of the United States. I would like to share with you a few thoughts about the choices confronting the civil rights community in this nation. For many years, no institution of American government has been as close a friend to civil rights as the United States Supreme Court.

Make no mistake, I do not mean for a moment to denigrate the quite considerable contributions to the enhancement of civil rights by presidents, recent Congresses, other federal courts, and the legislatures and judiciaries of many states.

It is now 1989, however, and we must recognize that the Supreme Court's approach to civil rights cases has changed markedly. The most recent Supreme Court opinions vividly illustrate this changed judicial attitude. In *Richmond v. Croson*,[2] the Court took a broad swipe at affirmative action, making it extraordinarily hard for any state or city to fashion a race-conscious remedial program that will survive its constitutional scrutiny. Indeed, the Court went so far as to express its doubts that the effects of past racial discrimination are still felt in the city of Richmond, and in society as a whole.

And in a series of cases interpreting federal civil rights statutes, the Court imposed new and stringent procedural requirements that make it more and more difficult for the civil rights plaintiff to gain vindication.[3]

Justice Marshall made these remarks before the Second Circuit Judicial Conference on Sept. 8, 1989. 125 F.R.D. 197, 201 (1989).
1. 490 U.S. 435 (1989).
2. 488 U.S. 469 (1989).
3. See, *e.g.*, Price Waterhouse v. Hopkins, 490 U. S. 228 (1989); Martin v. Wilks,

The most striking feature of this term's opinions was the expansiveness of their holdings; they often addressed broad issues, wholly unnecessary to the decisions. To strike down the set-aside plan in *Richmond*, for example, there was no need to decide anything other than that the plan was too imprecisely tailored. Instead, the Court chose to deliver a discourse on the narrow limits within which states and localities may engage in affirmative action, and on the special infirmities of plans passed by cities with minority leaders. The Court was even more aggressive in revisiting settled statutory issues under Section 1981 and Title VII. In *Patterson v. McLean Credit Union*,[4] the Court took the extraordinary step of calling for rebriefing on a question that no party had raised: whether the Court, in the 1976 case of *Runyon v. McCrary*,[5] had wrongly held Section 1981 to apply to private acts of racial discrimination.

And in *Ward's Cove v. Antonio*,[6] the Court implicitly overruled *Griggs v. Duke Power Co.*,[7] another established precedent which had required employers to bear the burden of justifying employment practices with a disparate impact on groups protected by Title VII. Henceforth, the burden will be on the employees to prove that these practices are unjustified. Such a shift of burden is uncalled for.

Stare decisis has special force on questions of statutory interpretation and Congress had expressed no dissatisfaction with either the *Runyon* or *Griggs* decisions. Thus it is difficult to characterize last term's decisions as a product of anything other than a retrenching of the civil rights agenda. In the past thirty-five years, we have truly come full circle. We are back where we started.

Regardless of my disappointment with last term's civil rights decisions, we must do more than dwell on past battles. The important question now is where the civil rights struggle should go from here.

One answer, I suppose, is nowhere at all—to stay put. With the school desegregation and voting rights cases and with the passage of federal anti-discrimination statutes, the argument goes, the principal civil rights battles have already been won, and the structural protections necessary to assure racial equality over the long run are already in place, and we can trust the Supreme Court to ensure that they remain so.

This argument is unpersuasive for several reasons. Affirmative action, no less than the active effort to alleviate concrete economic hardship,

---

490 U.S. 755 (1989); Lorance v. AT&T Technologies, Inc., 490 U.S. 900 (1989); Will v. Michigan Department of State Police, 491 U.S. 58 (1989); Jett v. Dallas Independent School District, 491 U.S. 701 (1989).
4. 491 U.S. 164 (1989).
5. 427 U.S. 160 (1976).
6. 490 U.S. 642 (1989).
7. 401 U.S. 424 (1971).

hastens relief efforts while the victims are still around to be helped. And to those who claim that present statutes already afford enough relief to victims of ongoing discrimination, I say, look to the case of Brenda Patterson. She alleged that she had been victimized by a pattern of systematic racial harassment at work—but the Supreme Court told her that, even accepting her allegations as true, federal statutory relief was unavailable.

We must avoid complacency for another reason. The Court's decisions last term put at risk not only the civil rights of minorities, but of all citizens.

History teaches that when the Supreme Court has been willing to shortchange the equality rights of minority groups, other basic personal civil liberties like the rights to free speech and to personal security against unreasonable searches and seizures are also threatened.

We forget at our peril that less than a generation after the Supreme Court held separate to be equal in *Plessy v. Ferguson*,[8] it held in the *Schenck*[9] and *Debs*[10] decisions that the first amendment allowed the United States to convict under the Espionage Act persons who distributed antiwar pamphlets and delivered antiwar speeches. It was less than a decade after the Supreme Court upheld the internment of Japanese citizens[11] that, in *Dennis v. United States*,[12] it affirmed the conviction of Communist Party agitators under the Smith Act. On the other side of the ledger, it is no coincidence that during the three decades beginning with *Brown v. Board of Education*, the Court was taking its most expansive view not only of the equal protection clause, but also of the liberties safeguarded by the Bill of Rights.

That the fates of equal rights and liberty rights are inexorably intertwined was never more apparent than in the opinions handed down last term. The right to be free from searches, which are not justified by probable cause, was dealt yet another heavy blow in the drug testing cases.[13] The scope of the right to reproductive liberty was called into considerable question by the *Webster* decision.[14] Although the right to free expression was preserved in several celebrated cases, it lost ground, too, most particularly in *Ward v. Rock Against Racism*,[15] which greatly broadened the government's power to impose "time, place and manner" restrictions on speech.

Looming on the horizon are attacks on the right to be free from the state establishment of religion: in a separate opinion in the crèche-and-menorah case, four members of the Court served notice that they are

8. 163 U.S. 537 (1896).
9. Schenck v. United States, 249 U.S. 47 (1919).
10. Debs v. United States, 249 U.S. 211 (1919).
11. Korematsu v. United States, 323 U.S. 214 (1944).
12. 341 U.S. 494 (1951).
13. National Treasury Employees Union v. Von Raab, 489 U.S. 656 (1989); Skinner v. Railway Labor Executives' Association, 489 U.S. 602 (1989).
14. Webster v. Reproductive Health Services, 492 U.S. 490 (1989).
15. 491 U.S. 781 (1989).

ready to replace today's establishment clause inquiry with a test that those who seek to break down the wall between church and state will find far easier to satisfy.[16] We dare not forget that these, too, are civil rights, and that they apparently are in grave danger.

The response to the Court's decisions is not inaction; the Supreme Court remains the institution charged with protecting constitutionally guaranteed rights and liberties. Those seeking to vindicate civil rights or equality rights must continue to press this Court for the enforcement of constitutional and statutory mandates. Moreover, the recent decisions suggest alternate methods to further the goals of equality in contexts other than judicial forums.

For example, state legislatures can act to strengthen the hands of those seeking judicial redress. A lesson of the *Richmond* case is that detailed legislative fact-finding is critical. Civil rights lawyers will stand a far better chance in federal constitutional litigation over affirmative action if they are armed with a state legislature's documented findings of past discrimination in a particular area. Thus persons interested in the cause of racial equality can ensure that legislators have access to empirical studies and historical facts that will form the bedrock of acceptable factual findings.

Most importantly, there is Congress. With the mere passage of corrective legislation, Congress can in an instant regain the ground, which was lost last term in the realm of statutory civil rights. And by prevailing upon Congress to do so, we can send a message to the Court – that the hyper-technical language games played by the Court last term in its interpretations of civil rights enactments are simply not accurate ways to read Congress's broad intent in the civil rights area.

In closing, let me emphasize that while we need not and should not give up on the Supreme Court, and while federal litigation on civil rights issues still can succeed, in the 1990s we must broaden our perspective and target other governmental bodies as well as the traditional protector of our liberties.

Paraphrasing President Kennedy, those who wish to assure the continued protection of important civil rights should "ask not what the Supreme Court alone can do for civil rights: ask what you can do to help the cause of civil rights."

Today, the answer to that question lies in bringing pressure to bear on all branches of federal and state governmental units including the Court and to urge them to undertake the battles for civil liberties that remain to be won. With that goal as our guide, let us go forward together to advance civil rights and liberty rights with the fervor we have shown in the past.

16. Allegheny Co. v. American Civil Liberties Union, Greater Pittsburgh Chapter 492 U.S. 573, 663 (1989) (Kennedy, J., concurring).

6. Associate Justices David Souter, Sandra Day O'Connor, Thurgood Marshall, Harry Blackmun, and Byron White, at Howard University School of Law, February 1991. Courtesy Donna R. Banks.

THE 1990S

Justice Marshall's nonjudicial opinions and writings slowed due to ill health during the early 1990s. In 1992, however, Justice Marshall gave a rare interview to the *American Bar Assocation Journal* covering a wide range of topics. During the interview, conducted by Gary A. Hengstler, the publisher of the journal, Marshall acknowledged his mentor Charles Hamilton Houston and reaffirmed that at Howard University School of Law, Houston had taught "that we be social engineers rather than lawyers . . . and I had early decided that's what I wanted to do."

Marshall addressed questions concerning racism in the military during World War II and suggested that the Supreme Court had wrongly decided *City of Richmond v. Croson*, which struck down as unconstitutional economic affirmative action enhancements for minorities. Marshall commented that it was his view that "a state or city can give its citizens more than our Constitution provides. . . . In Croson, this Court held that the Constitution prevented it. I can't believe that."[1]

In a speech delivered on September 6, 1990, before the Annual Judicial Conference of the Second Circuit, Marshall asserts his belief that "the most important institutional mission of the judiciary [i]n or out of the governmental scheme . . . must be a detached independent judiciary that has the final legitimate authority to ensure that political majorities, caught up in the passions of the moment, do not trample the rights of minorities."[2] This statement may be interpreted indirectly critical of the Supreme Court decisions bowing to political winds that either did not support minority concerns or were intent on turning back the clock on civil rights gains, or both.

Six months before Justice Marshall died, he received the Medal of Liberty in Philadelphia on July 4, 1992. Upon receiving this prestigious award, he remarked that if America believes that on the "racial side that we have accomplished everything, I feel obliged to tell you that it is

1. Gary A. Hengstler, Looking Back, *infra*, at 303, 307.
2. Thurgood Marshall, Mission of the Judiciary, before the Annual Judicial Conference, Second Circuit, Sept. 6, 1990, 136 F.R.D. 236, 236 (1990).

not so."[3] Thus, near the end of seven decades of fighting racism and near the end of his rich life, Marshall was inclined to see the nation as it was, still trapped by divisions of racism. Justice Marshall's remarks were not bitter, but marked by disappointment. Despite his seventy years as an advocate for the rights of his people and other disenfranchised minorities of the nation, the goal of liberty for all was still some ways off, though not out of reach.

The legacy of Thurgood Marshall takes many forms. When he announced his retirement from the Supreme Court, he was asked how he would characterize his legacy. He answered, "I don't know what legacy is left. That's up to the people . . ."

3. Thurgood Marshall, We Must Dissent, *infra*, at 311.

Looking Back

[Thurgood Marshall . . . talked] about his years battling for civil rights, starting with his college days spent arguing with fellow students Cab Calloway, Langston Hughes and "several others" at Lincoln University in Oxford, Pennsylvania. "Lincoln was a school of all Negroes with one or two exceptions," he recalls. "And an all-white faculty. We argued over general principles. And we were brainwashed. We discussed it [discrimination]. What we discussed was, why did we have to take it? Why shouldn't we do something about it?

"The leader of that group at Lincoln was a guy named U. S. Tate. He was the leader who said we ought to do something about it. We desegregated the theater in the little town of Oxford. I guess that's what started the whole thing in my life."

Lincoln was a turning point in his life. Until then, he had been taught to go along with segregation and "learn to take it." Asked if it were true that his father ordered him to fight if he were ever called "nigger," Marshall quickly replies, "Yes. Get in business right then and there! And I have to this very day."

After a brief pause, his demeanor softens. "One or two times I did take a little—in court." The idea of a Supreme Court justice ever having had to take racial slurs in court of law momentarily startles me. Then I recall that racial bias prevented him from attending the law school at the University of Maryland, sending him instead to Howard Law School, where he came under the influence of Charles Houston in 1930.

"Charles Houston, the vice dean of my law school, insisted that we be social engineers rather than lawyers," he reflects. "And I had early decided that's what I wanted to do. I did a lot of it while I was still in law school. For example, I started on the primary cases during my second year of law school. I helped." (States such as Texas, until challenged, had held all-white primary elections.)

Gary A. Hengstler, *Justice Thurgood Marshall Looking Back: Reflections on a Life Well Spent*, 78 A.B.A. J. 57 (June 1992). Hengstler is the editor and publisher of the *ABA Journal*. Reprinted by permission of the *ABA Journal*. Footnotes not in original.

In 1935 he took on the University of Maryland and succeeded, for the first time in American history, in getting a court to order a school to admit a black student.

After becoming chief counsel to the NAACP Legal Defense Fund, Marshall faced one of his more intriguing challenges in 1951, when news reports claimed that black soldiers serving under Gen. Douglas MacArthur in Korea had been court-martialed on false or exaggerated charges.

"When Truman sent you to the Far East," I begin.

"Truman didn't send me," Marshall quickly corrects. "He didn't send me. What happened was a newspaper reporter, a Negro from the Afro-American newspaper in Baltimore, reported when he came back from his trip over there that he saw this large group of Negroes—20, 30 or 40—all handcuffed, and he tried to find out what this was all about.

"And he couldn't find out. He thought something ought to be done about it. And he reported that to the board of the NAACP. They said somebody ought go over there and find out. Guess who they figured. They decided I should go. I almost didn't go because MacArthur blocked it every way he could. The only way Truman fits in was that I had to get to Truman to get over there, to get permission to go. And he gave the orders, so that's why I got over there.

"The great thing was that everybody was so interested that the NAACP even took out a $100,000 life insurance policy, which, now you would think is a great idea. When I got on the plane and looked at [the policy] it was not valid in Korea and Japan—which was where I was going. And then I looked at my passport. And it was stamped, 'Not Valid.' I went over there and spent a lot of time there. But Truman didn't order me."

But what did he find when he got there?

"I talked with all of the people, every one of them there. I spent about a month in Tokyo. Every day, five days a week, I went to the stockade and talked to one Negro after another. And a couple of Mexicans, too. I got all the leads I needed.

"Then I went to Korea and talked to the men themselves who were in [the accused black soldiers'] companies.

"Then one day we found the records which MacArthur was hiding. I think he was going to deep-six them, myself. But you can't prove that. We looked at them, and they were just unbelievable.

"[The proceedings] were what was known in the military as 'drum head' court-martials, which means they were held late at night out of anybody's knowing. And automatic guilt.

"One of them, I remember, was [of] a man who was convicted of bad conduct in the presence of the enemy, which meant that he was deserting. And in looking through the record, there was a captain, no, a major, who was a medical man, and a first lieutenant nurse who testified under oath that on that particular date, he was in their hospital. Both of them said that they weren't testifying from records that they had, they saw him and they knew it! And he was sentenced to life.

"We had one other record where the court-martial was in three stages. I read the thing. Then I got Col. Martin, who was with me, and one of us read it and the other timed it with a stopwatch. The entire thing was either eighteen or twenty-eight minutes. That was another life sentence. But I got them all overruled, every one."

The troops were all returned to active duty?

"No, they were not all returned. Most of them were returned, but all of their sentences were cut. The leader of the group, I think his name was Lt. Gilbert, [got] a cut in his sentence. He was sentenced to life and that was reduced to about five years."

By the time Marshall led the team that won the monumental *Brown v. Board of Education* case, he already had established himself as one of the nation's premier litigators. Interestingly, he would do away with one of the litigator's tools, the peremptory challenge.

"I would not use them," he muses. "I would be opposed to them. They are there, and I have used them, but I have talked to a hundred prominent, practicing lawyers who quietly will tell you they are willing to take the first twelve [prospective jurors].

"Because you can never tell what's on somebody's mind. If a person is dead-set against you and wants to do you in, he would be the very person who would say, 'Oh, I had no prejudice at all.' That's the only way he can do you in." And to illustrate his contention, he recalls an instance that happened early in his trial career.

"[It was] in Washington. I was with a local lawyer when I was a youngster, and he struck a woman off the jury, a white woman. He didn't pay attention to her, but she stayed there during the whole trial, two days. And the guy was convicted.

"As we were walking out in the hall, she came up and said, 'Mr. [Nathan A.] Dobbins, you remember me?'

"'Of course,' he said.

"'Why did you strike me from the jury?' she said.

"'Well, . . .' he said.

"'Because I am white?' she said.

"'Well, if you want to say it, that is the reason. That was the reason, because you're white,' he said.

"'For your information, I am not white, and would not have convicted your man. Goodbye!' she said.

"I'll never forget that as long as I live. She stayed there to tell him."

Because of the civil rights mountain Marshall formed throughout his legal career, including twenty-nine victories in thirty-two arguments before the Supreme Court, it is all too easy to forget that he also established an enviable record on the bench. Of the 150 opinions he authored after his appointment to the Second U.S. Circuit Court of Appeals by President Kennedy, not one was overturned.

In the '60s, I reminded Marshall, he once argued fiercely with Malcolm X over which philosophy—Black Nationalism or integration—would better serve black people. So I ask if the renewed interest in Malcolm X's life has changed Marshall's attitude toward him.

"I still see no reason to say he is a great person, a great Negro," Marshall reports. "And I just ask a simple question: What did he ever do? Name me one concrete thing he ever did."

President Lyndon Johnson named Marshall solicitor general in 1965 and appointed him to the Supreme Court in 1967 after a bitter confirmation opposed by four Southern senators on the Judiciary Committee. Shortly before he died, Johnson told Marshall that he believed that his appointment, and not the Vietnam War, was what ultimately cost him the presidency. I ask if he shared Johnson's assessment of the appointment. But Marshall merely shrugs and says, "How do I know?"

Once on the Court, he regularly found himself dissenting as the Warren Court gave way to the Burger and Rehnquist Courts.[1] But always there was the passionate, stubborn focus on the rights of the individual in those dissents—in particular, his belief that the death penalty was unconstitutional.

Marshall was the only member on the Court to have defended a man accused of murder, and I question to what extent those experiences shaped his views.

"Well, I don't know whether that . . . well, it did," he starts slowly. "It did because I lost the death case in private practice. The reason why I took the case was that it was a classmate of mine in high school. And I lost it; and when the time of execution came up, I felt so bad about it— that maybe I was responsible—that I decided I was going to go and see the execution.

"A white reporter from the daily *Morning Sun* newspaper in Baltimore was a good friend of mine. And when I told him, he said, 'Now wait a minute. You do whatever you want to do, but I have to go to them. I am required to.' And he gave the number [of executions] he had been to, something like a dozen or more. He told me, 'I have been to blank

---

1. Warren Burger was on the Court from 1969 to 1986. He was appointed to the Court and as Chief Justice by President Richard M. Nixon. *See* Joan Biskupic, *Ex-Chief Justice Warren Burger Dead, at 87; Court Helped Define Social Changes*, WASH. POST, June 26, 1995, at 1.

number of executions, and I have puked at every one of them. Now if you feel you want to go, go ahead.'

"And I chickened out. I didn't go. But I just, I am not for [the death penalty]. And I still am against it. I don't see what's gained by it."

Because it is evident that the current Court is not inclined to get rid of the death penalty, I ask Marshall what he thinks can be done to get more qualified lawyers for murder defendants at the trial and appellate levels.

"I have no comment on that. I am not going to get involved in anything," Marshall replies brusquely. "I am retired."

So I shift to some of his dissents in right to privacy cases and ask if he thinks the pendulum will swing back with future Courts. But he deflects this, too, with an "I don't know."

I plod on, noting that in a recent *ABA Journal* article, several black politicians alleged that a higher percentage of black officials were targeted for investigation and surveillance by the government than their white counterparts. I ask him whether he ever felt that he was the target of a probe by any administration.

"Well, I know my phone's been tapped regularly," he says matter-of-factly. "I don't know but that it's tapped now. And I don't care. Because all they're going to hear is my wife's gossiping and me cursing. So what difference does it make? I don't know. Maybe they didn't. I don't know."

Marshall wants it made clear, however, that any doubts about his political opponents do not extend to his treatments within the Supreme Court family. "Here in the building there has never been a problem. Never. There have never been any racial feelings. Some of my best friends have been the people here in this Court. We've got an awfully close-knit group."

For most of his career, Marshall has advocated federal intervention to protect the rights of minorities and to spur affirmative action. Yet in *City of Richmond v. Croson*,[2] he seemed to have switched tactics in his dissent, arguing that because local leaders had developed a far more effective plan for affirmative action, the Court ought to defer to local expertise. Isn't that a reversal of his position?

"Well, no," he says. "I believe a state or a city can give its citizens more due process and equal protection than our Constitution provides. I don't think it should limit what they do. In that case, this Court held that the Constitution prevented it. I can't believe that. I don't believe the Constitution prevents you from giving me something if you want to do it. I think it just means the state can give more but is not allowed to give less."

2. City of Richmond v. J. A. Croson Company, 488 U.S. 469 (1989).

While American has come a long way, there are, however, fears of a perceived retrenchment in civil and individual rights. Where does Marshall see the nation on that score?

"There's another benefit I have, you see. I did a lot of study of foreign law when I was drawing the constitutions for those African countries. And comparatively, I think our Constitution is the best of all, with a few exceptions, like Kenya, where I drew the whole schedule of rights.

"Whereas we have one phrase—due process of law—the section I wrote on due process was three or four pages. I spelled it out. You can't take anybody's land there unless you have a hearing and give them an adequate price for the land. And if they don't like it, they can litigate it in the high court. You don't have to start at the lower level. That's due process, I think."

That line of thought prompts Marshall to reflect on the concept of original intent and how the Constitution should be applied in our times.

"I think in our government, for example, we have never used a couple of phrases. Now I don't know how far you're going on privileges and immunities and things like that. I just think it is a living document. And more and more, I think that's true. This guy that just died from Harvard, Paul Freund, that was his whole belief. It's not what those people [the Constitution's authors] wanted. They didn't have anything in those days that we have now."

As an elder statesman of the profession, Marshall has probably seen it all. I note that the profession has been undergoing a lot of criticism in the past year.

"Always," he interjects.

What does he think about Vice President [Dan] Quayle's notion that we have too many lawyers?[3]

"Where did he practice law? And when?" Marshall shoots back. "How does he know that? What does he know about the practice of law? What does he know about it?"

Well, what about the administration's view that the legal system and lawyers have hurt America's economy and competitiveness? Has he seen any evidence of that over the years?

"Not at all. All lawyers have been picked on, that's all I know," he remarks. "Lawyers are the whipping boys. Everybody whips them."

Within the profession, there has been much concern about a decline in professionalism, particularly among the younger lawyers. Here Marshall sadly agrees.

3. *See* Talbot D'Aleberte, *Justice for All: A Response to the Vice-President*, TRIAL, May 22, 1992, at 55–56 (responding to the Vice President's charge "that U.S. lawyers are responsible for a litigation explosion clogging the courts and sapping our competitive strength").

"It's steadily going down. I fortunately started in [East] Baltimore with a lawyer, a colored man, who graduated from Yale Law School in 1888, and he was a terrific guy. He taught me the difference—that when he first started practicing, it was an insult to ask a lawyer for his signature. It was an insult to ask him to swear. And now you have to get six affidavits and everything else.

"Someplace along the line, it deteriorated. I think it has. I know it has. For example, when I first started practicing, I said one day, 'Mr. McQuinn, I've got a problem.[4] These white lawyers, they run into me in the hall, and they call me by my first name. Why can't they call me Mister like everybody else?'

"'No problem,' he said.

"'What do you mean?' I said.

"'Make it your order of business that whenever a white man calls you by your first name, go straight to the phone book, find his first name and the next time you see him, call him by his first name,' he said.

"And it worked."

Marshall then recalls the days when he was not permitted to be a member of the bar association. "It was interesting. They didn't let us in the bar association. They wouldn't admit Negroes. And they had a very good library in Baltimore at the bar association. But it was housed in the courthouse. And we raised the point and the court ruled that they had to let us in whether we were members of the bar or not. Because it was in the courthouse. So we got it for free. They had to pay and we didn't pay."

Marshall says he drew more personal satisfaction from his days as a practicing lawyer than from sitting on the bench. That makes me wonder why, after he began to achieve success in his brilliant career, he declined offers to go to big firms and make more money.

"I thought I had a commitment. And once I got involved in it, I figured I had to stay with it.

"I'll tell you, a member of our board of directors at the NAACP, Charlie Studin, was a very wealthy lawyer—he had gobs of money. We were walking from the board meeting one day, late in the afternoon, and I remember him saying, 'You know, Thurgood, you know I know how much you make. And I guess you can imagine how much I make, but it suddenly dawns on me that I make so much more than you, but you have so much more fun.' And I can remember my answer to him: 'Let's trade.' But I mean I enjoyed my work. And when you won, it was a helluva feeling . . ." What advice does he give to black lawyers today?

4. The lawyer's name was actually Warner T. McGuinn and he had graduated from Yale in 1887. McGuinn started a practice in Baltimore in 1890. *See* J. Clay Smith, Jr., Emancipation: The Making of the Black Lawyer, 1844–1944, 147 (1993) (McGuinn's photograph is in the photograph section).

"None. I don't," he crisply replies. . . . "I would answer any question, but I wouldn't volunteer advice. And it ends up that one of them [his son Thurgood Marshall, Jr.] gave up a job paying $100,000 and some with the biggest law firm here to go to work for [U.S. Senator] Ted Kennedy, and I said, 'With all that money I spent on your education, why did you take that?' You know what he said? 'I know somebody else who didn't give a damn about money, too.'"[5]

"And my other son [John William Marshall] is a state trooper, a state policeman, and he had the same kind of education, he graduated from Georgetown.[6] And you know what he said? 'I want to work for the people.' So that's their way, not based on money. And I mentioned it to Lewis Powell on our Court, and Lewis said, 'Yeah, I understand you. But I just remembered that a friend of mine who was the president of the biggest bank in Richmond was a former state trooper.' So I said, 'Whew! I have something to look forward to.'"

5. Thurgood Marshall, Jr., was graduated from the University of Virginia Law School. *See Family Drama Unfurls at Supreme Court,* St. Petersburg Times, June 26, 1991, at 4A.
6. *See* Simeon Booker, *Ticker Tape,* Jet, March 11, 1993 at 11.

We Must Dissent

Well, now that I'm here and having received these tokens, I might say this is about the most I've ever had of any kind of, what should I say, recognition now. But the best I can say to the committee is thank you for these medals. Thank you for the check. For all of you who are out here on this day. I say thank you for coming, and thanks for being here and what you represent, and I will tell you that my children and my grand-children who are here appreciate it, too.

But, as I said earlier today, for fear that some people might think on the racial side that we have accomplished everything, I feel obliged to tell you that that is not so.

I have these few words for you. As someone who relishes the ability to do and say whatever I damn please, independence is a concept near and dear to me. Because you were kind enough to invite me here, I'm not going to bore you with any long speech. What I'd like to do is share a few stories, a few anecdotes of people who actually have understood the meaning of liberty and struggle against the odds to become free.

I think of these people because of the risks that they have taken and the courage they have displayed. You know when I was trying these cases in the South, the people, the local people whom I represented, stayed there and faced the other side, and the dangers. And they were not afraid. They stayed there.

Well, you know what I did? When the case was over, I'd get the fastest thing out of there. So I want at all times to recognize those who stayed there. I value them not only because of the kind of people they were, but because of the kind of nation they insisted we become. I respect them not because of the influence they wielded, but because of the power they

One of Justice Marshall's last public statements prior to retirement was on July 4, 1992, when he received the Medal of Liberty in Philadelphia. *See* Steve Brooks, *Thurgood Marshall Awarded Liberty Medal*, PHIL. NEW OBSERVER, July 8, 1992 at 1. Other recipients of the medal prior to Marshall include Polish activist Lech Walesa, then President of Poland (1989), former President Jimmy Carter (1990), and Costa Rican President Oscar Arias Sanchez and the charity Doctors Without Borders (corecipients) (1991), *id.* at 18.

seized. It is useful, I think, to recall their stories, not to dwell on the past, but to see concrete evidence of what was in order to gain the inspiration for what can be.

Do you remember Heman Marion Sweatt?[1] He was an ordinary person, but he had an extraordinary dream to live in a world which Afro-Americans and whites alike were afforded equal opportunity to sharpen their skills and to hone their skills, to sharpen their minds. Unfortunately, officials at the University of Texas Law School did not share his vision. Constrained by the shackles of prejudice, incapable of seeing people, and seeing them for what they were, they denied Heman Marion Sweatt admission to the Law School of the University of Texas, as you will remember, solely because of his color—the color which just didn't happen to be theirs, a little more sunburned.

It was a devastating blow and a stinging rejection, a painful reminder of the chasm that separated the white from the Negro. But Heman Sweatt held on to what racism tried to snuff out, a sense of self, and a recognition of place, a determination to obtain the best, and a refusal to settle for anything else. Heman Marion Sweatt knew what the white segregationists tried to forget that none of us, Afro, White, or Blue will ever rest until we are all truly free.

Heman Sweatt did not pursue liberty alone. Just a few years earlier a couple named Shelley tried to do what the white Americans had done for years, live in a decent neighborhood, in the neighborhood of their choice. But to white homeowners in Missouri such audacity was too threatening to be tolerated, in their view. The whites belong in one world, because Negroes were in another, and they could not see the similarities that linked them to the Shelleys—the common desire to earn a living, to raise children, to own and care for a home. They saw only difference. I guess to them if the United States was indeed a melting pot, the Negro either didn't get into the pot, or he certainly never got melted down. Whatever the reason for myopic vision, the Shelleys were forced to do whatever Negroes had to do for years—use the only weapon they had, their right to a day in court to gain the rights to which they were constitutionally entitled.

Fortunately for our history, the Shelleys won their suit,[2] but even if they had lost, they would have known more freedom than the Whites who tried to shut them out should ever know.

Racism separates, but it never liberates. Hatred generates fear, and fear, once given a foothold, binds, consumes, and imprisons. Nothing is gained from prejudice. No one benefits from racism.

1. Heman Sweatt was the plaintiff in Sweatt v. Painter, 339 U.S. 629 (1950).
2. Shelley v. Kraemer, 334 U.S. 1 (1948).

As I think back on these courageous people who came before, I wonder what becomes of the challenge the Sweatts and the Shelleys provided. They worked for liberty. They fought for freedom. They insisted upon justice. They were optimistic, as I was, that racial interaction would lead to understanding, and in turn would produce healing and redemption. They were hopeful, as I was that America would grow toward justice and expand toward equality.

Who would have thought that in the wake of Smith against Allwright, and Shelley against Kraemer, and Brown against the Board of Education,[3] that I would be giving a talk now on the anniversary of our nation's independence? I would have predicted that I would have spoken with much pride and optimism of the enormous progress this nation has already made. But as I survey the world Heman Marion Sweatt and the Shelleys left behind, I wish I could say that racism and prejudice were only distant memories. I wish I could say that this nation had traveled far along the road to social justice and that liberty and equality were just around the corner. I wish I could say that America had come to appreciate diversity and to see and accept similarities.

But as I look around, I see not a nation of unity, but a nation of division: Afro and white, indigenous and immigrant, rich and poor, educated and illiterate. Even many educated white people and successful Negroes have given up on integration, and lost hope in equality. They see nothing in common, except the need to flee, as fast as they can, farther from our inner cities.

A Pullman porter once told me, when I was a kid, that he had been in almost every city in the country. He said he never was in a city where he had to put his hand in front of his face to know he was a Negro. Well, I'm afraid that I've been in every city in this country, and it's thirty or forty years after what he said. And I hate to tell you, what he said is still true.

But there's a price to be paid for division and isolation as the recent events in California indicate. Look around. Can't you see the tension in Watts, California? Can't you feel the fear in Scarsdale? Can't you sense the alienation in Simi Valley? The despair in the South Bronx and Brooklyn?[4] It's all around you. We cannot play hostage. Democracy just cannot flourish amid fear. Liberty cannot bloom with hate. Justice cannot take root amid fear.

3. *Id.*, Brown v. Board of Education, 347 U.S. 483 (1954); Smith v. Allwright, 321 U.S. 649 (1944).
4. *See, e.g.*, Brooklyn: R. W. Apple, Jr., *Specials to the New York Times*, N.Y. TIMES, June 18, 1992, at 1 (racism "'attacked in Brooklyn' by Governor Bill Clinton"). Scarsdale: *Country Club: Racism Expose*, NEWSDAY, Aug. 17, 1992, at 83; Simi Valley: Jana Mazanec, *Simi Valley Still Bears Scars*, USA TODAY, June 8, 1992, at 3A.

America must get to work. In the chilled climate in which we live, we must go against the prevailing winds. We must dissent from the indifference. We must dissent from the apathy. We must dissent from the fear, the hatred, and the mistrust. We must dissent from a nation that buried its head in the sand waiting in vain for the needs of its poor, its elderly, and its sick to disappear and just blow away. We must dissent from a government that has left its young without jobs, education, or hope. We must dissent from the poverty of vision and timeless absence of moral leadership. We must dissent, because America can do better, because America has no choice but to do better.

The legal system can force open doors, and sometimes even knock down walls, but it cannot build bridges. That job belongs to you and me. The country can't do it. Afro and white, rich and poor, educated and illiterate, our fates are bound together. We can run from each other, but we cannot escape each other. We will only attain freedom if we learn to appreciate what is different, and muster the courage to discover what is fundamentally the same. America's diversity offers so much richness and opportunity. Take a chance, won't you? Knock down the fences, which divide. Tear apart the walls that imprison you. Reach out. Freedom lies just on the other side. We shall have liberty for all. Thank you.

Appendix: The Fairness of the Reorganization Plan in Industrial Corporations

Most of the writers on the subject of reorganizations have not distinguished between reorganization as applied to railroad corporations and as applied to industrial corporations. The majority of the citations in support of their respective theories concerning the fairness of the plans are cases involving railroad corporations. No doubt, the reason has been that until recently few cases on reorganizations of industrial corporations have been before the courts because the usual procedure in cases of insolvency of industrial corporations had been some form of liquidation. However, since the recent depression, numerous large industrial corporations have been forced to make reorganizations because of the impossibility of sale of large properties at any public sales. It is, therefore, time to review the law as to reorganizations in industrial corporations.

I. Different Types of Actions in Which the Courts Have Considered the Fairness of the Reorganization Plan

The most direct form of proceedings to bring the reorganization plan before the court seems to be in the nature of a bill to set aside the reorganization plan. In *Ecker v. Kentucky Refining Company*,[1] bankruptcy proceedings were threatened and the stockholders and creditors agreed upon a reorganization plan. Plaintiff, owner of 1 percent of the stock, was the only dissenting stockholder. In a bill to set aside the reorganization plan bought by the stockholder, the court went into the reorganization plan and held that it was fair and consequently refused to set it aside. Nevertheless, an individual stockholder was given the right to question

This paper, dated May 13, 1933, appears to have been completed for Professor Alfred Joseph Buscheck's Corporations course during Justice Marshall's final semester at Howard University School of Law. Marshall received his law degree on June 9, 1933. Thurgood Marshall's name appears on the cover sheet of the paper, which runs eighteen legal-sized pages. The footnotes that follow are Marshall's. In the original version they were designated by letters. Some of the text and footnotes have been omitted.
1. 144 Ky. 264, 138 S.W. 264 (1911).

the reorganization plan in a direct court proceedings. Where a corporation attempted to promulgate a reorganization plan and to have sections of the proposed amendments to its charter, a preferred stockholder, as an individual, was allowed to question the reorganization plan and to have sections of the proposed amendments enjoined.[2]

The above cases might seem extreme in that they allow single minority stockholders in their individual capacities to question the reorganization plan. Similar actions by groups of minority stockholders have been entertained by the courts and the right to institute such proceedings is based upon the right of the minority stockholders to maintain derivative suits.[3]

Bondholders should have at least an equal opportunity to question the plans. In a recent case in New York,[4] a group of bondholders filed a bill to enjoin the placing into operation of a proposed reorganization plan. The court in this case went into the reorganization plan and granted relief.

Where a corporation transfers all its assets to another corporation pursuant to a reorganization plan, the court will entertain a bill to set aside the transfer and in doing so will go into the fairness of the plan.[5] In the M'Clean case the bill was in the nature of a derivative suit and was against certain of the directors of the former corporation. However, the corporation was not considered as an indispensable party; the court saying:

It was their (the directors') duty to get in the outstandings, reduce them to cash, pay the creditors, and distribute the balance, if any, to the stockholders. No creditor now complains. Any assets in the hands of the trustees are not for the corporation, as such, but for the stockholders, subject to the claims of the creditors. Any sum recovered would not pass to the treasury of this corporation, but to the corpus of the trust estate. The stockholders sue in their own right, not in the right of the corporation.[6]

Thus an individual stockholder was allowed to maintain a bill to set aside a sale under a reorganization plan and the stockholders were allowed to intervene.[7]

Where a corporation is before the court and a receiver has been

2. Yoakam v. Providence Biltmore Hotel Co., D.C. Rhode Island, 54 F.2d 533 (1929).
3. Abbott v. Waltham Watch Co., 260 Mass. 81, 156 N.E. 897 (1927).
4. Bergelt v. Roberts, 258 N.Y.S. 905 (1932), aff. 258 N.Y.S. 1086.
5. Finch v. Warrior Cement Corporation 16 Del. Ch. 44, 141 A 54 (1926); M'Clean v. Bradley, D.C., N.D. Ohio, 282 F. 1011 (1922).
6. Id. at 1017.
7. Eagleson v. Pacific Timber Co., 270 F. 1008 (D.C. Del. 1920).

appointed and a reorganization plan proposed, a minority creditor may appeal that order approving the reorganization plan and go into the fairness of the plan.[8] . . .

The next most direct method of attacking the reorganization plan is by filing a petition to intervene in a foreclosure proceedings. Prior to 1932, individual bondholders had been at quite a disadvantage in contesting and proposing reorganization plans. The individual stockholders by the common law and under statute have had the right to inspect the books of the corporation and thereby obtain the names and addresses of the stockholders so as to organize. As a matter of fact, the stockholders are already organized to a degree even before foreclosure is threatened. The bondholders never had such an opportunity. They never were organized at all and seldom knew the names or addresses of the other bondholders. The records are kept in the hands of the mortgage holder. These trustees usually will not furnish lists of the names of the other bondholders and it has been impossible for them to organize. The trustee usually proposes the reorganization plan on behalf of the bondholders and communicates with individual bondholders and obtain authority to act for them. The individuals, having only the one plan, agree to it.

When the trustee proposes his plan to the court in a foreclosure proceedings, minority bondholders have been denied the right to intervene. The reason for refusing the right to intervene has followed that given in railroad foreclosure cases and is stated by one judge as:

The rule, however, creates an exception to the general principle that all interested should join in the controversy. It is a rule of convenience to facilitate the conduct of the suit. It proceeds upon the assumption that the *cestui que* trust can be fully and fairly represented and protected in his rights by the trustee or representative. A rule of convenience must, however, give way when rights are involved. If it appears that the trustee refuses or neglects to act, or stands in a hostile position or has assumed a position prejudicial to the interests of the *cestui que* trust, the rule of convenience is put aside. And the *cestui que* trust must be admitted to represent his rights because in such cases the trustee had not (represented) and cannot fully and faithfully represent them.[9]

Thus it seems that the so-called rule of convenience places the burden upon the bondholders to establish the partiality or fraud in order to be permitted to intervene.

Last year the New York Supreme Court recognized the injustices of such a rule and, upon considering the hardships of such a rule, allowed

8. Corriel v. Morris White Inc., 54 F.2d 255 (2 Cir. 1931).
9. Continental and C Trust Bank v. Allis-Chambers, 200 F. 600, 606–607 (E.D. Wis., 1912), quoting Farmers' Loan & Trust Company v. North Pacific R.R. Co., 66 F. 169, 174 (1895).

a group of bondholders to intervene in a foreclosure proceedings. Judge [Thomas J.] Coff stated:

> The petitioners have no means of pointing out to those situated similarly with themselves where in they consider that the plan of the Commonwealth Bond Corporation is not for the best interests of all. . . . In the case at bar, the petitioning group have some definite ideas. Perhaps their plan is the better one . . .[10]

The same court allowed an even more direct relief in *Bergelt v. Roberts.*[11] . . . In this case the court held that the minority bondholders, in suits to enjoin corporate reorganization plan on the ground of adversary interests of the organization dominating the plan, was entitled to compel a disclosure of names and addresses of other bondholders.[12] . . .

The law as to the right of stockholders to intervene is not so clear cut. They have often been denied the right to intervene for the purpose of contesting the reorganization plan. The case of *Conley v. International Pump Co.*[13] has often been cited and relied upon as supporting this general proposition. However, the decision in that case is very limited. The right was denied there because the receivers who drew the reorganization plan had been appointed by some or all of the proposed interveners and the proposed interveners had not mentioned that plan to this receiver . . .[14]

II. The "Fairness" of the Reorganization Plan

In considering reorganization plans in industrial corporations the courts have made certain rules as to the fairness of the plans. The decisions for the most part have followed those concerning reorganizations of railroads. In these decisions the courts have seemed to find little or no distinction between the type of plan for a railroad and that for an industrial corporation.

Certain rules have been established as to the position of the person or committee proposing and representing the reorganization plan. They

10. Bank of Manhattan Trust Co. v. Silrap Construction Co., Inc., 259 N.Y.S. 935, 936 (Sept. 1932).
11. *Supra* note 4.
12. *Supra* note 9, at 174 (Farmers' Loan) (original quote in text of the case in Marshall's paper omitted). *See also* Clinton Trust 142–144 v. Joralemon St. Corp., 267 A.D. 789, N.Y. App. Div. 142–144 (March 1933).
13. 237 F. 286 (1915).
14. The Court stated: "It is an unusual and an unnecessary act to permit a few stockholders who applied for and obtained a receivership in the company's own state, to intervene in the same suit to which the receiver is a party, and advance a defense which they have not communicated to the receiver himself." *Id.* at 287.

have usually been considered as standing in a position similar to fiduciaries and under a duty to act in good faith.[15] In *Edenborn v. Sim*[16] a syndicate was organized for the purpose of purchasing the United States Iron Company and provided that the defendant and two others should be managers. The plan was to later sell the property to the corporation as reorganized. This was done and later it was discovered that one of the managers was personally interested in the property sold to the reorganized corporation. Plaintiffs rescinded their contracts and brought actions for the amount of their subscriptions that they had said: "Consideration of the agreement satisfies us that the defendant, as manager, was made the agent of himself and of every other subscriber separately in order to reply any interference of partnership between the subscribers."[17] . . .

All the courts seem to agree that the reorganization plan must be for a bona fide purpose. It cannot be used to "freeze out" the minority. Thus where stock was held in trust or the owner and the majority of the stockholders agreed to transfer all the assets of the corporation to another company of which they were the sole stockholders under the proposed reorganization plan, the holder of the minority stock contested the plan and upon the transfer being made the minority stockholder was allowed to maintain a bill for an accounting against the members of the new corporation. The basis of the bill was that the majority fixed the price so low that they failed [to mention] the value of the good will in the sale price and thereby succeeded in "freezing out" the minority as to this amount of the value of the property . . .[18]

Conclusion

As mentioned at the outset, the law as to reorganization plans for industrial corporations is very limited. The cases here reviewed are too few in number to support any theory as to what is the settled law on this subject, and they represent the bulk of cases on this particular point. One idea, however, is apparent from a reading of the cases and that is that the reorganization plans for industrial corporations upon being brought before the courts will be controlled by the decisions handed down by the courts in regard to the large railroad reorganizations.

The purpose of this paper has been twofold: (1) to review the law as to reorganizations of industrial corporations in the past, and future

15. Clinton Trust, *supra* note 12, 142–144.
16. 206 F. 275 (2d Cir. 1913).
17. *Id.* at 277. In this case it was held that there was constructive fraud but there could be no rescission because the parties could not be placed in status quo.
18. Nave-McCord Mercantile Co. v. Ranney, 29 F.2d 383 (1928).

(2) thereby to forecast, in a measure, what the law will be in the future. The modern trend is well exemplified by the three New York cases cited above. The effect of these [cases] will no doubt be felt in all future reorganization plans, in that, a holder of one bond is given the right to come into court and if he has a bona fide intention may question the plan and go even further and propose a plan of his own.

Bibliography

Barnard, William D. *Dixiecrats and Democrats: Alabama Politics, 1942–1950* (1974).
Bass, Jack. Frank Johnson: Legal Giant, *New York Law Journal* 19 (Aug. 16, 1999).
———. *Taming the Storm: The Life and Times of Judge Frank M. Johnson, Jr. and the South's Fight over Civil Rights* (1993).
Bell, Derrick A. Brown v. Board of Education and the Interest-Convergence Dilemma. *Harvard Law Review* 518 (1980).
———. *Race Racism and American Law* (1973 ed.).
Bell, Derrick, ed. *Shades of Brown: New Perspectives on School Desegregation* (1980).
Bickel, Alexander. *The Least Dangerous Branch: The Supreme Court at the Bar of Politics* (1962).
Bland, Randall W. *Private Pressure on Public Law: The Legal Career of Justice Thurgood Marshall* (1993).
Blaustein, Albert P., and Clarence Clyde Ferguson, Jr. *Desegregation and the Law: The Meaning and Effect of the School Segregation Cases* (1957).
Bowles, Chester. *Promises to Keep: My Years in Public Life, 1941–1969* (1971).
Brady, Paul L. *A Certain Blindness: A Black Family's Quest for the Promise of America* (1990).
Branch, Taylor. *Parting the Waters: America in the King Years, 1954–63* (1988).
Brooks, Thomas R. *Walls Come Tumbling Down: A History of the Civil Rights Movement, 1940–1970* (1974).
Brownell, Herbert. Civil Rights in the 1950s, 69 *Tulane Law Review* 781 (1995).
Bunche, Ralph J. *A World View of Race* 97 (1936) (Booklet).
Burch, Alan Robert. Charles Hamilton Houston, The Texas White Primary and Centralization of the NAACP's Litigation Strategy, 21 *Thurgood Marshall Law Review* 95 (1995).
Burns, Haywood. From Brown to Bakke and Back: Race, Law, and Social Change in America. 110 *Daedalus* 219 (Spring 1981).
Cain, Alfred E., and Walter Christmas. *The Negro Heritage Library* (1966).
Caro, Robert A. *The Years of Lyndon Johnson*, vol. 2, *Master of the Senate* (2002).
Carson, Clayborne, ed. *The Papers of Martin Luther King, Jr., Rediscovering Precious Values* (1994).
Carter, Robert. Equal Education Opportunity for Negroes—Abstractions or Reality, in John H. McCord, *With All Deliberate Speed: Civil Rights Theory and Reality* (1969).
———. In Tribute: Charles Hamilton Houston, 111 *Harvard Law Review* 2149 (1998).

Chang, David. The Bus Stops Here: Defining the Constitutional Right of Equal Educational Opportunity and an Appropriate Remedial Process, 63 *Boston University Law Review* 1 (1983).

Clark, Kenneth B. (issue ed.). Desegregation: An Appraisal of the Evidence, 9 *Journal of Social Issues* 1 (1953).

Cook, Anthony E. Beyond Critical Legal Studies: The Reconstructive Theology of Dr. Martin Luther King, Jr., 103 *Harvard Law Review* 985 (1990).

Corwin, Edward S. *"The Higher Law": The Background of American Constitutional Law* (1955).

Cummings, Homer, and Carl McFarland. *Federal Justice: Chapters in the History of Justice and the Federal Executive* (1937).

Darrow, Clarence. The Futility of the Death Penalty, 80 *The Forum* 327 (Sept. 1928).

Davidson, Scott J., W. Stuart, and Judith Hall Howard. The Riffing of Brown: De-Integrating Public School Facilities, 17 *Harvard Civil Rights Civil Liberties Law Review* 443 (1982).

Davis, Michael D., and Carter R. Hunter. *Thurgood Marshall: Warrior at the Bar, Rebel on the Bench* (1994).

Dowling, Ann, ed. *Twenty-Five Years Since Brown: A Commemorative Booklet* (1978).

Felman, Stephen M. American Legal Thought from Premodernism to Postmodernism (2000).

Fisher, Ada Lois Sipuel. *A Matter of Black and White: The Autobiography of Ada Lois Sipuel Fisher* (1996).

Flack, Horace Edgar. *The Adoption of the Fourteenth Amendment* (1908).

Forman, James. *Sammy Young, Jr. The First Black College Student to Die in the Black Liberation Movement* (1968).

Franklin, John Hope. *Reconstruction: After the Civil War* (1961).

———. *From Slavery to Freedom: A History of Negro Americans* (1967).

Friedman, Leon, ed. *Argument: The Oral Argument Before the Supreme Court in Brown v. Board of Education of Topeka, 1952–55* (1969).

Garlan, Edwin N. *Legal Realism and Justice* (1941).

Gillette, Michael L. Blacks Challenge the White University, 86 *Southwestern Historical Quarterly* 111 (Oct. 1982).

Gillette, William. *Retreat from Reconstruction, 1869–1879* (1979).

Goldman, Roger and David Gallen. *Thurgood Marshall: Justice for All* (1992).

Graglia, Lino A. *Disaster by Decree: The Supreme Court Decisions on Race and the Schools* (1976).

Greenberg, Jack. *Crusaders in the Courts: How a Dedicated Band of Lawyers Fought for the Civil Rights Revolution* (1994).

Gunter, Gerald. *Learned Hand, The Man and the Judge* (1994).

Gutermann, Paul Eric. School Desegregation Doctrine: The Interaction Between Violation and Remedy, 30 *Case Western Reserve Law Review* 780 (1980).

Hand, Learned. *The Spirit of Liberty* (1954).

Harris, Robert. *The Quest for Equality: The Constitution, Congress and the Supreme Court* (1960).

Hastie, William H. Charles Hamilton Houston, 35 *Journal of Negro History* 335 (July 1950).

———. Toward an Equalitarian Legal Order, 1930–1950, 407 *Annals* 18 (1973).

Hendel, Samuel. *Charles Evans Hughes and the Supreme Court* (1951).

Henken, Louis, et al. *Human Rights* (1999).

Higginbotham, Jr., A. Leon. *In the Matter of Color: Race and the American Legal Process: The Colonial Period* (1978).

Hill, Oliver W. *The Big Bang: Brown v. Board of Education and Beyond* (2000) (With Jonathan K. Stubbs).

Hines, Darlene Clark. *Black Victory: The Rise and Fall of the White Primary in Texas* (1979).

Jackson, Jesse. Justice Thurgood Marshall: The Struggle Personified, 35 *Howard Law Journal* 73 (1991)

Jones, Leon. *From Brown to Boston: Desegregation in Education 1954–1974* (1979).

———. School Desegregation in Retrospect and in Prospect, 47 *Journal of Negro Education* 46 (Winter 1978).

Kalodner, Howard J., and James J. Fishman, eds. *Limits of Justice: The Court's Role in School Desegregation* (1978).

Kaufman, Irving R. Chilling Judicial Independence, 88 *Yale Law Journal* 681 (1979).

Keys, V. O. *Southern Politics in State and Nation* (1949).

Keyssar, Alexander. *The Right to Vote: The Contested History of Democracy in the United States* (2000).

King, Jr., Martin Luther. *Where Do We Go from Here: Chaos or Community* (1968).

Kluger, Richard. *Simple Justice: The History of Brown v. Board of Education and Black Americas Struggle for Equality* (1976).

Kurland, Philip B., and Gerhard Casper, eds. *Landmark Briefs and Arguments of the Supreme Court of the United States: Constitutional Law* volumes 49 and 49A, *Brown v. Board of Education* (1954 and 1955) (1975).

Levin, Betsy. The Courts, Congress, and Educational Adequacy: The Equal Protection Predicament, 39 *Maryland Law Review* 263 (1979).

Lewis, John. *Walking With the Wind: A Memoir of the Movement* (1998).

Marshall, Ray F., and Vernon Briggs, Jr. *The Negro and Apprenticeship* (1967).

Marshall, Thurgood. The Cry for Freedom, in *Rhetoric of Racial Revolt* 318 (1960) (Roy L. Hill ed.).

———. An Evaluation of Recent Efforts to Achieve Radial Integration in Education Through Resort to the Courts, 21 *Journal of Negro Education* 316 (1952).

———. Justice Murphy and Civil Rights, 48 Michigan Law Review 745 (1950).

———. The Rise and Collapse of the White Democratic Primary, 26 *Journal of Negro Education* 249 (1957).

Mason, Alpheus T. Harlan Fiske Stone: Pillar of the Law (1955).

Masters, Isabell. The Life and Legacy of Oliver Brown, The First Listed Plaintiff of Brown v. Board of Education, Topeka, Kansas. Ph.D. diss., University of Oklahoma (1980).

McCary, Peyton. Freedom: Constitutional Law: Yes, But What Have They Done to Black People Lately? The Role of Historical Evidence in the Virginia Board Case, 1275 *Chicago-Kent Law Review* (1995).

McDougall, Harold A. Social Movements, Law, and Implementation: A Clinical Dimension for the New Legal Process, 75 *Cornell Law Review* 83 (1989).

McKinley, Carlyle. *An Appeal to Pharaoh* (1906).

McNeil, Genna Rae. *Groundwork: Charles Hamilton Houston and the Struggle for Civil Rights* (1983).

Metcalf, George R. From Little Rock to Boston: The History of School Desegregation. *Contributions to the Study of Education*, no. 8. (1983).

Miller, Loren. *The Petitioners: The Story of the United States Supreme Court and the Negro* (1966).

Motley, Constance Baker. Standing on His Shoulders: Thurgood Marshall's Early Career, in *Thurgood Marshall: Memorial Tributes in the Congress of the United States* 254 (U.S. Government Printing Office, 1994).

Murphy, Bruce. *Fortas: The Rise of a Supreme Court Justice* (1988).

Murphy, Jay. Can Public Schools Be Private? 7 *Alabama Law Review* 48 (Fall 1954).

Nelson, Bernard H. *The Fourteenth Amendment and the Negro Since 1920* (1946).

Nichols, Lee. *Breakthrough on the Color Front* (1954).

Northrop, Herbert R. Organized Labor and Negro Workers, 51 *Journal of Political Economics* 206 (June 1943).

Note, Legal Realism and the Race Question: Some Realism About Realism on Race Relations, 108 *Harvard Law Review* 1607 (1995).

Note, Right of Negroes to Vote in State Primaries, 43 *Harvard Law Review* 467 (1930).

Ogletree, Charles. *Why Has the G.O.P. Kept Blacks Off Federal Courts?* N.Y. TIMES, Aug. 18, 2000, at 27.

Orum, Anthony M. Black Students in Protest: A Study of the Origins of the Black Student Movement (1974) (Pamphlet).

Patterson, James T. *Brown v. Board of Education: A Civil Rights Milestone and Its Troubled Legacy* (2001).

Peeks, E. *The Long Struggle for Black Power* (1971).

Peltason, J. W. *Fifty-Eight Lonely Men: Southern Federal Judges and School Desegregation* (1961).

———. The Missouri Plan for the Selection of Judges, 20 *Missouri Studies* 1 (1945).

Plummer, Brenda Gale. *Rising Wind: Black Americans and U.S. Foreign Affairs, 1935–1960* (1996).

Polk, L., ed. 2 *The Constitution and the Supreme Court* (1966).

Potter, Lou. Liberators: *Fighting Two Fronts in World War II* (1992).

Prentice, Robert A. Supreme Court Rhetoric, 25 *Arizona Law Review* 85 (Winter 1983).

Pusey, Merlo J. *Charles Evans Hughes* (1951).

Reed, Merl E. *Seed Time for the Modern Civil Rights Movement: The President's Committee on Fair Employment Practice, 1941–1946* (1991).

Reno, Janet. Civil Rights: A Challenge of Conscience, 27 *Cumberland Law Review* 381 (1996–97).

Reske, Henry J. The Diverse Legacy of Warren Burger, 81 *American Bar Association Journal* 36 (August 1995).

Ripple, Kenneth F. Thurgood Marshall and the Forgotten Legacy of Brown v. Board of Education, 55 *Notre Dame Lawyer* 471 (April 1980).

Rist, Ray C., and Ronald J. Anson, eds. *Education, Social Science, and the Judicial Process,* Policy Analysis and Education Series (1977).

Rowan, Carl. *Dream Makers, Dream Breakers: The World of Justice Thurgood Marshall* (1993).

Schultz, Harry Richard. Brown versus Topeka: A Legacy of Courage and Struggle. Ed.D. diss., Ball State University, 1971.

Shoemaker, Don, ed. *With All Deliberate Speed: Segregation-Desegregation in Southern Schools* (1957).

Smith, Jr., J. Clay. *Emancipation: The Making of the Black Lawyer, 1844–1944* (1993).

———. Forgotten Hero, 98 *Harvard Law Journal* 482 (1984).

———. In Memoriam Professor Frank D. Reeves—Towards a Houstonian School of Jurisprudence and the Study of Pure Legal Existence, 18 *Howard Law Journal* 1 (1973).

———. Thurgood Marshall: An Heir of Charles Hamilton Houston, 20 *Hastings Constitutional Law Quarterly* 503 (1993).

Speer, Hugh W. *The Case of the Century: A Historical and Social Perspective on Brown v. Board of Education of Topeka with Present and Future Implications.* Kansas City, Mo.: University of Missouri (1968).

Stein, Sylvia, and Angela Dorn, eds. *From Slavery to the Supreme Court: The African-American Journey Through the Federal Courts* (1992).

Sutherland, Arthur E., ed. *Government Under Law* (1968).

Ten Broek, J. *Equal Under Law* (1956).

Tushnet, Mark V. *Making Civil Rights Law: Thurgood Marshall and the Supreme Court, 1956–1961* (1994).

Tuttle, Jr., William M. *Race Riot: Chicago in the Red Summer of 1919* (1970).

Vandever, Elizabeth Jane. Brown vs. Board of Education of Topeka: Anatomy of a Decision. Ph.D. diss., University of Kansas, 1971.

Vose, Clement. *Caucasians Only: The Supreme Court, the NAACP, and the Restrictive Covenant Cases* (1959).

Ware, Gilbert. *William Hastie: Grace Under Pressure* (1984).

Warren, Earl. *A Republic If You Can Keep It* (1972).

Weaver, Robert C. *Negro Labor: A National Problem* (1946).

White, Walter. *A Man Called White: The Autobiography of Walter White* (1948).

Whiter, Darien A. *The Legal 100: A Ranking of the Individuals Who Have Most Influenced the Law* (1997).

Whitfield, Stephen J. *A Death in the Delta: The Story of Emmett Till* (1988).

Wilkins, Roy. *Standing Fast: The Autobiography of Roy Wilkins* (1984).

Wilkinson, J. Harvie III. *From Brown to Bakke: The Supreme Court and School Integration: 1954–78* (1979).

Williams, Jamye Coleman, and McDonald Williams, eds. *The Negro Speaks: The Rhetoric of Contemporary Black Leaders* (1970).

Williams, Juan. *Eyes on the Prize* (1988).

———. *Thurgood Marshall: An American Revolutionary* (1998).

Wolters, Raymond. *The Burden of Brown: Thirty Years of School Desegregation* (1984).

Wood, Virginia. *Due Process of Law: 1932–1949* (1972).

Woodward, C. Vann. *The Strange Career of Jim Crow* (1966).

Index

Acknowledgments

I am grateful to several individuals and institutions that helped me assemble Thurgood Marshall's speeches and writings. This enterprise was supported by research grants provided by Alice Gresham Bullock, Dean of Howard University School of Law. I acknowledge the assistance provided to me by the administrative staff: Delphyne Bruner, Carolyn Minor, Chantell Randall, and Christine Wade, who helped type several of the Marshall manuscripts, and Jesse Dunn, who copied them. My thanks to Jason Crump, Aquanetta A. L. Knight, and Gail Heath, my legal assistants.

I acknowledge the support of Ms. Cecilia S. Marshall, and the advice and support of Kevin T. Baine, Karen Hastie Williams, and Jennelle Byrd. My gratitude extends to Jack and Lovell Olender and their foundation for generous and sustained support of this and other academic projects, and Hanes Walton, Jr., who located photographs and manuscripts for me at the Lyndon B. Johnson Library.

The following institutions have been very generous in their leads to Marshall's speeches and writings and in sharing them for inclusion in *Supreme Justice: American Bar Association Journal,* American College of Trial Lawyers, Amistad Research Center, *The Barrister* student newspaper at Howard University School of Law, Crisis Publishing Co., Inc., Dillard University Library, Federal Bar Council, *Georgia Law Review,* Harvard University Press, *Howard Law Journal, Journal of Negro Education,* Kalamazoo College, Library of Congress, *Michigan Law Review,* Moorland Spingarn Research Center at Howard University, National Archives and Records Service, *New York University Law Review, Record of the Association of the Bar of the City of New York, Texas Southern University Law Review,* Tuskegee University, *U.S. News and World Report,* and World Jurist Association.

In supporting roles, the following people have provided encouragement and assistance toward completion of *Supreme Justice*: Arthur

Affleck, Alaina K. Benford, Jason A. Christian, Jacoui Coleman, Steven M. Edwards, Gary A. Hengstler, Margaret Henneberry, the late Sylvia T. Johnson, Dr. James F. Jones, Jr., Joshua P. Jones, Venola Jones, Dorothy A. Kelly, Susan J. LeClair, Corlie McCormick, Jr., J. W. Peltason, Laura Smith, Stager C. Smith, Opio L. Sokoni, Joseph Steinberg, Jamye Coleman Williams, McDonald Williams, Jacqueline C. Young, Robert A. Young, and the library staff at Howard University School of Law, and the Moorland Spingarn Research Center, Howard University.

Finally, my thanks and appreciation to Patti Grace Smith, for her advice, support, and encouragement to complete this project, and to Justice Thurgood Marshall, whom I promised to compile this work in 1992.